# Rodgers &
# Hammerstein

# RODGERS & HAMMERSTEIN

## ETHAN MORDDEN

HARRY N. ABRAMS, INC., PUBLISHERS, NEW YORK

Editor: Robert Morton
Copy Editor: Peter Simon
Designer: Liz Trovato
Photo Editor: John K. Crowley


Library of Congress Cataloging-in-Publication Data

Mordden, Ethan.
    Rodgers & Hammerstein / Ethan Mordden.
        p.      cm.
    Includes bibliographical references and index.
    ISBN 0-8109-1567-7
    1. Rodgers, Richard, 1902–1979   Musicals.   2. Hammerstein, Oscar,
1895–1960.   3. Musicals—History and criticism.   I. Title.
II. Title: Rodgers and Hammerstein.
ML410.R6315M7   1992
782.1′4′0922—dc20   91-46586   CIP   MN

Printed and bound in Japan

On the preceding pages:
Endpapers: *Oklahoma!*
First—The dream ballet in *Oklahoma!* featured dancers
in the actors' roles. The original Laurey (center among the
women) and Curly (at left of men) were "played" by
Katharine Sergava and Marc Platt.
Next—Yul Brynner and Deborah Kerr break into the
"Shall We Dance?" polka in the movie *The King and I.*
Opposite—*Allegro:* "The Children's Dance."

# Acknowledgments

Although this book was written with the friendly cooperation of the Rodgers and Hammerstein office and families, the author maintained absolute control of the manuscript from preparation through publication. This volume therefore represents one writer's analysis of the work of Rodgers and Hammerstein, and not an "official" view.

The author is greatly indebted to the following for granting interviews: Agnes de Mille, John Fearnley, James Hammerstein, Dorothy Rodgers, Stephen Sondheim, and Elaine Steinbeck. He thanks as well his colleague Ken Mandelbaum for many stimulating conversations about the world of musical comedy and for exposure to arcane research material. At Abrams, Bob Morton superintended the project with wisdom and enthusiasm that can only be called classic; and, at the Rodgers and Hammerstein office, Ted Chapin and Bert Fink greatly enriched this undertaking with expertise, warm support, and trust.

Right—*The Sound of Music*: Mary and the kids in "Do Re Mi." Next pages—*The King and I*: the schoolroom. (Left to center are Gertrude Lawrence, Dorothy Sarnoff, Doretta Morrow, Sandy Kennedy, Johnny Stewart.) Following pages—the *Sound of Music* movie: Julie Andrews leads the kids on what appears to be a major Alpine hike.

Two classic R & H couples: above, Curly and Laurey (Alfred Drake and Joan Roberts) and, left, Emile and Nellie (Ezio Pinza and Mary Martin).

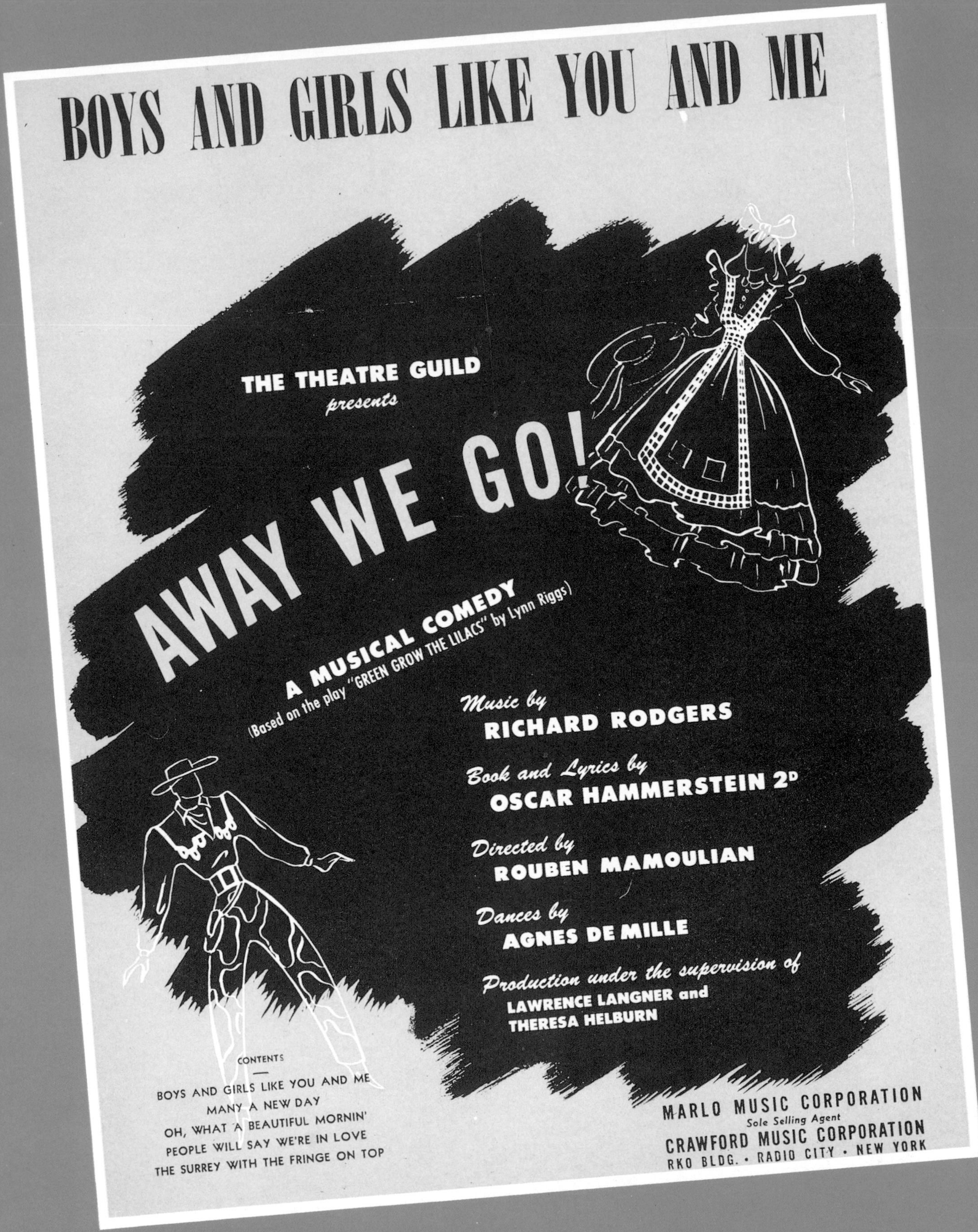

BOYS AND GIRLS LIKE YOU AND ME
THE THEATRE GUILD
presents
AWAY WE GO!
A MUSICAL COMEDY
(Based on the play "GREEN GROW THE LILACS" by Lynn Riggs)
Music by
RICHARD RODGERS
Book and Lyrics by
OSCAR HAMMERSTEIN 2D
Directed by
ROUBEN MAMOULIAN
Dances by
AGNES DE MILLE
Production under the supervision of
LAWRENCE LANGNER and
THERESA HELBURN
CONTENTS
BOYS AND GIRLS LIKE YOU AND ME
MANY A NEW DAY
OH, WHAT A BEAUTIFUL MORNIN'
PEOPLE WILL SAY WE'RE IN LOVE
THE SURREY WITH THE FRINGE ON TOP
MARLO MUSIC CORPORATION
Sole Selling Agent
CRAWFORD MUSIC CORPORATION
RKO BLDG. • RADIO CITY • NEW YORK

# Oklahoma!

In the summer of 1941, the Westport Country Playhouse staged a revival of Lynn Riggs' *Green Grow the Lilacs*, a look at the folkways of settlers in the territory that became the state of Oklahoma. *Green Grow the Lilacs* had failed on Broadway in 1931, with

*Oklahoma!*: "The Farmer and the Cowman."

its oafish dialect—"I ain't wantin' to do no hoe-down till mornin', and what would I want to see the sun come up fur, a-peekin' purty and fine, alongside of you?"—and its now charming, now unsettling triangle romance of egotistical cowboy, hard-edged farm girl, and disgusting ranch hand. But it went over well at Westport, and no one was more content than Theresa Helburn, one of the directors of the Theatre Guild.

The Guild had produced the original *Green Grow the Lilacs*, mainly at Helburn's insistence, and she looked back fondly on that production. The Guild had persuaded Riggs to allow a heavy interpolation of folk songs such as "Old Paint" and "Skip to My Lou," partly for atmosphere but also to endear the characters to the public. Apparently, something about Franchot Tone, as the cowboy, loping onstage to sing "Git Along, Little Dogies" gave the show a bit of a lift. The Westport revival built upon this, adding in not only folk songs but a square dance, choreographed by Gene Kelly, the Broadway dancer who had recently achieved stardom as the irresistible cad/hero of the Richard Rodgers and Lorenz Hart show *Pal Joey* (1940). Watching the audience warming to *Green Grow the Lilacs* as they hadn't done in 1931, Helburn realized that the closer the play got to being a musical, the better it went over. More music, more lift. She began to wonder what the piece might be like with a wholly original score. And she asked Richard Rodgers to come up and have a look.

A pensive Oscar Hammerstein (in a rare pose seated at the piano) and watchful Teresa Helburn audition would-be choristers.

Rodgers immediately saw the possibilities, but his partner, Hart, thought *Green Grow the Lilacs* would make a dud of a musical, and in any case was scarcely interested in working at all. Unstable, distracted, and inclined to the enervating pleasures of the demimonde, Hart had grown increasingly disengaged in the last few years of his two-decade partnership with Rodgers. Though he continued to discuss projects with Rodgers, and though he seemed eager and refreshed while working on what was to prove to be their final new show, *By Jupiter* (1942), Hart was more and more an unavailable talent. Rodgers, considering his own future, felt miserable and guilty, but Rodgers was desperate. Nothing mattered more to him than his work. As he himself put it, "I had to think about a life without Larry Hart."

He had to think about a new partner, too, and he had the man, Oscar Hammerstein II. However, by 1942 Hammerstein was very nearly a has-been. The coauthor of some of the biggest hits of the 1920s (including *Rose-Marie, The Desert Song, Show Boat,* and *The New Moon*), Hammerstein had slipped into a losing streak after *Music in the Air* (1932), with five New York and London flops in a row—some of them raving disasters—and a string of mostly unsuccessful films. True, Hammerstein won an Academy Award for Best Song (with Jerome Kern) in 1941, for "The Last Time I Saw Paris." Still, what's Best Song to the man who wrote *Show Boat?* Hammerstein's work was Broadway work; yet for ten years Broadway had not been in a Hammerstein mood.

Rodgers, on the other hand, was a king on Broadway. He'd had some failures, certainly, but since returning from Hollywood for *Jumbo* (1935) Rodgers and Hart had enjoyed a spectacular prime, with *On Your Toes* (1936), *Babes in Arms* (1937), *I'd Rather Be Right* (1937), *The Boys from Syracuse* (1938), *Too Many Girls* (1939), *Higher and Higher* (1940)— their sole flop in this series—and especially *Pal Joey,* controversial for its low-down nightclub setting but, among the cognoscenti, an instant classic.

So there was something jarring in the ultra-successful Rodgers teaming up with the embattled Hammerstein—and something even more jarring in the *kinds* of musicals that the two were used to writing. Look at those Hammerstein hits of the 1920s—Mounties and Indians in French Canada; foreign legionnaires, Arab freedom fighters, and dangerous love in a sheik's tent; nostalgic Americana and race relations along the Mississippi; pirates, nobles, and revolutionary democrats in old New Orleans. Hammerstein was operetta: majestic, committed, passionate. Rodgers was musical comedy: trim, sassy, come-as-you-are. Rodgers was ballet versus hoofing, kids putting on a show in a barn, a spoof of the New Deal. And Rodgers was above all contemporary, right on the money with what was urban, jazzy, smart. Hammerstein was a pioneer: of a form that had died in the 1930s. By 1942 he seemed a bit like Old Father Hubbard, bare cupboard and all. Operetta had come up empty. And look what happened when Hammerstein tried musical comedy—with Jerome Kern, no less—in *Very Warm for May* (1939): mixed reviews and dead houses.

Another problem was Hammerstein's reluctance to take Hart's place while there was the slightest spark of work left in him. At first, Hammerstein said no. Rodgers apparently made oblique overtures to Ira Gershwin, without question the closest possible replacement for Hart in talent and philosophy, in the worldliness of their sentimentality and the tricks leaping out of their rhymes. Gershwin, however, was still trying to decide if there was life after George, who had died in 1937. Ira had written *Lady in the Dark* with Kurt Weill and Moss Hart in 1940, but now he was contemplating light work in Hollywood and mourning his genius brother. Howard Dietz, who was stylistically not unlike Hart and Ira Gershwin, seemed to have broken with partner Arthur Schwartz. But Broadway was moonlighting for Dietz; he worked full-time for Metro-Goldwyn-Mayer as head of publicity.

No matter: for Rodgers wanted Hammerstein, and for good reasons. First of all, the man who had written *Show Boat* could not ever be counted out, no matter how many failures he had suffered. Second, Hammerstein had been for some time Jerome Kern's main collaborator, and it was Kern whose wealth of melody, ingenious formal constructions, and versatility of mood had enchanted Rodgers in boyhood and fired him with the need to try to do what Kern could do. How better could Rodgers reestablish his youthful ambition and intensity than by hooking up with the man who had composed the poetry for most of Kern's greatest scores? Then, too, Hammerstein was a librettist as well as a lyricist—in fact, the man who forced the revolution from makeshift scripts built around star comics, hit tunes, and dance numbers to scripts that told a story. No one knew better than Rodgers the troubles an unruly or pointless or witless book could cause. A great score is what makes a show a classic for the ages, but a solid book is what makes a show a hit *in its season*. Though Rodgers and Hart got their start working as a trio with the dependable, sassy Herbert Fields on book, their post-Fields years were spent searching for a book writer or writing the lines themselves, not always successfully. Hammerstein offered, among other gifts, book insurance.

There is one other thing. At the age of fourteen, Rodgers had attended a performance of a Columbia varsity show with his older brother, Mortimer, a Columbia man, and Morty took Dick backstage to meet one of the actors and coauthors—Oscar Hammerstein II. The collegiate Hammerstein made the bedazzled youngster feel perhaps even more welcome in the theatre than Kern's music did, less the spectator and more the participant, closer to the stage. Kern was a sighting, but Hammerstein was contact.

### Dramatis Personae, 1943

Left, Aunt Eller (Betty Garde) referees when Laurey (Joan Roberts) and Gertie Cummings (Jane Lawrence) fight for ownership of Curly (Alfred Drake). Below, the Peddler (Joseph Buloff) has flirted with Ado Annie Carnes (Celeste Holm), to the annoyance of her father (Ralph Riggs). Actually, old man Carnes prefers the Peddler to Annie's real boyfriend, Will Parker (Lee Dixon). At lower left, Will Parker sings of "the modren world" in "Kansas City."

"That afternoon," Rodgers wrote in his memoirs, "I went home with one irrevocable decision." That was to "go to Columbia and...write the Varsity Show." Didn't he really mean to "go to Broadway and write musicals"? So, in 1942, the notion of Rodgers joining forces with Hammerstein was stimulating adventurism, excellent history, and an act of rejuvenation.

But *Green Grow the Lilacs* as a musical? What a dreadful idea for a show! The great seminal works of musical theatre, however unconventional, tend to draw their energy from contemporary artistic evolutions. *Show Boat* seemed awfully epic for 1927, but *Show Boat*'s authors, Kern and Hammerstein, were becoming seignorial in the organically unified composition, producer Florenz Ziegfeld was an adept in the art of spending money, and the cast was very promising. *Show Boat* was daring, not dreadful. *West Side Story* (1957), for all its darkness, marked a meeting of two crucial strains in the postwar musical, sophisticated musicianship and the hegemony of dance. *West*

New York City's mayor, Fiorello La Guardia, flanked by Teresa Helburn and Richard Rodgers, visits backstage and meets Curly and Laurey, the Peddler, and the villain of the piece, Jud Fry (Howard da Silva, at left in suspenders), along with the rest of the company.

*Side Story* was extraordinary, not dreadful. *Follies* (1971) found the emerging "concept musical" in the hands of its masters—Stephen Sondheim, Hal Prince, Michael Bennett, and Boris Aronson. *Follies* was evolutionary, not dreadful.

But *Oklahoma!*, the musical that Rodgers and Hammerstein made of *Green Grow the Lilacs,* ran directly against the form and feeling of the musicals of its day. The age was conservative, mainly because Depression economics had cut down on the experimentation of the 1920s. Realistic subject matter and sophisticated musicality were prohibited, because a vastly diminished audience had made slick fun and hit tunes essential. It is notable that the few departures from convention, Kurt Weill and Paul Green's *Johnny Johnson* (1936) and Marc Blitzstein's *The Cradle Will Rock* (1937), were produced by noncommercial organizations, the Group and Federal Theatres, respectively.* (At that, *The Cradle*'s militant leftist stance scared the Feds at the last minute, forcing the company to scorn their padlocked house and strike out to perform on their own.)

We can take the measure of Broadway's idea of an acceptable musical in the big show that directly preceded *Oklahoma!* on Broadway, *Something for the Boys* (1943). Here's smarts: Ethel Merman starring and, as the posters crowed, "Cole Porter songs." Heavy names. *Oklahoma!*'s principals, by contrast, were apprentices or unknowns—and, as for "Rodgers and Hammerstein songs," who knew what these would be like? *Something for the Boys'* book writers were the practiced Herbert and Dorothy Fields, who could do trim and gutsy in their sleep. Its producer was Michael Todd, its director Hassard Short: the one a champion dealer in "legs and laffs" and the other a consummate showman. That's a nuanced team—coarse enough for the gents and stylish enough for the ladies. Everybody's welcome.

Compare Todd and Short with *Oklahoma!*'s Theatre Guild and Rouben Mamoulian: the Guild a producer of art and the Lunts in its heyday in the 1920s and 1930s but by now in grave financial trouble; and Mamoulian a once-distinguished Broadway director who had bombed out in Hollywood. Like Hammerstein, Mamoulian had the gift but, lately, not the luck—and show biz is superstitious. Bad luck can be catching.

Putting aside the personnel, *Something for the Boys* and *Oklahoma!* make a more telling comparison, that between a sure thing and an absolutely guaranteed miss. What was sure about *Something for the Boys* was its conventional construction, as a diversion planned to do literally nothing but divert.

---

*\*Cabin in the Sky* (1940) and *Lady in the Dark* (1941), mounted by commercial producers, were certainly unconventional, the first in its erotic black fantasy and the second in its unique format of spoken drama *containing* mini-opera dream sequences. However, *Cabin* failed, and *Lady* was on one level a vehicle for the amazing Gertrude Lawrence, *hors concours.*

This classic *Oklahoma!* photograph shows the cast storming the footlights to put over the title song. The picture was featured on the original 78 rpm cast album and is still in use today on the CD reissue.

The plot, implausible if not precisely science fiction, is a frame for the star, the Cole Porter songs, and about equal amounts of comedy, verve, and spectacle: three cousins from the urban Northeast jointly inherit property in Texas. (Theme for gags: slickers in hickland; and note to set designer: use the Alamo.) The property lies near an air force base, so the cousins renovate the place as a hotel for servicemen's wives (thus provisioning the chorus, the men in uniform and the wives in matching war-work pantsuits and, later, ball gowns). The hotel is mistaken for a bordello and placed off-limits, about the only thing that actually *happens* in the entire evening—but it's good for the love story, because Merman is one of the cousins and her intended is a sergeant. (Note to Porter: prepare another Porter-Merman torch song, latest in the line of "I Get a Kick Out of You [*Anything Goes*, 1934], "Down in the Depths" [*Red, Hot, and Blue!*, 1936], and "Make It Another Old-Fashioned, Please" [*Panama Hattie*, 1940].) Obviously, the setting and plot will emphasize the contemporary. This is very much a wartime show. But Porter, master of the timely allusion, will further underline the air of the here and now in a song about America's latest genre of show-biz star, "The Leader of a Big-Time Band," and lyrics in other songs will refer to such as Gene Autry, Dorothy Lamour, Diana Barrymore, the "meatless day" (because of rationing), Ovaltine, and Admiral Nimitz and General Eisenhower. The plot will be resolved by baldest contrivance, when Merman picks up radio transmissions through Carborundum in her teeth, saves a distressed plane, and thus ends the military ban on her hotel.

But so what? The entire show was a bald contrivance. The story didn't matter, and the characters were types—city wisecrackers, the true-blue hero,

ingenues demure and catty, and Merman, *sui generis* but a genre nonetheless. *Something for the Boys* was not a thing-in-itself but a well-organized collection of things: Merman, Cole Porter songs, city-country comedy, and Todd's cuties. It was not an absurd mess; on the contrary, it was state-of-the-art. But it was not a penetrating art. To hear the score by itself, one would not have the slightest idea what occurs in the story. Except for the opening number, in which an attorney seeks out the three cousins one by one and informs them of the terms of the will, not a single lyric — not a line anywhere — develops the concept of kinship, or hotels for servicemen's wives, or what little else was in *Something for the Boys* that hadn't already been in a thousand shows. "When We're Home on the Range," as the cousins prepare to leave for Texas, and "He's a Right Guy" — yes, the latest Porter-Merman torch song — do fit into the Fieldses' tale. But "There's a Happy Land in the Sky" and "By the Mississinewah" defy any sense of time and place; "When My Baby Goes to Town," "Could It Be You?," "Hey, Good-Lookin'," and "I'm in Love with a Soldier Boy" might have been written for any show of the day; and "See That You're Born in Texas" finds the citizens of San Antonio doing patter on famous Texans in a voice that belongs to Cole Porter — "Say, in a sweater, who looks better

*Oklahoma!*'s low-budget production led scenic designer Lemuel Ayers to create a series of backdrops (Laurey's farm is shown here) in front of which small sidepieces (such as the farmhouse porch) could be moved. The picture opposite shows a second porch-against-backdrop combination.

### "Many a New Day"

Although the number began with the full ensemble (*above*), the vocal featured only Laurey and the singers (*right*). Then (*below*) the dancers took over. At far right is a close-up of one of the many performers who became prominent in the show, Joan McCracken.

than Missus Sheridan's Ann?"—and not to the average (or even aberrant) San Antonian.

The weakest aspect of *Something for the Boys* is that it isn't about anything but the desire to entertain. However, that only looks weak today. In 1943, that was its strength. What else should a musical want to do but entertain? This is why *Oklahoma!*'s prospects seemed dim when it was an idea, and in rehearsal, and out of town. *Oklahoma!* didn't sound entertaining. It *was*, it turned out—but, also, *Oklahoma!* is about something, just as *Green Grow the Lilacs* is. Under the story of who gets to take Laurey to the dance, Riggs' play is a consideration of how a relatively primitive but orderly community deals with brutish lawlessness in its preparation to enter civilization—that is, to assume American statehood. Laurey's hired hand Jeeter is the brute, a rutting slimebag who plumes so fierce a sense of self that he destroys those who offend it:

LAUREY: Onct I passed a farm house and it was night....
And this farm house was burnin' up. An' it was
burnin' bright, too. Black night it was, like I
said. Flames licked and licked at the red-hot
chimbley, and finally it fell, too, and that was
the last of that house.... And the farmer's wife jist
set there by the side of the road, moanin' and takin'
on.... She kept sayin' over and over—"Now my home's
burnt up. 'F I'd a-jist give him a piece of cold
pork or sump'n. If I'd jist a-fed him!"

### Two More Numbers

Rouben Mamoulian's sororal grouping (*top*) — or is it de Mille's? — gives a feminist look to "Out of My Dreams." Below, we included this performance snapshot of "All Er Nothin'" because of its rare view of Lemuel Ayers' curious abstract cornflower curtain.

Jeeter is the challenge to republican entitlement, Riggs observes. Remove him, and not only can Curly marry Laurey, but the territory can enter the Union and its folk marry their history and future to the American epic.

*Oklahoma!* includes this idea but builds upon it as well. Not only can Oklahoma become a state: Oklahoma *must*. Statehood is an affirmation of individuality within citizenship, of liberty within the corporation. But only when antagonistic factions make peace can the Union emerge. From a single line in Riggs, Aunt Eller's "Why, we're territory folks — we orter hang together," came "The Farmer and the Cowman":

> And when this territory is a state,
> And jines the union jist like all the others,
> The farmer and the cowman and the merchant
> Must all behave theirsel's and act like brothers.

Yes. But only when individuals pursue a fair and responsible and personal agenda can the Union prosper. In a speech that Hammerstein amplified from

Riggs' original, Curly—the cowman about to marry a farmer—tells Laurey:

I'll be the happiest man alive soon as we're married.
Oh, I got to learn to be a farmer, I see that! Quit
a-thinkin' about th'owin' the rope, and start in to git
my hands blistered a new way! Oh, things is changin'
right and left! Buy up mowin' machines, cut down the
prairies! Shoe yer horses, drag them plows under the sod!
They gonna make a state outa this, they gonna put it
in the Union! Country a-changin', got to change with
it! Bring up a pair of boys, new stock, to keep up
'th the way things is goin' in this here crazy country!
Now I got you to he'p me—I'll mount to sumpin yit!

This is fine art, but, in 1943, doubtful commerce. At least *Oklahoma!* was fresh, to put it mildly. There had been western musicals before—*Something for the Boys,* remember, takes place in Texas, and there were as well *The Red Petticoat* (1912), *Rio Rita* (1927), *Rainbow* (1928), and *Whoopee* (1928). But how many musicals had there been that were about what being American entails? Maybe all this talk about how unfit *Oklahoma!* was for commercial success simply failed to see how valuable such a piece might be in 1943, when

Before the show opened in New York under its final title, sheet music was released (see page 16) with rather unfocused artwork. After the Broadway premiere, the sheet music cover (*right*) went from a vapid view of people to an idealization of Oklahoma itself.

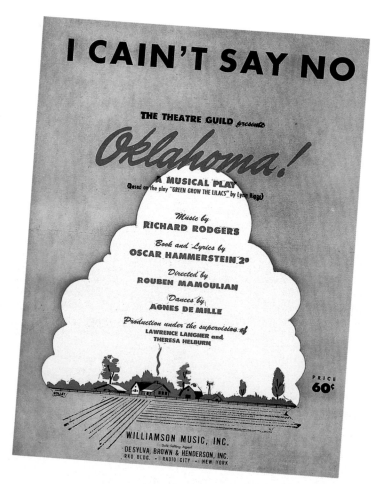

the nation was fighting for the privilege of remaining American.

In short, this show had a grip on what people were feeling at the time, so in the end its dowdy setting and unusual composition did not hurt it. By the rules of its day *Oklahoma!* was bizarre: but *Oklahoma!* changed the rules. These now read: one, Don't start with a star; start with a story; two, Don't paste fun onto the show; find the fun within the action; and three, The songs and dances define the characters or further the narrative.

So *Oklahoma!* couldn't use wisecracking New Yorkers "picturing" the rustics for our benefit. *Oklahoma!* shattered the picturing approach. The whole thing is written to see Oklahoma through Oklahoman eyes—which is why it so famously opens not with a bunch of chorus people telling *us* about the place (as *Something for the Boys* more or less does) but with a single native describing the place *to himself* in his terms: "Oh, What a Beautiful Mornin'" as opposed to "See That You're Born in Texas."

We feel the show's sense of self-identification very strongly in the choreography. It was Theresa Helburn who brought Agnes de Mille into the project, having seen de Mille's ballet *Rodeo,* for *Rodeo*'s settings alone—corral and ranch house—were highly apropos. So was its theme, on how women (are forced to) style themselves in a fundamentally masculine environment. De Mille's look at a tomboy who finally turns into a belle at the social had abundant humor, and she included pop dancing along with the traditional ballet, with a square dance interval (complete with one dancer calling out the steps) and even a tap solo.

At the time, however, the two new partners weren't sure if ballet would fit into their show. Rodgers was an old campaigner in the use of high-fashion dance in musical comedy—not only in George Balanchine's blending of hoof and toe in *On Your Toes* but in two other Balanchine shows—and *I'd Rather Be Right*'s "Sweet Sixty-Five" led into a dream fantasy choreographed by Charles Weidman, a maestro of modern dance. But then fancy dance was the thing in the 1930s, and not in 1942. *Oklahoma!* was going to be an unusually unified composition. Wouldn't ballet—even ballet as lyrically western as *Rodeo*—seem excrescent? Moreover, de Mille's experience in the musical counted just Cole Porter's London show *Nymph Errant* (1933) and getting fired from the Ed Wynn vehicle *Hooray for What* (1937). Something else must have been on everyone's mind—ballet dancers look funny. Actually, they don't; but the prevailing Broadway maxim in the hiring of chorus women was "Casting for talent is bad for business." Looks count.

Nevertheless, *Oklahoma!* had the breaking of maxims built into every part of it, and de Mille was hired. Came then her first meeting with Hammerstein, and she straightaway tackled this question of what kind of women she could hire. *Talent* counts:

First, I informed him, I must insist that there be no one in the chorus
I didn't approve. I sat up quite straight; as I spoke I looked
very severe. "Oh pshaw!" he murmured. He was sorry to hear I was
going to take that attitude—there was his regular girl, and
Lawrence Langner had two, and Dick Rodgers always counted on
some. For one beat, I took him literally, there being no trace
of anything except earnestness in his face, and then I relaxed on
that score for the rest of my life.

De Mille gave *Oklahoma!* precisely the mixture of ballet and pop she had
invented for *Rodeo:* contemporary social-hall for "Kansas City," women's
romanticism (laced with comedy) for "Many a New Day," frontier chivalry
for "The Farmer and the Cowman," and some old-fashioned musical-comedy
flirtation spoof for "All er Nothin'."

In the end, the choreographer did have to fight to hire Diana Adams,
Joan McCracken, and Katherine Sergava, whose look was thought just a little
too Ballets Russes for the rest of the line. All the same, de Mille folded
herself beautifully into musical comedy, even as she helped Rodgers and
Hammerstein expand the definition of what musical comedy could be.

"Kansas City," for instance, isn't the usual dance-after-the-vocal that
Broadway depended on. The song is Will Parker's description of the new-
fangled American civilization that he has seen on his trip east. (Hammer-
stein, again, is tipping us over into the future, reminding us that American
history is made by adventurers—"They've gone about as fur as they c'n go!")
As Will finishes his last chorus, he breaks into a two-step. "What you doin',
Will?" someone asks. Will demonstrates this latest metropolitan novelty
("That's all they're dancin' nowadays," he explains. "The waltz is through.
Ketch on to it?"), dancing Aunt Eller around the yard. But that's about as fur
as she c'n go. So the music now cuts into a stop-time version of the song as Will
introduces another advantage of modern life, hoofing. The other male dancers
take it up, building the number to its climax. It's the same *kind* of dancing
that other musicals had, but, arising casually out of the situation, it's more
pointed, more stimulating. It pulls the story right into the dance.

De Mille's most potent contribution was the dream ballet that ends Act
One, "Laurey Makes Up Her Mind." The famous joke about *Oklahoma!*
is that this historically crucial show is in fact about nothing more than who
will take Laurey to the dance. No—it's about how Americans comprehend
their destiny. But the *plot* of the show is thin, indeed, giving us only Laurey,
the dance, and the two men fighting for the right to take her.

It comes to a head just before the intermission. Loving Curly yet in some
strange way contemptuous of him as well, and fearful of, yet fascinated

by, Jud,* Laurey tries to puzzle it out. Who *will* take her to the dance?—and Hammerstein had a dandy idea: she'll dream that she's queen of the circus, and de Mille can stage a circus ballet!

"Why a circus?" de Mille asks.

"Because we need something bright and full and grand to close Act One."

De Mille objects: people don't have dreams like that. "They dream," she says, "about their anxieties, their fears. Laurey should dream about what she's most afraid of. Nice girls dream rather dirty dreams, you know."

Jud's disgusting, but Curly's too nice. Curly is "Oh, What a Beautiful Mornin'." Jud is a collection of naughty postcards. French. You know—the cancan?

"*Circus* ballet?" says de Mille. "We've got to get inside that girl's mind!"

This de Mille did. Her version of the dream—using dancing counterparts for Laurey, Curly, and Jud—encapsulates the drama through Laurey's eyes, pitting Curly's romance and neighborly community against Jud's postcard girls, who sneer at Laurey and go into that cancan, to an almost Offenbachian arrangement of "I Cain't Say No." De Mille has termed her ballets "playwrighting," mainly because they articulate wishes and fears that the characters themselves cannot express. Jud's rough sensuality intrigues Laurey—or does she want to tease the headstrong Curly? Could she be afraid of what Jud will do to Curly if she rejects Jud? Is she simply unwilling to give up her freedom? Hammerstein's script plays with all the possibilities, but de Mille's choreography steers straight to Laurey's approach-avoidance relation to Jud. As the dream ends, Jud kills Curly and carries Laurey off; suddenly the real-life Jud is shaking Laurey awake and, distracted, she leaves for the dance with him as Curly looks on crestfallen.

That's the first-act curtain, one of the great ones ever for its clarity, artistry, and commanding air of suspense.† Never before in a musical had a self-contained ballet so embraced the action surrounding it. There had been dream ballets before—Charles Weidman's in *I'd Rather Be Right,* for instance—and certainly Balanchine's *On Your Toes* ballets, "La Princesse Zenobia" and

## Laureys and Curlys

Clockwise from top left are: Evelyn Wyckoff and John Raitt on the national tour; New York replacements Betty Jane Watson and Harold (later Howard) Keel; and later revivals featuring Shirley Jones and Jack Cassidy, Louise O'Brien and Peter Palmer, and Susan Watson and John Davidson.

---

*Jud is Lynn Riggs' Jeeter, renamed in the musical to avoid reminding the audience of Jeeter Lester, the patriarchal grotesque of Jack Kirkland's play *Tobacco Road,* which ended its precedent-setting eight-year run less than two years before *Oklahoma!* opened.

†Because *Oklahoma!*'s status as evergreen classic has made it and the ballet so familiar, directors have sought to reclaim its original air of surprise by modifications in staging. Hammerstein's sons William and James—in the 1979 New York and 1980 London revivals, respectively—intensified the dream by, in New York, bringing the curtain down as the dream Jud carried off the dream Laurey; and, in London, having the real Laurey watch her dream unfolding and staging the Curly-Jud fight not with the ballet counterparts but with the real Curly and Jud. (James decided against these innovations before the opening: the spectator Laurey seemed intrusive, and the actors playing Curly and Jud got so exhausted during the fight that they couldn't go on with the show.)

"Slaughter on Tenth Avenue," essentialized the show's conflict of Ballets Russes and street strut, in "Zenobia"'s Diaghilev spoof and "Slaughter"'s downtown elegy. Maybe a movement was building in the late 1930s, but not till de Mille and *Oklahoma!* did sophisticated dance find its place in the musical—not in a niche, or as some exotic jewel, but systematically, elementally. At a de Mille gala in 1983, Jerome Robbins said, "People are always discussing who was the first to use ballet…to tell a story. I don't think that's important. What's important is that Agnes did it and made it stick."

More individual even than the dancing and the propulsive sense of nationhood that rises through the evening to the full cast's swelling delivery of the title song is the *Oklahoma!* score itself, unique to its characters and plot. We have a wonderful instance of this in a song that the new partners wrote and then discarded, so early on that the arranger's copy refers to the show itself as *Green Grow the Lilacs,* the working title. The song is "When Ah Go Out Walkin' with Mah Baby," a cakewalk in the style of the old-time "coon song."* Apparently, it was planned as Will Parker's first-act solo, representing the ragtime he has heard in Kansas City:

> When Ah goes out walkin' with mah baby,
> Stars are dancin' in mah baby's eyes!
> When Ah do the cakewalk with mah baby,
> Me and mah baby always wins de prize!

It's a trim piece, stylish archeology—but it has nothing to do with Will Parker. Furthermore, it virtually demands a follow-up ragtime dance, which would date a show whose informing energy is progressive, futuristic. So our boys abandoned "When Ah Go Out Walkin'" and replaced it with "Kansas City," which provided the same up-tempo spirit but spoke very clearly of the modernistic swing in American life, the hill beyond the hill. Best of all, "Kansas City" could cue in not ragtime but the aforementioned hoofing, the timeless brush-kick and ball-change steps that would respect *Oklahoma!*'s period without emphasizing the past. *Green Grow the Lilacs* is about what *was;* *Oklahoma!* has to be about what *will be.*

Then, too, the entire score is a treasury of ingenious constructions—the fiddler's reel shape of "The Farmer and the Cowman"; the deadpan spoof of "Pore Jud Is Daid," using a funeral march and recitative for a comic song; the filthy, sullen dissonance that opens Jud's solo, "Lonely Room," stalked by lowering chords in the brass till the strings lead in a tune of macabre beauty; the

---

*I don't like the term any more than you do, but that's what Tin Pan Alley called an ersatz black-culture number around the turn of the century. To euphemize history would be to forgive it.

bowlegged vamp that launches the refrain of "All er Nothin'," as if Will Parker were not merely courting Ado Annie but swaggering around her as a rooster claims a hen; the upward-rushing bass octaves that streak into "Oklahoma":

which then immediately retreat under the vocal in what musicians call inverted diminution:

It's a historian's cliché that Hammerstein avoided the banality of an "I love you" lyric by having Curly and Laurey trying to worm out of making a confession, in "People Will Say We're in Love." Less often remarked is the way the preceding dialogue runs so directly into the number that the two lovers pursue their devious conversation during the verse:

LAUREY: Why do they think up stories that link my name with yours?
CURLY: Why do the neighbors gossip all day behind their doors?

and are still bickering during the refrain—the most crucial section, remember, of what is supposed to be the show's big love song:

LAUREY: (singing) Don't start collecting things.
CURLY: (speaking) Like whut?
LAUREY: (singing) Give me my rose and my glove.

Rodgers' most ingenious invention was the composing of "Many a New Day" entirely in one musical idea. The usual AABA structure of the Broadway theatre song of the day gives us a melody, the melody repeated, a *counter*melody (for variation), then the original melody again (for relief). "Many a New Day," however, is *all* A sections, the heroine's willfulness dramatized in a single melody lightly hammered upon, flippant triplet phrases capped by determined half notes:

The countermelody impishly provides not contrast but variation. Laurey is capricious, yes, but what she mainly is is stubborn:

This casually brilliant craftsmanship runs even into the dance arrangements, as when the verse of "Many a New Day" is transformed by modal reharmonizing into the "heartland vista" sound popularized by Aaron Copland in *Appalachian Spring* and *Rodeo*. Or consider the scoring of the opening of Act One, pulsing strings supporting birdcalls on flute and oboe. Consider the canny use of reprises, often just a snatch of melody to cap a scene, as when an ambivalent Laurey starts an encore of "People Will Say We're in Love" but bursts into tears and runs off to sample the Elixir of Egypt to divine her true intentions. Aunt Eller knows better: it's *got* to be Curly, and Eller takes up the tune in a hum to put a button on the scene. It's comic, but it's wise as well: not "people will say" but *everyone knows* they're in love.

Best of all, consider "The Surrey with the Fringe on Top," possibly the greatest "musical scene" between *Show Boat* and *Follies*. Hammerstein in particular had spent decades trying to free the musical of its rigid alternation of dialogue and song, augmenting certain numbers into an expansive blend of speech, chant, and full-out song to create a cross between play and opera. Of course, the "Surrey" number is basic, simple. But it moves from an improvisation (for all his detailed description, Curly is inventing the surrey from scratch) to a caress, from a rhythm number to a love song, from a catalogue to a mood piece.

Not only Hammerstein's lyric but also Rodgers' melody starts with the regulated beat of the horses' hooves, the leaping and scrambling of the minor fauna dodging the surrey wheels, and the fluttering of the surrey's decorations. We *see* it: in the music. After Curly's verse and chorus, Aunt Eller and Laurey quiz Curly on the accoutrements, Eller egging him on and Laurey skeptical but enchanted. Again, as in "People Will Say We're in Love," it's a conversation but it's sung; or it's a song that functions as a scene from a play. Something is *happening*. Curly, a natural-born performer, really starts turning it on:

When we hit that road, hell for leather,
Cats and dogs'll dance in the heather.

This of course irritates Laurey, and she and Curly pursue their eternal wrangling, refereed by Aunt Eller. Meanwhile the song per se has halted, yet the orchestra plays under the spoken lines, developing its tone to match that of the characters. So when Curly envisions the ride homeward, the tune's bumping and cantering has been smoothed out, *con sentimento,* into a lullaby:

> The sun is swimmin' on the rim of a hill,
> The moon is takin' a header,
> And jist as I'm thinkin' all the earth is still,
> A lark'll wake up in the medder.

That's perfect theatre poetry: picturesque, direct, and persuasive.

This could as well be said of the musical-comedy book that Hammerstein made of Lynn Riggs' play. Hammerstein was the ideal adapter — his inventions are as well judged as his retentions. *Oklahoma!* isn't merely faithful to the spirit of *Green Grow the Lilacs.* Whole scenes are reproduced almost line for line, most strategically the establishing dialogue for Curly and Aunt Eller and then Laurey; the smokehouse challenge scene for Curly and Jeeter; and the last Curly-Laurey scene, in which they become engaged. But when Hammerstein adds to Riggs he doesn't amend: he tightens and penetrates. Take Will Parker and Ado Annie, the secondary, "comic" couple traditional to all forms of music theatre — Papageno and Papagena in *Die Zauberflöte (The Magic Flute),* Jacquino and Marzelline in *Fidelio,* Gustl and Mi in *Das Land des Lächelns (The Land of Smiles),* Benny and Susan in *The Desert Song,* Bobby and Babe in *Good News!.* Will Parker doesn't appear in *Green Grow the Lilacs;* Curly mentions the name in passing. Annie *is* in the play, but as little more than a walk-on — a wallflower at that! Hammerstein's boy-crazy Annie effects a balance in dramatic weight, as her absurd love triangle with Will and the peddler sets off the more serious triangle of Curly, Laurey, and Jud, especially as Annie is reckless where Laurey is hesitantly thoughtful. When Annie's father arranges a shotgun wedding for Annie and the peddler — a charmer, perhaps, but as wrong for Annie as Will is right — Annie is content. Heck, a wedding is a wedding. As Hammerstein observed of *Oklahoma!*'s characters, "They're very pleasant people to spend the evening with, but not one of them has a brain in his head."

Laurey is probably the most pleasant of all, certainly the most interesting — so willful yet so contemplative, so briskly independent in "Many a New Day" yet so wistful in "Out of My Dreams." Hammerstein liked strong women characters. Rodgers' shows with Lorenz Hart tend to be "couples" shows (like *Dearest Enemy, A Connecticut Yankee, Too Many Girls)* or male-lead shows *(On Your Toes, I'd Rather Be Right, By Jupiter).* Hammerstein wrote about heroines. During his youthful prime in the 1920s, other men's operettas were about a student prince or a D'Artagnan. Hammerstein's operettas featured powerful women leads—*Rose-Marie, The Desert Song, Show Boat, Sweet Adeline.* In fact, most stage directors find *Oklahoma!* the most durable of the Rodgers and Hammerstein canon mainly because Laurey is so enigmatic, so capable of reinterpretation, that each production feels like a new show.

Typically, then, Laurey was the trickiest role to cast originally. The Theatre Guild wanted to try Shirley Temple, but Rodgers had had his eye on Mary Martin ever since she had sliced off her cut of fame singing "My Heart Belongs to Daddy" in Cole Porter's *Leave It to Me!* (1938). Laurey was offered to Martin, but at the same time Vinton Freedley proposed to star her in the new Vernon Duke musical *Dancing in the Streets.* Folklore tells us that Martin flipped a coin and *Dancing in the Streets* won. But, in early 1943, *Oklahoma!* looked like a bomb waiting to go off—"Helburn's folly," they were calling it—while the slick *Dancing in the Streets* not only seemed promising but was going to be built around Martin. (One of the songs, "Got a Bran' New Daddy," was a kind of sequel to Martin's signature tune.) In any case, Martin joined *Dancing in the Streets* and had the bemusing experience of playing the show's Boston tryout the same weeks that *Oklahoma!* did. They didn't go to New York together, however: *Dancing in the Streets* closed in Boston.

Actually, none of *Oklahoma!*'s principals should be hard to cast. These are not star parts,* though Curly and (especially) Ado Annie have been known to make stars of their players, starting with the originals, Alfred Drake and Celeste Holm. Drake may seem an odd choice as a cowboy, since he later established a persona as a debonair ham, in *Kiss Me, Kate; Kismet;* and *Kean.* But then Curly is something of an entertainer—he's the guy telling the tall stories at the cookout. And Drake's opulent baritone served the part well. Remember, Curly has five big numbers and a reprise to get through, an unusual share of the singing for a musical of 1943.†

Rodgers knew Drake from *Babes in Arms* (in which he sang the title song), and Hammerstein knew the Laurey, Joan Roberts, from *Sunny River* (1941), probably the worst debacle of all in his flop period, a big, exotic operetta with music by Sigmund Romberg that closed in little more than a month. As we'll see, Rodgers and Hammerstein preferred to work with actors they were familiar with—however obscure—than to try out new talent. They were tireless auditioners, but they also knew the difference between a five-minute per-

---

*Stars do on occasion play them, for any one of the seven leads is big enough to support a major name. So now Jane Powell will head the cast as Laurey, now John Davidson as Curly, now Jamie Farr (the cross-dressing Klinger on television's *M\*A\*S\*H*) as the peddler. Even Aunt Ellers can star: Jean Stapleton topped the bills in that role in California in 1990.

†To be fair, Ethel Merman had seven numbers in *Something for the Boys.* But Merman was a trumpet beyond comparison.

formance for five or six people and filling the house all night. They liked experience. Betty Garde, the Aunt Eller, was a well-known radio actress, and Lee Dixon, the Will Parker, had come back from an unsuccessful term in Hollywood musicals. (He's the one dancing on the giant typewriter keyboard with Ruby Keeler in "Too Marvelous for Words" in the Warner film *Ready, Willing and Able*.)

These are sensible choices, though Dixon's drinking eventually destroyed him. History can only marvel at the casting of Howard da Silva as Jud, for da Silva, a fine actor, lacked both the voice and the sleazy hots the role needs.* But Joseph Buloff was an ideal peddler. Buloff was a veteran of the Yiddish theatre, and the peddler, technically Persian, is not really the Jewish comic Buloff made of him. But Rodgers recalled Buloff from the film *They Met in Argentina* (1941), for which Rodgers and Hart had written the songs. In the movie, as a South American rancher's wily employee and with his Jewish inflection only somewhat transmuted into go-everywhere Spanish, Buloff is more or less irresistible. Take away his cranky tantrums, and you have the peddler: sly, guilty, invariably bewildered when caught.

With the cast assembled, *Oklahoma!* went into rehearsal at the Guild's flagship home, the Guild Theatre (now the Virginia), under the title *Away We Go!*, drawn from square dance calls such as de Mille had used in *Rodeo*. Hammerstein, Mamoulian, and the actors worked in one place, generally on stage; Rodgers, conductor Jay Blackton, de Mille, and the singing and dancing choruses† worked in the basement. Theresa Helburn, caressing her folly, ran back and forth, exhorting and heartening and suggesting. It was her idea that the authors write "a song about the earth."

"What do you mean?" Hammerstein asked. The *earth?*

"Oh, I don't know," she answered. "Just a song about the earth. The land."

They did write it: that was "Oklahoma."

De Mille, working on what would in effect be her first Broadway musical and acutely aware of her colleagues, saw in Hammerstein a serene expertise that was at its most impressive when everyone else was in a panic.

Mamoulian, for instance. Mamoulian was what they call "temperamental"—and de Mille was no Squirrel Nutkin when defending her province. The

---

*Jud too often goes to an actor of questionable voice or an opera singer who lacks what the French call the *physique du rôle*. Perhaps not till the 1979 Broadway revival was Jud perfectly cast, with Martin Vidnovic, a singing actor of unquestionable vocal bite. Consider that Vidnovic also played Lun Tha (in *The King and I*) and the hero of *Brigadoon* on Broadway. Now try to picture Howard da Silva in those parts.

†The bigger musicals hired two separate choruses on the notion that singers can't dance and dancers can't sing. Depression economics had cut into this somewhat. But the rise of dance in the late 1930s reemphasized the need for a Balanchine or Weidman to hire a corps he could count on, and *Oklahoma!* observed the separations. By the 1960s, the rise of the choreographer-director had reintegrated the chorus, and today the ensemble must sing and dance equally well.

director and the choreographer did not really get along. After all, de Mille was not only the obvious choice for her job but a comer, the one on the production team who was most likely to get very famous very fast. "Mamoo" felt threatened. Nevertheless, has-been or not, he had a splendid comprehension of how music guides and exalts the drama. As Rodgers saw it, this unconventional project "required someone who was both creative and not too steeped in the conventions of traditional Broadway musical comedy"—someone who would know the drill yet not need to march to it.

Of them all, de Mille thought Rodgers the most adventurous, "one of the most astute theatre men in the world. He concerns himself zestfully and relentlessly with every detail of production….This might be interfering if he were not sensitive, sensible, and greatly experienced." Come up with an idea, and Mamoo would shout, "Impossible!," and the Guild would cry, "Too expensive!" It was Rodgers, every time, who said, "Let's try it and see."

Even as rehearsals proceeded, the Guild was still raising the money to erect the sets, sew the costumes, and take *Away We Go!* out of town for its tryout. The Guild was so hungry and the show so unusual that Helburn's gang had to audition the piece to potential investors along what Rodgers called "the penthouse circuit." Rodgers would play the piano, Hammerstein would outline the story (and sing Jud's part, in his engagingly ghoulish baritone, in "Pore Jud Is Daid"), and Alfred Drake and Joan Roberts would introduce the ballads. All right, the story is odd and the characters are unfamiliar. But given such compelling and sheerly attractive songs as these, wouldn't *Away We Go!* go over? Decades later, those connected with the show looked back with amusement on one such evening in particular, when the Guild cohort gave its spiel in the apartment of Natalie Spencer, so grande a dame that she had a ballroom. This

## The *Oklahoma!* Phenomenon

At left, a department store window shows the *Oklahoma!* influence in fashion. Far left, below, Terry Helburn, Agnes de Mille, Hammerstein, Mamoulian, Rodgers, and Lawrence Langner and Armina Marshall of the Theatre Guild hit the cake. Lower left, the show passes its two thousandth performance. The show card at right for a showing of the film in Poland was one of the few posters that Rodgers hung in his office, because he was amused that the Polish designer had neglected to include the names of the authors. And, below right, a Ziggy comic strip reveals how strongly the show's score became embedded in the nation's consciousness.

was the fanciest gathering that *Away We Go!* had yet faced: several chapters of the Blue Book, with *two* pianos in attendance. Not a backer came forward.

Meanwhile, one Saturday afternoon, Mamoo decided to "put the first act together." That is, the actors and singers with whom *he* had been working and the dancers with whom de Mille had been working would join forces for the first time, so the production staff could see what it had. Mamoo and de Mille sat in the orchestra as Curly sauntered onstage and sang of the mornin' and the surrey; as Will Parker led off "Kansas City," and the chorus "cowboys" whom Curly and Laurey had scarcely met kicked into the dance of the future; as Ado Annie checked in. The full chorus followed, boys and girls, singers and dancers intermingled, the play really starting to happen. This is not just lines and scenes and songs: this is a *feeling*. And when Laurey and the singers finished their section of "Many a New Day" and de Mille's corps took the stage to interpret what Laurey feels and wants but cannot directly express, stage manager Elaine Steinbeck ran to the phone, called Rodgers—Hammerstein was in the country that weekend—and said, "You'd better get down here quick."

Because, for the first time, the absolute dead-on rightness of Mamoulian, de Mille, and the cast, of Riggs' story and what Rodgers and Hammerstein had wrought of it, had been made palpable, visible. The story led directly to the music—made it necessary—the actors fell effortlessly into melody, and the dancers extrapolated what the melody was *about*. Suddenly the show became something very real that was just about to occur.

The Guild got the rest of its backing from various show biz figures, and *Away We Go!* went to New Haven for its shakeout. Here the legend begins: the smart money comes up from New York, takes one look—Mike Todd saw the first act, quoth "No gags, no gals, no chance!" and fled—then heads back to town glowing with tales of doom.

In fact, as sometimes happens with classic works, the initial "failure" has been exaggerated. Audiences took to the show from the start, and while Todd did fail to see that a musical could be very unlike his own *Something for the Boys* and still succeed, he did explain that he left early to bail a friend out of jail.

Certainly, some Broadway insiders displayed a suspicious lack of belief in a piece that was shortly to make the biggest hit in musical history. Perhaps some of them felt overwhelmed by, and resentful of, the play's high quality. *Something for the Boys* could be taken in stride—gags, gals, and chance was business as usual. But *Away We Go!* said, I'm something better. The people who created me have higher instincts. Now, Broadway loves hits, but genius makes it uncomfortable. If Rodgers and Hammerstein are that good, what does that make the rest of us?

By the Boston stand, between New Haven and New York, it was clear that

*Away We Go!* was looking very, very good. Still, there was a lot of tinkering, egged on by the now triumphant yet always watchful, prudent Helburn. And there were three major changes, first of the title. *Away We Go!* sounded like those pointless musical comedies of the early 1900s—*High Jinks, Stop! Look! Listen!, Step This Way, Cheer Up, Fancy Free, Head over Heels, Come Along.* The title *Oklahoma* had been considered, but it seemed to overemphasize the show's uncommercial setting. Bad enough that the opening moments of the show's overture—the first point of contact between work and public— sounded like a monstrous barn dance. Must the title *advertise* it? However, by the end of the three days in New Haven, it was obvious that the western setting and sound style were among the show's charms—and someone suggested that an exclamation point might put less weight on corral and prairie and more on theatrical excitement. *Oklahoma!* it was.*

A major problem had to be solved in the big second act scene that leads to Curly's proposal and Laurey's acceptance. *Oklahoma!*'s second act is notably short on new numbers. There are just four (the first act has ten, plus the ballet), and the sole ballad, "Boys and Girls Like You and Me," in effect Curly and Laurey's love duet, was not going over. It's a lovely song, very delicately composed, and was planned to touch once again on the idea that these Oklahomans are on the verge of realizing their destiny:

Songs and kings and many things
Have their day and are gone.
But boys and girls like you and me,
We go on and on.

The number needs more than a few hearings to take in, more hearings than the dramatic moment could stand. So the authors dropped the song in favor of a reprise of "People Will Say We're in Love," skillfully threaded into the dialogue. A solo violin creeps in under Curly and Laurey's kiss of reconciliation. Curly gets so excited that Laurey says they'll hear him "all the way to Catoosie!" "Let 'em," Curly replies, and suddenly he's singing, "Let people say we're in love"—and the song, reworded from a challenge piece into a duet, becomes the love song it always wanted to be.

One thing remained to be done. Curly had originally sung "Oklahoma" as a solo to Laurey, joining the farmers and cowmen in their incipient republican alliance in that Laurey owns a farm and cowboy Curly will thus become a farmer. Maybe this was too big an idea for a solo. "Oklahoma" was turned over to the full cast, and de Mille worked up a tap solo for George Church (who also

*The advertising, programs, and sheet music had all been printed up before the change of title, so for the two weeks in Boston the old title held.

### *Oklahoma!*: The Movie

A publicity shot on the set presents Gloria Grahame, Eddie Albert, Rod Steiger, Shirley Jones, Gordon MacRae, Barbara Lawrence, Gene Nelson, and Charlotte Greenwood.

danced Jud in the dream ballet). No, that didn't quite do it. Church's solo went out, and now Mamoulian pulled his people down to the footlights in a great line from stage right to stage left to share that final, shouted *"Yeow!,"* not as actors with their public but as Americans, all together. The night this new staging went in, the show exploded. All its parts were in place; everything was as fine as it could be. Oddly, the hectoring Helburn and the polishing Mamoulian were still at it. An entrance must be tightened, a laugh secured! In a famous story, Rodgers shuts down a late-night production meeting by asking them all, "Do you know what's wrong with this show? *Nothing.* Now, everybody pipe down and let's go to bed."

*Oklahoma!* opened in New York, swept the world, and announced the revolution in the writing and staging of musicals. Just its original Broadway run tells us how phenomenally successful the show was. Hit musicals of that day ran a season—four hundred performances or so, followed by a national tour of, at most, eighteen months. *Oklahoma!* opened at the St. James Theatre on March 31, 1943, and closed there on May 29, 1948, counting 2,212 performances—five years and two months. The touring company, like the show's original tryout, began with three days in New Haven, in October of 1943. It finished up in Philadelphia in May 1954, nine and a half years later.

Another telling aspect of the craze for *Oklahoma!* was the scarcity of tickets, unusual in a day when even hit shows didn't enjoy sell-out weeks, as happens now. Stories were told of the stunts that people would resort to to get in, although my favorite such is about two people who simply and quite honestly requested their way in. A young couple showed up at the St. James box office, hoping against hope that there might be something—a cancellation, perhaps? Nothing. The man was in uniform, and he mentioned that he was shipping out for Europe the next day. The ticket seller silently pushed over a pair, fifth row center.

They were my parents.

The national tour, headed at first by Harry Stockwell, Evelyn Wyckoff, Pamela Britton, Walter Donahue, and David Burns, proved an even hotter ticket than Drake, Roberts, and company, because traditional scheduling techniques for a touring show could not foresee the immense demand for seats. A few cities got open runs, whereby the show stayed put as long as the public came—sixty weeks in Chicago, twenty in Philadelphia. But for some towns, the typical split week (for instance, a show plays Monday to Wednesday in Omaha and then Thursday to Saturday in Kansas City) simply couldn't accommodate all interested parties. *Oklahoma!* wasn't a sellout; it was a turnaway.

This irked some regional critics, already annoyed that the news from New York and the huge popularity of the score had in effect robbed them of their rights. Moreover, as with those skeptical Broadwayites on *Away We Go!*'s first night in New Haven, few of them were ready to deal with a musical this rich and dark yet basic and even patriotic. "It is the show of the year, and perhaps of several years," the reluctant William Leonard reported of *Oklahoma!* in a now defunct Chicago paper. But *"Oklahoma!* will be remembered not for its contributions to the theatre, nor because it marked a new departure or the beginning or end of an era but primarily for its immense popular appeal and attendant box-office records." And why is it popular? Because in a time when "the night clubs were jammed with welders and high-school kids" and "the radio was so full of swing that they even needled you with jive commercials between programs…along came a show brimming with sweetness and nostalgia." In short, *"Oklahoma!*'s success doesn't lie in its drama, its music, its dancing, its decor or its personnel. It's in that delicious change of pace after a deluge of sophistication."

Leonard got it so precisely wrong that his lack of judgment might almost be called inspired. Not only did *Oklahoma!*'s success lie in its drama, music, dancing, and so on, but it is so well remembered as marking a historical and artistic departure that legends have grown up giving *Oklahoma!* credit for a great deal that actually happened before it. For instance, careless historians rave about *Oklahoma!*'s daring raising of the curtain on an almost bare, near-silent stage—Aunt Eller churning butter and Curly launching "Oh, What a Beautiful Mornin'" a cappella. However, a number of earlier musicals avoided the opening chorus, or at any rate a populous stage colorfully in motion. It was uncommon but not innovative. *Peggy-Ann* (1926), *Music in the Air* (1932), *Anything Goes* (1934), *Pal Joey,* and *Lady in the Dark* (1941), to name only the most famous titles, all began as intimately as *Oklahoma!*—and, remember, *Oklahoma!*'s opening comes directly from *Green Grow the Lilacs.* It wasn't dreamed up; it was there already in Riggs' text, waiting to become a song.

Another false legend concerns *Oklahoma!*'s costuming, the women's high collars and long skirts cited as if every musical before it had been a burlesque show. Yes, Mike Todd was startled, but apparently Mike Todd had never seen a period piece, like *Blossom Time* (1921), *The Student Prince* (1924), or *The Great Waltz* (1934), wherein the opportunities for a showgirl parade are limited.

Then there is this notion that *Oklahoma!* utterly broke the rules by going out there with youngsters, not stars; Rodgers and Hammerstein themselves mentioned this at times. Yes, producers liked to build their shows around a Merman or Bolger if they could. Hiring the talent first and developing the story later had been routine for decades—but so was the production of shows that were not vehicles and did not have stars. Rodgers' own *The Boys from Syracuse* and *Too Many Girls,* respectively five and four years before *Oklahoma!*, used casts of unknowns. Or consider Hammerstein's *Very Warm for May* (1939) principals—Grace McDonald, Richard Quine, Jack Whiting, Eve Arden, Hiram Sherman, and Donald Brian. These were unknowns, one familiar but hardly imposing name (Whiting), and one semi-forgotten veteran (Brian, New York's original Danilo in *The Merry Widow*).

Still another myth tells us that Decca's 78 album of the cast and orchestra running through the overture, ten songs, and a reprise finale not used in the theatre, DA 359, was the first American original cast show recording. This ignores recordings made in the 1930s of Harold Rome's *Pins and Needles* (1937) and Marc Blitzstein's *The Cradle Will Rock* (1937), though as both were piano-accompanied on disc (as they were in the theatre) they failed to provide the excitement of a big Broadway musical caught just as it sounded onstage—the essence, really, of what we mean by the term "original cast album."

Anyway, the reason why Decca's Jack Kapp was so ready to give *Oklahoma!* a full-sized, authentic, dramatic rendering with the same people who performed it in the theatre was that he had just done it the year before, with Irving Berlin's *This Is the Army* (1942), an all-soldier revue. The recording was made to raise money for Army Emergency Relief—Berlin waived his royalties, and Decca agreed to make back only its expenses and contribute the rest. The album, DA 340, could easily have been just a few cuts made by any handy artists, as Victor's studio-devised *This Is the Army* in fact was: Brad Reynolds, Harry Harding, Fats Waller, a pickup choir, and a Victor house orchestra. Not the show's cast: a gang. This had long been the way American record producers recorded show music, but for some reason Kapp saw the possibilities in a reading of the score as it was heard in the theatre. It was an idea made of lightning, for this "original cast album" concept became the musical's most powerful support after the first-night notices and, more historically, the means by which old shows remain vivid. Again: a solid script makes a show a hit, but a popular score makes a show a classic—and recordings make a score popular.

*Oklahoma!*'s recording sold so well that Decca (and, soon enough, other labels) made the preserving of hit shows a major practice. Decca even issued an appendix album of the three songs the first album had omitted—"It's a Scandal! It's a Outrage!," "Lonely Room" (sung, however, by Curly—Alfred Drake—rather than the vocally less capable Howard da Silva), and two sides, dance music and all, of "The Farmer and the Cowman." What matters isn't which show copped the first thoroughly in situ recording but which show best profited by this new theatrical approach to the recording of Broadway. *This Is the Army*'s pleasant but unexceptional numbers vanished when the show did, not because the military setting dated them but because, like *Something for the Boys'* songs, they were a string of pop tunes. *Oklahoma!*'s score arrested the ear because, from one end to the other, a story was being processed, characters came forth, *ideas* were told.

This marked another aspect of the Rodgers and Hammerstein revolution, scores that became nationally familiar not as a melody or two but as wholes. Granted, "It's a Scandal!" and "Lonely Room" are obscure. Nevertheless, this is a work we think of from number to number, opening to finale. No previous musical—not *Rose-Marie*, not *The Desert Song*, not even *Show Boat*—could have claimed as much. *Anything Goes* is thought of as Cole Porter's master score because he got five hits out of it, but the remaining numbers, such as "Bon Voyage," "Where Are the Men?," "There'll Always Be a Lady Fair," and "Be Like the Bluebird," fell away to nothing. *Oklahoma!*'s score became known not for its hits but more or less in its entirety, and this inspired

The great 1979 revival with Laurence Guittard and Christine Andreas gave full measure to the show's moody side (*above*); its sexual ambivalence (in the dream ballet, *above right*); and its fun (*below right*), as Harry Groener leads the "The Farmer and The Cowman" dance.

other writers to create scores whose artistry (and appeal) would filter right through the evening.

The most immediate sign that *Oklahoma!* had invented something new lay in an amazing constancy of production. With the New York run, the tour, another tour by the cast that closed the show in New York, foreign productions, and stock and amateur mountings along with major revivals, the show became furniture in the American art showroom, permanently on display. A very faithful film version in 1955 capped the notion that *Oklahoma!* will always be with us. Rodgers and Hammerstein produced it themselves and cast it brilliantly—Gordon MacRae and Shirley Jones as the lovers; Gene Nelson and Gloria Grahame as the comics, he in the best role of a somewhat disappointed career and she, a queen of *noir,* greatly refreshing as Annie; Eddie Albert as a, for once, persuasively seductive peddler; Rod Steiger as a truly disgusting Jud; and Charlotte Greenwood, the authors' first choice as Aunt Eller in 1943, at last claiming her role. Best of all, though the cast ranges vocally from the true to the untried, everyone does his own singing, and does it well.

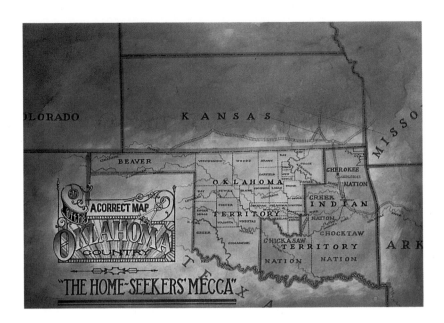

The 1979 show curtain, designed by Michael J. Hotopp and Paul DePass, troubled to locate the town of Claremore, near which fictional *Oklahoma!* takes place.

De Mille of course re-created her dances for the film, for by 1955 balletic dance—and especially de Mille–type balletic dance—had become the idealistic musical's badge of identification. De Mille had gone on to the two Rodgers and Hammerstein shows immediately after *Oklahoma!,* but she had also gone on to *One Touch of Venus* (1943), *Bloomer Girl* (1944), and *Brigadoon* (1947) in the emerging new era that *Oklahoma!* seemed to inaugurate. De Mille appeared to be so basic to the "musical play" as a whole that, though she had been hired for *Oklahoma!* at a set fee ($1,500, plus $500 after the show had paid off), the impact of her work made it necessary for the Guild to negotiate a bonus of $50 a week (this during the New Haven tryout), and four and a half years into the run de Mille was finally assigned a share of the gross—½ of 1 percent.

What made *Oklahoma!* so great? Years later, Rodgers observed of it that "all the individual parts complement each other....The orchestrations sound the way the costumes look." Hammerstein said it's not the "tangibles" but the "spirit." They're both right. As with that magical first run-through of Act One, the parts fitted together because the intentions behind the work were inspired and fearless.

Rodgers and Hammerstein pulled it off by rejecting Broadway's rules on the very nature of entertainment. What confidence they must have had! Yet, to the last minute, Hammerstein, at least, had no idea how *Oklahoma!* was going to play. After all, he had seen good work fail before, especially during the preceding eleven years. Just before the New York premiere he told his wife, Dorothy, "I really hope they like this one, because it's the only way I know how to write."

# State Fair

With *Oklahoma!* settled in at the St. James Theatre to break Broadway's record as the longest-running musical, Rodgers had found a new partner and Hammerstein had ended his time of hard luck. Further to solidify their teaming, the two men opened an

This portrait of Rodgers and Hart was taken on the Paramount lot in Hollywood in the early 1930s.

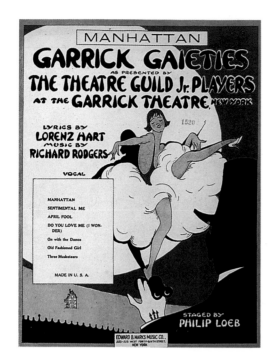

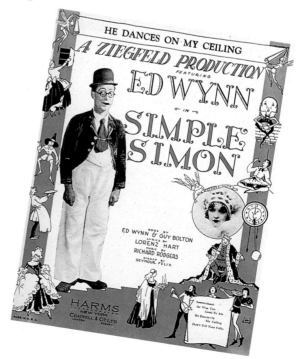

office to oversee business dealings on *Oklahoma!* and their future projects. Moreover, the office could provide a headquarters for their insistent search for new performing talent, and, while they were at it, serve as a base for the production of shows written by others. This last function was probably more to Rodgers' taste than to Hammerstein's. Though both were vastly experienced in all phases of play production, Hammerstein preferred to travel or relax when not writing or rehearsing his own shows. Ironically, it was Hammerstein who had been born in a trunk, the grandson of the furiously brilliant cigar manufacturer, vaudeville magnate, and opera impresario Oscar Hammerstein, and both the nephew and son of more strictly theatrical Hammersteins. But Oscar II liked a day off. It was Rodgers who was the irrepressible devotee, so eager to get into another theatre that, between his own shows, he'd put on those of other writers.

So the two men were now a team, a going concern, R & H. Oddly, they had taken very different, almost antagonistic paths to reach this revolutionary concord. For instance, Rodgers' form had always been musical comedy, to the romantically soigné lyrics of Lorenz Hart and to brassy wisenheimer scripts of no great moment. "Larry and I simply could not wait around for the odd chance that something novel and worthwhile would turn up," Rodgers wrote in his memoirs, *Musical Stages.* "We had to accept the best offers we could get." What made Rodgers and Hart fresh despite the scripts was their inventive scores, the lyricist's facetious, sorrowful wisdom lifted by the composer's dancing heart. "Falling in love with love," Hart could warn, "is falling for make believe." But he would set his warning against Rodgers' serenely flowing melody. That was their charm: Rodgers' wistfulness balancing Hart's regret.

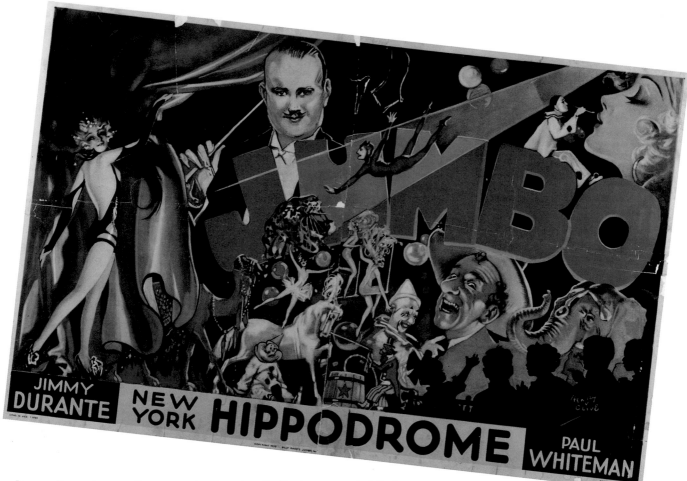

It was city poetry, penthouse music. Occasionally the two expanded their form. *A Connecticut Yankee* (1927) waggishly borrowed the through-sung "finaletto" more common in operetta than in musical comedy; *Chee-Chee* (1928) utilized longish musical scenes rather than a program of songs; and most of the scores they wrote for Hollywood used "rhythmic dialogue," lyrics spoken, not sung, to musical accompaniment.

Still, Rodgers and Hart basically wrote unreconstructed musical comedy. Oscar Hammerstein, on the other hand, was attracted to operetta, more intense than musical comedy not only musically but dramatically. In musical comedy, boy gets girl. In operetta, boy gets girl while exculpating himself of a capital crime (*The Yeomen of the Guard, Rose-Marie,*) rising from beggar to prince (*The Vagabond King, Kismet*), running an anti-imperialist crusade (*Eileen, The Desert Song, The New Moon*), running an *imperialist* crusade (*Song of the Flame*), composing great music (*Song of Norway*), or learning that human existence is low and cruel (*Candide*). Some operettas are so dire that boy doesn't even get girl (*The Student Prince, Bitter Sweet*).

When R & H started out, they wrote in the form Rodgers was used to, musical comedy. *Oklahoma!* was billed as a "musical play," if only to distinguish it from *Something for the Boys.* But it is nevertheless a musical comedy, trim,

fleet, and down-to-earth. Later, the team would realign their elements in favor of operetta—more voice, more intensity, more of the picturesque settings and enthralled sensibilities that operetta thrived on, the form Hammerstein was used to and did his best work in. Yet by then the very words "musical play" were a kind of euphemism for "operetta"—but operetta reinvented, smoothed out and rationalized.

It was R & H who reinvented it. But that's not until *Carousel*, one chapter hence. For now, it is worth noting how the two men redeveloped their work habits to suit each other. For one thing, their youth of prolific, even spend-thrift composition was over. Rodgers and Hart wrote six scores in 1926, Hammerstein two or three shows a year from 1922 to 1928. No more. When *Oklahoma!* opened in 1943, Rodgers was forty and Hammerstein forty-seven. They could afford to slow down.

Neither man had ever been given to churning out material, but the hell-bent-for-heaven pace of Twenties Broadway, somewhat abated in the 1930s, did not allow for the creation of a great many *unique* musicals. Yes, Rodgers and Hart's *Peggy-Ann* and *Love Me Tonight* stand among the great individual works in, respectively, theatre and film; and, again, Hammerstein wrote *Show Boat*. Still, much of their work in that era employed the standard song spots, the old jokes, and the familiar characters, at least partly because the very bases of those musicals—the stories—were standard, old, and familiar.

The R & H show, however, is a unique show, and the hallmark of their com-position is contemplation. R & H generally create one show every two years, leaving plenty of time for discussion, wondering, trying out. How do the princi-pals regard each other? What kind of voice should one hear from a cowboy, New England working girls, a Burmese slave, a mother abbess? What music goes with a clambake, a child's first steps, the death of a king? Where's the humor in World War II? How does the ocean sound?

Then, too, the writing of the script became the fundamental act of composi-tion, a clear break with the procedures of the 1920s and 1930s. In their youth, both Rodgers and Hammerstein had at times to work *around* the script,* whereas now they invariably worked *through* it. The two men's conversations and Hammerstein's notes would lead to a sort of Platonic conception of the work, from which would flow everything from love songs to comedy lines. If the R & H revolution could be boiled down to three words, they would read, Story is Everything.

*Collaborating with Jerome Kern on *Sunny* (1925)—just two years, by the way, before their extraordinarily virtuous *Show Boat*—Hammerstein could scarcely tell the story straight on, what with the star's demands, the producer's wheedling, and the need to fit a colorful miscellany into the whole, even unto the placing of a specialty performer's spot by a certain hour of the clock each evening. Boy and girl may have reached a sore point in their romance, but at ten chimes out came the blissfully irrelevant Ukelele Ike—as specified by contract—to do his ten minutes.

## Rodgers Before Hammerstein

A retrospective of Rodgers and Hart gives us visual keys to their quirky, fleet and sassy style in: the mock-operetta *Dearest Enemy* (*left, top*); the satirically experimental *Peggy-Ann* (*left, center*); the sexy Ernst Lubitsch film *Love Me Tonight*, with Jeanette Macdonald and Maurice Chevalier (*left, bottom*); the dance-crazed *On Your Toes*, with Ray Bolger and Vera Zorina (*left*); and (*below*) the college romp *Too Many Girls*, here with Desi Arnaz leading the "Spic and Spanish" number.

One arresting backstage detail: from *Oklahoma!* on, the lyrics were written first. This ran directly counter to the old practice. Show music was almost always composed before it was versified: melody to which words were added. There were sound reasons for this, relating to the tremendous power of the music publishing business when the American musical was establishing itself in the late nineteenth century. Melody sold sheet music, for performance by the home pianist, the amateur soprano and baritone, the Light Opera Society. True, the "novelty song" was based on its (silly) lyrics. But the money was on the music—on "After the Ball," for example, so vast a hit from 1892 into the early 1900s that Kern and Hammerstein used it at *Show Boat*'s narrative climax to essentialize the show's nostalgic panorama. Simply to quote the abundantly familiar melody was to take an entire public back to its youth. The money was on the music.

Anyway, there were no great lyricists before the 1900s, no P. G. Wodehouse, Ira Gershwin, Lorenz Hart. No Oscar Hammerstein. Lyrics were generical, routine, moon in spoon by the light of the June. Naturally, then, the generation of Victor Herbert, Broadway's greatest melodist in the very early 1900s, adhered to the practice of building songs around tunes, and Herbert's successors Sigmund Romberg, Rudolf Friml, Jerome Kern, George Gershwin—and Richard Rodgers (with Lorenz Hart)—accepted the tradition. But Hammerstein had always wanted to "compose" a song around its intellectual ideas rather than its sheer sound; and Rodgers liked setting words to music. It gave them both the opportunity to think, from the first, in terms of character—what the people in their shows are saying, wishing, fearing. Hammerstein had been reasoning with the musical since the early 1920s, making it orderly: a plausible story. Now, with Rodgers, he would make the musical characterological: a human comedy.

*Oklahoma!*'s unprecedented success made R & H emergent figures, veterans though they were. It's a youthful work, exuberant, like *The Garrick Gaieties* that had launched the career of Rodgers and Hart two decades earlier. The authors could have been twenty. What would come next?—but the two men separated for projects of personal importance before pursuing their partnership. Hammerstein honored his operaphile grandfather with a new translation of Georges Bizet's *Carmen,* reset in the contemporary American South as *Carmen Jones* in a spectacular production that had Broadway in awe. Rodgers honored his buddy Hart with a revival of *A Connecticut Yankee* for which they wrote six new songs and expanded a part for one of Hart's favorite people, Vivienne Segal. Nevertheless, it was the end of Hart. Hospitalized for exposure, a systemic breakdown, or suicidal despair—you call it—he passed away during a civil-defense blackout.

That was how R & H closed 1943, the year they inaugurated not only their

## Hammerstein Before Rodgers

Below, young Oscar (*seated*) appears with his ear-
liest professional collaborator, composer Herbert
Stothart, with whom he wrote his first four musicals and two smash hits, *Wildflower* and *Rose-
Marie*. A retrospective of Hammerstein's early
career reveals the intensely romantic nature of his
work. At right Paul Gregory and Margaret Schilling
appear in *Children of Dreams*, the first, and for
many years the only "through-sung" movie — virtually a filmed opera. Irene Dunne (*center*) starred
in *High, Wide and Handsome*, the first and at this
writing still the only movie to contain elephants,
corrupt capitalists, oil wells, a circus and Dorothy
Lamour. Last, (*below, right*) is a curiosity: a
Hammerstein–Otto Harbach operetta with music
by Jerome Kern that tried out in St. Louis in 1938
as *Gentlemen Unafraid* and never reached New
York. We offer a ballad from its equally obscure
revision called *Hayfoot, Strawfoot*.

partnership but an era of musical human comedies: shows *about something*, organically conceived, and with, wherever possible, Agnes de Mille choreography and an original cast album. So of course their next piece explodes that definition. It was their only original film and, to my mind, the one dud of their seventeen-year career, *State Fair* (1945).

Our entry into World War II had led Hollywood into a cycle of musicals of patriotic nostalgia, costume pictures designed to rediscover a pure, a fundamental Americana: *Yankee Doodle Dandy* (1942), *My Gal Sal* (1942), *For Me and My Gal* (1942), *Hello, Frisco, Hello* (1943), *Coney Island* (1943), *Meet Me in St. Louis* (1944), *Can't Help Singing* (1944). Obviously, *Oklahoma!* recommended R & H as coming masters in this field, and Twentieth Century–Fox had just the property, *State Fair*, from Phil Stong's novel about a rural Iowa family's adventure at the annual provincial fete of livestock showing, mincemeat and pickle tasting, and midway strolling. Fox had filmed it in 1933 with Will Rogers as the father, Janet Gaynor and Norman Z. Foster as his children, and Lew Ayres and Sally Eilers as the slickers with whom the two kids become romantically involved. Now Fox's chief, Darryl Zanuck, proposed to turn the tale into a big-budget Technicolor musical, and sent for R & H.

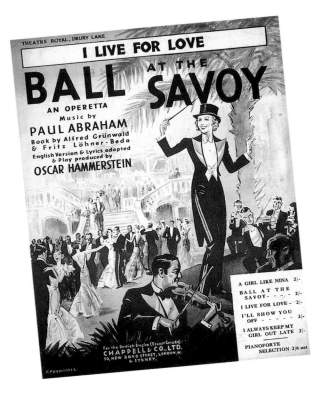

Howevever, just as *Oklahoma!* made R & H the apparent poets of Americana, *Oklahoma!* had made them very secure, which is to say independent, poets. *State Fair* sounded right to them, and Hammerstein agreed to write the screenplay (adapting Sonya Levien and Paul Green's 1933 script) as well as collaborate with Rodgers on the songs. But they were not about to work in Hollywood itself, where each had had highly variable experiences, especially with producers like Zanuck. R & H would write *State Fair* on the condition that they could write it, from Fade In to Fade Out, in the East.

Zanuck agreed, the film went through composition and shooting without major incidents, and it was greeted relatively warmly on its release, in August of 1945 (just before the start of the state fair season, as it happens). The six-number score was tuneful, the color avid, Walter Lang's direction professional, and the cast appealing. Will Rogers' wonderfully bemused, almost cynically optimistic village patriarch was an irreplaceable paragon, but his successor Charles Winninger was by then one of Hollywood's favorite fathers; Jeanne Crain and Dick Haymes as the country kids were two of the studio's more emergent stars; Dana Andrews was a natural as Crain's beau, a brash reporter; and Vivian Blaine as Haymes' date was a prize exponent of the Tough Tomato School of Musico-Dramatic Art (though Zanuck had planned the role for Alice Faye, who suddenly retired from filmmaking that year with *Fallen Angel*). Haymes and Blaine could even sing, a rare talent in a Fox musical, where the dubbing of unmusical voices was as routine as tails on RKO's Astaire.

### Pal Joey

This Rodgers and Hart show marked the apex of the fundamental American form in musical theatre: urbane, brash, and sexy musical comedy. Rodgers and Hammerstein virtually replaced this form with the rural, sensitive, and idealistic *Oklahoma!*, but meanwhile let's enjoy a *Pal Joey* scrapbook. Top: cast members Janet Davis, Van Johnson, June Havoc, Leila Ernst, and Sondra Barrett are en route to the Philadelphia tryout. Center: Jo Mielziner's design for Act One, Scene Two places the audience "inside" the shop, looking out at actors on the street. Below: during the run of *Pal Joey* some of the cast competed in the Broadway Bowling League. Here, Betty Hutton and Ethel Merman represented *Hattie*, but the *Joey* team had the delectable Vivienne Segal (*far right*).

### Some Yearbook Candids

Above, Oscar (*left*) appears in a college show; right, Dick dresses as Zeppo Marx for a costume party; opposite, the two Dorothys with their husbands.

Still, there was a general feeling that *State Fair* was a letdown. As a Fox musical it was acceptable; as the follow-up to *Oklahoma!* it lacked atmosphere and passion. *State Fair*'s Iowa is not felt, *experienced*, as *Oklahoma!*'s Indian territory is. Where is the whimsy of Curly's made-up surrey, the hunger of Jud's "Lonely Room"? Where's, even, the stupid merriment of Ado Annie? Hammerstein's *State Fair* script is flat—and where is the *dance* that keeps lifting, expanding, deepening *Oklahoma!?*

Moreover, R & H did not truly apply themselves to the film medium, though their early talkies were often experimental, Rodgers in his aforementioned "rhythmic dialogue" and Hammerstein in the through-sung *Children of Dreams* (1931), a kind of pop opera fifty years *avant le genre*. *State Fair* does show some technical expertise. The opening, "Our State Fair," gives us a neat sense of the Frake family spread, as the tune is passed from one character to another, including Winninger's prize pig, Blue Boy, grunting out a chorus; and "It's a Grand Night for Singing," at the fair, seems to have been similarly conceived to catch the various principals at different spots on their Night Out on the midway, even if director Lang didn't quite go for it and pull the whole fair into the number.

R & H's most cinematic conception is "It Might as Well Be Spring," heroine Jeanne Crain's establishing character number. It comes very early, just after "Our State Fair," and the authors naturalize it with a bit of dialogue between

verse and chorus, as Crain's mother, Fay Bainter, calls upstairs to her. Then, in a reprise, Crain fancies her beau ideal as a combination of "Ronald Colman, Charles Boyer, and Bing"—and Fox processes voice-over imitations of these stars, one after the other, the great lovers emoting in High Brit and French accent and Bing moaning his "Buh buh boo" as Crain pensively delights.

Perhaps *State Fair*'s problem is that there are too many "performance" numbers, onstage or at a party, and not enough of that R & H specialty the character song, like "Spring." Hammerstein, without a real situation to depict, is put off center; and "All I Owe Ioway" must be the worst song R & H ever wrote. "Spring" won the Academy Award as Best Song, and it was such a big hit for so long that it made the film almost legendary. This is the tail wagging the dog. It's a fine piece, wonderfully listless yet flushed in its description of a teenage girl's romantic yearnings, and with a classic instance of a Rodgers "wrong note," deliberately jarring the ear for emphasis on the line "jumpy as a puppet on a string":

Note the discordant F natural (at the arrow) on "string," harmonically the most remote note possible at that moment and suggestive of the off-kilter wistfulness of spring fever attacking in fall. Hammerstein got his main chance in "Isn't It Kinda Fun," picturing two kids pretending to be in love but—this is *so* Hammerstein—wondering if maybe they really are:

Maybe you'll never be the love of my life,
Maybe I'm not the boy of your dreams,
But isn't it kinda fun to look in each other's eyes,
Swapping romantic gleams?

In Rodgers' bouncy melody, its syncopations reminiscent of his jazzy youth with Lorenz Hart, the song suggests a story, characters, maybe Dick Haymes' first date with Vivian Blaine. In fact, it's presented as no more than a potential pop hit that Haymes and Blaine plug at the piano. Everyone's *performing* in *State Fair,* showing off. No one's truly undergoing anything. Yes, undergoing does lie, mildly, in the story. But not in the score.

  "'Nice,' I believe, would be the word for it," wrote John McCarten in *The New Yorker;* that's aptly faint praise. Of course, *nice* is how R & H were generally perceived, though their shows deal with murder, racism, adultery, and fascism. Nice is not *State Fair's* problem: lack of grip is. The senior Frakes' obsession with his pig and her pickles is foolish, and their kids, for all their longings, lack drive. Tuptim and Lun Tha, in *The King and I,* are no older than the Frake kids, yet how much more R & H were to make of their longings, even in a subplot. Most important, what is great about R & H is the way they blend all elements of theatre into something unique and substantial. What we want after *Oklahoma!* is another R & H show, not a vapid movie with some R & H songs.

  The film was by no means a disgrace, and it proved quite profitable. But, like most Fox movies, it was seldom seen on television in the 1950s, when Astaire and Rogers, Busby Berkeley Depression backstagers, and Judy Garland and Gene Kelly were being acculturated as national treasures. In the wake of the big R & H hit shows—*Oklahoma!, Carousel, South Pacific,* and *The King and I*—an original R & H *movie* must have seemed an enticing curiosity. Yet *State Fair* was little more than a famous title and an echo of "It Might as Well Be Spring." Still, even into the 1960s, in an elevator or on a train, one could hear someone whistling "Our State Fair," virtually a throwaway bit, albeit to one of Rodgers' catchiest tunes, as direct and simple as a folk song:

Refrain *(Brightly)*

Suddenly, in 1962, Fox produced a remake in color and CinemaScope, and if the 1945 version is underpowered, the later one is a bomb. Jose Ferrer's direc-

***State Fair:*** **Four Principals**

Left, in 1945 country girl (Jeanne Crain) loves city boy (Dana Andrews). Below, in 1962, city girl (Ann-Margret) loves country boy (Pat Boone).

This still of the "Isn't It Kinda Fun" number in the remake typifies the sensitivity and taste of the production in general.

tion is windy, Richard Breen's script (from Hammerstein's adaptation of Levien and Green) loses most of the Hammerstein points about how home-bodies need a little adventure to appreciate the stability of home life, and the original's few vital moments now seem dead. R & H's skillful expansion of "It Might as Well Be Spring" throughout the farm sequence was thrown out, and Pamela Tiffin—dubbed, like Jeanne Crain—sings only a verse and chorus, *netto,* mostly in a wide-screen shot designed to make a picture out of her isolation. OK, what CinemaScope; but it's empty.

The pickles-and-mincemeat tasting, amusing in 1945 for the taster's fastidious gurglings and for views of Mother Frake's haughty, preening rival, is now led by Wally Cox at his least inspired (and the pickles are missing). We had hoped for some gala CinemaScoping of "It's a Grand Night for Singing," with the midway in eruption—but Ferrer gives the scene less than Lang had done. Ferrer even repeats Lang's use of the Frake boy and his date on a Ferris wheel, drearily. (And why does the camera cut away from the singers to Wally Cox for a reaction shot that never happens?)

Worse yet, in keeping with the Sixties notion that an important musical is a Very Long Musical, Fox bloated dialogue and added five new songs by Rodgers—words as well as music, for Hammerstein had died in 1960. The new numbers—"More Than Just a Friend" (which Father sings to Blue Boy); Mother Frake's advice to her daughter, "Never Say 'No' (to a man)"; two love songs, "Willing and Eager" and "This Isn't Heaven"; and "The Little Things in Texas"—are so awful that it's hard to believe Rodgers wrote them, especially since, that same year, he produced a truly wonderful (and lyrically quite inventive) score for *No Strings,* the only stage show with lyrics entirely by him. At least "That's for Me" turns from a floor number to a story song, the Frake boy's joyful solo in the gallery of a drag-racing stadium, after he meets and falls for his girl of choice. The number works better this way because R & H weren't floor-number writers. They wrote for character and situation—and, frankly, "That's For Me" sounds a little characterful for a pop tune.*

The worst aspect of the 1962 *State Fair* is the uncharismatic casting. Tom Ewell is, if nothing else, correct as the father, and Pat Boone makes an engaging son. But as the daughter Pamela Tiffin reminds us that her sole distinction as an actress is that she was once married to magazine editor Clay Felker. The usually superb Ann-Margret, Boone's temporary love light, is hurt by Ferrer's "just do it" direction and a disgusting production number based on "Isn't It Kinda Fun," which starts as a Dutch-boy-and-girl caper and turns into a

---

*One of the 1945 *State Fair* songs, "All I Owe Ioway," was dropped, as the setting had been moved to Texas to take advantage of footage of the Dallas skyline and the real-life Texas fair. The 1990 video re-release of the remake tries to tighten up the loose pacing by omitting "This Isn't Heaven" and "The Little Things in Texas."

### Rodgers Without Hammerstein, Hammerstein Without Rodgers

Just after *Oklahoma!* the two men separated for solo projects. Rodgers and a fading Lorenz Hart updated *A Connecticut Yankee* (*right*), and Hammerstein Americanized Bizet in *Carmen Jones* (*top*) with Muriel Smith, at center, in the Habañera, "Dat's Love." In 1946 Hammerstein revived *Show Boat*. At left center, Queenie (Helen Dowdy) keeps order during the "No Shoes" dance. (Note the segregated theatre entrance doors.) Below, Captain Andy accompanies the play-within-the-play, *The Parson's Bride*; left to right are Ralph Dumke, Jan Clayton, Charles Fredericks, and, on the balcony Ethel Owen, not to mention Howard Frank and Duncan Scott, two rustics so taken with the melodrama that they shoot the villain off the stage. One of Hammerstein's most intense aperçus is that theatre *matters*.

hellcat-and-beatnik-chorus-boys lounge act in virulent orange and black. Charmless Bobby Darin takes Dana Andrews' old part, the newspaperman, updated to a television reporter; and Darin's puffy look mars his close-ups.

There is but one real star on view, Alice Faye, at last claiming a piece of the film she missed out on but now, seventeen years later, playing the mother. Fay Bainter, in 1945, made her concerned, sweet, and dowdy, the modest center of her family. Faye, the Broadway kid of countless backstagers and bios, doesn't know from mothers. She looks drawn, bored, even dour. Some comeback.

Kibitzers might like to imagine a livelier cast of actors available for a *State Fair* remake in 1962. Ann Sothern and Percy Kilbride would have made a colorful duo of the Senior Frakes, especially as Kilbride (who has a small part in the 1945 version) was one of Fox's standard Rustic Characters in the 1940s and '50s. Let's keep Boone as the son and partner him with Sheree North; and what about Ann-Margret as the *daughter*, with James Franciscus as the reporter—it's really better as a non-singing part, anyway. And, to revitalize the mincemeat scene, we insist on Buster Keaton, Margaret Hamilton, and Billy Barty for cameos as the judges.

In all, the 1945 *State Fair*'s lack of smarts and surprise did not temper R & H's reputation, for, while it was the project that they next worked on after *Oklahoma!*, it came out five months after the premiere of their second Broadway partnership. This R & H show was bolder and darker than *Oklahoma!*, much more daring, and, while not their biggest success, will almost certainly prove to be their masterpiece.

# Carousel

On paper, *Carousel* reads as a close follow-up to *Oklahoma!:* another Theatre Guild production based on an old Theatre Guild play; another period piece of regional Americana directed by Rouben Mamoulian with choreography by Agnes de Mille;

Bambi Linn, playing Louise, the daughter of Billy and Julie, makes her joyfully defiant entrance at the start of the second-act ballet. Left: Julie (Jan Clayton) and Billy (John Raitt) just before the final curtain—"I love you, Julie. Know that I loved you."

another tale of lovers who don't get along well (and she's got an elderly woman relative and he gets into trouble with the law, just as in *Oklahoma!*).

It was also another idea for an R & H musical from the officious, the meticulous, the copious Theresa Helburn, this time pitching her camp on Ferenc Molnár's *Liliom* (1909), as adapted into English by Benjamin F. Glazer for the Guild in 1921. In the familiar story, R & H balk at treating a tale set in Budapest, as World War II has taken the romance out of Europe as a setting for musicals. "So," Helburn counters, "we'll set it in New Orleans." To which Hammerstein, contemplating the "zis" and "zose" of Creole dialect, says "No way."

What this story leaves out is that Hammerstein had already had his dose of New Orleans in the six-week bomb *Sunny River,* three years earlier. Hammerstein wasn't backing away from tricky possibilities: he *knew* a New Orleans musical wouldn't work—not for him, anyway.

Then someone said, "Let's set it in New England."

Suddenly the show seemed possible, even attractive. The locale, in the time of the late nineteenth century, allowed for such vivid background material as an amusement park, a clambake, a hornpipe for sailors on shore leave, and a little-old-schoolhouse graduation day. The two leads, Billy and Julie, were sufficiently different from Curly and Laurey to inspire entirely different songs—consider the plangent, almost doomed feeling of "If I Loved You" and "What's the Use of Wond'rin' " after "People Will Say We're in Love" or "Many a New Day." The very source marked a refreshing break from *Oklahoma!,* for where *Green Grow the Lilacs* is a "folk play," striving to conceptualize a people through their dialect and social structures, *Liliom* is a fantasy about a thuggish yet attractive loser whose restless, defensive personality destroys his marriage, his life, and even a last pathetic attempt to redeem himself after death.*

But then, *Carousel* really *had* to be entirely unlike *Oklahoma!*. How else to follow a triumph than with something incomparable? Most important, though, *Oklahoma!* was billed as a "musical play," *Carousel*, similarly billed, was more nearly the show in which R & H unveiled this new genre, in which all the musical's elements blended harmoniously into something with the passion of operetta and the delight of musical comedy—but a *sensible* operetta, a *penetrating* musical comedy: the kind of show Hammerstein and Jerome Kern invented in *Show Boat* and, to a lesser extent, in *Sweet Adeline* (1929), *Music in the Air* (1932), and *Three Sisters* (London, 1934). The term "musical

---

*The character's name is Andreas Zavocki, but Liliom—Hungarian for "lily"—is his nickname, emphasizing his blunt, assertive nature by irony. It's akin to a tough street kid's being known as "Creampuff."

### The Lovers Meet

Above, Billy and Julie share a lingering glance as the jealous Mrs. Mullin (Jean Casto, *right of center*) smolders; Julie's cousin Nettie (Christine Johnson, *center*) looks on. Julie's friend Carrie (Jean Darling, *left*) seems startled, but then, above right, congratulates Julie on her new "feller." Right, "If I Loved You."

## Subplots

One of the strengths of R & H is the way that their secondary principals are integrated into the main plot—as opposed to, say, the somewhat irrelevant presences of *Brigadoon*'s wisecracking Jeff or *Kiss Me, Kate*'s Lois Lane and Bill Calhoun. Left, Carrie's beau Mr. Snow (Eric Mattson) personifies the hypocritical social climate that creates yet destroys Billy. Below, Jigger Craigin (Murvyn Vye), menacingly flirting with Carrie and representing Mr. Snow's opposite, is the actual agent of Billy's destruction.

play" was not new; operettas with the slightest pretensions had been bandying it since the early 1920s. What was new was R & H's use of it for their hybrid form of...what? Musical-comedy opera?

We see this first of all in the profusion of musical scenes, song spots that rise far above what Broadway usually thought of as a "number." *Oklahoma!* has that extended sequence of dialogue and song built around "The Surrey with the Fringe on Top." But more than half of *Carousel*'s score develops that pattern—in Billy's seven-minute "Soliloquy," a kind of cluster of melodies tracing the character's growth from the cocksure man's man to a fearfully tender father; in the way "You're a Queer One, Julie Jordan"* does not end but glides into a snatch of dialogue culminating in a question to which the answer is "Mister Snow"; in the first ensemble scene, a women-versus-the-men sing-off that seems about to subside when it suddenly bursts into "June Is Bustin' Out All Over," then finds apotheosis in a women's dance in celebration of spring and rebirth, scored so beautifully that, de Mille recalls, "you could feel the noon heat in the woodwinds"; in the very lengthy scene near the start of Act Two that begins as a comic triangle (for Jigger, the flirtatious Carrie, and Mister Snow) and grows into a disquisition on romance, the tunes themselves moving from spoof ("Geraniums in the Winder") through pseudo-folk song ("Stonecutters Cut It on Stone") to art song ("What's the Use of Wond'rin' "); or even in the way Rodgers quotes from his own score from scene to scene, carrying the "weaving theme" from "Julie Jordan" into "If I Loved You," or retaining the downward-marching octaves of "Give it to 'em good, Carrie, give it to 'em good!," from "June Is Bustin' Out All Over"—the very noise of New England obstinacy—in the lead-in to "What's the Use of Wond'rin'."

Of course, "If I Loved You" is *Carousel*'s musical-scene showpiece, twelve and a half minutes of duet in which two people have the first conversation of their lives and, more or less, decide to love till death—presently—do them part. It's an amazing scene, because so much that can't be stated in dialogue can be phrased in music—Billy singing what he dares not say and Julie feeling what she is afraid to know. They speak very directly to each other, yet they're both lying. *If* I loved you? They talk about nothing—the sky, the sea, taking, giving up. "The tide's creepin' up on the beach like a thief," Billy observes, "afraid to be caught stealin' the land." Billy's coming up on Julie like a thief, afraid to be caught making a claim upon someone so fair and right. But nothing is as potent in Hammerstein's world as a troubled love that *has* to be. Following Hammerstein's lead, Rodgers is spendthrift, tossing out melody as

---

*This, the oddest song title in Broadway's first century of musical theatre, testifies to the pointed nature of R & H's songwriting. Look at *Oklahoma!*'s titles—here and there unusual ("Pore Jud Is Daid"), not to mention in regional dialect. But "You're a Queer One, Julie Jordan" is less a title than a slice of conversation—like much else in R & H, something utterly new in musicals.

if it were water and he a well. Blossoms fall. "The wind brings them down," Julie observes, in the Molnár-Glazer original, translated into *Carousel*'s New Englandese as, "The blossoms are jest comin' down by theirselves." Then —the Hammerstein touch, finalizing the romance—"Jest their time to, I reckon." Troubled but accepting, she turns to Billy for the kiss.

*Carousel* is the musical with extra music, an opera with book scenes. *Oklahoma!* can be done in grammar schools, but *Carousel* needs *voice*: two sopranos (Julie, Carrie), mezzo (Nettie), tenor (Mister Snow), baritone (Billy), bass (Jigger). Or consider the extraordinary opening. Musicals of the 1940s always, but *always*, began with an orchestral medley of the potential Big Tunes. *Carousel* begins with the sound of a carousel's pipe organ starting up, a little out of tune:

Relaxing into key, D Major, that first theme, has been transformed into a serene waltz:

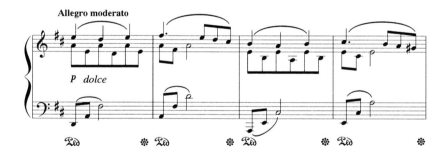

and the curtain of the Majestic Theatre has risen on an amusement park in full cry: sailors, fishermen, girls from the local textile mill, a few families, an ice-cream man, and of course the carousel, just then slowing to a stop. *Oklahoma!*, we know, gets all the (wrong) credit for having discovered a new way to start a musical—*Carousel* is the show whose opening, a six-and-a-half-minute pantomime to music, really startled Broadway. It's not a dance, exactly. It's what one might call "acting in tempo," staged by the bickering Mamoulian and de Mille in tandem. As "The Carousel Waltz" variously tootles, glides, and plows along, three principals emerge from the throng: heroine Julie, her friend Carrie, and hero Billy, the carousel barker who

### Calamity

Jigger's robbery plan fails and Billy dies a suicide. Right, we catch the show in the moment that it turns into fantasy, for as Julie and Nettie pray over Billy a Heavenly Friend (Jay Velie) arrives to take him Beyond. Below right, given a chance to revisit his loved ones on earth, Billy steals a present for them from the Starkeeper (Russell Collins).

flirts, amiably, unconcernedly, with Julie. Other characters catch our notice — Mr. Bascombe, the pompous mill owner; Mrs. Mullin, the widow who runs the carousel and, apparently, Billy; a juggler; a dancing bear; an acrobat. But what draws us in is the intensity with which Julie regards Billy — the way she stands frozen, staring at him, while everyone else at the fair is swaying to the rhythm of Billy's spiel. And as Julie and Billy ride together on the swirling carousel, and the stage picture surges with the excitement of the crowd, and the orchestra storms to a climax, and the curtain falls, we realize that R & H have not only skipped the overture *and* the opening number but the exposition as well. They have plunged into the story, right into the middle of it, in the most intense first scene any musical had ever had.

As it happens, Molnár had opened *Liliom* with the same scene. But *Liliom's* prologue, though unscripted, is not a pantomime — it's mostly shouting and ad libs — and was not performed to music. Again, as with *Green Grow the Lilacs* and *Oklahoma!*, Hammerstein knew what to retain from his source; and Rodgers knew how the music should work for it. What is most interesting is that *Carousel* was not the first musical to open with an establishing pantomime: *Sunny River* had begun with a "Pictorial Overture" something like "The Carousel Waltz," though more devoted to presenting New Orleans than

## The Lovers Part

Compare Jo Mielziner's design for the final scene, Louise's high school graduation (*above*) with the scene in performance (*right*). Now wearing mutton-chop whiskers as Dr. Seldon, Starkeeper Russell Collins is at the lectern; Bambi Linn sits at far right in the first row of students; Christine Johnson and Jay Velie flank Jan Clayton and John Raitt.

launching the plot. However, few people had seen *Sunny River,* and one wonders if Sigmund Romberg could have equaled the dazzling variety of tunes Rodgers lets flow in *Carousel's* prelude.

For "The Carousel Waltz" is not merely a suite of tunes in "carousel time," so to say, but a deceptively sophisticated interweaving of themes. For instance, the melody quoted above immediately turns up in a third guise:

and its "back half" (marked "A") then turns into an emphatic rhythmic figure that will urge the music along right to the last page:

The transformations and developments continue. The *un poco lento, ben cantabile* ("somewhat slower, strongly sung") section introduces a new theme:

but the motive marked "B" is our first theme back again in a fourth variation. By the time Rodgers rides his music right into the tumult of the action, themes are crashing into themes, as when the original melody, in the brass, marries a passionate new idea in the strings:

**The De Mille Touch**

Above: a joyous women's rite of spring follows "June Is Bustin' Out All Over." Below: Louise and two hooligans (Ralph Linn and Robert Tucker) face down Mr. Snow and his brood in the second-act ballet.

The effortlessly soaring velvet of the famous "Rodgers waltz" is noteworthy, certainly: but other composers wrote soaring waltzes. What made Rodgers' waltzes special was their absolutely contemporary sound. When Herbert, Romberg, Friml, or even Kern wrote waltzes, their very atmosphere summoned up Vienna, May wine, candlelit ballrooms. When Rodgers wrote a waltz—"The Most Beautiful Girl in the World," "Falling in Love with Love," "Wait till You See Her"—it said *here and now*. Indeed, by the 1920s, when Rodgers and Hart began, the waltz was out-of-date in America, supplanted by the tense new dances of "jazz," and composers usually reserved the waltz for nostalgia or operetta. Yet, two decades later, Rodgers could waltz Hammerstein's lyric for "Out of My Dreams" and still sound as up-to-the-minute as anything in *Something for the Boys*.

In short, *Carousel* is a very *musical* play—and more: an ecumenical one. Its strong nineteenth-century New England flavor hides a universal view of gender relationships and the class system that gives *Carousel* greater reach than the slighter, funnier, more compact genre that R & H now thought of as "musical comedy." As Stephen Sondheim puts it, "*Oklahoma!* is about a picnic; *Carousel* is about life and death." The folkish tang that made *Oklahoma!* sweet makes *Carousel* timeless—in the almost primitive spring-means-rebirth atavism of "June Is Bustin' Out All Over" or the weary wisdom of exploited women in "Stonecutters Cut It on Stone":

> I never see it yet to fail.
> I never see it fail.
> A girl who's in love with any man
> Is doomed to weep and wail.

With Rodgers' square-cut tune backing up Hammerstein's observation, we are on the verge of a kind of extrapolated folk song, something drawing upon eternal verities—as, indeed, Hammerstein loved to do, in such numbers as "Ol' Man River," "'Twas Not So Long Ago," "The Folks Who Live on the Hill" (before Rodgers), and "A Fellow Needs a Girl" and "All at Once You Love Her" (with Rodgers), not to mention "Edelweiss," which many people think actually *is* a folk song. *Carousel*'s "You'll Never Walk Alone" has been loved and hated for precisely this naive yet knowing air, though what arrests the ear is less Hammerstein's message than the utter break it marks in Rodgers' career. True, nothing that he composed for *Oklahoma!* sounds like the music he had been writing with Lorenz Hart. But in *Carousel*—and especially in "You'll Never Walk Alone"—we meet an even more reconstructed Rodgers, hymnlike, diatonic, simple in an overwhelming way. As we shall see, this is another effect of the musical play: it draws authors into compositional styles they don't know they had in them.

What an amazing play *Liliom* must be, to have pulled all this out of R & H. Or perhaps their adaptation is *very* adapted? Is *Carousel* only "suggested by" *Liliom?* Nothing of the kind. As with *Green Grow the Lilacs* and *Oklahoma!*, *Liliom* is *Carousel* without the songs—*almost*. Billy, Julie, Carrie, and the slimy villain, Jigger Craigin, are all in *Liliom* as they are in *Carousel*, at times line for line. Nettie Fowler, Julie's cousin, is in Molnár her aunt, one Mother Hollunder, but she was changed from a grumbly crone into a clambake-running Earth Mother. Carrie's stuffy fiancé, Mister Snow, is in Molnár an obsequious servant; Hammerstein rebuilt him as a little tycoon-on-the-rise to enlarge the tale's social background.

*Liliom*'s characters are almost entirely working-class, resentful or respectful of the system and its officials. One of the protagonist's most destructive impulses is his compulsion to bait authority, anyone from an aunt to a policeman. Hammerstein not only retained this, but, in turning Liliom into Billy, shows us more of the great world of grace and plenty that Billy has imagined as lying outside his reach—the world, in fact, that Hammerstein's reinvented Mister Snow takes Carrie into when he turns from fisherman into canning magnate, a world free not only of want but of oppressive policemen.

This is why Billy is so tragically determined to steal: to rear his child in a freer environment. And this is why, when *Liliom* and *Carousel* slip into fantasy, the dead hero enters an afterworld as claustrophobic and rule bound as his life had been. "Liliom's Heaven," Molnár's adapter Benjamin Glazer wrote, "is the Heaven of his own imagining...an irrational jumble of priest's purgatory, police magistrate's justice, and his own limited conception of good deeds and evil." In short, a courtroom. Hammerstein's first idea was to transmute this into what his New England roughneck would envision: Mr. and Mrs. God, austere and judgmental in their front parlor, the kind of people Billy has been willfully affronting all his life. It was a good idea but, for a musical, dreary. Audiences in Boston hated it; it was probably their idea of heaven, too. So Hammerstein veered to the fanciful, rewriting his heaven as a vast, open space of dry-ice clouds and stars hung on strings, with a Starkeeper—God?—and a businesslike man in a business suit who leads Billy to the beyond and then back to earth to try to redeem his ne'er-do-well life.

*Carousel* emphasizes "simple" people, but then so did Hammerstein. "I'm more at home with characters who haven't got a big vocabulary," he told the interviewer Arnold Michaelis. "You find people who are primitive in their education—they're more likely, I think, to say what they mean. They haven't got the subtle tools to cover up their meaning." It is interesting that, starting work on *Carousel*, R & H kept walking up dead ends until they attempted Billy's "Soliloquy." Somehow, laying out the drives and fears of a simple man unleashed their powers.

Casting, however, was not simple. One of the reasons *Carousel* is less frequently revived than *Oklahoma!* or *South Pacific* is the difficulty in getting a Billy Bigelow who can not only sing but act. Today we think of it as a star part, though the original *Carousel* cast was even more unknown than *Oklahoma!*'s crew, and still are: for besides John Raitt and, to a lesser extent, Jan Clayton, who has heard of Jean Darling (Carrie), Eric Mattson (Mister Snow), Christine Johnson (Nettie), Murvyn Vye (Jigger), or Jean Casto (Mrs. Mullin)?*

But then, given the way that R & H worked, a batch of unknowns was practically inevitable, at least at this early stage in the R & H revolution. In the 1920s, when both men were getting started, musicals were written loosely, mainly to accommodate the stars and specialty talent but also in the hope that rehearsals would inspire something hot for Act Two. By the 1930s, the rise of such thorough librettists as Herbert Fields and Moss Hart had tightened musical-comedy composition—but even these men had to write around the hired talent.

R & H, on the other hand, wrote the *entire* show and *then* cast it. The text didn't have to suit the available talent; the talent had to suit the text. This explains the incessant Tuesday auditions in the R & H office, the permanently open door. Who knew what character in what next show might step in? That's how R & H found John Raitt, in the spring of 1944. They promptly put him into the *Oklahoma!* touring company as Curly, to try him out. He tried out fine.

*Carousel* followed *Oklahoma!*'s route out of town, from a few days' shakeout in New Haven to several weeks' stay in Boston—and Agnes de Mille, for one, never ceased to applaud the ruthless sense of purpose with which R & H solved their shows' problems. Through the 1950s and 1960s, de Mille was to suffer failures on Broadway for various reasons out of her control—weak books, hard-sell concepts, productions overbalanced to favor a star. At staff meetings, the honchos would say, "Well, we've got to fix that scene," or, "That song should be replaced." It was all talk. *Chez* R & H it was all action: yellow pads, notes, and a schedule of attack—rewrite that scene Monday, put the new song in Wednesday afternoon, and so on.

In fact, *Carousel* was in trouble out of town. Act Two felt long and dour, not only in Billy's adventure in the afterworld but in de Mille's Big Ballet catching up on what had happened to Billy's wife and daughter in the fifteen years when he had been…away. De Mille's Act One dances fell beautifully into place. As in *Oklahoma!,* they set forth women's lyricism (in "Many a New Day" and, here, in the women's dance following "June Is Bustin' Out All Over") and men's

*Actually, Jean Darling had been much seen, if not heard: she had played the delectable Darla in MGM's *Our Gang* comedy shorts in the 1930s.

energy (in "Kansas City" and, here, in the "Hornpipe" after "Blow High, Blow Low"). But the Big Ballet—in *Oklahoma!* the dream that closes Act One and in *Carousel* a long narrative in the middle of Act Two—was not going over. De Mille fondly recalls a stylization of the birth of Billy's daughter, Louise: a group of women sympathetically encircling Julie (an echo of the staging of "What's the Use of Wond'rin'," earlier in the act), pressing tightly and more tightly upon her till a clap of thunder brought Louise forth, defiant and fully grown. The ballet and its travails so bore upon de Mille in New Haven that in one tormented moment she told Hammerstein that she hated her work and hated herself, and Hammerstein grabbed her and growled, "Be careful— you're speaking of the woman I love."

And embraced her.

Needless to say, R & H solved *Carousel*'s problems: by cutting down the sec-ond-act book, rephrasing the heaven sequence, and letting de Mille restyle parts of the ballet. Louise was no longer "born." Now she simply appeared at the ballet's start, romping on the beach, bellicose and free. She enjoys a dalli-ance with the cynosure of a carnival troupe (as did her mother) and angrily confronts the bourgeoisie (as did her father). *Now* the ballet stopped the show. One night in Boston, the applause was so intense that Jean Darling tried three times—and three times failed—to launch the next scene. The fourth attempt took—but then the Louise, Bambi Linn, reentered, and the Colonial Theatre so rocked with cheers that Linn had to step out of character and take a bow.

*Carousel* opened in New York—at the Majestic Theatre, directly across from *Oklahoma!* at the St. James—on April 19, 1945. The critics were dazzled, the show ran 890 performances—twenty-six months—and the score, like *Oklahoma!*'s, immediately became popular not as a small set of big tunes but almost as a whole. Decca's original cast album unfortunately reduced the musical scenes to kernels—the operatic "If I Loved You" was boiled down to verse and chorus, as if Irving Berlin had written it, but a ready corps of bari-tones and sopranos kept the show in hearing for twenty years. In London it followed *Oklahoma!* into the Drury Lane, affirming a solid regime of R & H that lasted (through *South Pacific* and *The King and I*) into 1956.*

After a while, however, *Carousel* fell behind the other R & H hits, though it remained popular on the summer tent circuit and in New York City Center revivals into the mid-1960s. At the time, decent Billys were relatively easy to come by, though as early as 1954, at the City Center, we note the obscure Chris

*This was Hammerstein's second reign at London's most historic theatre. In the 1920s, a consecu-tive run of *Rose-Marie, The Desert Song,* and  *Show Boat,* all starring Edith Day, made the Drury Lane an outpost of American operetta, and of librettos by Oscar Hammerstein II.

Robinson playing with the soon-to-be-prominent Jo Sullivan, Barbara Cook (as Carrie), John Conte, and some of the original dancers. Three years later the City Center built a *Carousel* around Howard Keel—so much so that the Julie, Janet Blair, walked out, to be replaced by Cook. Oddly, another star part emerged from this revival, for after Keel, Cook, and company, the posters promised "as 'THE STARKEEPER,' none other than the beloved VICTOR MOORE." The original Starkeeper, Russell Collins, a veteran of the Group Theatre and the first Johnny Johnson (in Kurt Weill's musical of that name of 1936), was no better known than anyone else on stage. But Moore's billing glamorized the role. At Lincoln Center in 1965, Edward Everett Horton got comparable billing (though he could not fairly, or even imaginatively, have been called "beloved"), and even Parker Fennelly, back at the City Center in 1966, retained this special announcement. Ironically, the Billy of that revival, Bruce

### The Film Version

Left: Carrie (Barbara Ruick), Mr. Snow (Robert Rounseville), and Jigger (Cameron Mitchell) in the clambake scene. Below: the crew sets up for the "June" number on location in Boothbay Harbor, Maine.

Yarnell, was perhaps the last of the dependable Billys. *Carousel* was going to become scarce.

Certainly the debased film version, somewhat miscast and with the score vastly cut (two songs had been dropped, and, after a draggy preview, much more music was sliced out of the release print), has done nothing for the show's reputation. Twentieth Century–Fox, producers of *State Fair* and re-distributors of the *Oklahoma!* film (on its general release after a year of road show screenings), again officiated. What a soggy piece of gingerbread they made of it. Yes, we have the advantage of location filming in Maine. "Boothbay Harbor was simply perfect!" Arne Brucker rhapsodized, thirty-four years later, in the *Boothbay Harbor Register.* Well, consider the quality of the locals hired as extras—Whitmore Garland, Myrle Sproul, Mary Sue Gould, Maxine Thiboutot, Lyall Ritcher (among many others). How can you go wrong? Consider choreographer Rod Alexander throwing out de Mille's Act One dances for a raucous imitation of Michael Kidd after "June" and blithely re-creating de Mille's second-act ballet, though de Mille was to receive no credit.* Consider that Frank Sinatra was hired to play Billy. Gordon MacRae, the last-minute substitute for Sinatra, had been radiant as Curly, but he lacks Billy's power; Shirley Jones' Julie, Barbara Ruick's Carrie, Robert Rounseville's Mister Snow, Claramae Turner's Nettie, and Cameron Mitchell's Jigger are all correct but uninspired; and director Henry King lacks the slightest understanding of what a musical is. In the event, most of the Boothbay Harbor footage was cut after those first previews, including "Blow High, Blow Low." "Audiences never got to see Cameron Mitchell cavort," Arne Brucker laments.

The trouble is, with stage revivals thin on the ground, *Carousel: The Movie* is our only *Carousel*, which makes a tricky proposition trickier. The show is already problematical in its very size (the props include a working carousel) and its feelings (your husband, father, or brother gets killed in Act Two). This must have been especially difficult during the original run, at the end of World War II, when so many of the women in the audience were in fact widows. Yes, Billy does hearten Julie and Louise, in a scene totally invented by Hammerstein (and endorsed by Molnár, a Hitler refugee in America and *Carousel*'s first enthusiast). "I loved you, Julie," Billy tells her. "Know that I loved you!" Still, the guy *is* dead.

But, then, Hammerstein often asks us to accept tragic events, because people of various fates have been placed on earth to influence each other's lives, sometimes climactically. We see this particularly in *Show Boat*, wherein a series of coincidences persuades us that these people aren't just bumping

*Shamefully, de Mille had to go to court to get credit for her (purloined) work. This marked the end of her relationship with R & H on every level.

into, but *revising*, each other, playing out a mutual destiny. We know, from the "If I Loved You" scene, that Billy and Julie cannot give each other up. Love is their fate, as sure as blossoms fall from trees: "Jest their time to, I reckon." Billy and Julie aren't merely a marriage, but a concatenation of feelings that don't coincide yet are bound to be joined. This is *Carousel*'s hard part—a layabout thug who is not above hitting his wife gets killed during an armed robbery, then invites the public's tears just for showing up a generation later to whisper pep mottos into his survivors' ears.

Yes, it's sentimental, especially with "You'll Never Walk Alone" surging through it. However, Billy *is* led off to the afterworld, his mission accomplished but he himself to be cut off forever from the only people who could love or understand him. Then Hammerstein does something so natural, and so right, and so terrifying, that it throws the entire show onto a higher level, still

*Carousel* is the R & H "women's show," much of it told from a woman's point of view. Above, note the sympathetic Julie (Barbara Cook) and the shyly radiant Carrie (Pat Stanley) in Carrie's reprise of "Mr. Snow," at the City Center in 1957. At right, the Takarazuka Theatre of Japan mounted a *Carousel* entirely cast with women. Actually, Takarazuka performs all its shows this way, even (or especially) *Me and My Girl*.

sentimental but epically so. For, given that Hammerstein liked the notion that certain people are meant to serve a purpose, was it Billy's life's agenda to stimulate the introspective Julie or Julie's to soften the hard-edged Billy? Which of the two is *Carousel*'s protagonist? Hammerstein evens it out in the finale—the post-Molnár scene, so to say—wherein he improves upon *Liliom*'s fantasy, naturalizes it, by recasting the Starkeeper as the old country doctor who delivers the address at the high school graduation of Julie and Billy's daughter.

Merging the Starkeeper and Doctor Seldon is no stunt. God walks among us. For, in the moment just before the curtain falls, as "You'll Never Walk Alone" rises to its climax and the invisible Billy, having heartened his family, is taken away, the doctor nods and smiles as if he had seen the whole thing and always had known it could—and in fact was going to—happen. Julie and Billy have each redeemed the other, and Doctor Seldon becomes something of an angel on earth.

And Hammerstein was something of a healer. He used the very word about himself—in embarrassment, certainly. Nevertheless, he said, "I see plays and read books that emphasize the seamy side of life, and the frenetic side, and the tragic side. And I don't deny the existence of the tragic and the frenetic. But I say that somebody has to keep saying that that isn't all that there is to life....We're very likely to get thrown off our balance if we have such a preponderance of artists expressing the 'waste land' philosophy."

So we see how truly suited Richard Rodgers and Oscar Hammerstein II were, in the way the musical-comedy composer and the operetta lyricist developed a "healing" art as interested in discussing the advantages of community or analyzing the nature of love as in entertaining. But this is not what makes *Carousel* great. This is what makes *Carousel* a parable: "How the Ne'er-do-well Makes Good." What makes *Carousel* great is what finally implanted the musical play on Broadway as the form that all major musical works inevitably must take: one-of-a-kind stories that sing deeply in character and that dance to express what words and music cannot, so that each show will be unlike all other shows. *Oklahoma!* was a great event. But not till *Carousel* was Rodgers' ability to *concentrate* on what was happening in the story so intensely felt; or was Hammerstein's poetry so liberated, inventive, unique, as when Carrie accuses Julie of being eccentric and Julie, neither denying nor affirming, explains, "I like to watch the river meet the sea."

Brooks Atkinson took a second look at *Carousel* in 1954 and predicted that it would turn out to be "the finest of the [R & H] creations." It's darker than *Oklahoma!,* not as amusing as *South Pacific,* and lacks the invigorating exoticism of *The King and I.* Still, "if it were not so enjoyable, it would probably turn out to be opera." Atkinson meant that *Carousel* is like art, only better.

# Allegro

In the opening scene of *Allegro*, the "Greek" chorus (preceding page) and townspeople hail the birth of Joseph Taylor, Jr., in 1905. At right are Grandma Taylor (Muriel O'Malley), Joe's mother (Annamary Dickey), and his father (William Ching), a small-town doctor. Above, despite a flawed negative, we wanted to present the all-important scene in which little Joey (seen only in a dim back-projection) takes his first steps, to the coaching of Grandma and Mother. This leads into a choral piece, "One Foot, Other Foot." Above right, a "Children's Dance" follows, introducing Joe's childhood sweetheart, Jenny Brinker (danced by Kathryn Lee, center). But we still haven't seen Joe himself: characters address him by speaking to the audience. Time passes, Grandma dies, and, years later (*right*) as Joe is about to go off to college, we see his parents reaffirm their love in "A Fellow Needs a Girl." At far right, above, we see Joe's first dance as a Freshman. A Charleston (done to Rodgers and Hart's "Mountain Greenery") reminds us that this is the 1920s. Then (far right, below) the dance turns elegant as the kids imagine themselves as sophisticates.

During the dance, the Greek chorus decides to hunt for Joe in the crowd and when we find someone counting (*below*) "One Foot, Other Foot," the chorus cries "That's our boy!" Right, Joe does some dating, here with Beulah (Gloria Wills), who sings "So Far." Bottom right, Joe's buddy and fellow premed, Charlie Townsend (John Conte), has plenty of girls on his mind even in the lecture hall.

But Joe thinks only of Jenny (now a young woman, played by Roberta Jonay). Jenny is vain and selfish and Joe's mother knows it. But she dies, and, above, Joe and Jenny marry. Note the presence of Grandma—in Joe's thoughts that day—and his late mother (right of Jenny), who attends the ceremony and urges the bride to take her vows seriously. (In this photograph of the national tour, Joe is played by James Jewell).

Act Two opens during the Depression when Jenny and other penniless young housewives (*left*) sing "Money Isn't Everything." But Jenny doesn't really think so.

Jenny manipulates Joe into leaving his hometown for Chicago, where she sets up a salon for wealthy wastrels (*above*) and helps him build his practice. Joe is now rich and useless, a "healer" of hypochondriacs and (*right*) under much social pressure. A new character now appears, Joe's nurse, Emily (Lisa Kirk).

Emily loves Joe and loathes Jenny. Stomping out of one of Jenny's soirées, Emily sings "The Gentleman Is a Dope" (*left*), the number that made Lisa Kirk a star. Following this, de Mille renders modern life in a Big Ballet (*below*) as frantic, neurotic, scattered—not (as the show's title suggests) "allegro," which simply means lively.

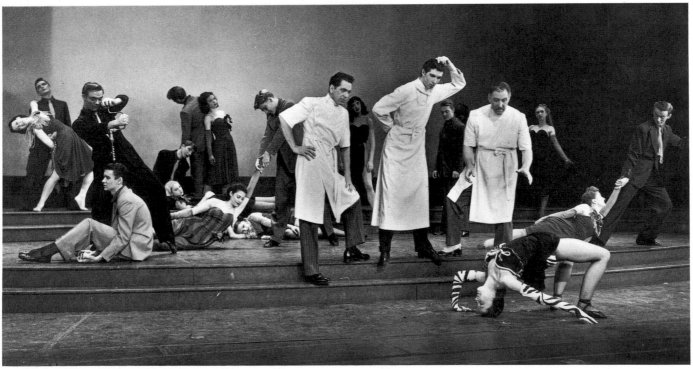

Joe discovers Jenny's adultery and, thoroughly disenchanted with his life, he turns down the post of Physician-in-Chief at the big-city hospital to return to his real home, taking Emily and Charlie with him. In the final scene (*above*), as Joe (again played by James Jewell) "learns to walk" again, to the coaching of Grandma and Mother, the audience hears a last vindicating reprise of "One Foot, Other Foot."

After reading *Allegro*'s script, Agnes de Mille asked Oscar Hammerstein II what the show was about.

"It's about a man who can't fulfill his life's work," said Hammerstein, "because of personal and professional pressures."

"That's a wonderful premise," said de Mille. "But you haven't written that story."

This was one week before rehearsals were to begin, in the summer of 1947; and de Mille was not only choreographing but directing the entire piece.

She hadn't truly wanted to, for what she had seen of the script—it was finished, but tentatively—and heard of the score did not sound worthy to follow *Oklahoma!* and *Carousel*. But history was looking over her shoulder. It was the first time a choreographer (and, more important to de Mille, a woman) had been invited to direct a musical. And surely, whatever she felt about the composition, she must have been attracted to the authors' vision of a great empty stage almost ceaselessly in motion, with crowd upon crowd of actors, singers, and dancers now undergoing the action and then musing abstractedly upon it, here a pin strip of light spotting a character and there an eruption of chorus and dance. It was a kind of ballet theatre.

History was looking over R & H's shoulders as well, for, with *Oklahoma!* still running and *Carousel* just closed, and with "Oh, What a Beautiful Mornin'," "People Will Say We're in Love," "It Might as Well Be Spring," "If I Loved You," and "You'll Never Walk Alone" enjoying a density of popularity beyond the reach of any previous Broadway masters, the world was eager to see what the boys would come up with next. (So was the Theatre Guild. As with *Carousel*, they would be "presenting," rather than actually producing, *Allegro*—R & H were in charge—but even an "in name only" role promised to be lucrative.)

It isn't clear whether R & H actually chose to up the stakes in the musical play or it just turned out that they did, but in either case *Allegro* was so original a musical, so thoroughly reconceived in its format, that its words and music were no more crucial than its staging plan. Here was a show whose visuals mattered as much as the text.

*Allegro* was, in fact, the first "concept musical," as we now call them: shows written around a unique and thematically explanatory staging plan, as in *Cabaret*'s commentative numbers in the Kit Kat Klub, or in *Follies*'s abandoned theatre of passé showstoppers and dead souls. *Allegro* was also the first big commercial musical that set out to be uncommercial. True, *Show Boat* had broken rules, but *Show Boat* had a very strong story, a presold title, and a great deal of old-time musical-comedy diversion. *Pal Joey* had broken rules, but *Pal Joey* was all the same an up-tempo song-and-dance show. *On the Town* had broken rules, but *On the Town* was at heart a farce with a lot of ballet, easy to love and ready to be admired. These and other nonconformist shows found ways to defy convention while appealing to conventional theatregoers. *Allegro* shattered every rule in the musical-comedy handbook.

Of course, it was really the *musical-play* handbook, the R & H formula, that is best summed up as "There is no formula: tell a good story with genius." The story Hammerstein told in *Allegro* seemed to denounce urban life in favor of the small town: country doctors are self-sacrificing while city doctors attend cocktail parties and have pianos in their offices. The story Hammerstein had had in mind, however, appears to be somewhat autobiographical. Like the protagonist Joe Taylor, Hammerstein lost his mother when very young, left an adulterous wife,* and found himself too often the public figure and rather less the private man he essentially was. However, Hammerstein actually seems to have modeled *Allegro*'s protagonist on a friend, a doctor whose life corresponded in many details to Joe Taylor's. This friend may even have had an affair with his nurse (though in *Allegro* Joe and Emily get together only seconds before the final curtain) and did finally give up his big-city practice to move to the country, apparently to retire, rather than to purify his ethics.

*Allegro* was the fourth R & H work but their first original, Hammerstein's attempt to air some personal matters while treating, as he said, "the integrity of doctors, a big subject." Somewhere or other Hammerstein has gotten the reputation of a tireless adapter, when in fact the bulk of his musicals were original, including *all* his extraordinarily influential shows with Kern, Romberg, Friml, and Youmans (except *Show Boat,* and even there, while respecting the spirit of Ferber, Hammerstein invented most of what happens in the action of the show). Still, the bulk of R & H is adaptations, so *Allegro* stands out as the first show (of only two) that they put together from scratch.

Some musicals are written, some thrown together. This musical was *conceived.* Not a song, not a scene was planned without the authors' having some idea of how it was going to look and behave. To start with, they devised a playing area unlike any other of the age, a vast, open area like the *orchestra* of the ancient Greek theatre, backed by projections on a cyclorama and "placed" here and there by bits of scenery whisked on and off from the wings. For the first time since the old days of the one-set-per-act musical—the days, virtually, of Gilbert and Sullivan and the Gaiety shows—there would be no delay in the playing of a piece, no "stage waits" between scenes (as the orchestra rampaged through an echo of the score and the audience sat in limbo), no need for little scenes "in one" (downstage in front of a curtain, as stagehands shoved and hauled behind it). Aside from the intermission, *Allegro* could be

*Myra Finn, whom Hammerstein allowed to divorce him so that he could marry Dorothy Blanchard.

played absolutely continuously. It was designer Jo Mielziner who worked out the mechanics by which such plans could be implemented, and Mielziner proved such a wizard that he became, after orchestrator Robert Russell Bennett, the most constant of the R & H artistic team, handling settings and lighting from *Carousel* right through *Pipe Dream*, five shows later.

A bare stage, a little furniture, curtains, projections. It sounds simple. Yet in physical terms *Allegro* ended up as one of the biggest musicals since the Depression economy had tightened Broadway's production budgets. Even *Show Boat* wasn't much bigger than this: eighteen principals, twenty-two dancers, and thirty-eight singers; thirty-five players in the pit; and, despite the "bare stage," such a host of supplementary visuals to keep in play that it took forty stagehands to run the show, twice as many as the average big musical with conventional scenery.

One reason for *Allegro*'s great size was the use of a third chorus, in addition to the usual singing ensemble and dancing corps. This was the "Greek chorus" that urged on the action and explained subtexts to the audience. Actually, this chorus resembled that of Aeschylus, Sophocles, and Euripides only in limited ways. A true Greek chorus has two major functions: to dispute with the protagonist and, alone, to elaborate poetically on the events of the play. *Allegro*'s chorus has considerably more various duties and addresses the public far more than it does the protagonist, almost as if it doesn't know what to say to him. This may be why Joe Taylor never comes through as a character: if his own Greek chorus finds him remote, where does that leave us?

Moreover, Joe Taylor is possibly the first romantic lead in an American musical who has very little to sing—a ditty about being lonely at college, a love song, and a few lines of the title number. But then, no one in *Allegro* has much to sing, for R & H made a certain decision in the writing of this score—something like the opposite of *Carousel*, with its operatic grandeur. *Allegro* has only one musical scene, though music pumps through it. Instead, it has bits and pieces, occasionally a full-out song, and, naturally, plenty of dances. There is no "The Surrey with the Fringe on Top," no "Soliloquy." This is a kind of deconstruction of theatre music, to match the show's deconstruction of traditional theatre design. Musicals before *Allegro*—the serious ones, which is to say the operettas—tended to be dense and methodical. *Allegro* is airy, mercurial, as its title suggests. Just before the infant Joe Taylor takes his first steps, the chorus, speaking for him, says, "Maybe going forward is easier than standing still!" *Allegro*, like *Show Boat, Pal Joey, Lady in the Dark, On the Town*—and *Oklahoma!* and *Carousel*, for that matter—was a show that went forward.

Rumors of the bare stage, the Greek chorus, and the extraordinary look of the piece excited interest in the theatre community, and, for the average theatregoer who had taken in *Oklahoma!* and *Carousel*, *Allegro* was, to put

Jo Mielziner's design for the Freshman Dance.

it mildly, a hot ticket. It may well have been the most eagerly awaited show in history—certainly to that date, the most widely covered in advance press reports. *Life* and *Time* gave it cover stories, *Life* brandishing three of the chorus dancers and *Time,* for some reason, picturing Hammerstein without Rodgers. As with *Oklahoma!* and *Carousel,* the tryout consisted of a brief road test in New Haven's Shubert Theatre followed by a lengthy polishing period at the Colonial in Boston. But *Allegro's* first night in New Haven stands out for mishaps. It is, in fact, one of the theatre's legendary disasters.

First, dancer Ray Harrison caught his leg in one of the grooves cut to run Mielziner's scenery and was seen limping offstage in his colleagues' arms. Shortly after, William Ching (playing Joseph Taylor, Sr.) noticed, during a tender scene with his wife, that a wall piece was about to fall and spent all of "A Fellow Needs a Girl" holding his house up. Later, during "Come Home," smoke began to seep into the theatre, and, just before panic broke out, Joshua Logan rose in his seat and bawled out, "It's just an alley fire! Everybody *sit down!*" (It was, in fact, some trash burning in a can in the alley outside the building—as Logan, a veteran of New Haven tryouts at the Shubert, had guessed.)

The most famous of the evening's accidents occurred late in Act Two, while Lisa Kirk was singing "The Gentleman Is a Dope." Like Ray Harrison, she got caught in a groove and pitched forward—but she happened to be standing right at the edge of the stage. The story, as told, has her crashing into the orchestra pit; but the New Haven Shubert Theatre didn't have an orchestra pit. When musicals played there, the orchestra sat on the auditorium floor, as in nineteenth-century opera houses, the fiddle bows cutting into spectators' views and those in the front rows overwhelmed by noise. So Kirk couldn't crash very far—she fell onto the biggest woodwind section in musical history, and the players simply helped her back onto the stage as she went on singing.

The Kirk story, carried back to New York by the usual first-night gossips, was all over The Street by the next day. Unwisely inspired, Kirk apparently decided to prolong her notoriety by taking the same spill during the same number at the next performance. Hammerstein went back to her dressing room and told her that if she tried it again she'd be fired.

Rodgers looks on as de Mille (on the couch) drills the dancers.

In Boston *Allegro* ran more smoothly, and the town's leading critic, Elliott Norton, *raved.* "*Allegro* has everything," he began; and he ended by calling it "the most remarkable musical show I have ever seen." Seven hundred fifty thousand dollars were sitting in the box office* on the afternoon of the New York opening, October 10, 1947, when R & H invited a host of associates and employees to look in on one last run-through. The house went wild with tears and cheers; that night, at the premiere, the audience that mattered sat on its hands. As de Mille's husband, Walter Prude, put it, *Allegro* went over "like a wet firecracker."

The reviews were widely divided. Robert Coleman of the *Daily Mirror* said, "*Allegro* is perfection." Wolcott Gibbs of *The New Yorker* called it "a shocking disappointment." In *The New York Times,* Brooks Atkinson thought R & H had "just missed the final splendor of a perfect work of art." Robert Garland, in the *Journal-American,* suggested that the authors "confused 'allegro' with, say, 'lento,' which means 'slow,' 'unhurried,' and even downright 'serious.'" Ward Morehouse of the *Sun* probably was the most accurate—"distinguished and tumultuous," he called it. "It takes its place alongside of *Oklahoma!* and *Carousel* as a theatrical piece of taste, imagination, and showmanship.... [It has] a simple story but it becomes frequently touching and occasionally exalted." George Jean Nathan, who delighted in debunking shows by asserting that they had looted earlier works with which they had at best tenuous links, wrote a special piece in the *Journal-American,* lifting his leg on *Allegro* like a dog at a hydrant. (Nathan's idea of a good show was *Something for the Boys.*) *Allegro* struck him as "a combination of the poorer elements of Andreyev's *The Life of Man* ... and of Wilder's *Our Town* ... and with an old D. W. Griffith going-forth-to-greet-the-dawn ending. Mixed into the dish is not only such

*Today this sounds like lunch money, but at a time when the top ticket prices for musicals had just reached $6, one hundred thousand was considered a very heavy advance, and twice that was unheard of.

hokum mush as the familiar wedding scene and the ghost of a mother who re-turns at intervals to keep her son from error, but a cocktail party chatter-box number paraphrased from an old Noël Coward show, a college number dittoed from an earlier George Abbott one, and various other elements hardly rivaling the daisy in freshness."

"Nobody is neutral about *Allegro,*" wrote Wayne Abrams in the *Chicago Sun.* "The Hammerstein-Rodgers-de Mille musical play is nigh unto perfect or a dismal flop. There's that much room for disagreement." Yet until *Allegro* there was generally a consensus on Broadway about which were the great shows, the good shows, the worthlessly amusing shows, the bombs. Who but a grump or a zany didn't like *No, No, Nanette, Music in the Air, Anything Goes, Lady in the Dark?* Musicals generally weren't controversial before R & H.* Controversy was the province of dramatists—Eugene O'Neill, Thornton Wilder, William Saroyan.

R & H had turned the musical into a form capable of inspiring contro-versy: important. That's what "musical play" meant: *theatre,* like O'Neill's or Saroyan's except with music. Theatre that had to be staged by artists like Mamoulian or de Mille, not the amiable hacks who put *No, No, Nanette* and *Anything Goes* on stage, or who worked out the "combinations" for the hoof-ing chorus. Theatre that had to be performed by acting singers. Theatre for which new technologies had to be devised simply to work out the visuals. Theatre that invented a new category of entertainment every time it raised its curtain.

The *Allegro* debate surged on in the press, over cocktails, at the fashionable dinner table; who shall be praised, who blamed, for each element of the show? Never had a musical had such impact on the culture. Musicals, till this point, tended to make their effect very gradually, as over the years the melodies of *The Student Prince* or *Rose-Marie* ingratiated themselves. Suddenly, be-cause R & H had made the author's profile so visible, the musical was telling, immediate, *news.*

Yet *Allegro* itself was not appreciated. R & H were faulted for not writing "Oh, What a Beautiful Mornin'" again. *No one* outside the theatre community noticed what an amazing invention Jo Mielziner's design constituted. The cast didn't enjoy the popularity of *Oklahoma!'s* Alfred Drake or Celeste Holm or *Carousel's* John Raitt and Jan Clayton—but then perhaps there were too many principals for any one of them to matter. Certainly, *Allegro* has no role as beguiling as Ado Annie or as weighty as Billy Bigelow. Some of *Allegro's*

*\*Pal Joey,* the apparent exception, was almost universally agreed to be a fine show, even by those who disliked its shady subject matter. Folklore tells that the piece failed at first, not to succeed till the famous 1952 revival. On the contrary, the 1940 original was a big hit, lasting 374 perfor-mances, a long run by 1940 standards.

people are little more than generic—the dedicated country doctor, the self-ish young bride,* the nurse who loves the doctor's son.

Of all involved in *Allegro,* only de Mille got her due praise. The *Times'* dance critic, who had been mugging her ballets, phoned her to tell her how amazed he was by how beautifully the whole thing moved. "Laurey Makes Up Her Mind" was keen psychology and *Carousel's* "Hornpipe" a celebration of the physical, the animal. But *Allegro's* four major dances startled, amid the kaleidoscopically shifting patterns in the book scenes, for their warmth and point. Joe Taylor's freshman mixer featured the interdisciplinary pas de deux of Annabelle Lyon on the ballerina's toe and Harrison Muller in tap shoes. The "Money Isn't Everything" dance considered the role of the postwar wife, cut off from the possibility of gainful employment (as veterans edge back into the work force) yet cowed into trying to run a household on an allowance. The first act's Big Ballet was the "Children's Dance," a look at the rituals of recreation and courtship among the innocent, and the second act's Big Ballet, to the title song, shattered those social codes in a view of the young doctor wandering helplessly among broken, tortured, and (literally) crucified victims.

"Agnes, what are you *doing* to us?" R & H cried when they saw the "Allegro" ballet in rehearsal. So de Mille refashioned it from the tragic to the satiric, to ridicule the high-tension triviality of modern life. Another R & H regular, dance arranger Trude Rittmann, emphasized the anarchic, scattered nature of Our Times by flashing quotations of five of the show's melodies through a wiry, rhythm-crazed din. The ballet marked a climax of sorts—not only as *Allegro's* major statement on how the social life can be harmful to the individual, but also as the last piece of choreography Agnes de Mille created for the R & H musical play.

De Mille had indeed stood up to the history looking over her shoulder. Her directing as well as choreographing of *Allegro* made possible the rise of the director-choreographer—of Michael Kidd and *Li'l Abner* (1956), *Destry Rides Again* (1959), and the darkly grandiose *The Rothschilds* (1970); of Bob Fosse and *Redhead* (1959), *Sweet Charity* (1966), the impishly commentative *Pippin* (1972), and the "all public life is a performance" metaphor-vaudeville of *Chicago* (1975); of Jerome Robbins and *Peter Pan* (1954), the sexy-romantic *West Side Story* (1957), and the ecstatically tribal *Fiddler on the Roof* (1964); of Michael Bennett and *A Chorus Line* (1975) and *Dreamgirls* (1981); and of

*This was Roberta Jonay, probably the most obscure name to play ingenue lead in an R & H show. The joke along The Street had it that the most efficient way to disappear was to play the woman lead in R & H's musical plays. Joan Roberts did go on to *Are You with It* and *Marinka* and replaced Nanette Fabray in *High Button Shoes;* and Clayton was graduated to the 1946 *Show Boat,* an MGM contract, and the first cast of the television series *Lassie.* Still: Betta St. John? Isabel Bigley? Miyoshi Umeki? Lauri Peters? Not to mention Roberta Jonay.

Victor's original-cast 78 rpm set of *Allegro* (see page 86) sold so poorly that not until the mid-1960s was there an LP reissue (*above*). Both album covers sport variations of the same design, the show's original poster logo, which was finally used on the second LP issue a decade later (*below*).

Tommy Tune and *Nine* (1982), *My One and Only* (1983), and the astonishingly dark, *and* romantic, *and* commentative *Grand Hotel* (1989). In his autobiography, Rodgers wrote that Hammerstein took over *Allegro*'s direction from an overworked de Mille. No. The *Allegro* that went to New Haven was solely de Mille's work. But she ceded direction of a few book scenes to Hammerstein during the Boston weeks because he was doing so much last-minute rewriting that she had no chance to read and reflect upon the new pages before staging them while reworking the dances and drilling her vast corps.

Installed on Broadway, *Allegro* ran out its season, from October to July. It closed after 315 performances, enough for most good-sized musicals to recoup on, but not for one with a cast of seventy-eight, an orchestra of thirty-five, and a small army of backstage help. Ironically, another musical, with a few semi-somebodies in its cast, a score by Hollywood unknowns, and based on a minor novel set way in the past—a musical with so little potential it could only get a booking at the very unpopular New Century Theatre, off the track at Seventh Avenue and Fifty-eighth Street—opened the night before *Allegro* and turned out to be the season's hit. It got hot so fast they had to move it down to the Shubert Theatre, half a block east of *Allegro*. The show was *High Button Shoes*—and this may have added to *Allegro*'s ills, for nothing deflates reviews of a Big Show like a Little Show that ends up Big first.

Nevertheless, *Allegro* continued to create headlines—for backstage antagonisms. These are a common problem on Broadway, but they don't usually make the papers. *Carousel,* for instance, was vexed by a chorus woman of no talent and great arrogance who was under the protection of someone high up on the production team—odd, after de Mille's charming *Oklahoma!* anecdote in which Hammerstein ridiculed the very notion of such practices. But the theatre is a volatile world, the tango of opportunism and art—and what's glamour but a reckless ego in heavy makeup? De Mille called a *Carousel* production meeting, demanding that the offending chorus woman be fired.

"And there was Theresa Helburn," de Mille recalled long after, "her mean eyes glinting, looking from one of us to the other. [Lawrence] Langner. [Armina] Marshall. And all Terry could ask was, 'Who's keeping her?'"

*Allegro* had comparable trouble, and this time the press made it known. In the spring of 1948, de Mille had dancer Frances Rainer fired because her work was inadequate. Rainer claimed she had been penalized for union militancy. Actors' Equity sided with Rainer, and, to avoid arbitration (and more bad PR), the Guild rehired Rainer, over de Mille's vociferous protest. A bit later, *Allegro* was in the papers again when the Guild dropped eight of the ensemble and six orchestra players to cut costs for a run through the summer. One of the fired chorus men, Charles Tate, likened his cause to Rainer's: punished for hardline unionism.

Harold Rome's demobilization revue *Call Me Mister* had to vacate the Majestic to make way for *Allegro*, as ticket buyers lined Forty-fourth Street.

So *Allegro* was still news, prominent, res publica, even after having been sidelined as inferior to *High Button Shoes*, a tuneful and smartly staged show (the one with Robbins' famous "Mack Sennett Ballet") but all the same a vacuous romp. Had a dancer been fired from *High Button Shoes*—or from *Allegro*'s other coeval hits, *Finian's Rainbow* and *Brigadoon*—no one would have heard of it outside the theatre community. R & H were by now some- what beyond Broadway, larger than "theatre," more famous, even, than their shows.

After a summer's wait, *Allegro*'s company set off on a national tour, with John Battles' and Lisa Kirk's understudies taking over as Joe and the nurse. The nation received it as New York had: some were enthralled, some mystified, some bored. There were to be no foreign productions, no major revivals, no *Oklahoma!*-sweeps-the-world prestige. *Allegro* has been heard from here and there—in music tents, at the St. Louis "Muni" in 1955, at Connecticut's Goodspeed Opera House in 1968, at New York's Equity Library Theatre in 1978. But, as national events go, *Allegro* is gone forever.

How can a musical excite such disparate reactions, be so important one year yet so forgotten after? *Allegro* is a work of genius—but *Allegro* has problems. First of all, it's *serious*. Not *Carousel* serious, because *Carousel* has Carrie. *Allegro* is serious, period, grave and self-absorbed. Second, *Allegro* is a show on an idea rather than on a character. When de Mille told Hammerstein he hadn't told the tale he'd had in mind, she may have meant that he didn't have a lead character. A protagonist, yes: idealistic, country bred, confused. But that's all Joe Taylor is. In a show as filled with personali- ties as this, someone has to catch our sympathy—and nobody does. One might argue that *Allegro*'s people are archetypal, its story a fable. But R & H made *believable relationships* the key element in the writing of musicals; they threw out the musical-comedy "types." *Allegro* deals in the homey, all- wise grandma, the unworthy minx fiancée, the happy-go-lucky best friend, the ignored yet loving Eve Arden nurse, the rich, idiotic hypochondriac. *Types.*

*Allegro*'s production was flawed, too. The wonderful open playing area certainly made *Allegro* unique in the annals of the musical. But the back projections—crucial in defining mood or setting locale for the bare stage—never quite worked. Some of them were fuzzy, hard to "read," and a few, like the giant spoon of medicine in Joe's infancy, looked grotesque. Other innovations, such as a set of costumes dyed red in front and black from behind to allow dancers literally to "disappear" against a black background when they turned, could not be brought off.

Then, too, did not R & H disassemble their score a bit too much, assigning major numbers to minor characters and avoiding the exuberance of an emotionally expansive number like "June Is Bustin' Out All Over"? At least the big ballad, "You Are Never Away," one of Rodgers' loveliest melodies, utilizes *Allegro*'s unique production style to turn what would normally be a solo into a sort of "solo with Freudian chorus": an intimate love song for thirty singers, an actor, and a dancer. Even better known is "The Gentleman Is a Dope," a classic torch song that catches Hammerstein in a savvy mood:

> The gentleman is a dope,
> A man of many faults,
> A clumsy Joe
> Who wouldn't know
> A rumba from a waltz.

The other, soaring Hammerstein is most present in "Come Home," bluntly sentimental and so committed that it's hard not to share his vision of a loving, protective, person-scaled community:

> You will find a world of honest friends who miss you,
> You will shake the hands of men whose hands are strong,
> And when all their wives and kids run up and kiss you,
> You will know that you are back where you belong.

However, some of the score just isn't worthy. Though the first-act finale wedding climaxes impressively with the chorus sopranos on a top C, it opens with the generic scene-setting chorus that R & H themselves had outmoded, Rodgers bumping along on empty and Hammerstein tossing clichés:

> What a lovely day for a wedding!
> Not a cloud to darken the sky.
> It's a treat to meet at a wedding,
> To laugh and to gossip and to cry.

And the second-act opening, "Money Isn't Everything," is strangely plodding for a Rodgers waltz, not to mention one of Hammerstein's lamest comedy lyrics:

> Your Carnegie dress
> Will be more or less
> Of a handkerchief round your hip,
> Sewed on to you so
> That your slip won't show —
> And whatever you show won't slip!

Nevertheless, *Allegro*'s need to expose a few of civilization's Big Lies is very strongly felt. It's sad to know that, much later, when Hammerstein was told that he had cancer and was presently going to die, it was *Allegro* that he turned to, hoping that a rewrite would correct its flaws. Apparently Hammerstein was going to de-emphasize the first act–country, second act–city (really, the four-legs-good, two-legs-bad) feeling of the show, and to try to cure Joe, Jr.'s ailing marriage. But Joe is so simple and undemanding a guy that country life would suit him beautifully. Why *not* send him back to his place of choice? As for his marriage, his wife is consistently rendered as a materialistic opportunist. Why save a marriage with so unworthy a partner? One of the hooks that keep Act One sharp is this very courtship, by a fine young man, of a selfish jerk. Isn't it Hammerstein's premise that the two Joe Taylors are by a far shot too good for the world they work so hard for? Hammerstein got it right the first time, and *Allegro*, flaws and all, is a beautiful, strange, and terribly moving piece, "tumultuous and exalted," as first-nighter Ward Morehouse had said—tumultuous because that's how R & H saw the age they were discussing, and exalted because their view of the ageless village discovers a rhapsodic sense of community. To extend Sondheim's simile, *Oklahoma!* is about a picnic; *Allegro* is an ethic.

Let's do some history, while we're at it. As I've said, *Allegro* happens to be the first "concept" musical, presentational rather than representational, the "entertainment" that challenges its public and is generally thought to be the antithesis of the R & H–style show: *Fiddler on the Roof, Cabaret, Company, Follies, Chicago, Pacific Overtures, Grand Hotel.* The symbolic character of Anatevka's Fiddler, invisible to all but Tevye; *Cabaret*'s and *Company*'s and *Chicago*'s use of time and place as relative and ambiguous, rather than linear and spatial; *Follies'* ghosts; and *Pacific Overtures'* essay in sheer theatrical method were all anticipated in *Allegro,* and the fact that all the later works are *Allegro*'s superiors as compositions does not detract from its achievement in having opened up such startling possibilities. Oh yes, they were startling—it took a decade before they could even begin to be fulfilled. "Maybe going forward is easier than standing still!" R & H announced in *Allegro.*

And maybe it isn't.

# South Pacific

We presume that it's *Tales of the South Pacific* that Martin grips with such pleasure as the book's author, James Michener, stands at left, with Oscar, Dick and Joshua Logan. Left: on Rodgers' copy of the famous Philippe Halsman study of Mary Martin's Nellie Forbush, she wrote "Dick— See! You're my honeybun today and every day—Love, Mary."

"I wish I could tell you about the South Pacific," is how James Michener begins his cycle of stories called *Tales of the South Pacific:*

> The way it actually was: the endless ocean. The infinite specks of corals we called islands. Coconut palms nodding gracefully toward the ocean. Reefs upon which waves broke into spray, and inner lagoons, lovely beyond description. I wish I could tell you about the sweating jungle, the full moon rising behind the volcanoes, and the waiting. The waiting. The timeless, repetitive waiting.

One can see why R & H were intrigued. Michener's writing is plain, but he persuasively limns a wide range of characters: American Seabees and nurses, French adventurers, and Tonkinese natives; and he explores a frustratingly beautiful and perilous place far away on the edge of the earth.

But look at the problems. Here was another serious subject—war stories, no less. And how were R & H to get the vastness of the sea, the color of the vegetation, the heat and boredom and loneliness onto the stage? And what of the choreography that R & H had made essential to the musical? Military drills? Fertility rites?

However, R & H seemed to thrive on tackling problems—making *Oklahoma!*'s dialect and odd costumes into values rather than obstructions, empathizing with *Carousel*'s difficult hero, universalizing *Allegro*'s doctors. Thus far, only *State Fair* had posed no challenge, which is probably why it's so tame. However, *South Pacific* confronted R & H with something that had been fundamental in the musical for a century but which they had made absolutely unnecessary: the star.

*South Pacific*, of course, had two stars, Mary Martin and Ezio Pinza. "What do you want, two basses?" Martin cried, when R & H approached her. What they wanted was their first woman lead who wasn't a soprano but rather a "belt," in the line of Ethel Merman and Judy Garland instead of Marilyn Miller and Jeanette MacDonald. *South Pacific*'s Nellie Forbush was going to be a musical-comedy heroine in a musical play. *Oklahoma!*'s Laurey and *Carousel*'s Julie and Carrie, though they don't demand opera singers per se, do need women with reasonably high singing voices. Ado Annie is a belter, but she is hardly *Oklahoma!*'s leading woman. And *Allegro*'s Jenny Brinker is a dancer—she doesn't sing a note by herself in the entire show.

So Nellie was something new in R & H, carrying a goodly share of the score on a "Broadway" voice (though legit sopranos with a solid chest range have played the role). But Pinza was an old hand on Broadway—Broadway and Thirty-ninth Street, the Metropolitan Opera. However, *South Pacific* was to be his first musical, and his name, on the posters, was questionable. Not for many years had a celebrated opera singer gone into a musical—*obscure* opera sing-

Left, Joshua Logan demonstrates a bit of business using Ezio Pinza's stage children Barbara Luna and Michael DeLeon. Below, Mary tries it as Pinza looks on.

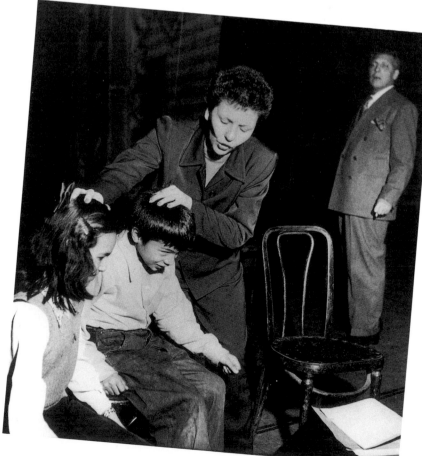

## The Look of *South Pacific*

Top left, a set design by Jo Mielziner and, above, a costume design by Motley. Bottom left, though this photograph is a bit unclear, we include it to demonstrate the original production's dazzling use of color to summon up an exotic locale.

ers, yes; and Grace Moore had established herself as a musical-comedy diva before venturing into the opera house. But casting for strong voices was a facet of the musical play. *Oklahoma!,* a musical comedy despite its billing, depends on a *solid* baritone for Curly—Broadway voices couldn't last out eight Curlys a week—and *Carousel* runs so insistently upon voice that the first "crossover" recording of a musical (that is, with an opera cast) was Victor's 1955 reading of *Carousel,** with Robert Merrill and Patrice Munsel. Even *Allegro*'s mother, Annamary Dickey, who sang but two songs, had been on the Met roster—and, looking ahead, we see more opera singers to come in the original productions of *The King and I, Pipe Dream,* and *The Sound of Music.*

So the use of Pinza was typical R&H—another surprise and obviously another first-class voice. In a way, Martin with Pinza symbolizes the R&H musical play—her musical-comedy élan confronting his opera majesty. Pinza

*Record buffs will recall Victor's 1935 album of *Porgy and Bess* with Met singers Lawrence Tibbett and Helen Jepson; but *Porgy* is an opera in the first place, so opera singers can hardly cross into it.

may have been a little *too* opera. Because the lingua franca backstage at the Met during Pinza's reign was Italian, he had never had to master English, and now, in *South Pacific,* his diction was so vexing that at one point the show's director, Joshua Logan, demanded that Pinza be replaced.

He demanded in vain, because R & H, who sided with Pinza, owned 51 percent of the show, as coproducers with Logan and Leland Hayward, the two who had originally bought Michener's book for adaptation. Oddly, at first they didn't know what they were going to do with it. (Surely it seemed most potential as a movie, wherein the great ocean and mysterious islands could be most easily visualized.) Apparently Logan blurted out something about it to Rodgers, against Hayward's strict orders for secrecy. Perhaps Logan was freeing an unconscious wish to direct an R & H musical of the book, nudging Rodgers to nudge Hammerstein—after all, he knew both men well, having staged three Rodgers and Hart shows as well as, for R & H as producers, *Annie Get Your Gun.* In any case, R & H certainly did want to write *South Pacific*—but only if they could control the show, Logan and Hayward to be in effect silent partners.

Hayward was furious and Logan helpless. Said Hayward to Logan, "You're going to regret this," and—as we shall see—Logan greatly did. But Rodgers told Hammerstein that he was never going to let a producer dictate to him the terms under which he would work. He had had his run-ins with tone-deaf producers, more concerned about the ingenue's lighting than about the flow of a scene, and one incident in particular grated on him all his life, when he and Lorenz Hart worked on *I'd Rather Be Right* (1937). This was a star show, for starters: George M. Cohan as FDR. The book, by George S. Kaufman and Moss Hart, was strong, a very, very funny political satire, like George and Ira Gershwin's *Of Thee I Sing* (1931), also with a book coauthored by Kaufman. And Kaufman directed both shows. But where *Of Thee I Sing* had let loose a medley of first-rate Gershwin, whole scenes through-sung in operetta-finale style, *I'd Rather Be Right* somehow cramped Rodgers and Hart. What with working with the dry-voiced Cohan, contriving somewhat unmotivated musical interludes between the book scenes, and trying to find character in a show with no character but the star, Rodgers and Hart came up with a second-rate score, one lifted into greatness in one song, "Everybody Loves You (when you're asleep)." This was the opening of Act Two, carefully keyed into the whole in that *I'd Rather Be Right* represents the dream of a penniless young couple who envision FDR trying to balance the national budget so they can get married; and "Everybody Loves You" found the boy asleep and his girl musing on this idyll of guiltless bliss amid an evening of noise and shenanigans. The number was expert theatre writing, defining character (except for this song, the girl is a cipher) while slyly supporting the show's construction (in the use

### The Characters of *South Pacific*

Emile de Becque (Ezio Pinza, *left*) meets Nellie who celebrates their love (*below*) in "A Wonderful Guy." At left, below, the horny Seabees bellow "There Is Nothing Like a Dame." Note Myron McCormick, fifth from left, as Luther Billis, a one-man corporation of get-rich-quick schemes, everything from hand laundry to the selling of souvenirs.

of the "sleeping" motif to reinstate the "dream" frame after the intermission). It was also expert Rodgers and Hart, almost bizarrely beautiful, with a particularly evocative verse.

But Kaufman was in charge of the show, and Kaufman hated the song. He found tenderness problematical; Kaufman's idea of a musical was, if not political satire, something with the Marx Brothers.* "Have You Met Miss Jones?," *I'd Rather Be Right*'s other major ballad, was OK by Kaufman—love as a foxtrot. But the more intense "Everybody Loves You" went out, not to be heard till it was retrieved as cabaret caviar in the 1960s, and *I'd Rather Be Right* proved a triumph for everybody *but* Rodgers and Hart. Rodgers had logged another instruction in the art of making theatre: *run your own show.* Now that he and Hammerstein had overwhelming power, they were going to keep it. Along The Street, some said that R & H's lawyer, Howard Rheinheimer, was the one who fortified their ironclad defenses. Nevertheless, the two authors presented a united front as businessmen.

*South Pacific* was the first time since *Oklahoma!* that all R & H production meetings included "outside" associates on the highest level. The Theatre

---

*Kaufman worked on two of the three Marx Broadway shows, *The Cocoanuts* (1925) and *Animal Crackers* (1928).

Guild had "presented" *Carousel* and *Allegro*, but, for *South Pacific*, Hayward's and Logan's names joined R & H on the top line of the posters. It was at one such meeting, at Joshua Logan's apartment, that Rodgers finally found the way to get the sound of the ocean into the theatre. As production assistant John Fearnley recalled it, Rodgers was suffering from back trouble and spent meetings lying on the floor, his legs propped up on sofa cushions. Hammerstein arrived with the lyrics to "Bali Ha'i." Rodgers looked them over.

Now, "Bali Ha'i" is potent verse, simple and smooth, but dense. Michener's island of Bali-Ha'i (as he spells it) is all-purpose exotica. "It was small," he tells:

> Like a jewel, it could be perceived in one loving glance. It was neat.
> It had majestic cliffs facing the open sea. It had a jagged hill to
> give it character. It was green like something ever youthful, and it
> seemed to curve itself like a woman into the rough shadows formed
> by the volcanoes on the greater island of Vanicoro.

That's pure Michener: plain, aching to lyricize, but limited by talent. The unlimited Hammerstein's Bali H'ai is much richer, a symbolic place, of healing and liberation, where the troubled find calm and the repressed find release:

> Your own special hopes,
> Your own special dreams
> Bloom on de hillside
> And shine in de streams.

### The Characters, Continued

Above, earnest Lieutenant Cable (William Tabbert) meets Bloody Mary (Juanita Hall): "You damn saxy man!" Mary wants Cable to marry her daughter, Liat. On the taboo isle of Bali Ha'i (*below*) Cable sings "Younger Than Springtime" to Liat (Betta St. John).

This is, by synecdoche, the R & H view of the south Pacific in general, as a moral testing ground that challenges the bourgeois American's prejudices. Heroine Nellie Forbush passes the test after some resistance; secondary hero Joe Cable fails…and dies.

Obviously, a lyric that so beautifully encapsulated the theme *and* the atmosphere of the show immediately inspired Rodgers. According to legend, he rose from the floor, took the lyric into another room, and came back ten minutes later with a finished song.

"Not so," says Fearnley. After ten minutes, Rodgers had composed only the first three notes of the lyric, the tones that accompany the words "Bali Ha'i":

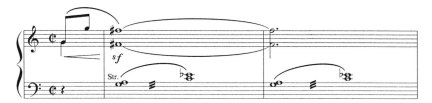

With their seascape placed and notated, R & H considered how they were to match Mary Martin's "Broadway" voice to Ezio Pinza's *basso cantante.* The solution was simple: don't match them at all. Let them sing not together but alternately, so that her gamine's belt and his opera-house bravura could characterize their two very different cultures without having to blend into some forced love duet. Thus, "Bright Canary Yellow," a number R & H wrote for the two stars, finds them singing the same music but *separately,* one after the other, she the romantic:

> The sky is a bright canary yellow
> And the sea is a robin's egg blue.
> It makes you wish, when you fall asleep,
> You will dream about the view.

And he the realist:

> Bizarre and improbable and pretty
> As a page from the fairytale books.
> It makes you wish that the world could be
> As lovely as it looks.

The yearning melody is attractive and the sentiments characterful; but R & H gave the music a second set of lyrics for Nellie alone (under the title "Loneliness of Evening"), then a third set as a duet again, he singing of the loneliness of evening while she sang of the loneliness of *sunrise,* emphasizing the gap in their ages. Still, as the couple's first number together, the song lacked drama. The music suggested a pair who are comfortable in their own company—but they are strangers, and the moment needed anxiety, suspense. "Loneliness of Evening," in Nellie's solo version, was reassigned to a scene later in the show,* and the first "duet" spot was given an entirely new number, "Twin Soliloquies." Sandwiched between Nellie's first solo ("A Cockeyed Optimist") and Emile's ("Some Enchanted Evening"), "Twin Soliloquies" is a pair of interior monologues set to a pulsing melody that grows in power and tension till it climaxes, *in the orchestra,* as Emile crosses the stage with filled brandy snifters, hands one to Nellie, and they drink, hiding the tension that the music relays to us: a kind of opera without singing. By the time the pair actually do sing together, at the end of Act One, on a reprise of "A Cockeyed Optimist," the audience has grown used to the different qualities of their voices; and Martin's "two basses" concern proved groundless. (For all that, Julie and Billy in *Carousel,* two shows earlier, never sing together at *all,* not even in the whole twelve and a half minutes of the "If I Loved You" scene.)

*Dropped during tryouts, the song was quietly published on its own in 1951 and finally used in the 1965 remake of *Cinderella,* as a solo for the Prince. Note Hammerstein's fondness for the phrase "bright canary yellow": it turns up, sky and all, in the first line of "A Cockeyed Optimist."

This rising octave that immediately falls a semitone comprises at once the most stable and the most unstable intervals in music, a protean—an exotic—sound that gave Rodgers just the tool he needed to build the sprawling Pacific geography on the stage. "This," he announced to his colleagues, "is not only the beginning of the song, but the beginning of the show." From the first moment of the overture, with the brass booming out the three notes, the audience would feel itself, like Nellie, Cable, and the other Americans, drawn into an alien and beautiful and perilous world.

The biggest of all problems in turning *Tales of the South Pacific* into a musical lay in placing a narrative center in Michener's scattered episodes. It may have been Michener's setting and atmosphere that first attracted R&H, but their musical play, as a form, is above all about relationships. The book's nineteen stories feature many leading and assistant characters and jump from the amusing to the serious: where's the heart of the piece? In the end, *South Pacific* drew on bits here and there but mainly on three tales: "Our Heroine" (for the Nellie-Emile story), "Fo' Dolla'" (for the Cable-Liat subplot), and "A Boar's Tooth" (for the comic figure, Luther Billis). It is becoming a commonplace that *South Pacific* varied the traditional setup of a "deep" main couple balanced by a prankish second couple (as in *Oklahoma!:* Curly and Laurey "lightened" by Will Parker and Ado Annie) by having *two* deep couples. Rodgers himself pointed this out. But Nellie is a fundamentally comic character who is put through a serious test, and, despite Emile's operatic grandeur, much of their story is the stuff of musical comedy, charm and high spirits, from the pensively sunny "A Cockeyed Optimist" to the spoofy "Honey Bun." What R&H did to tradition was less to vary it than to naturalize it, finding the humor in the deep people and the tragedy in the light.

Oddly, one problem that R&H had overlooked in planning *South Pacific* was Hammerstein's lack of sympathy for, even knowledge of, military life. Chugging methodically through the first scene, between Nellie and Emile, Hammerstein hit the necessary points—the splendid fascination of the locale, the biracial children who will threaten the romance, the strange, shy attraction of the two ill-sorted principals. Then came the first scene among the sailors, and Hammerstein stopped dead. Luckily, director Joshua Logan had had military experience, and he went down to Hammerstein's farm in Doylestown, Pennsylvania, to help out. That answered one difficulty but created another—for by the time Logan left Doylestown he was in effect the coauthor of *South Pacific*'s book, entitled, he presumed, to credit and royalties.

That R&H refused to give him. After the three shows with Rodgers as sole author of the book, Hammerstein thought it would besmirch his reputation to collaborate; and assigning Logan author's royalties ran counter to R&H business principles. In the end, Logan's contribution to the script was too great to be ignored, and his name did join Hammerstein's on the posters as coauthor of the book. All the same, Logan got no more money than he was entitled to as director, and while he could have held out for a legal solution, he would probably not have ended up as the director of *South Pacific,* or anything else R&H controlled. Logan was too attached to the piece—and too certain of its success—to throw it away. As Hayward had warned, he was definitely regretting this. Yet who else could have made a *South Pacific* for Logan to direct in the first place? Harold Arlen and E.Y. Harburg? Lerner and Loewe? Cole Porter? Other authors might have been far more generous in their terms, but other authors didn't write shows that made directors famous. *Oklahoma!* and *Carousel* saved Rouben Mamoulian's sinking career. *Allegro* created the concept of the choreographer-director. *South Pacific,* coming just after another military show directed and cowritten by Logan, *Mister Roberts* (1948), crowned Logan as a king of The Street. For comparison, did anyone know—or, really, care—who had staged Arlen and Harburg's *Bloomer Girl* (1944), or Lerner and Loewe's *Brigadoon* (1947), or Porter's *Kiss Me, Kate* (1948)?—all shows, mind you, heavily under the R&H influence.*

Logan's directing *South Pacific* brings up one last problem: where to fit in the choreography? Moreover, *South Pacific'*s two love plots, the Luther Billis comedy, and the show's macguffin, a military maneuver known as Operation Alligator, made for so much text that there wasn't much room for dance. So Logan ended up as *South Pacific'*s choreographer as well, overseeing what were designed to look like impromptu movements or amateur performances—the sailors' cutups during "Bloody Mary" and their restless pacing of "There Is Nothin' Like a Dame,"† Liat's body language during "Happy Talk," the Thanksgiving variety show. The R&H formula was "Don't have a formula," so, just when it looked as if R&H had formulated de Mille, they dropped the choreographer altogether.

But for the very mixed reaction to *Allegro,* one might say that success was becoming absurdly monotonous for the team. The New Haven premiere more or less stunned its public. There wasn't much to do between there and the New York opening, on April 7, 1949, but restage "I'm in Love with a Wonderful Guy," cut "Loneliness of Evening" and Cable's "My Girl Back Home," replace Emile's second act solo, "Will You Marry Me?," with "This Nearly Was Mine," and let

---

*\*Bloomer Girl'*s direction was credited to Harburg himself and one William Schorr, which sounds like director trouble to me. *Brigadoon'*s director, Robert Lewis, was a distinguished thespian, but the staging honors on that one went to the choreographer, our own Agnes de Mille. *Kiss Me, Kate* was staged by John C. Wilson, a dependable hack.

†*"Feel it in your crotch!"* Logan shouted at the actors when he staged the number, sending this horny group stamping off this way and that randy gang slinking off that way. A dance of the loins, so to say. It looked sloppy—natural—and went over tremendously, except on the national tour, for conductor Franz Allers gave the sailors Prussian brushups till they looked like hussars on dress parade, and Logan's air of casual misery was destroyed.

### The Recording of *South Pacific*

Is this a Caravaggio, or is it Mary, Dick, and Ezio listening to a playback? At left is conductor Salvatore dell-Isola with Barbara Luna, gloomy because she's only in two cuts.

Emlyn Williams—playwright, actor, and Logan's friend—trim the text the hard way, seeking out the unnecessary phrase, the redundant adjective. *South Pacific* came into town a sure thing, and in some ways it was the biggest hit R&H ever had. *Oklahoma!* ran longer. *Carousel* is the opera. *The Sound of Music* made more money. However, *Oklahoma!* was, in 1943, a novelty; *Carousel* is grim; and *The Sound of Music* really broke its records as a movie. *South Pacific* was a vastly profitable, state-of-the-art joy. It ran for 1,925 performances—nearly five years—at a time when Broadway was filled with R&H musicals. Not their own: those of their imitators. *South Pacific* was running against itself, for by 1949 major musicals were rationalized, choreographed thematically, and scored for character. Think of it this way: *Oklahoma!* was up against *Something for the Boys. South Pacific* was up against...well, *Oklahoma!*, whose national tour dropped in on the Broadway Theatre, eight blocks north of *South Pacific*, for two months in the summer of 1951.

Even then, two years after it had opened, *South Pacific* was selling out.

Scarcity of tickets had become not only a source of insiders' jokes but a scandal, as the attorney general's office wanted (but could not find a way) to investigate the connection between box-office staff and ticket agents' under-the-counter markups. Why this unstoppable triumph two years into a run? At that time, comparably, *Oklahoma!* was down to a mere 90 percent capacity, and *Carousel* was about to close.

One reason was the performers, and not only Pinza and Martin. Cable and Billis—the earnest preppy and the engaging hustler—shouldn't be hard to cast. Yet has anyone since William Tabbert quite caught the sorrowful wonder of the buttoned-up youth grown wide-eyed at the discovery of his own sensuality? Has anyone but Myron McCormick surrounded the appetitiveness of Luther Billis, as figged out in his rascal drollery as a Restoration fop? Both men stayed with the show for the entire run. Juanita Hall, the Bloody Mary, made such an impression that, even though Rodgers came to prefer the more richly vocalized Mary of Muriel Smith (Hammerstein's original Carmen Jones in 1943, as it happens) in London, he let Hall play Mary in the film—dubbed, we have to say, by Smith.

Perhaps it was the *South Pacific* production as a whole that made the show so imposing, its unique look in which one scene "dissolved" as the next simultaneously slithered in. Certainly, Logan was most highly praised for this. Except this was in fact one of the many innovations first tried out in *Allegro*, two years before. It had not stood out then because everything about *Allegro* was unusual, and because the quick-change exit of one group of performers as the next group enters doesn't seem unexpected on a bare stage. What else are the actors going to do in that bizarre limbo but walk on and off at the same time? That's what they do in ballet, and *Allegro* at times looked like a vast dance with words. However, amid *South Pacific*'s *representational* sets, the coincidental motion of actors leaving and arriving was a shock—not least in the first set change, when de Becque and his children, departing upstage, were suddenly obscured by a line of Seabees leaping on from the wings to launch "Bloody Mary (is the girl I love)."

What really distinguished *South Pacific* from the three preceding R & H shows was its sense of fun. If *Oklahoma!* is a musical comedy calling itself a musical play, *South Pacific* is a musical play that acts like a musical comedy. Two of its leads are comics, most of its score is delightful rather than moving, and its dancing is not artful but silly. It's a serious show to an extent—race relations are what drive it. But side by side with Cable's acerbic "(You've got to be) Carefully Taught" is Nellie doing lovable things with a hat during "I'm in Love with a Wonderful Guy," Bloody Mary learning blue language from the Seabees, Billis gyrating his stomach muscles to animate the tattoo of a ship appointed there, the Seabees hunking and bellowing their way

### The Auld Lang Syne of
### *South Pacific*

On Martin's last performance in New York, Rodgers, Hammerstein, Logan, and coproducer Leland Hayward trooped onstage in costume with what appeared to be an airplane propeller. Inside it was a diamond-and-pearl bracelet for Mary. "I learned later," she wrote in her memoirs, "that Nancy Hayward had helped choose the design, from Schlumberger's." That's good to know.

through "There Is Nothin' Like a Dame," Nellie's drag act with Billis in "Honey Bun," and other merry adventures.

Or maybe it's just the R & H effect: a great composition. Unique characters fully brought forth. A compelling story against a colorful background. Or even: the most popular score ever written. For here is a show whose *every number* is well known. *Oklahoma!* had the forgettable "It's a Scandal! It's a Outrage!" and *Carousel* "Geraniums in the Winder." *The King and I* will have "Western People Funny" and *The Sound of Music* "An Ordinary Couple." *South Pacific* is *nothing but hits*—yet not one of them could have fit into another show. "Dites-moi"? "Bloody Mary"? "Happy Talk"? "This Nearly Was Mine"?* There's a nice up-to-the-minute air about Rodgers' tunes here and there, as if he had decided to create pop styles rather than respect them. "I'm Gonna Wash That Man Right Out-a My Hair" is of, yet beyond, its time, something of a twelve-bar blues on a frolic. And what is "Some Enchanted Evening," an aria? It's *grand*. But then R & H had been creating pop styles since "The Surrey with the Fringe on Top." Nothing before 1943 sounded even remotely like that.

"Bali Ha'i" and "Happy Talk," Bloody Mary's numbers, are the "exotic" entries—though we notice that it is really Robert Russell Bennett's orchestration, rather than Rodgers' melodies, that makes the geographical indications, for Rodgers doesn't deal in pastiche. This is an American score. One thinks of the famous tale of Kern and Hammerstein planning a show about Marco Polo's trip to China, and Hammerstein asking Kern what their show will have to sound like, and Kern replying, "It'll be good Jewish music." That's *South*

---

*Musically the climax of the evening, "This Nearly Was Mine" calls up quotations of earlier songs in the orchestra parts—of "Bali Ha'i" (in the brass) during the introduction, then of "Some Enchanted Evening" and "I'm in Love with a Wonderful Guy" (in the woodwinds) during the refrain. As it happens, one *South Pacific* song *did* fit into another show: "Will You Marry Me?," the number that preceded "This Nearly Was Mine" in the same spot, was later used in *Pipe Dream,* presented as a pop tune sung at a party.

*Pacific,* too. "I'm in Love with a Wonderful Guy" might be the center of the score, with its take-no-prisoners bounce, its "typical" American girl who describes her romance by spouting clichés—clichés that, for the most part, Hammerstein simply invented ("corny as Kansas in August"). Sure enough, over the years they have become clichés.*

If prizewinning is a measurement, *South Pacific* was without question the most successful R & H show, with eight Tony and nine Donaldson awards, the Pulitzer Prize for drama (most remarkable for a musical but especially one in a season that counted plays by Maxwell Anderson, Arthur Miller—*Death of a Salesman,* in fact—Tennessee Williams, Sidney Kingsley, and Clifford Odets, not to mention Jean-Paul Sartre and Groucho Marx), and a gold record for Columbia's cast recording, though this was almost immediately overtaken by Decca's *Oklahoma!,* the disc that everyone bought in 1949 and 1950 to try on his brand-new LP phonograph as a transition sampler. In sheer numbers, *Oklahoma!* held the record over *South Pacific* as the best-selling album (because so many households bought *Oklahoma!* twice, first as a set of 78s and then as an LP) till *My Fair Lady* overwhelmed them both in 1956.

Following *Oklahoma!* and *Carousel* into London's Drury Lane in 1951, *South Pacific* exasperated the English critics. "Why do all the good musicals have to be American?" they seemed to say, without verbalizing the idea. "A fiendishly clever rehash of the old stuff," says a jerk on the *London Daily Express.* "All right in its way," allows the *News Chronicle.* "South Soporific," the *Daily Mail* declares. They were irritated particularly at the show's noble attitude toward racism, a sore spot for many spectators then and now. Some find Hammerstein's moralizing self-congratulatory, his "Carefully Taught" patly virtuous. (Would the show be stronger if it used the word "nigger"? Michener does.) On the other hand, the American musical looks back on a venerable tradition in the treatment of racism, partly because so many show people were Irish, Jewish, or black and partly because the bohemian show biz subculture tended to evangelically liberal politics. Hammerstein, remember, had dealt with racism in *Show Boat,* and his colleague E. Y. Harburg reopened the question in *Bloomer Girl* (1944) and *Finian's Rainbow* (1947). *South Pacific* was timely and bold; and what's wrong with being noble?

Harold Hobson (of the *Sunday Times*) and Kenneth Tynan (of the *Spectator*) knew what they had before them. But it was of no matter, for after *Oklahoma!* and *Carousel* the English did not need to be told whether or not to like *South Pacific.* In her autobiography, Mary Martin recalls coming out of the

*The piling of similes builds to a marvelous line: "I'm bromidic and bright as a moon-happy night pouring light on the dew." Except isn't "bromidic" a bit advanced for the backward Nellie? She'd be unlikely to know the word, much less use it. This was a rare slip for the fastidiously simple Hammerstein; perhaps his only other such is Will Parker's picture of himself in "All er Nothin'" as a homebody "all complete with slippers and pipe." What would a cowboy know about slippers?

## The Physical Production of *South Pacific*

As the first scene ended, (*below*) Pinza and his two children were seen walking upstage center, toward the ocean. Abruptly, the Seabees ran in from both sides of the stage down at the footlights, while a "traveler" curtain closed behind them, allowing stagehands to clear away the two moveable pieces (*center*). Keeping the same backdrop, a view of Bali Ha'i, a change of frame and new moveable pieces created the second scene (*bottom*).

**From Stage to Screen**

Above is "Happy Talk" on Broadway, with Hall, St. John, and Tabbert. Below is the movie version, with France Nuyen, Hall, and John Kerr. Opposite: "I'm Gonna Wash That Man Right Out of My Hair," with Martin, above, and Mitzi Gaynor, below.

Drury Lane the night before the opening to find a horde of people braving a heavy rain to line up for "on the day" gallery seats. They begged Martin for a song, and, with Joshua Logan and Martin's husband, Richard Halliday, standing by, she gave them her two big solos a cappella. They loved it, as London loved the show. Martin was the work's sole star there (with fellow Americans Wilbur Evans, Muriel Smith, and Ray Walston; the English Peter Grant played Cable), emphasizing Nellie Forbush as the role, along with Peter Pan, that remained her most memorable. By the way, another thing Martin mentions in her book is that Smith, London's Bloody Mary—like New York's Juanita Hall a black woman—had trouble finding a hotel room.

The *South Pacific* movie, released in 1958, fails to recapture the excitement of the stage show yet does not reinvent the tale as film. Logan, stilling his regrets about R & H business practices, directed. But Logan was not a great director of film. Yes, he opens it up. We're in planes, we're on islands, we see a boar's tooth ceremony on Bali Ha'i. Cable and Liat go for a swim. Emile and Cable dig in on their mission, with foliage and binoculars. It's all competent, but it hardly suggests a show that had been universally regarded as Broadway magic less than a decade earlier.

The casting's not at fault. Rossano Brazzi presents, for once, a very attractive Emile, and Mitzi Gaynor is a most appealing Nellie. As I've said, Bloody Mary splits the difference between New York and London, Muriel Smith dubbing Juanita Hall on the vocals. There is other dubbing as well—Giorgio Tozzi for Brazzi and Bill Lee for John Kerr's Cable. The entire score is sung; better, the dropped "My Girl Back Home" is restored, so we can see and hear how we

## The Physical Production, Continued

During the song "Bali Ha'i" the lighting dimmed on the actors to emphasize the beckoning island, below. Below, yet another combination of backdrop, frame, and moveable sidepieces created the "backstage" area for the Thanksgiving variety show.

like it. Critics groaned at Logan's absurd use of colored filters for the musical scenes—utter a song cue and the screen goes Krakatoa puce—but this is a cavil. What hurt the film is Logan's normalization of the show's larger-than-life personality. R & H startle you; the movie doesn't.

For instance, onstage *South Pacific*'s curtain rises on two Polynesian children singing a song (in French) so short that it's over in literally thirty seconds. The kids leave just before a navy nurse and a French planter enter, apparently on a date but also apparently utter strangers. Small talk ensues. Songs: what she believes in; what he needs. It's mystifying and fascinating—the Polynesians and the whites, the navy and the civilian, the young woman and the older man, her naïveté and his passion, a dense mix (not to mention the festively shocking lack of ceremony in the two stars' entrance). That is R & H: rich shows. The *South Pacific* movie isn't rich, from the drab opening inside Cable's plane to the perfunctorily exotic look of the location shots on Bali Ha'i. One reason why we never see the place in the show, except for the inside of a hut, is that Bali Ha'i is more a concept than a locale. It's dreamland, a place few of us ever get to. But Logan takes us there, and it looks like your high school with coconuts.

Even onstage, *South Pacific* is not easy to keep in trim. Of all the big R & H titles only *Carousel* is tougher to revive. *South Pacific* needs stars, or at least very special performers. Rodgers brought it back in 1967 at Lincoln Center with Tozzi and Florence Henderson, capably, and London saw a reasonably lively production in 1988 with Gemma Craven as a charming, spirited Nellie and Bertice Reading full of the devil as Bloody Mary; but the men were weak. Even less compelling was the New York City Opera's try the year before. Without stars, the piece lacked punch.

Perhaps the best modern revival was the 1985 staging in Los Angeles with Richard Kiley, Meg Bussert, Brent Barrett, and Novella Nelson (an extraordinarily intense Mary). Director A. J. Antoon threw out the *d'après* Logan approach of so many revivals to address the work as if it were new: spare but evocative set pieces instantaneously lowered and raised over a bare stage; the famous between-scenes crossovers cut; and a choreographer on hand. Kiley may have been a bit miscast and Bussert weak on Nellie's serious side, but the show took on a fleet and even contemporary feeling, as when the departure of the Seabees on Operation Alligator, originally a mass exit down front from stage right to stage left (to distract the audience from the scenery being changed behind the curtain), now exploited the big empty stage as the soldiers marched all the way upstage and off left while chanting the words of "Honey Bun"—which suddenly sounded exactly like the kind of hup-two rhyming ditty that servicemen favor during drills.

The 1940s was in some ways the greatest decade of the American musical. In the 1910s, Victor Herbert oversaw the development of the available genres, from story-strong operetta through star-concentrated extravaganza to the now forgotten smash hit that inspired the Kern-Bolton-Wodehouse "Princess" shows, *The Only Girl* (1914). The 1920s saw Hammerstein's revolution in the "normalization" of the book. The 1930s brought in the integration of dance, vast experiments in design, the reappointment of the star comic as a salient element rather than the central one, and the politicization of musical comedy as an agent of the liberal agenda. Still, it was the 1940s, urged along by many writers but led, really, by R & H, that pulled all this into constant and ever inventive play.

It must be admitted that many of the greatest shows of the decade have dated—in a thudding overuse of the de Millian Big Ballet, in the plot through-line's clumsy accommodation of humor, or in a Popular Front innocence (in *Finian's Rainbow*'s absurdly effortless defeat of racism, for instance). But the R & H shows don't have this problem, despite those Big Ballets, strongly denoted comics, and an emphasis on the liberal worldview—in *Carousel*'s attempt to "understand" Billy's outlaw mentality, *Allegro*'s mistrust of big-money medicine, and *South Pacific*'s exorcism of Nellie's bigotry. On the contrary, R & H use the specific to treat the universal—in balancing Nellie-Emile with Cable-Liat, for example. Why is one American able to conquer her prejudices while the other surrenders to his? Because he's so embedded in his Rittenhouse Square way of life that he can't imagine breaking out of it. Nellie, though a southern woman, is inner-directed, eccentric, capable of seeing herself anywhere. "Do you think I'm crazy, too?" she asks Emile, early on. "They all do over at the Fleet Hospital." Because she makes her own culture wherever she goes. She's not a cockeyed optimist. She's a strong, free soul, and her roots, unlike those of the likable but repressed Lieutenant Cable, aren't her curse. Cable despises racism, but he's willing to live with it—which is why he must die. Nellie, who has worn racism like skin, unthinkingly, contemplates it and, in horror, throws it off. To put it another way: Cable needs Bali Ha'i but cannot use it. Nellie doesn't need it.

This is an unusual comparison to be able to make about two principals in a musical, especially in the season that hosted *Where's Charley?*, Mike Todd's Bobby Clark farrago *As the Girls Go*, a Sigmund Romberg operetta called *My Romance* that was based on a play that was antique when it was new in 1913, numerous small-change revues, and Cole Porter's musically adventurous but psychologically flat *Kiss Me, Kate*. Among R & H's revolutions we have to list strength of theme. They didn't know it at the time, but they were building shows to last.

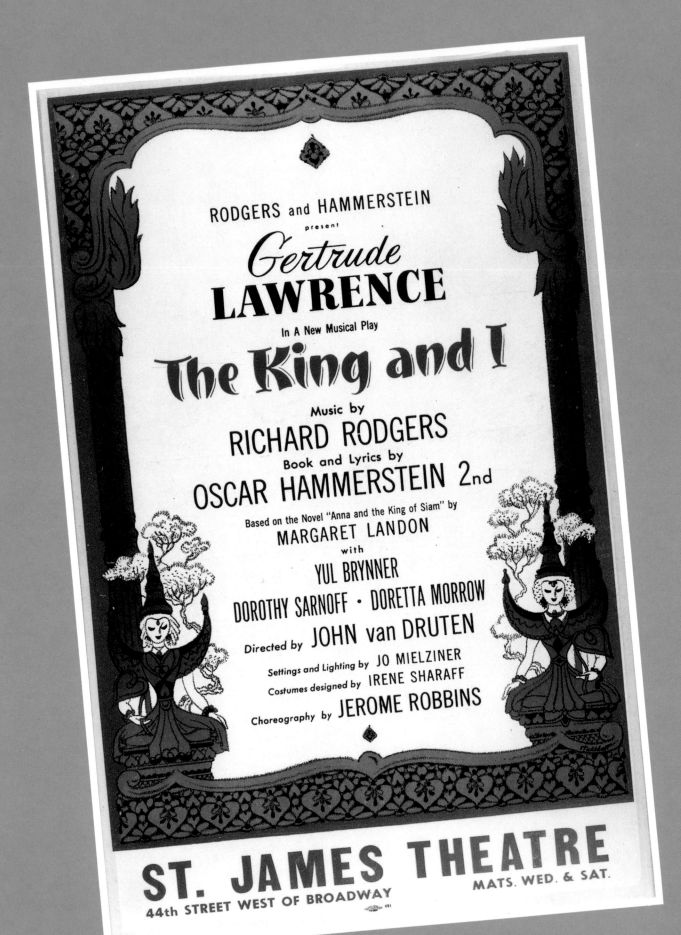

# The King and I

The odd thing was, they were somewhat uneasy partners. They worked well as a unit, the methodical Hammerstein playing nicely to the more impetuous Rodgers, and Rodgers' interest in the producing side of theatre complementing Hammerstein's

This publicity still of Yul Brynner and Gertrude Lawrence illustrates not a moment in the show but the confrontational feeling of Anna and the King's relationship.

more strictly thespian abilities as a director. Still, as personalities they never built a relationship as warm as the one that Rodgers had had with Hart or Hammerstein with Kern. Rodgers could be curt, stingy with his enthusiasm; the impish Hart enjoyed that, taking it as part of the game. But Hammerstein, used to the touchy but outgiving Kern and the humming, joking Romberg, found it austere, unappreciative.

For some reason, Hammerstein seems never to have confronted Rodgers about this, and a certain tension collected between them—tension that Rodgers wasn't aware of. When Hammerstein, after days of meticulous labor, sent Rodgers a lyric and Rodgers responded with, "It's perfectly adequate" (which, translated from the Rodgersese, meant, "It's your usual brilliant work and will make a superb song"), Hammerstein felt greatly let down. If that's what Rodgers meant, why didn't Rodgers *say* it?

Yet they were without question the most *professionally* harmonious team in theatre history: producers as well as writers, the main shareholders in the biggest grossing series of shows of their time, two minds so in key that no one can recall their having disagreed on anything from the booking of a theatre to the casting of a walk-on. And consider how adaptable the two were: at home on the biggest budgets (*Allegro*) as well as the smallest (*Oklahoma!*), following musical comedy (*Oklahoma!*) with operetta (*Carousel*), comfortable with unknowns (*Allegro*) and stars (*South Pacific*), *protégeurs* of the dance yet producing *South Pacific* without a choreographer. They had done just about everything that mattered in the musical theatre of their day except a star vehicle—that is, a show not merely offering a star but wholly erected around one.

Rodgers had logged plenty of such experience with Hart, contriving *Betsy* (1926) for Belle Baker, *Simple Simon* (1930) for Ed Wynn, *I'd Rather Be Right* for George M. Cohan, *By Jupiter* (1942) for Ray Bolger. Hammerstein had had less exposure to the star turn, as he had been concentrating on operetta, and there were few if any operetta stars; the big names headlined in musical comedy. Still, Hammerstein and Kern had designed *Sweet Adeline* (1929) for Helen Morgan as a follow-up showcase after her Julie in *Show Boat*. Of course, *South Pacific* had Mary Martin and Ezio Pinza, and certain considerations had to be made on their behalfs. But *South Pacific* was not subservient to its leads—and the two Big Names were hired *after* most of the show was written.

Vehicles can be frustrating, for building a structure around a particular personality-talent means subsuming most elements of composition in the presentation of that personality, but *within the limits of its talent*. Rodgers once remarked that he ultimately rejoiced that Mary Martin had turned *Oklahoma!* down, for in joining Martin to the role of Laurey he and Hammerstein would have ended in writing a somewhat different play, per-

### A Panoply of Annas and Kings

Left are Lawrence and Brynner at the time of the 1961 premiere. Below is Alfred Drake, Brynner's vacation replacement in 1952, with the second Anna, Constance Carpenter. Below, left, Brynner and Patricia Morison, with whom he closed the show in 1954.

## More Annas and Kings

Farley Granger and Barbara Cook (*top*) at New York's City Center in 1960 and, at center, Michael Kermoyan and Constance Towers, at the City Center in 1968. Below is "Shall We Dance?" in Japan.

haps not as good a one. And Martin, at the time, was less than a top-rank star. Imagine how differently weighted *Oklahoma!* would have been if it had been fashioned as a Mary Martin vehicle in the first place: with a much less vigorous Curly (in order to protect the star's prestige); with "Oh, What a Beautiful Mornin'" deleted (an opening that impressive would detract attention from the star's subsequent entrance); with Ado Annie's role cut down (again, to defend the star from competition); with Act One's Big Ballet either cut (because Martin's character must be handed over to a dancer, bad for fame) or completely revamped to allow Martin to do her own dancing; with at least one big solo for Martin added into Act Two (even if the story doesn't need one; even if it can't use one); and with the title song dropped (because it temporarily suggests that the Indian Territory folk as a whole are the show's star, making Martin seem insignificant). It's a matter of balance.

So R & H were no more than amused when Gertrude Lawrence decided that they must write her next show: for Lawrence, star of stars, had been playing nothing but vehicles since the 1920s. By 1950, these authors and this actress were such large figures that negotiations had to be conducted through go-betweens, Lawrence's agent, Fanny Holtzman, and Hammerstein's wife, Dorothy, a friend of Holtzman's. Dorothy was not sanguine about an R & H & Lawrence show. Lawrence was sheer wild magic on stage, but Lawrence was difficult. Her thin soprano was wayward, apt to flat; and her top notes, precarious a decade earlier when she could barely hit a top G to cap "The Saga of Jenny" in *Lady in the Dark*, were by now resting in peace. Turn your back on her for a moment and she'd sweep onstage from some totally unexpected entry, or improvise dance steps and throw the ensemble off, or turn up in a new costume. She was tough on her fellow actors, hell on directors.

No wonder Dorothy was leery. Why should R & H work for Gertrude Lawrence? "She'll want it all," she told Holtzman.

"That's just what we would have said!" Hammerstein observed to Rodgers, recounting the exchange.

But Lawrence had an irresistible proposal: Gertrude Lawrence starring in the R & H version of *Anna and the King of Siam*. Margaret Landon's nonfiction novel of 1944 had been a best-seller, then a hit film two years later with Rex Harrison and Irene Dunne. It's easy to see the tale's fascination—a Western woman battling for democratic fairness (and feminism) in the patriarchal, totalitarian East. And of course this West versus East could serve as a background for an arresting relationship, for the Westerner is amazingly iron willed, while the king is a despot struggling to become a president, half barbarian and half republican.

In fact, that relationship is scarcely to be found in Landon's book, and the King himself appears only sporadically. Landon was far more interested in re-creating the Bangkok that Anna Leonowens knew in the five years that she spent as the royal schoolmistress: the customs, festivals, religion, and people, all surveyed by the absolute power of the King. *Anna and the King of Siam* is in some ways a terrifying book. Landon commented that she realized how different twentieth-century Siam was from the Siam of the 1860s when she visited the country between the two world wars and "never saw a single person who had been branded."

Landon's book is less a novel than a chronicle—plotless, spinning out episode after episode on court intrigue, the boredom and despair of harem life, the King's occasional diplomatic forays. This is not the stuff of good theatre. Theatre is *story*. It was the movie version that found a solution, expanding the role of the King, suggesting in slight ways an attraction between Dunne and Harrison, and building up one of Landon's episodes, on the concubine Tuptim, who escapes from the palace disguised as a priest, is tried on a false charge of fornication, and is tortured and burned alive with her alleged lover. As R & H's *State Fair* studio, Twentieth Century–Fox, had produced the *Anna* film, setting up a screening was the work of a moment, and it was then that R & H comprehended that they were going to have to write a vehicle for Gertrude Lawrence. For now *Anna and the King of Siam* really was irresistible—and of course Lawrence had snapped up the rights for adaptation to the stage.

In truth, though the show's posters would read "based on the novel, *Anna and the King of Siam*, by Margaret Landon," R & H based *The King and I* on the movie script, by Sally Benson and Talbot Jennings. R & H not only followed the Benson-Jennings scenario (which includes the presentation of the royal wives and progeny that became the "March of the Siamese Children") but adopted the screenwriters' invention of the King's uniquely entry-level, furiously paced English, with its elaborately incorrect tenses, its emphasis on "scientific" (meaning all sorts of things, but especially "reasonable" and "male dominated"), its "et cetera, et cetera, et cetera." Landon's King speaks conventional English (though he does at one point berate Anna's ignorance of certain technical terms with, "It's clear that you aren't scientific!")

Still, as with *Oklahoma!* and *Carousel*, the change from script to musical wholly reimagines the piece. The details are, in part, the same, but the *feeling* is greatly altered: from *Green Grow the Lilacs'* regional "shucks" to *Oklahoma!*'s nationalistic "*yeow!*," from *Liliom*'s depression to *Carousel*'s ecstasy, and, here, from a duel of wits to a play of passions. From film to show, R & H dropped the death of Anna's son, Louis (in a horseback-riding accident); gentled the haughty Tuptim into a fragile and terribly sympathetic pupil who feeds exhaustively on Mrs. Anna's views on freedom; fleshed out Tuptim's conspirator and changed him from a priest, innocent of sensuality, into her lover. This may not seem like a great deal of revision, but it

### Behind the Scenes

Left, Lawrence and cast members in a party skit at the show's first anniversary party. At left, center, Dick, Gertie, and Oscar rehearse for a promotional appearance on the *Ed Sullivan Show*. Below, kids line up to audition as Prince Chulalongkorn's replacement. They don't look very Asian, but neither did the original Prince, Johnny Stewart. Bottom, at the 1952 Tony Awards, *The King and I* won for Best Musical, Best Book, Best Score, and Best Gertie. Here are Oscar, Gertie, Dick, and Brynner with other Tony evening participants Helen Hayes, Phil Silvers, and Judy Garland. The show also won Donaldson awards for Brynner, Doretta Morrow (Tuptim), choreographer Jerome Robbins, and set and costume designers Jo Mielziner and Irene Sharaff.

Mielziner's design for the "Small House of Uncle Thomas" ballet.

does center the work's hatred of slavery, as everyone is now part of the problem—the King; his second-in-command, the Kralahome; the King's head wife, Lady Thiang—or on the side of a solution—Anna; her son, Louis; Tuptim; her lover, Lun Tha; and even the next king, Chulalongkorn. The shift from film to musical also aggravates the Anna-King confrontation over Tuptim far more effectively. In the film they merely argue. In the musical they must come to grips with the very core of what they cannot abide in each other—her resistance to authority and his egomania. Moreover, this happens only moments after the "Shall We Dance?" scene, in which they have drawn closer to each other than ever before. Now, with Tuptim held down on the floor before them, the King orders her to be whipped.

> ANNA: She's only a child. She was running away because she was
> unhappy. Can't you understand that? Your Majesty, I beg of you—
> don't throw away everything you've done. This girl hurt your
> vanity. She didn't hurt your heart. You haven't got a heart. You've
> never loved anyone. You never will.
> (The King, stung by Anna's words, seeks a way to hurt her in
> return.)
> KING: I show you! (He snatches the whip from the Guard) Give!
> Give to me!
> ANNA: I cannot believe you are going to do this dreadful thing.

KING: You do not believe, eh? Maybe you will believe when you hear
   her screaming as you run down the hall!

ANNA: I am not going to run down the hall! I am going to stay here
   and watch you!

KING: Hold this girl! (The two Guards grab Tuptim's arms) I do this
   all myself.

ANNA: You *are* a barbarian!

KING: Down! Down! Down! (The Guards hold Tuptim down) Am I
   King, or am I not King? Am I to be cuckolded in my own palace?
   Am I to take orders from English schoolteacher?

ANNA: No, not orders...

KING: Silence!...(He hands the whip to the Kralahome) I am King,
   as I was born to be, and Siam to be governed in my way! (Tearing
   off his jacket) Not English way, not French way, not Chinese way.
   My way! (He flings the jacket at Anna and takes back the whip
   from the Kralahome) Barbarian, you say. There is no barbarian
   worse than a weak King, and I am strong King. You hear? Strong.
   (He stands over Tuptim, raises the whip, meets Anna's eyes,
   pauses, then, suddenly realizing he cannot do this is front of
   her, he hurls the whip from him and, in deep shame, runs from
   the room.)

Anna has destroyed the King. So fully has he come to depend on her for advice, support, and esteem that he cannot survive without them. Yet she has come to depend on him, to be the kind of man she can at once guide and admire. Seeing him as a savage shatters her idol.

The Tuptim subplot further roots the musical's anti-authoritarian theme in that "Hello, Young Lovers" is virtually an anticipation of Anna's taking Tuptim's side and thus becomes a hymn not only to love but to liberty. And of course the Big Ballet, "The Small House of Uncle Thomas," Tuptim's court entertainment, elaborates the situation of a slave hoping to flee a wicked master to join her lover. As with *South Pacific*'s Cable and Liat, the subplot is in one way the main plot, thematically explanatory. Anna and the King are the show: but Tuptim is what the show is about.

Obviously, this evening-long duel of politics and personalities yields first-rate acting opportunities. Anna may be anything from charmer to nag. Lawrence made her ultimately vulnerable, hurt more than defiant, in "Shall I Tell You What I Think of You?," but Barbara Cook (at the City Center in 1960) saw her as a tragic heroine (though her "Shall I Tell You" was truly outraged) and Sally Ann Howes (in London in 1973) made her self-righteous, almost a shrew. Some Annas dominate the King; some are dominated. It depends upon who is starring—for, oddly, a show that began as a vehicle for Anna eventually became a vehicle for the King, Yul Brynner.

What a natural Brynner was in the part!—hot, bald, and more or less Mongolian. This was Gable-as-Rhett casting. Yet R & H had first asked Rex Harrison, then Alfred Drake, then Noël Coward (who was also to direct), all in the tradition of Harrison's Limehouse-suave, fake-eyes King in the movie. Very *outer* Mongolia, a portrayal in cosmetics. R & H simply knew no Orientals. However, Mary Martin had played with Brynner in the Chinese pageant *Lute Song* (1946)—one of those odd intervals that Martin went through between her discovery singing "My Heart Belongs to Daddy" and her affirmation as the Heavenly Hoyden, on the national tour of *Annie Get Your Gun.* Martin recommended Brynner to R & H, and Brynner came to audition. "He was dressed casually and carried a guitar," Rodgers later recalled. "He scowled in our direction, sat down on the stage and crossed his legs, tailor-fashion, then plunked one whacking chord on his guitar and began to howl in a strange language....He looked savage, he sounded savage, and there was no denying that he projected a feeling of controlled ferocity.... Oscar and I looked at each other and nodded."

In the pre–R & H days, casting a vehicle was a cinch after you signed the star: anyone else would do, because everyone else was accessory. Once Ed Wynn or Marilyn Miller or the Astaires were in place, who cared who else was on hand? Can anyone name the featured players in Wynn's *The Laugh Parade* (1931) or Miller's *Sally* (1920), or the Astaires' *Lady, Be Good!* (1924)? However, R & H storytelling required stronger support than stars were used to— Brynner, though billed below the title in small letters, gave the ethereal Gertie far more stalwart "support" than she had had from the shtick comic Victor Moore and the genially repellent "juvenile" Oscar Shaw in *Oh, Kay!* (1926) or from the mincing Danny Kaye in *Lady in the Dark* (1941). Even Lawrence's partner of choice, Noël Coward, couldn't hold a stage as the brazen Brynner could.

On the other hand, in the pre–R & H days Brynner would never have been cast. One didn't overwhelm the star; one flattered her. But R & H had made strong casting as certain as strong narrative. They sometimes erred in the hiring of the juvenile (if that isn't too stately a term to encompass Joe Taylor, Jr., Lieutenant Cable, *Me and Juliet*'s Larry, *Cinderella*'s Prince, and *Flower Drum Song*'s Wang Ta), going for good singers but dullish actors; and Larry Douglas, *The King and I*'s Lun Tha, made no history. But R & H hired Murvyn Vye (*Carousel*'s Jigger and a solid singing actor) as the Kralahome and understudy to Brynner: and the smoothly plummy mezzo Dorothy Sarnoff as Lady Thiang and the lyric soprano Doretta Morrow as the hapless Tuptim were wonderful performers.

However, R & H really made a mistake in the hiring of the director, for after Joshua Logan and Coward turned it down R & H smiled upon John van Druten. An English playwright who had emigrated to America in 1925, when the censor banned his play *Young Woodley* and Broadway welcomed it, van Druten had enjoyed a couple of comedy hits in the 1940s, *The Voice of the Turtle* and *I Remember Mama,* the latter of which R & H commissioned from him for their first venture as producers of other writers' plays. Van Druten directed *Mama* as well, but he didn't know from Siam or musicals, and with this show the importance of the director in R & H permanently declined. Major names would still officiate—George Abbott, Harold Clurman, Gene Kelly. But the oomph that Mamoulian had given *Oklahoma!* and *Carousel,* and that de Mille had given *Allegro,* was defunct. The staging of *The King and I* was really managed by Brynner (whose no-nonsense tone and aggressive deltoids kept Lawrence in line), by old pro Hammerstein (who laid out the final form of the book scenes), and by Jerome Robbins, originally hired simply for the Big Ballet and to stage the "March of the Siamese Children" and the "Shall We Dance?" polka, but eventually to block out all the numbers and the between-scenes crossovers.

Robbins had more choreography to direct as the show developed out of town. In fact, the show did nothing but develop, from story conference to design meeting to production planning, till it became the most expensive show in Broadway history at $360,000, twice the cost of the average musical. Broadway wags asked, "Something actually cost more than *Allegro?*" The money went for Irene Sharaff's costumes, mostly, for Jo Mielziner's set plan was the least elaborate of the four R & H shows he had thus far designed, allowing for one main set (the throne room) and a number of front-stage drops (for the ship, Anna's room, and so on), with the entire stage cleared for "Uncle Thomas." As with all their shows after *Oklahoma!,* R & H had no trouble securing their backing; on the contrary, the author-producers dispensed shares like rich uncles at Christmas. Major investors included Twentieth Century–Fox; R & H's lawyer, Howard Rheinheimer; wives Dorothy Rodgers and Dorothy Hammerstein; Theatre Guild stalwarts Lawrence Langner, Armina Marshall, and Terry Helburn (the "mother of us all," one might say, as it was she who first got the notion that *Green Grow the Lilacs* would make a wonderful musical); Mary Martin; Billy Rose (who had produced Hammerstein's *Carmen Jones*); and *South Pacific*'s coproducers Leland Hayward and Joshua Logan.

Nevertheless, before *The King and I* opened in New York (on March 29, 1951, at the St. James Theatre) and made its palpable hit, the show looked like a tough sell. After the New Haven opening, Leland Hayward startled the authors by suggesting they close the show. *Oklahoma!* was "no gags, no gals, no chance"; *Carousel* was this *Hungarian* thing about death; *Allegro* was the Aeschylus musical; and *South Pacific* was race and war. And *The King and I?* "By its very nature," Hammerstein said, "the story will not permit the pace and lustiness of a play like *South Pacific* and I am now sharpening a very long knife for the first one who tells me that it hasn't the qualities of *South Pacific*. It is a very strange play and must be accepted on its own terms."

The piece had its comedy, its charm, its pageantry—"I Whistle a Happy Tune"; Anna's son and Prince Chulalongkorn reprising "A Puzzlement"; the exuberant East-goes-West polka, "Shall We Dance?"; and of course the "Uncle Thomas" spectacle. Still, what New Haven saw in *The King and I* was grim and brooding, a star show without a star turn, and the fifth R & H musical in a row that dealt with death—closes with it, even. In place of *South Pacific*'s "There Is Nothin' Like a Dame" and "Honey Bun" was an almost hieratic score, lyrical, pleading, more serious even than *Carousel*'s: Tuptim's plangent "My Lord and Master," lovely and passionate but over in a flash and not heard again but for a few bars of underscoring; the impatiently hectoring "Waiting," a trio for Anna, the King, and the Kralahome; two slow, grieving ballads in a row near the end of Act One, when the Kralahome and Lady Thiang each beg Anna to stay in Siam, his "Who Would Refuse?" and her "Now You Leave." Even "Uncle Thomas," for all its vivacity, is a grave and brutal matter, not one of de Mille's folkish daydreams but a look at slavery through the eyes of a slave.

The show was singing heavy, and R & H moved quickly. "Waiting" wasn't going over, and "Who Would Refuse?" was unnecessary. They were dropped, leaving Murvyn Vye's Kralahome without a note to sing; Vye left the show, replaced by John Juliano. The new, prankish "Western People Funny" enlivened the second-act opening; and "Something Wonderful," given to Lady Thiang in place of "Now You Leave," strengthened the end of Act One. "I Have Dreamed" was put in just before "Uncle Thomas," to ensure that the Tuptim–Lun Tha subplot didn't get lost. This, too, empowered the show melodically. The score was now more lyrical, fleeter.

Still, it needed lightening. Gertrude Lawrence had an idea—how about a number for her and the kids? And Mary Martin* had the tune—that soft-shoe she had rehearsed to in *South Pacific* while R & H were coming up with "Honey Bun." Remember? Mary asks. "Suddenly Lucky?"

Right. With new lyrics and a carefree fan dance, the number considerably brightened the middle of Act One and, incidentally, turned out to be one of the most popular of R & H titles, "Getting to Know You."

---

*Martin tells the story herself in her autobiography, but one wonders how she could have taken in *The King and I* on its tryout when she was still in *South Pacific* in New York: *The King* went out of town from late February to late March of 1951, and Martin played Nellie Forbush till June of that year.

*The King and I* is a big show, with six principals and (originally, at least) fifty-five other performers. Yet it is essentially about three people. It begins (*top left*) as Anna and her son Louis (Sandy Kennedy) bid farewell to their home culture in the person of Captain Orton (Charles Francis). They enter the king's world (*left center*) where Anna allies herself with his plans to make Siam more "scientific." Mrs. Anna also becomes a personal ally of Tuptim (Doretta Morrow) seen between Brynner and Lawrence. And, below left, it is Tuptim, seated at left, who presents as author and narrator "The Small House of Uncle Thomas," confronting the King with a picture of his own barbarism, but pleasing the visiting British delegation. That night (*right*), the King and Anna become more than allies. Yet, moments later (*below, center*), they break their bond over the question of Tuptim; she lies on the floor at right as the Kralahome (John Juliano) looks on. When the King dies (*below*) Anna decides to stay on to further the scientification of Siam.

The *King and I* score underwent the severest out-of-town alterations of all the R & H shows, yet it seems as fully thought out as that of *Carousel*. Consider Rodgers' treatment of the locale. As in *Oklahoma!*, *Carousel*, and *South Pacific*, he generally avoids pastiche; but so dense an atmosphere needs some support in the pit. Rodgers, dance arranger Trude Rittmann, and orchestrator Robert Russell Bennett agreed to leave most of it to incidental bits and an industrious percussion section (though much of the Siamese effect is handled by "horse's hooves," the wooden clopping pieces traditionally used in racing numbers). Still, Rodgers extended himself to find something not necessarily authentic but certainly suggestive, in the piercing seconds that frame "A Puzzlement":

or the sinuous flute runs that caress "We Kiss in a Shadow":

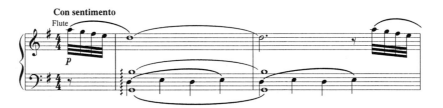

or the sullenly exotic 6/2 chords that impel "My Lord and Master":

Most notable is the use of soliloquy. The King's "A Puzzlement" is a triumph of game talent over sluggish material, for R & H found it difficult to "ensong" the King. He seemed one of those characters that cannot use music—not because of his brutality, because Jud Fry is brutal, and *his* solo, "Lonely Room," is a gem. Even violence has feelings. But the King's ambiguous nature, halfway between public executions and diplomatic banquets, seems to have baffled R & H somewhat. His sense of humor, in particular, lay out of reach. A comic trio for the King, Anna, and Lady Thiang, "Why? Why? Why?," in which the King compares the sensible East with the mystifying West, just didn't work; the number got as far as the arranger's writeout but was never performed and may not even have been rehearsed. True, the tiny "Song of the King," seldom recorded and never mentioned, but so basic that it was included in the movie, does illuminate the King's whimsy. And he has his share of "Shall We Dance?". Still, was the second principal of the show not to have a major solo? R & H finally found the King's voice in the *irony* of "A Puzzlement," incidentally underlining his ambivalence as he temporizes between tradition and progressivism:

> Shall I, then, be like my father
> And be wilfully unmovable and strong?
> Or is better to be right?
> Or am I right when I believe I may be wrong?

Hammerstein, of course, is totally progressive, leading the King to the necessary perception that his father was a blind tyrant, not "scientific." But Hammerstein is somewhat cynical here as well, a realist:

> And it puzzle me to learn
> That though a man may be in doubt of what he know,
> Very quickly will he fight,
> He'll fight to prove that what he does not know is so!

Anna, too, has her soliloquy, "Shall I Tell You What I Think of You?," another multifaceted musical scene like *Carousel*'s "Soliloquy." Six discrete sections make up this number, as Anna's mind freely ranges from indignant fury through regret to a withering sarcasm. The interior monologue, now a standard feature of the musical, is in fact an R & H invention. Before *Oklahoma!*, characters in musicals had solos, certainly—but they were always *songs*, the personality cut down to fit a tune. R & H widened the possibilities of the solo, psychoanalyzed it. "A Puzzlement" gives us such a rich view of the King's thinking—and feelings—that it alone maintains the character's prominence in the score, delivers him musically. "Shall I Tell You?" is even richer. Had it been Anna's only song, we would still know her.

The ballads are deceptively sophisticated. "We Kiss in a Shadow" at first seems like the simplest of tunes, with Tuptim and Lun Tha pretending to pray at the opposite sides of the stage, seated and immobile, staring straight ahead while they converse through the music. Anyone but Rodgers might have set Hammerstein's lyric as a waltz, following the natural 3/4 of the scan:

> We *kiss* in a *shad*ow,
> We *hide* from the *moon*.

In fact, Hammerstein gave his protégé, the very young Stephen Sondheim, a let's-see exercise—putting these words to music—and Sondheim came up with a waltz, pure 3/4. Too obvious. Rodgers heard the piece in 4/4, and though it sounds absolutely right that way, it is, in a way, aberrant. It is as if R & H were so into their own revolution that they could only do the unorthodox. "I Have Dreamed"—written, remember, at the eleventh hour, in Boston—doesn't seem unusual to the average ear, but it is very oddly structured, virtually one theme constantly repeated and developed till Rodgers caps it with a new tune at the very end. "Getting to Know You" is the same only more so, riding its first five notes (a triplet and two quarters) all the way through the refrain. Only musicians and academics fuss about these craftsman's sorties, yet they nevertheless concern all listeners, because composition this inventive affects the public as a whole in its freshness, its uniqueness. The AABA format of popular song was, by 1951, venerable; scores made up wholly of this AABA construction could sound tired even when new. Rodgers constantly broke away from it in his work with Hammerstein, which is one reason why their frequently heard scores never lose their appeal. They attend to situation and they unveil character, but also: they surprise you.

Most surprising of all in *The King and I* is the Big Ballet, "The Small House of Uncle Thomas." But it's not by Rodgers, and, unlike the Big Ballets in *Oklahoma!* and *Carousel*, it's not an arrangement of Rodgers' tunes (though "Hello, Young Lovers" and, briefly, "A Puzzlement" are quoted). It is, largely, original music composed by Trude Rittmann. This is unusual, for Rodgers habitually either wrote the dance music in his shows (as with *On Your Toes*'s "Slaughter on Tenth Avenue," "The Carousel Waltz," and *Cinderella*'s "Waltz for a Ball") or directed his dance arrangers to stick as closely as possible to the show's songs. Rittmann, dance arranger for most of the early R & H titles, would drive Rodgers crazy by dropping in allusions to European classical masters or some tidbit of her own—like the majestically lyrical D Flat Major theme in *Carousel*'s second-act ballet, which is actually a development of the "Soliloquy" (the "I guess he'll call me 'The old man'" line, heard just before it in the ballet) but is so fully expanded that audiences take it for an entirely new melody.

"It's not Rittmann and Hammerstein," Rodgers would tell her. "It's *Rodgers* and Hammerstein!"

Yet the special nature of "Uncle Thomas," its blend of Broadway smarts and Oriental theatre technique, called for something more than an "arrangement": a wholly new composition. Although it is true that, in this era, Kurt Weill and Leonard Bernstein troubled to write their own ballet music, Broadway production doesn't usually allow the composer the time to work out the accompaniment for the dances with the choreographer and the corps. It can be dreary, endless labor, time beating and cobbling, as the choreographer asks for "a kind of hopping sound" here and a "cancan in jazz" there. Anyway the composer is busy elsewhere, coaching the singers, conferring with the orchestrator, wheedling the producer, sulking with the lyricist. "Uncle Thomas," though Hammerstein's idea, was clearly going to be authored mainly by Jerome Robbins—so Rodgers left it to Rittmann, and he must have been happy with the results, for when he produced the Risë Stevens–Darren McGavin *King and I* at Lincoln Center in 1964, he made certain that the recording included a healthy chunk of the fifteen-minute "Uncle Thomas." This was unconventional largesse in a day when the average LP cast album ran at most fifty minutes, for it meant omitting some of the show's songs—the minor ones, to be sure, but nevertheless ones composed entirely by Rodgers. At that, it's amazing that no other *King and I* recording (except, to my knowledge, that of the Munich cast) has troubled to include even a taste of the piece, for its almost over-the-top theatre-of-gesture is studded with some of the show's most evocative moments: stage attendants crossing the scene between episodes swinging ratchets; Eliza and her baby (a doll) climbing a mountain formed by three boys; "King Simon of Legree" chasing Eliza with "scientific dogs who sniff and smell" (dancers in ferocious masks); the freezing and liquidizing of the river presented through the use of a giant silk scarf; and, of course, Tuptim's climactic loss of composure when she starts to beg the King for her freedom. "Uncle Thomas" may well be the most ingenious item in R & H, which makes it all the more interesting that, before Hammerstein realized that Robbins proposed to base the whole thing on artifice and suggestion, the author actually wanted trained poodles to perform Eliza's crossing of the ice.

Oddly, some of *The King and I*'s most difficult scenes—"Uncle Thomas" among them—seem to have fallen into place naturally, while the apparently simple moments went awry or fell flat. What could be more basic to the show than "Hello, Young Lovers," with Rodgers' exquisitely aching barcarole lines that cadence in waltz time (and which, despite the expansive feeling, limit the vocal range to one half step above an octave, to husband Gertrude Lawrence's debilitated instrument) and Hammerstein's confiding poetry? Yet the lyricist put the number through version after version as he struggled to give Anna the words that would establish her character, tell us of her past. From the start, he had in mind another extended musical scene (for Anna, her interpreter Lady Thiang, and the royal wives), as Anna's recollections were punctuated by dialogue and dissonant bits from the orchestra. Time after time, Hammerstein wrestled with the details of Anna's past, such as:

> I was dazzled by the splendor
> Of Calcutta and Bombay...

or:

> The celebrities were many
> And the parties very gay.
> (I recall a curry dinner
> And a certain Major Grey.)

Finally Hammerstein realized that the scene wasn't about where Anna had been or what she had seen but about how she felt, what she sympathized with, to strengthen the link with Tuptim that tragically shatters Anna's relationship with the King. At last Hammerstein had his lyric:

> I know how it feels to have wings on your heels,
> And to fly down the street in a trance.
> You fly down the street on the chance that you'll meet.
> And you meet—not really by chance.

Hammerstein sent it off to Rodgers, expecting some congratulations on having licked an imposing problem. But, as we know, that wasn't Rodgers' style. He took genius for granted. So Rodgers didn't get back to Hammerstein for days, at that about other matters, and he finally mentioned "Hello, Young Lovers" only in passing. "Quite satisfactory," he called it.

Hammerstein was, as they put it now, blown away and, in an episode that's in all the books, unburdened his feelings to Joshua Logan, recounting to Logan the many times he had had to restrain his temper in his meetings with Rodgers. It makes an odd scene, for Logan did his best to soothe Hammerstein even while nursing his own grudge against both R *and* H for the tough stand they had taken with him on *South Pacific*. Well, that's— *really*—show business.

Whatever abuse Hammerstein felt he was taking from Rodgers, he knew it was artistically worth it, for after five shows they were still at the summit of their powers, still persuading audiences to delight in being surprised. *The King and I* might well be the "other" R & H masterpiece, as fulfilled a composition as *Carousel*, less experimental but more tightly built. Of the Big Five —the musicals that chart the first eight years of the team's sixteen-year partnership—*Oklahoma!* is the exuberant ground breaker, *Carousel* the showpiece, *Allegro* the marvelous failure, and *South Pacific* the brooding treat, so mournful yet so elated. But *The King and I*, for all the difficulty R & H had in writing it, is the work that perfects their revolution. Only *Carousel* is as passionate, and even *Carousel*'s two leads aren't as fascinating as Anna and

### Anna and Her Kids

At right is the "Getting to Know You" dance with Deborah Kerr in the movie and (*below*) Constance Towers in the 1977 Brynner revival. By then, Brynner had become so basic as the King that he, not Anna, was the show's star. When Brynner went on vacation and Angela Lansbury (*bottom*) replaced Towers with a matchless, moving performance, ticket sales dropped off: *The King and I* had become *Anna and I.*

the King. This is the show that announces, "Now everything is possible, even a star vehicle in which the real star is the show itself, even a musical in which the two central lovers never kiss, scarcely even touch."

Despite excellent-to-good but not discerning reviews, *The King and I* quickly asserted itself as another smash in the style of *Oklahoma!* and *South Pacific*. Internationally, it proved even more universal in appeal than *Oklahoma!* (*South Pacific*, like *Carousel*, doesn't go over well in translation), and the movie is perhaps the best of the R&H adaptations, even admitting a mutilated score.* And among the public's memories of R&H, surely the happiest is Anna and the King leaping into their "Shall We Dance?" polka, that great mauve Irene Sharaff number sweeping the air as they whirl through the room.

It's strange how formidably the King confronts Anna in her own show, so to say. But it was Gertrude Lawrence who urged that Yul Brynner be given star billing—on her deathbed, for she died seventeen months into the run, at the age of fifty-four. After four decades in the theatre, Lawrence had hoped to go out in something consummate, with lengthy runs in New York and London and possibly the film version as well. (The last seems unlikely, for she was never a draw in movies; but it's pleasing to dream.) As Lawrence's health, unknown to

---

*The soundtrack album is misleading, as it includes prerecorded numbers that did not make it into the release print: "My Lord and Master," "Shall I Tell You What I Think of You?," and "I Have Dreamed."

all, succumbed to hepatitis, her always unsteady singing deteriorated so badly that spectators stirred uncomfortably and, so folklore tells, even booed her. (This is unbelievable. New York theatregoers are the most forgiving audience in the world. I actually heard a houseful of them clap—a little—after *Legs Diamond*.) R & H drafted a letter calling on Lawrence to relinquish the role rather than humiliate herself further. Gallantly, they never sent it.

Yul Brynner did assume stardom in the show, and though he quickly went to Hollywood to make his career playing in things like *The Ten Commandments, The Buccaneer,* and *The Magnificent Seven,* he never got another role as good as the King, not even as Dmitri Karamazov. In fact, Brynner won a Best Actor Oscar for the *King and I* movie, an unusual honor for a role in a musical. *The King and I* was the very center of Brynner, it seems: he has haunted the role in every revival without him (for no one has figured out a way to play the King that isn't a Brynner imitation), and in the end it is hard to know who made whom, the actor or the part. And, like Lawrence, Brynner died in the show, on his last tour, in 1985, felled by a cancer so turgid that at most performances he was cutting "A Puzzlement"* and less leaping into the polka than staggering into it.

When *The King and I* was new, of course, Rodgers had no idea what staying power it would develop, and he took exception to the reviews, which for some reason underrated him while praising Hammerstein: "It is not a great score according to Rodgers' standards"; "It is probably the weakest of Rodgers' scores"; "The most important work [is that of] Mr. Hammerstein." Richard Watts of the *Post*, revisiting the show four months later, wrote, "I was struck by the way we otherwise enthusiastic reviewers were lacking in appreciation of Rodgers' score." Truly, boys and girls, what great show has been appreciated on one viewing? Consider the original reviews of *Show Boat, Porgy and Bess, West Side Story, Company, Fiddler on the Roof,* all established classics. Are these works *comprehended* or, merely, at best, praised? Why would a Broadway veteran like Rodgers suddenly expect reviewers to get his work, especially as music is the most technical and thus the most privileged aspect of theatre?

Nevertheless, for the remainder of 1951 R & H suffered the equivalent of Gilbert and Sullivan's "carpet quarrel," and, to all visible intents, separated. They would certainly continue to collaborate; no one willingly walks out on making history of this quality. But the two temporarily put the firm of R & H on ice, no longer producing other men's plays and busying themselves with private projects: Rodgers with his score to accompany a television series of naval war foot-

A last look at Gertie, in her favorite *King and I* photograph.

Right, Deborah Kerr and Rita Moreno play the "Anna protects Tuptim" scene in the movie.

*This was an old habit of Brynner's. During the show's original three-year run—Brynner played the whole thing, less absences and vacations—he cut "A Puzzlement" 116 times.

age, *Victory at Sea*, and with a revival of *Pal Joey*; and Hammerstein with a revival of *Music in the Air*.

Rodgers used to joke that when he was with the diminutive Lorenz Hart, Broadway kibitzers would say, "The little guy's OK, but watch out for the big guy." Then, when he was with Hammerstein, they said, "The big guy's OK, but watch out for the little guy."

Well, as Stephen Sondheim puts it, the next R & H show was kind of about the big guy taking a poke at the little guy.

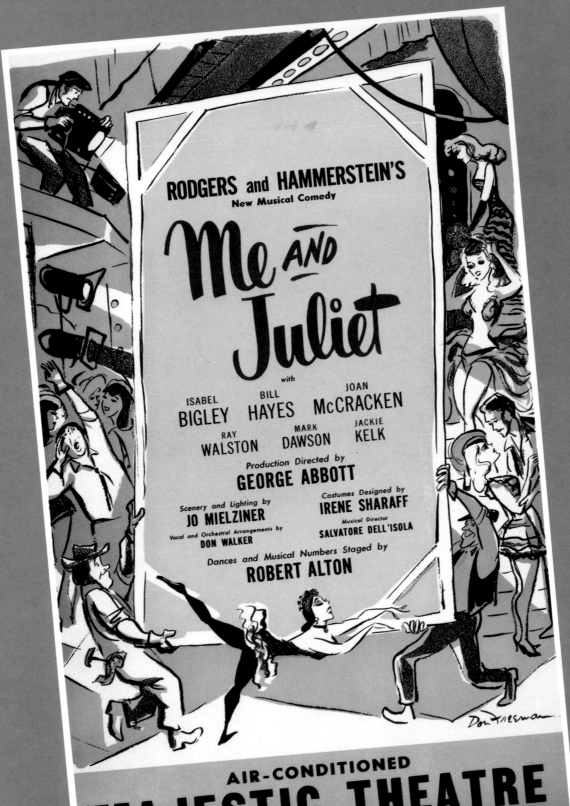

# Me and Juliet

Rodgers had been quietly toying with this idea for some six or seven years: a back-stager set entirely within a single theatre — in every part of it, from the dressing rooms up into the flies, moving almost cinematically through the building as the very world

Director George Abbott coaches Isabel Bigley in a big scene.

of the theatre is made comprehensible, sympathetic, to its public. Moreover, R&H could make another breakaway, in writing their first all-out and so-advertised musical comedy, something sassy and carefree like...well, *Something for the Boys.*

Hammerstein wasn't interested. But *Allegro* had been his baby, which Rodgers had helped to sire with some reluctance. Hammerstein owed him one. And, as they talked, the possibilities began to intrigue Hammerstein. For instance, the idea of starting the show with the curtain up on an empty stage—no overture—as if the audience were entering a theatre not at performance time but early in its day. Singers and dancers would drift in and warm up, a guy with a clipboard would call out orders, a rehearsal would begin...that sounded provocative. Today we're used to such effects; in the 1950s they were not only untried but unthought of. Hammerstein also liked Rodgers' idea of digging into the *real* life of the theatre—the look of thespian street attire, a taste of what auditions feel like, especially to the loser (and with the producer and choreographer conferring at the back of the auditorium), the drudgery that creates the magic, even unto a detail like a chorus boy's using a touch of a chorus girl's mascara to repair a hole in his tights, an effect Hammerstein had witnessed on his first job as assistant stage manager of the Rudolf Friml show *You're in Love* (1917).

Some sensational theatrical effects might be managed as well—shifting the show-within-a-show's very proscenium to the side of the stage during a performance to reveal what goes on in the wings, or pulling a blackout on a number only to have the lights come up again a few seconds later on the same number, with the dancers suddenly changed into rehearsal clothes.*

It's a given of R&H history that our boys would avoid the clichés of the backstage musicals. *What* backstage musicals? Broadway had never liked backstagers; Broadway already *is* backstage. The backstager was developed in *Hollywood*, as were the clichés. True, there have been a few stage musicals about putting on the show. One thinks immediately of *Kiss Me, Kate* and *A Chorus Line* along with Rodgers' *Babes in Arms* and Hammerstein's *Music in the Air* and *Very Warm for May* (not to mention *Show Boat*, so rich in subject matter that it does not seem like, but nevertheless is, a backstager). Still, the picture of a company pulling together against various threatening but ultimately surmountable odds and having a hit is Warner Brothers, not Broadway. There were no clichés for R&H to subvert because, as far as backstage musicals went, there were no clichés. Still, it was smart of the team to follow a few weeks in the life of an established hit (so we gather) in order to close in on the lives of its folk, rather than on the tension leading up to opening night.

*Both these effects were managed, but they were not appreciated till they were replicated in, respectively, *La Cage aux Folles* and *Dreamgirls.*

## People of the Theatre

At right is a rehearsal read-through: from left to right are Arthur Maxwell (who played the lead male singer), Jackie Kelk (the candy counter man), Mark Dawson (the electrician), Isabel Bigley (the chorus girl and Dawson's girlfriend), Bill Hayes (the assistant stage manager, who secretly loves the Bigley character), Joan McCracken (the lead female dancer), and Ray Walston (the stage manager). Bigley has the pivotal role: she must defy the overbearing Dawson and support the diffident Hayes. Below, Ray Walston and McCracken represent the techie and the gypsy. At right center, the "audience," onstage, is seen at the start of Act Two doing what the real-life audience had just been doing, enjoying the intermission. Below right, the chorus kids of the play-within-the-play here supposedly improvise a dance to the jazz trio that really was improvising.

What about the show-within-the-show? R & H decided it should be immediately intelligible, something to take for granted in order not to impinge upon the public's interest in the real-life characters. Every time the lights come up, we should know where we are—backstage or onstage, in clothes or costumes, singing what we feel or what we are paid to sing. In fact, Hammerstein thought, let's make the show-within something bizarre, to stand out and amaze us, the better to set off the plain life of the actor, with his and her dates and auditions and classes and the odd personal emergency. We shall imagine some rather advanced musical of the near future, something beyond even *Allegro*, with archetypal characters—a simple hero and his lovable Juliet, the rapacious Don Juan and his volatile Carmen. Then the audience will always know where it is. *Contrast* is the key. The show-within must look and sound, at every moment, as far from real life as possible.

Something else particularly excited Rodgers: a truly contemporary musical comedy would give him the chance to retrieve his saucy Rodgers and Hart mode—syncopation, lots of brass and percussion, hot stuff. Latin dances were sweeping the country, and Rodgers studded his score with markings for calypso, rumba, tango, samba, and "Tempo di Montuna," whatever that is. Furthermore, there was plenty of boogie and even an onstage jazz trio encouraged to improvise. The vocal arrangements—for the first time in R & H—suggested the Kay Thompson–Hugh Martin sound, about a decade old but still very popular then. *Me and Juliet* was going to be something new in R & H: not timeless but timely.

The songs themselves, then, found R & H going for impish, nimble, the sound of the Hit Parade as reimagined by R & H. The naive bounce of "It's Me," the cynical, slithery cool of "We Deserve Each Other," and the chromatic melody of "Marriage Type Love" really do invoke the youthful, Hartened Rodgers and a Hammerstein willing to loosen up and play Hart. Some of the cut songs go even further. "Meat and Potatoes" is such a risqué lyric that it shocked out-of-town critics ("We Deserve Each Other" replaced it), and "You Never Had It So Good" bears a wonderfully sleazy melody and a lyric that actually spoofs R & H:

I'll sew, I'll bake,
I'll try to make your evenings all enchanted.
My honeycake,
I'm yours to take, but don't take me for granted!

Furthermore, R & H went out of their way to assemble a typical *musical-comedy* production team, people not associated with operetta or the musical play: George Abbott to direct, along with choreographer Robert Alton (of, for instance, the original *Anything Goes, Leave It to Me!, Panama Hattie, Laffing*

*Room Only,* and *Hazel Flagg*) and orchestrator Don Walker, as opposed to the virtually inevitable but somewhat grandiose Robert Russell Bennett.

Somehow, something went wrong on the way to the premiere, May 28, 1953, at the Majestic Theatre. *Me and Juliet* was at the very least an enjoyable piece very beautifully produced. There were none of the technical miscalculations that had vexed *Allegro*; the show's sinewy, radiant visuals, moving from the tense backstage world into the suave fantasy of performance, were the talk of the town. The main plot was strong—a shy stage manager and a mousy inge-nue fall in love under the shadow of her murderously jealous lighting-man boyfriend.* The actors, all relative newcomers, were personable: Bill Hayes very sympathetic as the good guy fearful of the thug and Mark Dawson natu-ralizing the thug through good looks and mean-streets charm.† As the hero-ine, Isabel Bigley had—I always think—a weird quality, as one of those overacting nonactors. But she sang well. And Joan McCracken's Carmen crack-led (if I may) with the somewhat overproduced personality burnished with true talent that musical comedy dotes on. *Carousel* needs dignity, profundity; but musical comedy is sex and guts.

Interestingly, given R & H's emphasis on good voices, *Me and Juliet* called for principals who don't sing. Ray Walston, as the stage manager who loves McCracken but has a policy against dating members of his company (and McCracken is transferred from another show to *Me and Juliet* midway in Act One), was the show's actor, the guy who's so serious about theatre that he'd have a policy on fraternization in a fiercely incestuous field. George S. Irving, similarly nonsinging (though a baritone of operatic weight), was the show's stooge, in the absurdly comic role of *Me and Juliet*'s conductor, Dario. Irving played a portion of his part in the real-life orchestra pit, flirting with a myste-rious "Gardenia Lady" whom he believes is in the audience, and, in one of the show's funniest moments, lovingly soothed his orchestra when Juliet (Helena Scott) sang, then ruthlessly Wagnerized his orchestra when Me (Arthur Max-well) piped up.

It sounds wonderful; but something went wrong. It's not clear where the problem lay, for the idea itself was novel and compelling. It would seem that at some point R & H backed away from going too far with their own naturalism.

---

*It's not *Oklahoma!* again, despite the apparent correspondence, because the characters are dif-ferent. Curly is a show-off, Laurey wild and confused, and Jud a slug. *Me and Juliet*'s trio is less highly mettled, and Bob—the Jud counterpart—is less a psycho than a big man who is used to kicking people around. Anyway, the bully figure runs through Hammerstein's career, in *Rose-Marie, The New Moon, Golden Dawn, Rainbow,* and *High, Wide and Handsome,* not to list *Oklahoma!, Carousel* (Billy really is something of a hoodlum), and *The King and I* (the King, obviously). To Hammerstein, facing down the aggressor was a fundamental democratic act.

†William Tabbert, *South Pacific*'s Joe Cable, was to have played the hero but lost out because he looked too tall to be truly fearful of the towering Dawson. When R & H associate John Fearnley told Tabbert that the shorter Hayes had the part, Tabbert shucked off his platform shoes and shrank down to nothing. Too late—but, built up again, Tabbert copped the juvenile lead in *Fanny* a year later, ironically at the same theatre in which *Me and Juliet* played.

## Places of the Theatre

Below is the dressing room, where Bigley and McCracken sing "It's Me." At bottom, on the lighting bridge over the stage Mark Dawson (*right*, with Edwin Phillips) first learns that Bigley is involved with Hayes. Opposite, above, are McCracken and Arthur Maxwell in the alley leading to the stage door and opposite, below, the bar across the street, where Dawson sings "It Feels Good."

The backstage got a bit pretty, the real life a touch stylized. Yes, there was chorus dancer Buzz Miller repairing his tights with his colleague's mascara, truth in art. Still, somewhere along the way the curtain-up-on-a-bare-stage opening was dropped, along with the number that had launched the show, "Julius Baum Is Sweeping Up the Stage." And while *Me and Juliet* did run an overture in the middle of Act One, to signal the beginning of the show-within (and with vignettes of the cast psyching up behind the curtain and "conductor" George S. Irving plying his pantomime with the Gardenia Lady), the evening nevertheless began with the usual overture anyway, sapping the second overture of its surprise.

Nor were the authors able to articulate the theatre's relationship to its public. Bill Hayes' cue-in to "The Big Black Giant"—the audience, of course—calls theatregoers "the smartest people in the theatre, and the toughest…and the nicest." But Act Two opens in the lounge during the intermission, to show the audience what it looks like: a bunch of jerks who argue about whether the theatre is vital or dead—all this in one of the few "Rodgers waltzes" that could almost be called lumbering.

Worse yet was the show-within. What *was* it? "No one had thought it out," Abbott wrote in his memoirs. Hammerstein "was almost sphinxlike about it. He probably hoped that the choreographer would invent something, but Alton, completely at a loss [that is, without that plot and character material that Agnes de Mille and Jerome Robbins had drawn upon in *Oklahoma!*, *Carousel*, *Allegro*, and *The King and I*], just devised some Altonesque dances."

Surely Alton should have lightened the murky show-within by spoofing it—"satirizing Bob Alton," as John Fearnley saw it, for Alton was, after all, the presiding master of ensemble hoofing on Broadway in the late 1930s and in Hollywood in the early 1940s. The authors called in Jerome Robbins to see if he could—this is Fearnley again—"twist the dances around."

"I can do it," said Robbins. "But I won't. It would kill Bob Alton, and I can't do that."

This was one era saluting another. For while Alton represented the any-old-dance-will-do style of the old-fashioned musical, Robbins (along with de Mille, Michael Kidd, Bob Fosse, and Gower Champion) was going to reshape the function of choreography in the musical precisely because R & H had made a uniquely evocative kind of dance necessary. Recognizing this, Robbins could not bring himself to complete the symmetry and "execute" his predecessor Alton. It was a surprisingly gentle diplomacy from one of the meanest honchos of The Street.

All these problems were perhaps unavoidable, part of the risks involved in the collaborative process of putting on a big musical. But *Me and Juliet* suffered one problem that R & H really should have solved. Two problems, really:

the lyrics and the music. Unlike every other R & H stage score, this one simply isn't first-rate. It is tuneful and saucy. But the need to keep the show-within immediately effective at all times meant that *its* numbers (five of the evening's twelve, nearly half the play) had to be free-floating songs, without a context—what we might call high-quality pop tunes. Rodgers had tried this before, in *Pal Joey*, wherein half the score is nightclub floor numbers and the rest character songs for the principals. Unfortunately, *Me and Juliet* has so many principals that the score runs thin trying to characterize them all—and there is no room left for the situation songs that R & H emphasized, numbers like "The Surrey with the Fringe on Top" or "Pore Jud Is Daid," really *embedded* in the story.

Furthermore, if Rodgers is at less than his best, Hammerstein is out of his element. After *Carousel* and *The King and I*, he just doesn't *do* unreconstructed musical comedy. For instance, late in Act One we find Isabel Bigley and Joan McCracken in a dressing rooom preparing for a performance. A bit of dishing and teasing leads into "It's Me," a duet on how the theatre transforms the nobody into someone special. It's a cute idea for a song, but the lyrics are weak—not audacious, not *telling.* Similarly, Mark Dawson's solo, "It Feels Good," lacks the grip of the "Soliloquy" or "A Puzzlement," two comparable numbers, in which a difficult man shows himself to us. Billy and the King are rich characters; Dawson's character, Bob, is half there, not much more than a pushy guy drinking in a bar.

"Hammerstein's music drama redefined the singer of a song," Gerald Mast wrote in *Can't Help Singin'*. "While the voice, the I, of a Gershwin, Hart, or Porter lyric is an undefined surrogate for the lyricist himself, the voice, the I, of a Hammerstein lyric is an Oklahoma rancher, or a nurse from Little Rock, or a Victorian British schoolmarm." Exactly right. Hammerstein had no signature style: his characters did. It would appear that *Me and Juliet*'s characters never quite reached him.

Any other team might have been proud of the score. It produced one standard, "No Other Love (have I)," Hammerstein's verse applied to a theme from Rodgers' *Victory at Sea* suite. The jiving "Keep It Gay" and the briskly affectionate "Marriage Type Love" were popular for a few years. Listening to the *Me and Juliet* cast album, we clock agreeable music—but by 1953 the theatregoer, like Rodgers, was taking genius for granted.

We hear good voices on that record, a hallmark of R & H casting. Go back to the original-cast cuts of *Oklahoma!*, *Carousel*, *Allegro*…these are the strong voices of operetta bent to the realism of musical comedy (another demonstration of how the musical play is a hybrid of the American musical's two fundamental structures). Here and there, exceptions prove the rule—Howard da Silva's Jud (whose "Lonely Room," remember, was usurped by Alfred Drake on *Oklahoma!*'s appendix set) or John Conte's Charlie in *Allegro* (similarly replaced on the cast album, by a chorister, Robert Reeves). But even when moving into the vocally erratic world of musical comedy, R & H auditioned for tone and musicianship. *Me and Juliet*'s Joan McCracken, primarily a dancer, had the voice of a hoarse olive. But Bill Hayes, Isabel Bigley, Mark Dawson, Helena Scott, and Arthur Maxwell could have sung Romberg; and Hayes sounds especially winning in *Me and Juliet*'s best number, "The Big Black Giant." As I've said, this is about the audience, Hammerstein's main chance to relate to the most volatile constant in his profession. It's a strange piece, possibly the only R & H song that is admired as often as it is ridiculed, both then and now. Yet in its quietly valiant way it does express Hammerstein's belief that theatre is not just entertainment but instruction, therapy, and social reformation:

> Every night you fight the giant
> And maybe, if you win,
> You send him out a nicer giant
> Than he was when he came in...

This suggests a serious show, as all R & H works partly are; but *Me and Juliet* isn't serious. Unfortunately, *Me and Juliet* isn't very funny, either. Spirited, yes. Snappy, sure. But not *funny*. A funny musical comedy, in those days, was *Finian's Rainbow* (1947), loaded with sharp cracks about the internal contradictions of capitalism and democracy; or *Guys and Dolls* (1950), with its opulent Runyonland wisenheimers; or *Top Banana* (1951), a last look at the know-how of old-time burlesque.

It's a commonplace that Hammerstein was weak in comedy—that he has many an amusing or charming line but seldom an all-the-way, laugh-inducing lyric like Cole Porter's "Always True to You in My Fashion" or Frank Loesser's "Adelaide's Lament." Nor are the R & H scripts the kind of joke-a-minute texts that musical comedy strived for. However, going back to the librettos Hammerstein wrote in his days as Otto Harbach's cowriter and the collaborator of Sigmund Romberg and Jerome Kern, we find truly funny shows. The humor is traditional, but never corny or witless. It's fine, sure stuff, still vital today. *Show Boat*, for instance, is studded with pranks that read a little pat but which play beautifully on stage, as when Ravenal finally asks Captain Andy why he jumps whenever his obnoxious wife, Parthy Ann, calls, even after all these years. What has she got?

Expert Andys can put it over. What has she *got*? Why, she's got...she's got... well, after all, it's....And at length Andy looks Ravenal square in the eyes and says: "She's got a *mean disposition*."

There is much, much less of this in R & H, partly because of the shortage of the vaudevillian talents who could play these lines—the Charles Winningers and Irene Franklins—but mainly because R & H storytelling made vaudeville obsolete in the musical. *Show Boat* is epic, less about relationships than about a way of life, and so it has room for a certain amount of miscellaneous fun. The R & H musical play is not epic, despite the sense of national destiny that impels *Oklahoma!* or the forty-two years that *Allegro* covers. There is no room in such shows for anything but the characters, what they do, and how they feel. This is why *Me and Juliet*'s script disappoints. Here, for once, was an R & H show that *needed* miscellaneous fun—and didn't have it.

Nevertheless, the tryout did not reveal a show in trouble. *Me and Juliet* wasn't unfinished, simply unfulfilled. It opened in Cleveland rather than in New Haven because the physical production was too elaborate for the old Shubert—and its lack of an orchestra pit would have ruined the scenes in which conductor Dario leads his players. *Me and Juliet* was the biggest of the R & H shows, its backstage work even more complex than *Allegro*'s, with the most complicated set of lighting cues in the musical's history. There were eighty-five tons of scenery and "five giant tracks with synchronized motors in the fly-loft"—so Jo Mielziner told the *Christian Science Monitor*. "As the scenery moves, the audience will get the sensation that the auditorium is turning while the stage is standing still." All told, *Me and Juliet* cost $350,000, staggering for the time, and though *The King and I* had cost $10,000 more, that was only because of the many extraordinary costumes with which Irene Sharaff had dressed the "Uncle Thomas" ballet.

The play-within-the-play is deliberately stylized in look and action to contrast with the everyday feel of the backstage scenes. At left, Helena Scott is Juliet, Bob Fortier is Don Juan, Arthur Maxwell appears as the character called Me, and Svetlana McLee plays Carmen. Below, McCracken, Fortier, Gwen Harmon, and Maxwell go into their dance.

Cleveland loved the show, perhaps out of regional pride—it had been quite a few years since Broadway-bound shows regularly stopped off in Ohio—and the racy nature of some of the lyrics gave the piece some useful PR even as R&H replaced them. Boston got prideful as well, declaring an R&H week with a luncheon at the Algonquin Club including heavy dignitaries from the mayor to the lieutenant governor of Massachusetts. New York, too, held an R&H week, at the end of summer, for by then the team had three shows running on Broadway (*Me and Juliet* had joined *The King and I* and *South Pacific*, moved to the Broadway Theatre to make room for baby), and a revival of *Oklahoma!* was playing at the City Center.

*Me and Juliet*, however, was found wanting. The reviewers were kind but, almost to a man, unenthusiastic. Jo Mielziner got all the raves, and he certainly had mounted some glorious pictures. Yet the critics didn't realize that the many special effects had been written into the show in the first place. For instance, Mielziner's greatest triumph was the first-act finale, that moment when the very stage itself appeared to move ten feet to the right (that is, as if a movie camera had panned ten feet to the left) to show us not only the dancer-filled nightclub set but the wings where, every night, hero Bill Hayes and heroine Isabel Bigley shared a kiss just before she "enters" as a waitress, this timidly defiant tryst unseen by her psychotically jealous boyfriend, Mark Dawson, up on the lighting bridge.

Of course, *this* night Dawson is watching them. As they embrace, a spotlight catches them, then follows Bigley around the stage like an objective correlative for the infinitely angry eyes of Dawson above. Meanwhile, the dancers, aware that something is going very, very wrong, start to look up at the flies as they move to Alton's frantic choreography. Suddenly a sandbag drops, so close to the heroine that it dashes the tray from her hands, and as she races to the wings, and the dancers keep staring up in terror as they dance, the stage manager desperately gives a signal and the curtain falls.

It's one of the great first-act curtains ever tried, and it typifies the zest with which R&H approached the project. But it was perceived as simply more of Mielziner's stage wizardry. "Mechanically, the show is pure magic," said Walter Kerr. But he thought the authors had "come perilously close to writing a show-without-a-show." *Me and Juliet* ran ten months and made a profit, but it couldn't muster a tour, just seven weeks' worth of open run in Chicago. There was no movie and no foreign production, and, except for "No Other Love," the score quickly fell out of memory. R&H scores seem to become popular as wholes or not really popular at all. As with *Allegro,* even the hit tunes don't have the resonance that minor numbers from the classic R&H shows do.

The main problem with *Me and Juliet* would seem to be the authors' lack of ease in musical comedy. But, as we shall see, *The King and I* was really the last of their musical plays. The four R&H titles that follow *Me and Juliet*, no matter how they were announced on the posters, are all musical comedies, and all of value. R&H had seen *Me and Juliet* as a novelty; Hammerstein noted that "it's the first of our plays in which nobody dies." More important, it was the first of their plays without a powerful sense of destiny, of characters consequentially interconnected. In *Oklahoma!*, *Carousel*, *South Pacific*, and *The King and I* especially, the principals—whether noble or weak, just or impetuous—change each other's lives. *Me and Juliet*'s characters appear to be thrown together by chance and—except for the lovers—will part company unaffected by each other as soon as the show closes. This left Hammerstein with nothing to seek out in his people, and Rodgers with nothing to illustrate.

They did it for fun. Yet, as Kerr remarked, "So little of this spirit shines through. *Me and Juliet* seems more deeply in earnest and a lot less light-hearted than their more significant work."

It was a chastening experience; and, oddly, it drew the two men closer together, both as collaborators and as...well, almost friends.

Jo Mielziner's design for the first-act finale shows how the "stage" looked after it moved to reveal the "wings."

# Pipe Dream

*Me and Juliet* marked the first decade of R & H. In ten years they had transformed the American musical. Of course, this had been Hammerstein's work since the 1920s, and Rodgers' early film scores with Lorenz Hart were astonishingly well integrated.

Jo Mielziner's design for scene one, Doc's laboratory.
Opposite are the principals, William Johnson, Judy Tyler, and Helen Traubel.

R & H were figures of such importance by the mid-1950s that on March 28, 1954, for its twenty-fifth anniversary, General Foods sponsored a television salute to their career that ran on all four networks. Here, at top and left to right, are Tony Martin and Rosemary Clooney, Florence Henderson and Gordon MacRae, Mary Martin and Ezio Pinza, Patricia Morison and Yul Brynner; in the middle are Jan Clayton and John Raitt, Bill Hayes and Janice Rule; and at the bottom are Ed Sullivan, Groucho Marx, Jack Benny, and Edgar Bergen with Charlie McCarthy. In the foreground, Dick and Oscar.

And many a show before R & H had managed to ban the vaudeville. *Oklahoma!* did not invent the artistically organic musical. What *Oklahoma!* did was popularize it.

Broadway began to absorb the elements of R & H immediately. Six months after *Oklahoma!*, *One Touch of Venus* (1943) sported Agnes de Mille choreography, including a dream ballet. The following season, *Bloomer Girl* (1944) and *Up in Central Park* (1945) joined *Carousel* in depicting historical America with a strong sense of atmosphere and a somewhat solemn sociology, in *Bloomer Girl's* treatment of racism and in its keening Civil War Ballet (de Mille again) and in *Central Park's* look at an idealistic reporter fighting Boss Tweed's Tammany Hall.

The term "musical play" was becoming trendy, too—but, quite aside from how they billed their shows, authors veteran and fledgling were working wholly in the R & H format. Alan Jay Lerner and Frederick Loewe suffered two musical-comedy flops before they wrote *Brigadoon* (1947) according to R & H innovations (and including a new innovation, several crucial principals who don't sing a note). True, much of Broadway went its own way, as when Frank Loesser found an audacious new voice for pure musical comedy in *Guys and Dolls* (1950), or when Irving Berlin and the librettist team of Lindsay and Crouse tailored a dowdy shift to Ethel Merman's measurements in *Call Me Madam* (1950).

Still, the R & H influence—it could nearly be called a regime—did force many an author to sharpen his craft, to write *higher*. Even Cole Porter, the most unreconstructed of the old pros, turned against his *Something for the Boys* style in the very characterful scores for *Kiss Me, Kate* (1948) and *Out of This World* (1950)—and Porter stated outright that the reasons why were Rodgers and Hammerstein. Not that Porter had never written an integrated show before: *Jubilee* (1935), to my ear his finest score, dazzles with the elegance with which Porter brings eight principals to life while juggling the needs of the chorus and dancers. But *Jubilee's* music proved so rich and diverse that critics and public couldn't take it in; even its standards, "Begin the Beguine" and "Just One of Those Things," were ignored till years later. *Jubilee* failed, and after that a more prudent Porter stuck with easy-listening musical comedy. If R & H made the *Kiss Me, Kate* Porter necessary, they also made him possible.

They even inspired less experienced writers to outdo themselves. The composer-lyricist Harold Rome was so unattuned to narrative that he spent his first fifteen years exclusively in revue—five of them, most notably *Pins and Needles* (1937) and *Call Me Mister* (1946). When he finally tried a story show, in *Wish You Were Here* (1952), he was still working with the proletarian Jewish characters his revues had featured, but his next show, *Fanny* (1954), from

Marcel Pagnol's Marseilles trilogy, marked a departure in its French setting, quasi-operatic passions, and flavorful, haunting score. It was Rome breaking out of the Rome style, writing higher. Moreover, all of *Fanny*'s principals were R&H alumni—Ezio Pinza, Walter Slezak (actually a Hammerstein-only alumnus, having played the juvenile lead in the first production of *Music in the Air*), William Tabbert, and Florence Henderson, one of the Laureys on the national tour—and Joshua Logan directed and collaborated on the book. To top it off, *Fanny* was one of the few shows not by R&H that Hammerstein regretted not having written. He had been eager to do it, but David Merrick owned the rights to Pagnol's films, and Rodgers refused to work with Merrick, even for 51 percent.

The R&H influence outlasted R&H themselves, for while Hammerstein died in 1960, some of the next generation pursued the R&H narrative structure and musical dramatization. Consider Harvey Schmidt and Tom Jones' *110 in the Shade* (1963), a very R&H kind of adaptation (of N. Richard Nash's play *The Rainmaker*) in the way the original text is respected while opened up, not to mention such R&H ideas as an intense soliloquy to close Act One and folk-flavored de Mille choreography.* It is not that *Fanny* or *110 in the Shade* are ersatz R&H, but that the R&H approach is so vast of potential that its principles guided all kinds of writers for decades. Some say the R&H era ended with *Gypsy* (1959), as the last great linear narrative before the rise of the concept musical. But *Gypsy* is about three people, where R&H usually feature a large group of lead characters; and *Gypsy*'s dances are functional—rehearsals and performances—where R&H dances are extrapolative; and *Gypsy*'s score is vernacular and contemporary, where R&H sound timeless. Stephen Sondheim points to *My Fair Lady* as the end of the R&H regime in that it was the last marriage of operetta and musical comedy—the last great "musical play."

What is undebatable is that R&H had entirely changed the musical in ten years, not only in a difference of emphasis (for example, in the intently integrated scores of musical comedies such as *Finian's Rainbow* or *Guys and Dolls,* far more tightly executed than musical comedy had been in the early 1940s) but also of kind, of the very genres that were thought viable. In 1942, when R&H teamed up, the form of choice was musical comedy, whether bawdy (*By Jupiter,* 1942), carefree (*Best Foot Forward,* 1941), or artistically ambitious (*Lady in the Dark,* 1941). The revue, simpler to write because so loosely constructed, was in its prime, though debased from the thrill of spec-

---

*Schmidt at times even sounds like Rodgers, as in the flowing diatonicism of *110*'s "A Man and a Woman," punctuated by a stinging dissonance between the sung lines such as Rodgers sometimes employed; or, in *I Do! I Do!* (1966), in "My Cup Runneth Over," "The Snows of Yesteryear" (especially the bridge), and "What Is a Woman." And note, in the middle section of "The Father of the Bride," that when Robert Preston mentions "my own little girl," Schmidt quotes the vamp that launches *Carousel*'s "Soliloquy."

tacle that Florenz Ziegfeld had given it, the high-energy talent that George White had assembled, and the wit and sophistication it had known in the late 1920s and early 1930s. Operetta was dead. To take the 1941–42 and 1942–43 seasons as samples, Broadway saw a total of eleven musical comedies; sixteen revues (starring such as Ed Wynn, Gypsy Rose Lee, Irving Berlin—in his own *This Is the Army*—and Olsen and Johnson); one operetta; revivals of, among other shows, *Porgy and Bess, The Student Prince,* and *Die Fledermaus* (in English, retitled *Rosalinda,* and a surprise smash); and, at the very end of the period, *Oklahoma!.*

By contrast, in 1952, after the first five R & H shows, the revue was moribund and musical comedy was overshadowed by the musical play. A number of factors contributed to the death of the revue: the loss of its specialized talent to other mediums or to retirement and certainly competition from television's staple, the variety hour. But R & H had also put their kibosh on revue by popularizing the story score, thereby revealing the revue's contextless pop tunes as thin and unmotivated; and also by emphasizing elaborate production values, for the Forties revue suffered almost generically from low-budget presentation.

As for the rise of the musical play itself, this never threatened to overwhelm musical comedy by a sheer head count. Still, the musical play did bear an air of prestige that left the somewhat coarse—or, let's say, less pretentious—musical comedy as a kind of kid brother. Indeed, the musical play's often surging vocal component—the "If I Loved You" or "Some Enchanted Evening" syndrome, not to mention, say, "Come to Me, Bend to Me" or "So in Love"—actually revived operetta. After *Oklahoma!,* such works as *Song of Norway* (1944), *Rhapsody* (1944), *Marinka* (1945), *Polonaise* (1945), *Music in My Heart* (1947), *Magdalena* (1948), and *Kismet* (1953)—and even a few out-and-out operas—were not only produced but, sometimes, successful, even wildly so. *Song of Norway*'s improbable look at the life of Edvard Grieg, filled to the grim with irrelevant ballets (albeit by George Balanchine) and risible sentiments, was the sort of show that might have bombed even in the operetta-happy 1920s. Yet it ran over two years.

*Song of Norway* belongs to a subgenre that I feel compelled to term "floperetta," because most of them deserved to (and ultimately did). The floperetta, at heart, counters the R & H method with, one, an idiotic plot, two, idiotic characters, and, three, idiotic songs, and can be identified by three factors: one, the show was first mounted on the West Coast by Edwin Lester; two, it has a score by Robert Wright and George Forrest drawn from the music of an established classical composer; and, three, it starred Irra Petina. *Song of Norway,* with Lester, Wright and Forrest (adapting Grieg), and Petina, was floperetta at its best, so imagine what *Gypsy Lady* (1946) was like—

### R & H as Producers

At left is George Jenkins' design for John Van Druten's *I Remember Mama* (1944), R & H's most successful straight play, with Mady Christians as Mama, Oscar Homolka as terrible Uncle Chris and, in his Broadway debut, Marlon Brando as son Nils. Though Helen Hayes played Anita Loos' *Happy Birthday* (1946) in New York, Miriam Hopkins took it on tour (*bottom*), singing one of the few R & H numbers not written for a musical. Opposite, Irving Berlin's *Annie Get Your Gun* (1946) was the biggest hit of Ethel Merman's hit-filled career and the gem of the R & H production team. In a nice touch of cyclic history, all Berlin's work is now handled by the R & H office.

and no Petina, at that, a crucial error. Not all floperettas observed all three factors.* Tongues wagged when Wright and Forrest filled *Anya* (1965) with Rachmaninoff and Petina yet went with another producer, Fred R. Fehlhaber. A floperetta without the Lester touch was like...well, *Song of Turkey*, with Wright and Forrest adapting the music of Tughril Beg.

The point is that R & H did not make Broadway safe for operetta; on the contrary, they *absorbed* operetta into their format and made unreinvented operetta all the more extraneous. It is illustrative that, when R & H began producing shows by other writers, the one musical they staged was not an operetta and not a musical play, but a musical comedy—one, however, with an R & H sensibility, *Annie Get Your Gun* (1946). The show was lyricist Dorothy Fields' idea, and she was originally to have collaborated on the score with Jerome Kern, teaming up with her brother Herbert on the book. This, of course, sounds like the kind of musical the authors of *Oklahoma!* and *Carousel* would have wanted to produce—who better than the Jerome Kern of the "Princess" shows, *Show Boat*, and the ultra-jazzy Astaire-and-Rogers film *Swing Time* (1936) to adapt to the new Broadway of R & H, even in a vehicle for Ethel Merman? But Kern died, and R & H turned to Irving Berlin. Now, *this* seems strange, as Berlin was far more a pop writer than a musical narrator. Like Harold Rome, he had spent many years in revue rather than dare a story score. And didn't *Annie* need a country-style sound? What did Berlin know of hooting and hollering?

*There was one flopera, *My Darlin' Aida* (1952), trying Verdi on Hammerstein's *Carmen Jones* plan, without success.

"That part's easy," Hammerstein told him. "Just leave the final *g* off of every word that ends in *ing.*"

So Berlin went to work, hootin' and hollerin' in, amazingly, the R&H manner: not churning out ditties but finding the moments in the Fieldses' book that needled his muse. Berlin was turning so much of the script into score that finally he suggested that a portion of his royalties be reassigned to the Fieldses, as all the songs were being fathered by the story.

"That," said Hammerstein, "is how a musical *should* be written."

Suddenly, Berlin found himself building his music not out of "good ideas for songs," out of hooks and novelties, but out of his characters and their conflicts. As with the R&H shows, to hear the songs is to comprehend what is happening in the *book,* from "You Can't Get a Man with a Gun" and "The Girl That I Marry" through "They Say It's Wonderful" to "Anything You Can Do." *Annie Get Your Gun* demonstrates the reach of R&H even more than *Brigadoon, Kiss Me, Kate, Fanny,* or *110 in the Shade.* Those were the work of people who either had integrated shows in their past or were young enough not to know of any other way of writing. But by 1946 Berlin was fifty-eight, an old dog set in old ways. That he could so eagerly reequip his shop that late in what was probably the most successful songwriting career in history tells us how attractive the R&H mode had become.

Though they continued to run their own shows, R&H ceased to put on works by other authors after 1950. They had racked up an impressive count: seven new shows, including one all-time smash (*Annie Get Your Gun,* obviously), four hits, and only two flops, Graham Greene's *The Heart of the Matter* (which closed out of town) and John Steinbeck's *Burning Bright,* both in 1950. In Rodgers' memoirs, he explained this disengagement from non–R&H works in an unclear and somewhat unbelievable passage concerning his and Hammerstein's lack of profits "as producers." What? After *I Remember Mama's* two-year run and sales to Hollywood, radio, and television? After *Annie Get Your Gun?* Nor can it have been the failure of the Greene and Steinbeck plays; R&H weren't the men who let a few failures stop them. What seems more likely is that Hammerstein wanted more time to travel and to enjoy his Doylestown tennis matches, and that Rodgers was running out of the energy needed to sustain not only his own work but others' as well.

The R&H office now concentrated on R&H. The partners bought back the rights to their three Theatre Guild titles* and kept sharp eyes on R&H productions around the world — in fact, they had instituted the practice of sending Broadway shows to London in replicas of the originals, from the tempos in the overture to the timing of the final curtain. In the days of *Sally, Sunny,* and

*Oklahoma!* cost them $851,000, in six installments over three and a half years.

*No, No, Nanette,* American musicals tried the West End in heavy revisions addressed to the English audience, but when *Oklahoma!, Carousel, South Pacific,* and *The King and I* took over Drury Lane for a bit short of nine consecutive years, they did so uncompromisingly and authentically. In their wake, all sorts of Broadway musicals, from *The Pajama Game* and *The Music Man* to *Fiddler on the Roof* and *A Little Night Music,* almost invariably go over in facsimiles of the original productions.

Perhaps in response to all this, the two men's partnership began to run a little more smoothly on the personal level. Realizing what kind of history they had made together must have eased tensions somewhat. True, in a famous story, Hammerstein's doctor diagnoses an ulcer in 1959 and Hammerstein cries out, "An ulcer! That son of a bitch finally did it to me!" But in another story Hammerstein foresees that Rodgers will be sorely taken when he is left alone, and asks Stephen Sondheim to be ready to replace him as Rodgers' lyricist.

Clearly, we have something a trifle odd yet very natural, one partner who harbors grievances and another partner who thinks everything is fine. Actually, Rodgers admitted in his memoirs that he had been puzzled by the missing piece in his relationship with Hammerstein, even hurt at times. Maybe they should have slugged it out at some point, unburdened themselves. Kern would have. Hart was known to have done so.

In any case, at this point R & H stand at the height of their fame. *Me and Juliet* or no *Me and Juliet,* the two men are, without question, the most famous people in the theatre. And *that*'s when they write their only bomb: *Pipe Dream.*

Hammerstein always blamed *Pipe Dream* on Cy Feuer, half of the producing team of Feuer and (Ernest) Martin. "We do mug shows," Feuer told Hammerstein, probably thinking more of the gamblers of *Guys and Dolls* and the lecherous bohemians of *Can-Can* (1953) than of the Oxonians of *Where's Charley?* (1948) and the finishing-school belles of *The Boy Friend* (1954). "You," Feuer advised Hammerstein, "should do a mug show."

"We do family shows," Hammerstein replied.

Feuer and Martin's next show after *The Boy Friend* was Cole Porter's *Silk Stockings* (1955), *Ninotchka* with mug elements. In the works, however, they had what promised to be the mother of all mug shows, *The Bear Flag Café,* a musical using the setting and characters of John Steinbeck's novel *Cannery Row.* Steinbeck himself would write the book and Frank Loesser the score; and Henry Fonda would play Doc, the marine biologist saint of a northern California coastal town filled with ne'er-do-wells, layabouts, and whores whose life's work consists of hustling each other, bullshitting, and attending the occasional raucous party.

It's no *Guys and Dolls*—though, surely, a follow-up to that show is what Feuer and Martin had in mind. But then *Guys and Dolls'* source, the stories of Damon Runyon, begged for Broadway. Steinbeck is not so adaptable. Steinbeck is, in fact, a born writer *writing,* so filled with his own books that essential qualities are lost when they go into other mediums. True, there are several Steinbecks. The best known is the realist and social critic, the Steinbeck of *Of Mice and Men* and *The Grapes of Wrath,* which *can* be refashioned; movie buffs admire John Ford's classic *Grapes* of 1940, and more recently theatregoers enjoyed a stage version by Chicago's Steppenwolf troupe.

But there is also the impish fantasist Steinbeck, a spinner of antic parables of the colorfully humdrum life of Monterey, the Steinbeck of *Tortilla Flat* and *Cannery Row.* This Steinbeck does not go well into other mediums, and here's why:

> Cannery Row in Monterey in California is a poem, a stink, a grating
> noise, a quality of light, a tone, a habit, a nostalgia, a dream.

This is a mood piece, stories based more on how life feels than on individual action.

Musicals are about individual action, so Steinbeck found he had to compose a new story for the show: because *Cannery Row* doesn't have one. In fact, in the end Steinbeck decided not to write *The Bear Flag Café*'s libretto, but rather to write another novel set in Cannery Row, to provide the basis for the musical. At about that time Frank Loesser dropped out of the project, and R&H heard about it.

And R&H said, "We'll take it." This was the show that was to become *Pipe Dream.*

R&H struck a deal with Feuer and Martin, cutting them in on the future show's profits, and Hammerstein began to write the book as Steinbeck sent him manuscript pages, chapter by chapter. The new novel, *Sweet Thursday,* was to get unappreciative reviews, but it is one of Steinbeck's most congenial works, in the heavily authored style of Steinbeck the wag, cutting a wise and endlessly tolerant figure as the narrator, calling plenty of time-outs for ontological discourse (he'll start a chapter with "Some days are born ugly" or "Of all our murky inventions, guilt is at once the most devious, the most comic, the most powerful") and grandly undercutting his own gravity with digs and spoofs. One of his characters, Joe Elegant, the cook at the Bear Flag Café—a bordello, by the way—is writing a novel. The book he's working on sounds like Steinbeck's takeoff on a Steinbeck novel:

> His hero had been born in a state of shock and nothing subsequent
> had reassured him. When a symbol wasn't slapping him in the

mouth, a myth was kicking his feet out from under him. It was a book of moods, of dank rooms with cryptic wallpaper, of pale odors, of decaying dreams. There wasn't a character [in the book] who wouldn't have made the observation ward.

The new story that Steinbeck concocted for his novel sounded right for a musical. *Cannery Row*'s male leads were back: Doc, of course, and Mack, Hazel, and the rest of the gang of bums who live in an abandoned dump known as the Palace Flophouse. Dora, the Bear Flag's madam, had been replaced by her more usefully eccentric sister Fauna, and the love plot was provisioned with the introduction of Suzy, a hard-edged tramp whom Dora takes in and whom Doc falls in love with.

Doc and Suzy went down well with Hammerstein as his favorite kind of couple, culturally mismatched yet drawn to each other, he on the phlegmatic or moody side and she rather intense (as in *Wildflower, Rose-Marie, Song of the Flame, The Desert Song, The New Moon, High, Wide and Handsome;* and *Carousel, South Pacific,* and *The King and I*). At the same time, they were something new for Hammerstein to try out, for Doc is a restless and ambivalent man, dissatisfied with his quiet existence yet fearful of his ambitions, and Suzy has such low self-esteem that she has built up an abrasive facade that turns almost everyone away from her.

Everyone but Fauna. One of those soft-hearted madams beloved of fiction,* Fauna takes it upon herself to bring Doc and Suzy together. A subplot concerns the efforts of the Palace Flophouse boys to secure ownership of their sweet home, meanwhile raising the money to buy Doc a much-needed micro scope. The two story lines come to a point at a big party at which the boys succeed but at which Doc's approach-avoidance and Suzy's belligerence threaten to drive them apart forever. Suzy leaves the Bear Flag to move into an empty boiler pipe—thus the musical's title—and there it uncomfortably rests—till the dangerously helpful Hazel hears Suzy mention that if Doc broke his arm or something she'd bring him soup.

Ensues a short crossover scene "in one" as Hazel passes Mack. Mack waves, but Hazel, deep in thought, his arms behind him, misses it. His hands come around in front: he's carrying a baseball bat (as in: to break an arm with). Mack is puzzled. Blackout.

Clearly, what R & H had in mind was another musical comedy, though, as with all their shows except *Me and Juliet*, it was billed as a musical play. Typically for R & H, it was cast mainly with singers. As an actor, Fonda was the

### The Folk of Cannery Row

In *Pipe Dream*, Helen Traubel (*below*) played Fauna. As John Steinbeck wrote, "She was named Flora, but a gentleman bum said, 'Flora, you seem more a fauna-type to me.' 'Say, I like that,' she said. 'Mind if I keep it?'" At right, the lovers are Doc (William Johnson) and Suzy (Judy Tyler). Fauna plans to bring them together, but it is Hazel (Mike Kellin, *far right*) who actually pulls it off. Explaining his unusual name, Hazel says, "My mother had eight children in seven years and she kinda got mixed up." Below right is the show's finale: it's Sweet Thursday on Cannery Row as the Palace Flophouse boys present Doc with the, uh, microscope he needs. "Biggest one in the whole damn catalogue," says Mack. (Mack, the fifth and last principal, was played by G. D. Wallace, *at center*, holding his hat.)

*But not necessarily of Steinbeck. In *East of Eden* he created one of the coldest, cruelest bordello managers in literature. Moviegoers will recall Jo Van Fleet's dire rendering, as her son James Dean weeps and wonders. An Oscar for Jo.

perfect type for Doc, but it turned out that all the coaching in the world couldn't pull a voice out of him. David Wayne was "mentioned," and Russell Nype was signed; there were press reports that he would let a shaggy Steinbeckian hairdo grow in over his trademark crewcut. But in the end Doc was William Johnson, a dependable Broadway baritone—Ethel Merman's love interest in *Something for the Boys* and the lead in *Annie Get Your Gun* and *Kiss Me, Kate* in London. R&H wanted Janet Leigh for Suzy, but a movie contract made her unavailable. The boys must have been thinking heavy Hollywood, for both Rhonda Fleming and Arlene Dahl were rumored to be under consideration (though Feuer and Martin had originally wanted their *Boy Friend* star, Julie Andrews). Finally R&H found their Suzy in Judy Tyler, hauntingly deep-voiced and surprisingly tough for an ingenue, especially one who had been discovered playing Princess Summerfallwinterspring on television's *Howdy Doody Show*. Mack was another baritone, G. D. (later George) Wallace, and Hazel was the lovable bumpkin Mike Kellin. All this is solid casting—not the real *Cannery Row*, maybe, but as close as a musical can get. (And Kellin, at least, was an authentic mug.)

What about Fauna? Well, in 1954 R&H and their production team were in Hollywood, planning the first movie to be made from an R&H show, *Oklahoma!* One day at MGM they heard a woman in the next room erupting in the grandest yet most convivial laughter ever heard. It sounded like a cross between Margaret Dumont and Mount Etna, and someone said, "That's Fauna!"

Fauna was Helen Traubel, the great Wagnerian soprano and St. Louis Woman, literally both at once: for when the Met's Brünnhilde took up nightclub singing in the early 1950s, the Met manager, Rudolf Bing, fired her, claiming that she was lowering the tone of the house. Traubel was trying other lines of work now, mystery writing, television, movies—she was at MGM to make the Sigmund Romberg bio, *Deep in My Heart*—and the soprano was delighted at the opportunity to crash Broadway.

R&H were delighted, too, for after the misfire of *Me and Juliet* they felt that they finally had the musical comedy they should have done in the first place, one with interesting and vital and funny people, with atmosphere, with powerful feelings. Steinbeck's worldview, at least in *Sweet Thursday*, coincided with Hammerstein's, in the two men's belief that humankind is ultimately a pretty likable form of life, and Rodgers responded to Hammerstein's inspired lyrics with one of his most melodic scores. One doesn't think of either R or H as a gung ho guy, but the two were unquestionably stimulated by *Pipe Dream* and very eager to reassert their powers. For one thing, there were none of the stunts and tricks, the almost cinematic motion, of *Me and Juliet.* Jo Mielziner was again the designer, but this time he employed a relatively simple system of house-frame outlines against village-sights backdrops which emphasized playwrighting over stagecraft, and the director was no wizard of pictures like Rouben Mamoulian but Harold Clurman, one of the founders of the Group Theatre and a distinguished director of drama. The story, the score, and the characters were going to be all that *Pipe Dream* would be about.

All looked well. The *Oklahoma!* film had so occupied R & H that they couldn't finish writing *Pipe Dream* in time to hold their house of choice, the Majestic, and they lost it to *Fanny*—the first time an R & H show would not open at either the Majestic or the St. James, directly across the street. With the loss of so many theatre buildings in the post–World War II years and the concomitant consolidation of the theatre district, the four houses on Forty-fourth Street between Seventh and Eighth avenues had become almost totemic in their power, not only to attract customers but to represent the muscle of the producers occupying those theatres, especially the three that almost invariably hosted musicals, the Majestic, the St. James, and the Shubert. A few other theatres were considered very desirable—the Imperial, the Forty-sixth Street, the Winter Garden. But it must have irked R & H to lose the Majestic, house of houses and home of *Carousel, Allegro,* and *South Pacific.* (This was the theatre that Andrew Lloyd Webber, with all of Broadway to pick from, chose for *The Phantom of the Opera.*) Still, it's a measure of how much was expected from R & H that they were able to nab the Shubert—and yet of how faithless their audience could be, for while *Pipe Dream* racked up the biggest advance in history ($1,040,000), once the deflating reviews came out few tickets were sold. Ironically, this was the first show that the author-producers allowed to be sold to theatre parties, those grudging agglomerations that had become too systemic in theatregoing to be ignored. It was ironic because the presold theatre parties were what kept *Pipe Dream* going for its 246 performances, for between the capacity houses were some very dead nights, something that had never happened to *Allegro* or *Me and Juliet.* The running costs on those shows were so high that they had to close when business faltered, but the smaller *Pipe Dream* could endure an empty Monday or Tuesday night, play to a party on Wednesday, scrape through a sparsely settled Thursday, enjoy a solid weekend, then do it again; and again. Thus *Pipe Dream* managed to see out its season, from November 30, 1955, to the end of June 1956. But there was no joy in Mudville, and no tour, not even a *Me and Juliet* jaunt to Chicago. Today *Pipe Dream* is forgotten. Most ironic of all is that R & H had a firm belief in never, but *never*, investing in their own shows.

They broke it for *Pipe Dream,* put up the entire cost themselves, and lost a fortune.

What went wrong? Steinbeck, who remained close to the authors throughout the process and after, thought their version of Cannery Row wasn't salty enough. There's a famous line here: "You've turned my prostitute into a visiting nurse!" That is, Suzy's activities in the Bear Flag are glossed over in favor of the Big Scene in which she cooks soup for Doc after Hazel has broken his arm. Still, the show is clear on what Suzy is:

> SUZY: (lashing out—against herself as much as at Fauna) Don't he know I come off the road that night? Don't he know where I been ever since? I been here—with you—in this house!

Steinbeck also felt that the show lost the tender tragedy of a truly noble guy who is also a loser and who is compromising some of his nobility—he fervently and quite hopelessly believes—by marrying a whore. This is not to mention an abused but spirited woman who reluctantly mates with a man who will always resent her past. But this, too, is in the show, particularly at the big blowout, when Suzy, dressed as a bride in virginal white, sings "Will You Marry Me?," and the embarrassed Doc laughs at her.

Maybe R & H failed to capture the aura of disorderly conduct along Cannery Row. "Someone seems to have forgotten," Walter Kerr thought, "to bring along that gallon of good, red wine." Oddly, the rehearsal script reveals a somewhat more hard-edged treatment. When tryout audiences reacted uneasily at having to go slumming at an R & H show, the tough talk was gentled down.

There is another problem. An R & H show is a logical piece of work, and Steinbeck's characters are irrational people. Hammerstein has them bustling around doing things, setting up a scheme and working something out, where Steinbeck has them blowing with the breeze. These are people who refuse to fit into anything as methodical as a musical comedy, and the show turns them into puppets dangling on R & H strings.

Then there was the Traubel problem. *Pipe Dream*'s failure is traditionally blamed on Traubel, but a look at *Deep in My Heart* reveals a very engaging performer. Traubel herself admitted growing very uncomfortable in her role somewhere between rehearsals and New York, and even uncomfortable with her songs—incredibly, the woman whose Isolde had filled the Met was now so weak that she had to be miked, the first such instance in an R & H show.

Why wasn't Traubel replaced? One reason is that Hammerstein was running the show single-handed. Rodgers had gone into emergency surgery for cancer of the jaw on the first day of *Pipe Dream*'s rehearsals, and was either away or under sedation for the entire out-of-town tour. No matter how unequal Traubel might have proved, Hammerstein surely knew her background, as a kid growing up with a dream of joining Caruso and Melba on Victor's Red Seal records, the top of their line. Sadly, by the time Traubel had made her mark Kirsten Flagstad was America's Wagnerian soprano, and while Victor did sign Traubel it had also signed Flagstad, and thus seldom let Traubel challenge their lucrative Flagstad discs in the repertory that Traubel excelled in, forcing her instead into *Lieder* and devotional song, stuff anyone could do. When Traubel finally got a shot at Heavy Wagner, singing Brünnhilde's Immolation Scene under Toscanini, the conductor refused to release the test pressings because his set ran two sides longer than the Flagstad set, and he was convinced that Victor was out to sabotage his sales appeal. Traubel was caught in the cross fire. Then came the Met firing—and surely Hammerstein just wasn't willing to chalk another distress upon this woman's slate, especially without Rodgers to stand with him. Hammerstein did what he could, smoothing over the gulf between Traubel and director Clurman and beefing up Traubel's big first-act solo, "Sweet Thursday," with two kids to dance a cakewalk with her— the first R&H cakewalk since *Oklahoma!*'s "When Ah Go Out Walkin' with Mah Baby."*

On the other hand, there are many who claim that Traubel is taking a bum rap. R&H themselves—or at least Rodgers speaking for them—did say that the show was not well produced, that something got lost between composition and performance. But, basically, the show failed not because of Traubel but because the critics gave it bad reviews, and I believe that, had anyone else written it, it might have gotten good ones. As with all the R&H musical comedies, it isn't as comic as it ought to be. But it is *molto* musical. "That's a funny guy," observes someone of Doc in Steinbeck's novel the moment after he and Suzy first meet. "It takes all kinds," Suzy replies, and of that came *Pipe Dream*'s opening number, "All Kinds of People," one of the most ebullient statements of Hammerstein's worldview:

> One guy will kill you for dough,
> And one guy will rob you of lunch.
> One guy will help you and he makes you fall
> In love with the whole darn bunch.

A less frequently encountered Hammerstein is also heard from, and in the very next song, "The Tide Pool," in which sea creatures, predator and prey, are seen microcosmically as representatives of the struggle of all life:

> DOC: Hungry flowers that live on fish,
>     Scooping in whatever comes,
>     Crabs that grab another crab and chew its legs.
> SUZY: The dirty bums!

---

*Has anyone noticed how many R&H works have kids in them? The answer is nine out of eleven: *State Fair, Carousel, Allegro* (actually dancers playing kids), *South Pacific, The King and I, Pipe Dream, Cinderella, Flower Drum Song, The Sound of Music*. I feel a monograph is needed: *The Semiotics of Youth in R&H*.

Rodgers set it to a pounding 6/8 in b minor, something like a wailing march:

over which, at the end, the woodwinds and trumpets slither out a line suggesting the lunging and thrashing of this cannibal kingdom:

Despite the apparently opposing viewpoints, both songs are faithful to Steinbeck, because his survey, for all its patience with human failings and love of life's many insane little kindnesses, is nevertheless very firm in admitting how destructive humankind can be. More typically R & H are the ballads: Suzy's establishing character song, "Everybody's Got a Home but Me," say, or her duet with Fauna, "Suzy Is a Good Thing" (though that title comes verbatim off the pages of *Sweet Thursday*). After the Rodgers and Hart–like Rodgers of *Me and Juliet,* the purely melodic "Everybody's Got a Home but Me" reminds us how smoothed out the Hammerstein Rodgers became, diatonic rather than chromatic in his melody and measured out rather than syncopated. Hymn tunes, very like. However, the Flophouse gang's "A Lopsided Bus" bears a screwy gaiety, and "The Man I Used to Be" has a nice swing, as Doc, looking back on the good old days of man's carefree youth, watches his younger self go through a nimble soft-shoe then tries it himself, awkwardly, impossibly. Like *South Pacific, Pipe Dream* offered mainly "informal" choreography (by Boris Runanin, a ballerino who had played the dream Curly on Broadway near the end of *Oklahoma!*'s original run), as in Traubel's kicky "Sweet Thursday" parade or in the "Lopsided Bus" dance, a mad scramble of good-natured clodhoppers.

RCA Victor fudged Helen Traubel and William Johnson's star billing on its first *Pipe Dream* record jacket, so the names were covered with a "special advance edition" sticker, and a second printing (*below*) reverted to the contractual billing and used the show's poster logo.

One odd fact is that the neglected R&H shows are the modern-dress, "plain"-colored ones—*Allegro, Me and Juliet, Pipe Dream.* The classics are all costume pieces, with cowboys and bustles, military uniform, Oriental dress, Chinatown America, nuns and Nazis. Of the three contemporary shows, two pose unusual production challenges, but *Pipe Dream* is easy to stage and extremely revivable—I see it with Tyne Daly, Davis Gaines, and Andrea McArdle, with John Candy as Hazel. Ted Chapin, chief of the R&H office, would like to cast it with Muppets. Doc and Suzy would be played by humans, but Miss Piggy would tackle Fauna, Kermit would be Mac, and surely Fozzie Bear was born to play Hazel. I think it's a natural. "A Lopsided Bus" is a perfect Muppet raveup:

> On a lopsided, ramshackle bus
> We ride from day to day.
> We wobble around on a rock-happy road
> And rattle along on our way...

Dick adores Mary at *Pipe Dream*'s New York premiere in the Shubert Theatre.

and "All Kinds of People" cries out for the gentle earnestness with which Jim Henson's creatures articulated big ideas. Certain elements of the show would have to be sweetened, of course. But then, with *Pipe Dream,* in any form, there remains the difficulty of the script's normalization of Steinbeck's aberrant characters. His Monterey has never adapted well. MGM's 1942 film of *Tortilla Flat* is phony even for its day, and the same studio's 1982 try at *Cannery Row* (using, like *Pipe Dream,* the *Sweet Thursday* plot line) failed even with the very appropriate Nick Nolte as Doc and Debra Winger as Suzy, not to mention the endorsement of the ultimate Steinbeckian maverick, John Huston, for voice-over narration.

At least *Pipe Dream* did not harm Steinbeck's friendship with R&H. The novelist kept a low profile on opening night, but the next evening he attended the show, and his wife, Elaine, a veteran R&H stage manager, dragged him backstage to meet the cast. He found them surprisingly high and happy for a company whose work had been kiboshed so thoroughly; they loved the show and they loved Steinbeck. Then he and Elaine went to Sardi's, where they were shown to the celebrity section, to the left as you enter. The management sent champagne to their table, and to Steinbeck it just didn't feel like being the father of a big Broadway bomb. It felt like being the father of a wonderful musical by Rodgers and Hammerstein.

So he turned to Elaine and said, "Isn't the theatre marvelous?"

# Cinderella

Old Broadway musicals were a staple of television in the 1950s, especially musicals from the 1940s. They were so common they were routine, though networks would lure the public by terming them "spectaculars": Ann Sothern in *Lady in the Dark;* Mary Martin

Below, the production team: back row, left to right—choreographer Jonathan Lucas, Dick, Oscar; middle row—producer Richard Lewine, designer Jean Eckart; foregound—assistant Joseph Papp, director Ralph Nelson. Opposite, the star awaits her call.

and John Raitt in *Annie Get Your Gun;* Alfred Drake and Patricia Morison (the original stage stars) in *Kiss Me, Kate;* Barbara Cook and Keith Andes in *Bloomer Girl;* Nanette Fabray and Hal March in *High Button Shoes.* Older shows were also heard from—Ethel Merman re-created her Reno Sweeney in *Anything Goes* with Frank Sinatra and Bert Lahr; Drake, Patrice Munsel, and John Conte led *Naughty Marietta;* and there was even some Gilbert and Sullivan in *The Yeomen of the Guard,* with Drake, Cook, Celeste Holm, and *Me and Juliet*'s Bill Hayes.

There were original musicals as well—*Little Women, The Gift of the Magi, Pinocchio* (with Mickey Rooney), *High Tor* (from Maxwell Anderson's bizarre play, with an Arthur Schwartz–Howard Dietz score), Van Johnson in *The Pied Piper of Hamelin* (with a score in the Wright-and-Forrest floperetta style, drawn from Edvard Grieg and duplicating some of *Song of Norway*), Alfred Drake and Doretta Morrow in *Marco Polo* (with another floperetta score, this one from Rimski-Korsakov, and, though it is not by Wright and Forrest—kidding aside—it really sings).

Of all the television musicals, the one with by far the greatest impact was Mary Martin's *Peter Pan,* adapted from her West Coast Broadway staging and first telecast live and in color on NBC on March 7, 1955, then remounted in early 1956. Now CBS saw the appeal of a similar for-the-entire-family musical spectacular. Stories differ on what exactly happened next, but at some point the network, R&H, Julie Andrews, and *Cinderella* got into a huddle. As we know, R&H did family shows; so did Julie Andrews. She had been in that Schwartz-and-Dietz *High Tor,* with Bing Crosby, but, as that had aired just a few days before the opening of *My Fair Lady* (1956), Andrews had not been highly touted in the PR. "And presenting Julie Andrews," one read, rather late in the billing, way below Crosby's costar, Everett Sloane. However, in the 1950s nothing built a career like having a hit on Broadway, and *My Fair Lady* made Andrews very hot, and Andrews as Cinderella was almost unbearably hot, and Andrews as Cinderella in the R&H version—their first creation for television, remember—was as hot as whiskers on kittens. According to CBS, 107 million people saw the show, seen from 8:00 to 9:30 P.M. on March 31, 1957 (the fourteenth anniversary of *Oklahoma!*'s New York opening). One hundred seven million people is approximately enough warm bodies to sell out the Majestic Theatre at eight performances a week for a run of 214 years.

Here was another R&H musical comedy, without question their sunniest piece, untroubled by *Me and Juliet*'s thug or *Pipe Dream*'s man-woman ambivalence tango. The R&H *Cinderella* is nicer even than the fairy tale: the King and Queen are lovable Darby and Joan oldsters, the Stepmother and -sisters are selfish rather than vicious, and the Godmother is totally in command. She's another of Hammerstein's "destiny" figures, changing people's lives.

Left, the Prince (Jon Cypher) meets Cinderella (Julie Andrews) at the ball. Next morning (*below*), the stepsisters (Alice Ghostley and Kaye Ballard) and the stepmother (Ilka Chase) are peeved, but Cinderella is rapturous—"A lovely night!"

Above and opposite are William and Jean Eckart's costume designs for Cinderella and the King.

Well, certainly; that's her job, you say—but, as Hammerstein didn't like fantasy, he made her less a fairy waving a wand than an interloper poking at people to get the romance working. "Impossible!" she declares, "for a plain yellow pumpkin to become a golden carriage." But she's watching Cinderella carefully, almost *casing* her, to see how deeply she believes. In Hammerstein, you don't just deserve happiness; you have to work for it.

The casting of the show was in some ways typical R&H and in other ways surprising—for instance, Rodgers wanted Vic Damone as the Prince. Egad! *Cinderella* ended up with someone as unknown in his role as Julie Andrews was starred in hers, Jon Cypher, much later to break through to fame as the elegantly sleazy Chief of Police Fletcher Daniels on *Hill Street Blues*. Prince Charming is a tough part to pull off, and Cypher gave it his best, but he marred the history—this was a live telecast—by tripping on a stairway during the ball scene and then jumping ahead of the orchestra *twice* during his reprise of "Do I Love You Because You're Beautiful?"

Howard Lindsay and Dorothy Stickney, the King and Queen, and Ilka Chase, the Stepmother, were out of the R&H line, very suitable but nonsingers who virtually talked their way through their song lines, whereas R&H if anything favored singers over actors. However, the very vocal—and very funny—Step-sisters, Alice Ghostley and Kaye Ballard, were a real treat; Ghostley (as Joy) the dowdy one and Ballard (as Portia) a merry idiot, quoting Shakespeare's Portia's "quality of mercy" speech to the Prince at the ball just as Cinderella enters, and reading the phrase "droppeth from heaven" just as his eyes take in this vision descending a staircase. Comics with real voices are a little rare in R&H—one thinks of the more typically split-the-difference singer-comics like Celeste Holm, Betty Garde, and Joan McCracken.

Most characteristic of R&H, yet most startling, was Edith Adams' God-mother, startling because she was young—at the time she was playing Daisy Mae in *Li'l Abner* at the St. James—but characteristic because she had won her break through the usual R&H Tuesday auditions. Adams had impressed everyone, but at the time there was nothing for her—nothing at R&H. A bit later, George Abbott asked if anyone knew of a girl to play Eileen in *Wonderful Town*...and R&H knew of Adams. *Wonderful Town* led to *Li'l Abner* and then to *Cinderella,* which was why R&H regarded the cumbersome Tuesday hearings as essential, part of their business but also part of the making of theatre by *anybody*.

The making of *Cinderella* involved a protracted rehearsal period, almost as much as that of a stage show, with two preliminary kinescoped* run-throughs

*That is, the show was played before working cameras twice before the actual telecast, to polish any awkward movements or camera work.

that Rodgers referred to as "the New Haven and Boston tryouts." Even more significant was the publicity campaign, possibly the heaviest and most carefully concerted in television history—interviews, photo calls, anecdotes, exclusives, lunches, personal telephone hype to print editors from cast members, costume sketches for fashion people, demo albums for radio disc jockeys, press receptions, promo kits, full-page advertisements in the key ratings cities, and, one week before the performance, the personal appearance of R & H themselves on *The Ed Sullivan Show*, Rodgers conducting and Hammerstein reciting "Do I Love You Because You're Beautiful?," and Sullivan reminding America that *Cinderella* would preempt his show the following Sunday night. Highly influential as well was Columbia's cast album, released a few days before the telecast and snapped up by so many consumers that it recalls Victor's Caruso and Melba 78s, bought by the early-twentieth-century bourgeoisie to define themselves as "cultured."

But then it was a wonderful album. This is perhaps R & H's most infectious score, from the spoof of an old-fashioned opening chorus in "The Prince Is Giving a Ball," as the Town Crier runs through the catalog of the royal names (the King's include Sidney; "Sidney?" ask the dubious townsfolk; *"Sidney!"* the Town Crier insists), to the jiving piano obbligato in the Stepsisters' chorus of "A Lovely Night," another touch of the Rodgers of Rodgers and Hart. Obviously, the ninety-minute running time yielded a short score, only ten numbers compared with the fifteen or so titles a full-length stage score would comprise. But it's vintage R & H: "In My Own Little Corner" their most wistful character song (more so even than *Pipe Dream*'s "Everybody's Got a Home but Me"), "Ten Minutes Ago" the most luminous of love songs, and "Waltz for a

This implausible design for a reissue of the first cast recording was printed but never used.

Ball" a Rodgers dance suite to rank with "The Carousel Waltz."

Best of all is the musical scene building up to "A Lovely Night," the orchestra simulating the clopping tread of coach horses and the melody gently leaning on anxiously dissonant notes as Cinderella "imagines" the trip to the palace. It's romantic, tense—yet Hammerstein doesn't forget he has two comediennes to bring in:

> JOY AND PORTIA: You can guess till you're blue in the face,
>     But you can't even picture such a man.
> JOY: He is more than a prince...
> PORTIA: He's an ace!

There was talk of a Broadway mounting for the next season, but there is always such talk; Irra Petina could slap some guy in a cab and there would be talk that Edwin Lester would be taking it to Broadway, with a Wright-and-Forrest score drawn from the melodies of Henri Sauguet. However, *Cinderella* did reach London's West End, for the 1958 Christmas season, refashioned for the Palladium as a traditional English pantomime, with the Stepsisters in drag, the King built up as a comedy part, a cuddly bear character, and Tommy Steele starring as Buttons, the neglected but dauntless servant and Cinderella's confidant. The book was of course riddled with the shenanigans beloved of panto—bawdy humor, actors breaking out of character to game with the audience, and so on, all of this very out of style for an R&H show. (Apparently, R&H sold the show outright to producer Harold Fielding with no intention of collaborating on the production, the sole time they let London try its own version of R&H, rather than mount an authentic staging.)

The score was fiddled with, too, wholly reorchestrated and beefed up with three numbers from *Me and Juliet* that destroyed the neither-here-nor-there storybook aura that the original had rejoiced in. There was even an interpolation written by Steele, "You and I," an eleven o'clock silliness for him and the King. By R&H standards, this *Cinderella* was crass; but as a pantomime it was classy, cast with experts and introducing the young and enticingly mononymous Yana as the heroine in what was to prove her greatest (indeed, apparently her only) role. This panto *Cinderella* was a success and was revived two years later at the Adelphi Theatre, with Joan Heal replacing the elusive, mysterious Yana.

Because *Cinderella* had been televised before the days of tape and thus could only be screened in kinescope, CBS decided to restage it in 1965, this time to preserve the show in color for annual replays. Hammerstein had died by then, and trouble began when Rodgers commissioned an entirely new script (by Joseph Schrank) that lost Hammerstein's delicate blend of romance and jest, not to mention his amusingly timeless neverland. William and Jean Eckart had designed the original *Cinderella* in a kind of non-aligned bon ton, to suggest an unplaceable fantasy; the 1965 version looked implacably medieval, to match Schrank's "yon wench," and "slew a few dragons," and "rub some unicorn oil on it." Gone were Hammerstein's subtle variations, the rather touching relationship between the Prince and his parents, the sardonic young Godmother. Gone as well was the simple charm of the original cast. Taking top billing, for some vastly unknown reason, were Ginger Rogers and Walter Pidgeon as lifeless monarchs—Pidgeon seems so dense he might be on something—and Celeste Holm makes a cutesy-poo Godmother. Jo Van Fleet humiliates a fine reputation on both stage and screen with a Stepmother who manages to be drab and exaggerated at once, and as her daughters, Pat Carroll and Barbara Ruick haven't a single good line between them.

Why the new script? What was wrong with the old one? The dropping of the Royal Dressing Room Number is perhaps forgivable, as Schrank wrote in an early Meeting Scene for Cinderella and the Prince, allowing Rodgers to reclaim "Loneliness of Evening," deleted from *South Pacific*. On the other hand, that does give us rather a lot of Stuart Damon and Lesley Ann Warren (who in due course developed into a sharp song-and-dance comedienne; here she is raw and wrong). Why, with much larger playing areas than the cramped unit set of 1957, is the dancing so stupid? "The Prince Is Giving a Ball" looks like the Turkey Number in your second-grade Thanksgiving Pageant, and almost all of the "Waltz for a Ball" offers no more than Damon and Warren circling around while everyone else just stands there. (There is one choice moment, when Damon almost runs over Pat Carroll.)

Sad to say, it is this puerile and cliché-bound *Cinderella* that survived, first in many CBS airings and lately as a commercial videotape, as kinescoped copies of the original reside only in private collections. One wonders if we are ever to see the piece on stage. The English panto adaptation was perhaps too elaborate to become a fixture over there, and sporadic stagings of an expanded version of the American original (with "Boys and Girls Like You and Me" added for the King and Queen, a wonderful touch) at summer festivals did not outlast the 1960s. Still, a tale this audience-friendly and a score this brilliant need a truer setting than that plate of hash that Rodgers served up in 1965. Or—who knows?—CBS might give it a third try, with Julie Andrews as the Godmother this time. Impossible things, one hears, are happening every day—as are, to cue in the next chapter, a hundred million miracles.

# Flower Drum Song

R&H shows, especially their musical plays, tend to define a stable or coalescing community, then threaten it, then defeat the threat. In *Oklahoma!* the community is made of the somewhat uneasy truce of farmers and cowmen readying themselves for

Pat Suzuki, director Gene Kelly, and Miyoshi Umeki fake a dance step (nothing like this was in the show) for a publicity shot.

national citizenship; the threat is lawlessness and solipsism, represented by Jud Fry. *Allegro*'s community is not small-town life (as Hammerstein's script accidentally makes it appear), but the utopia of responsible men and women achieving personal fulfillment in work and love; the threat is, partly, the selfish wife, Jennie Brinker Taylor, and, more broadly, the demands of celebrity and the public life that sap a man's personal and professional energies. Even *Me and Juliet* offers a look at a community—that of the thespian, whose very stage is disrupted by another selfish thug.

*Carousel* and *South Pacific* are more complex. One might argue that they each oppose two different communities—*Carousel* in what eventually becomes a face-off between the good-natured society of fisherfolk and the pretentiousness of the rising burgher (Mister Snow) and his brood. The antisocial Billy is a threat to both, a bad husband and a parasite. *South Pacific*'s two communities are, one, that of the local Polynesians and French planters, and, two, that of the American armed forces. And the threat is as much racism as it is the Japanese enemy.

One reason why *The King and I* especially retains its interest in revival is that Hammerstein gives us not two communities but two opposing political viewpoints. The Siamese are not viewed as a community but as a court: wives, concubines, slaves, guards, priests. Background matter, really. And the British are scarcely there at all—a ship captain, a few envoys. The other R & H shows have many principals, more or less of equal weight, but *The King and I* is virtually a two-character plot, and there is no *outside* threat—each threatens the other.

In 1958, after the merry irrelevance of *Me and Juliet* and the resounding failure of *Pipe Dream*, some felt that *Flower Drum Song* presented R & H with a curiously ordinary subject. It looked like another musical comedy— a good one, certainly, and a hit. But where was the drive of *Oklahoma!*, the tortured elegy of *Carousel*, the thematic grandeur of *The King and I?* Actually, *Flower Drum Song* offered yet another cross section of a community, one split in two by separatist and cosmopolitan factions—the Chinese-American society of San Francisco.

The show's source, C. Y. Lee's novel of nearly the same title (R & H dropped Lee's definite article), is wholly unlike the other two novels that R & H drew upon. James Michener's novel is really a cycle of stories, Steinbeck's an extravagantly narrated comedy; and both feature a wide assortment of characters. *The Flower Drum Song* is simple and tight, the world as seen by a reactionary Chinese patriarch, so shaped by the "old ways" that though he lives in the United States he calls Americans "foreigners" and prides himself on knowing nothing of their way of life, not only of nightclubs but banks and hospitals.

Wang Chi-yang views himself as the center of the world, his ills as global in significance:

> After [his wife] had died, everything seemed to go wrong. The sons became wild and disobedient, the servants became lazy and untrustworthy, even the whole Chinese nation went to Communism.

Lee's narrative is studded with fascinating details of Chinese culture, but his main work lies in confronting the old man with irritating intrusions of the American world, in his busybody sister-in-law, Madam Tang, a Chinese who accommodates some of the foreigners' ways, and especially in his older son, Wang Ta, a docile young man slowly edging out of his father's grip.

That, really, is the book in toto, with the important addition of the three women who influence Wang Ta's maturity—the wholly Americanized playgirl, Linda Tung, the tragically lonely Helen Chao (who kills herself when Wang Ta jilts her), and the dutifully old-fashioned May Li. Ta finally squares off with his father when a jealous housemaid frames May Li in the theft of a golden clock that had belonged to Wang Chi-yang's late wife. Ta defends May Li and leaves his father's house with her; and, as the novel ends, the regretful old man makes a symbolically conciliatory gesture toward his son's adopted culture.

The novel has charm and point, and it's easy to see why it appealed to R&H. For one thing, nobody else would have done it. For another, the Oriental cast and Chinatown setting would be 1958's equivalent of *Oklahoma!*'s "no gags, no gals, no chance," another opportunity for our boys to rewrite the musical-comedy handbook. By chance, *Flower Drum Song* came about rather as *South Pacific* had done; here, instead of Joshua Logan's initiating the project and collaborating and coproducing with R&H, the third party was Joseph Fields, son of Lew (of Weber and) Fields and brother of Herbert and Dorothy, and a veteran author of comedies and musical-comedy books. Like Logan, Joseph Fields always wrote with a partner, and now Hammerstein was quite willing to share his byline, for he was sixty-three years old and not in robust health.

This time the work of adaptation would exact far more in invention and development than Michener or Steinbeck (or Riggs, Molnár, and Benson and Jennings) had demanded. Most of the events in Lee's book were deleted—Helen Chao's suicide, the clock episode, Wang Chi-yang's many little adventures in Chinatown, the infighting among his household servants. Old Man Wang himself was demoted from the dominant to an assistant figure, little more than a foil for his sister-in-law (now Madam Liang). The characters of Linda Tung (resurnamed Low) and a respelled Mei Li were enlarged to

### Characters and Themes

Above, Keye Luke (*right*) and his sister-in-law Juanita Hall (*left*) welcome Miyoshi Umeki (*center*, holding the flower drum) as the intended bride of Luke's older son. The son, however, played by Ed Kenney, is going Western. Below, he is seen The Morning After, having spent the night with Arabella Hong.

## Characters and Themes, Continued

The war of West versus East—central to *Flower Drum Song*—is echoed in the half-assimilated chorus people at top right and center. But R & H also dealt with the war of Youth versus Age, exemplified below, right in "The Other Generation," led by Patrick Adiarte (*center*), Keye Luke's other son.

Opposite, left, is a rehearsal shot of nightclub singer Pat Suzuki, representing ultra-Westernization, with the nightclub owner, here played by Larry Storch, who was replaced in Boston by Larry Blyden—both white men intended to play an Asian. Suzuki and Blyden (*far right*) are former lovers whose romance is on the skids until midway in Act Two, when they sing the idyllic "Sunday."

function as the two contrasting ideals in Ta's romantic life, the bold, free American woman and the tender Chinese woman, sex versus poetry. A new character, the brash nightclub owner, Sammy Fong, was devised to complete the duel of cultures, and to complicate the love plot as Linda's longtime boyfriend. Like Ta, Sammy is caught between the vivacious Linda and the sweet Mei Li, for while he and Linda are a perfect match as totally assimilated Chinese-Americans, Mei Li is officially Sammy's fiancée, as a picture bride contracted for by his parents years before.

All this meant that something of C. Y. Lee's power and point would be lost, first of all the formidable weight of his protagonist, Wang Chi-yang, decreeing and punishing, relishing his horror of the foreigners' ways and cultivating a cough as an emblem of authority. But his son Ta also lost some personality between novel and libretto, especially because of the high profile of the brassy Linda, the adorable Mei Li, and the pushy Sammy, who talks in nonstop slang. The novel is about a father; the musical is about two couples. Still, Hammerstein and Fields were careful to centralize Lee's battle of cultures and generations—and of course music and dance would be able to color this in as no novel could.

At right is a key scene in the show, for it is while watching American television that Umeki hits upon the solution to the show's romantic crisis: Blyden and Suzuki love each other and Kenney and Umeki love each other, but, according to the Chinese elders, Blyden must marry Umeki because they were pledged to one another as children, in the old-fashioned way. What Umeki is watching is a B-movie Western, at whose climax the heroine confesses to the Sheriff that she is a "wetback," unworthy of her fiancée. Below is Umeki's wedding day, when she suddenly tears off her veil and cries, "My back is wet!," and "I must give myself up! I will tell the Sheriff!"

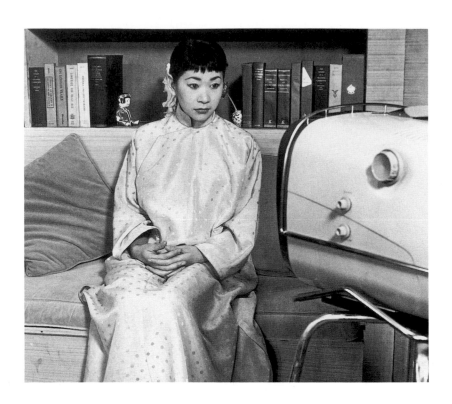

*Flower Drum Song*'s production staff marked a slight breakthrough for R & H, perhaps reflecting a decision to produce, above all, a *contemporary* show, state-of-the-art in look and sound. For one thing, the sets were designed not by the trusty Jo Mielziner but by Oliver Smith, known for his work in ballet and also for the pastel fantasy New York that he created for *On the Town* and the gloomily romantic, realistic New York that he built for *West Side Story*. Note that both these shows were dance musicals. Smith gave them a lot of air and space—and *Flower Drum Song*, too, would be a very fully danced event. This brings in another name new to the firm, Carol Haney, the charmingly bizarre Gladys in *The Pajama Game* on stage and on film, making her debut as a Broadway choreographer. The dance arranger, Luther Henderson, Jr., was similarly a newcomer, young and game; perhaps R & H felt that a mixture of veterans and debutants suited a show treating the war between the generations.

A rare moment that happened to be photographed: director Gene Kelly (*right*) in Boston, apparently saying to C. Y. Lee, Joseph Fields, and Richard Rodgers something like, "Kids, we're in trouble."

### The Dream Ballet

At right, below, Yuriko (dancing the role of Mei Li) arrives with her suite. Below, Ed Kenney (as Wang Ta) dallies with her and then (*right*), with Jo Anne Miya (dancing the part of Linda Low) — the two women representing the conflicting ideals of tenderness and sensuality.

Logically, then, the director might have been one of the younger choreographers, such as Bob Fosse or Gower Champion. The directing choreographer was becoming the norm; state-of-the-art meant letting a Michael Kidd direct and choreograph a *Li'l Abner* (1956), say—and had not R & H originated the approach when de Mille staged *Allegro*? In the event, R & H chose an older choreographer to direct *Flower Drum Song,* a man who was by now a stranger to Broadway: Gene Kelly. Perhaps his movie work would feed some new information into the tempo of the musical. Or he'd give it a new look. A motion. A savvy. Something.

Casting was hell, for there had been so little opportunity for Oriental actors in the theatre that there virtually were no Oriental actors. Most of the talent was picked up on the West Coast, and, by the time all the contracts were signed, this all-Chinese play counted a Hawaiian, a black, two Japanese, and a white among its principals alone. However, the rehearsal period revealed some striking casting strengths. Lines that read only well on the page were, viva voce, fairly dancing for joy. The senior roles were well filled by Keye Luke (the former "Number One Son" to Warner Oland in Hollywood's *Charlie Chan* series) and Juanita Hall (the original Bloody Mary), he almost too likable in his rages and she vocally worn but, as ever, fine company.

As the junior Wangs, the older Ed Kenney was on the dull side though (again and again, the standard R & H credential) a fine vocalist, and, as the younger Wang San, Pat Adiarte was one of the rare singing and dancing adolescents whom you wouldn't hope to see maimed in a trolley-car accident. The four made an engaging family:

WANG: Why are you not in school?
SAN: It is Saturday.
WANG: Always some excuse!

Or, when Wang Ta spends the night with Helen Chao:

WANG: (To Madam Liang) Another citizen for your Western world!
    This is the first time Ta has ever stayed away all night. What
    could he be doing?
MADAM LIANG: If this was a quiz program I could win
    a trip to Europe.

Most emergent among the cast were Pat Suzuki and Miyoshi Umeki as Ta's two loves, Suzuki for her lusty swagger and solid belt voice and Umeki for the fetching intimacy of her comedy and the dignity with which she brought off her dramatic scenes. The authors built this up during rehearsals, giving Umeki touching and humorous pantomimes, and writing in an amusing scene in which she naively takes television programming, from commercials to old films, as representative of American life. She fills a pause in conversation by singing, "Filter, flavor, flip-top box," and, in her gentle way, raves about the society she sees portrayed on *The Late Show*:

> MEI LI: In the movies every American has a beautiful automobile,
>     and a beautiful golden girl in a car, who wears wonderful clothes.
>     They all seem so happy, but I don't understand why they all go
>     around killing each other.

In a way, Umeki and Suzuki together demonstrate the opposing forces inherent in R&H, the musical play versus musical comedy: *Carousel* versus *Me and Juliet*, Ezio Pinza versus Mary Martin, "If I Loved You" versus "I Cain't Say No," Agnes de Mille versus "Honey Bun"...poetry versus sex. That competition *is* the American musical, and that is, especially, this particular musical — something of a musical comedy with musical-play elements.

The Boston tryout revealed a somewhat disconcerted work, slow to start and vexed by rough scenes and faulty projection of character. Gene Kelly had proved utterly out of his form as a director of a stage show, lacking the technical vocabulary for theatre production and unable to address the actors on that essential R&H element, relationships. Larry Storch was so at sea as Suzuki's vis-à-vis — too harsh, apparently — that he was fired, replaced by Larry Blyden (another white man as a Chinese and, by hap, Carol Haney's husband). Blyden agreed to take the part only if R&H gave him a big number, and they apparently cooked up "Don't Marry Me" inside of two hours, lyrics and all. It's a comic song, as Sammy Fong tries to edge out of his marriage contract and Mei Li plays it deadpan, and it may not sound like much as a composition, but onstage it played like dynamite, Blyden's wise guy balancing Umeki's porcelain doll. *Flower Drum Song* was what Hammerstein termed a "lucky" show:

Oliver Smith's sets demonstrate the hip, state-of-the-art feel of the original production. Opposite is The Three Family Association's headquarters, where disputes are settled according to Chinese law. At left is the garden of Old Man Wang's house.

the company turned out to have a lot of personality, and that seems to have taken care of any weaknesses the piece may have had as a composition. (Hammerstein himself thought the first quarter of Act One turgid yet strangely uncuttable.) And the play did in the end come off as contemporary, even youthful, as if R & H had observed another generational war occurring on their own Broadway, one that was making them look Old Guard rather than avant-garde. After all, even at their boldest and freshest, R & H represented a tradition that reached back to Victor Herbert and the "Princess" shows, when Broadway writers made their definitive break with masscult pop and forged an elite audience to support elite art.

The one element in *Flower Drum Song* that seemed somewhat old-fashioned was its dancing, because this was the one element that had most changed in the decade and a half since *Oklahoma!*. That first R & H work made a revolution in how the musical used choreography, changing it from decoration to character and mood and narrative. But eighteen months after *Oklahoma!* Jerome Robbins took the revolution a step further in *On the Town*, and, looking at the major dance shows of the years after *Flower Drum Song*, we see a breakaway from the stylized and the thematic into the natural: from dream ballets into "Hello, Dolly!" and "Who's That Woman?," the old vaudeville hoofing drawn back into the narrative. The fantasy, the Big Ballet that stood outside the story, is gone. Now the entertainment is direct, effortlessly integrated. This leads to *A Chorus Line,* a show that appears to be about dancing but is actually about growing up in America, and in which people dance only to audition or to pull off a curtain call.

*Flower Drum Song* was one of the last shows to feature the kind of choreographic structure that R & H had introduced in *Oklahoma!,* with plenty of incidental capers here and there but mainly one major set piece after a song in Act One and one major set piece after a song in Act Two, plus the Big Ballet.

Pat Suzuki pays back treacherous boyfriend Larry Blyden.

One year earlier, in *West Side Story,* Jerome Robbins cast, with a few exceptions, one ensemble for singing *and* dancing. *Flower Drum Song* observed the traditional separation of talents. So, after delivering "I Enjoy Being a Girl," Pat Suzuki made herself scarce and the dancers took over, simulating the eternal hunt of boy for girl, along with a touch of Chinese-American assimilation in a young Chinese girl working a Hula Hoop. Similarly, after singing "Sunday," Suzuki and Larry Blyden exited as blithely as possible as Haney brought on her troupe for more of the East-West thing in dancers bunched as three mandarins, five very Americanized Chinese women pursued by Americanized suitors, and three children in scout uniforms, everybody grouping and regrouping till the Hula Hoop kid reappears—this time with *two* hoops.

*Flower Drum Song*'s Big Ballet was not the last of its kind—the flawed but fascinating out-of-town casualty *Mata Hari* (1967) included a psychological dream (choreographed by Jack Cole) just like those in *Oklahoma!* and *Flower Drum Song*. In fact, *Flower Drum Song*'s ballet, just after the start of Act Two, is a kind of "Wang Ta Makes Up His Mind": between Mei Li of the poetry and Linda Low of the sex. Luther Henderson's use of Rodgers' tunes was free, with plenty of original themes and ingenious deviations. But then R & H wanted a new sound in this show; free and ingenious was the idea.

The score itself is nothing but songs—no musical scene, no waltz suite, no great surprise. Yet it is superb R & H, very melodic and poetic and organized so that "Chinese" numbers challenge "Americanized" numbers. Rodgers actually indulges in some Oriental pastiche here, as in the "title" song, as it were, "A Hundred Million Miracles," which, like "Bali Ha'i," lends its unique signature, the beating of a drum, to the opening and closing of the Overture. The tune isn't really Chinese; it simply makes a suggestively ethnic effect (and it certainly doesn't sound like anything else Rodgers wrote). "You Are Beautiful," the show's main love ballad, avoids pastiche but casts a kind of "faraway" spell during the underscored dialogue between verses, when the music is played on the mandolin. The most obtrusive touch of musical impressionism lies in the sharpened second (at the arrows) of "I Am Going to Like It Here":

Dick, Oscar, and coauthor/coproducer Joseph Fields stand by as Pat Suzuki cuts into the first-anniversary cake.

which transforms an extremely basic Western tune into a kind of Shanghai kiss. This is Mei Li's most establishing character song, and to define her sweetly insistent nature Hammerstein created an odd sonnet form with sparing use of rhyme but in which the second and fourth lines of each strophe become the first and third lines of the next strophe, a subtle and telling effect.

R & H extended themselves in the contrasting American numbers, though Robert Russell Bennett's orchestration makes "Grant Avenue" *lugubriously* jazzy, not as up-to-date as it thinks it is; and Hammerstein's lyric for "Chop Suey," on the diversity of American life, is so vague it feels pointless. Amusingly, R & H emphasized the denatured feel of the wholly Americanized Chinese-American in "Fan Tan Fannie," a throwaway nightclub number whose lines make a few Chinese references but whose music is a deliberately hollow echo of what we might call "Hong Kong soundtrack noises."

The score's best number is a ballad for Helen Chao that somehow fell by the wayside, though aficionados invariably mention it, "Love, Look Away." Rodgers gave it distinction by launching the melody on the seventh tone of the scale in the tonic chord, which comes across as a cry of despair; and Arabella Hong, another of those R & H opera singers, delivered it with great beauty.

*Flower Drum Song* brought R & H back to the St. James Theatre (home of *Oklahoma!* and *The King and I*), on December 1, 1958. It was well received, ran 600 performances, enjoyed an unusually successful tour lasting a year and a half (and taking in twenty-one weeks in Chicago and nine weeks in Philadelphia, sizable visits for the day), made another hit in London, and was faithfully turned into a movie.

Then it disappeared forever.

Apparently *Flower Drum Song* is half classic and half statistic, a much-loved show that most people don't ken. Obviously, casting a revival would be even harder than casting the original was, what with Actors' Equity and B. D. Wong examining birth certificates to ensure Ethnic Correctness, as in the case of *Miss Saigon*. But, more than that, the piece doesn't compel attention the way the R & H classics do. *Flower Drum Song* is a charm show, a kind of entertainment that we really don't have anymore—not a strange story, not an ingenious production, not an operatic score, but a pleasing and touching and delightful item with a lot of character. It's notable that R & H classics are generally musical plays; it's their musical comedies that haven't lasted. No doubt this is because musical comedies usually have less intense relationships than musical plays (or operettas), because the music doesn't have to work as hard, and once R & H began to drift into musical comedy they didn't have to work as hard, either. The amount of thought and labor they put into their art had not diminished. Hammerstein remained the tireless note taker, Rodgers the careful overseer of his music as it was delivered from lead sheet through his own arrangements on through the orchestra's parts. But the revolution was over: R & H had won. Ironically, their last work—another musical comedy, although a serious one—turned out to be their most successful work, or, at least, their most profitable. Some refer to it as the one with the nuns and the Nazis.

# The Sound of Music

Listen to the bizarre cast that the U.S. State Department pulled together for the production of Thornton Wilder's *The Skin of Our Teeth* that it sent to Paris as part of the "Salute to France" festival in 1955: George Abbott as Mr. Antrobus, Helen Hayes as

Left is the original poster, quickly dropped in favor of a photo of Mary and the kids.
Just as well: what do a drum, a tuba, a harp, and cymbals have to do with the Trapp family? What is this, *The Music Man?*

his wife, Don Murray as their son, Heller Halliday as their daughter, Florence Reed (in her original role) as the Fortune Teller, and Mary Martin as the campy yet Pirandellian temptress Sabina, the part created by Tallulah Bankhead. *What?* Martin the innocent, the Peter Pan? She was no temptress. Why, she had a daughter in the cast—Heller, Martin's child by her producer husband, Richard Halliday.

It was a disaster, and Martin knew it. So did the director who was to oversee the American televising of the production, Vincent J. Donehue. He re-coached Martin, Martin acquitted herself more or less with honor, and the two made a vow to work again together. It was Donehue who found the project, after screening a German movie about the life of Maria von Trapp, the Austrian woman who left a convent to (is there anyone in the Western world who doesn't already know this tale?) marry a widower baron, mother his brood, and escape with them when the Nazis annexed their country, and who ended up running a ski resort in Vermont.* Donehue saw Martin in the part, Martin saw it as a play directed by Donehue, and Howard Lindsay and Russel Crouse—who were going to write it—saw it with songs. Trapp Family songs, of course: folk tunes, hymns, and such, plus, as a treat, perhaps one or two numbers run up special for us by…well, how about Rodgers and Hammerstein? Our boys rightly pointed out that half-and-half scores never work. It should be all von Trapp numbers or all R & H; and they'd be happy to oblige as soon as they'd gotten *Flower Drum Song* out of the way.

Consider: Leland Hayward (of *South Pacific*) and Halliday coproducing (with R & H) a show with an R & H score starring Mary Martin, not to mention a book by Lindsay and Crouse (undistinguished talents but distinguished Broadway survivors, from *Anything Goes* and *Life with Father* in the 1930s to two Ethel Merman vehicles, *Call Me Madam* and *Happy Hunting*, in the 1950s). We are talking not about something that will necessarily make history in the aesthetics of the musical, but about something that makes an awfully imposing advance advertisement in *The New York Times*. A *popular* show, this—and, as we shall see, a fundamentally Hammersteinian piece. By chance, it was the sole R & H show for which he did not work on the book. Because Lindsay and Crouse had been brought in earlier and because Hammerstein would remain occupied with *Flower Drum Song* for the better part of a year, he and Rodgers agreed to write the score to fit into what by then would be a finished Lindsay and Crouse book.

---

*I know that I sometimes place a jest or two, but the Vermont part is as true as the rest. What isn't true is the "climb ev'ry mountain" ending of the movie, retained in the R & H show and *its* movie version, in which the von Trapps simply walk from Salzburg into Switzerland, about one hundred miles west-southwest. Italy is closer; the Venetian Alps border Austria about thirty miles due south of Salzburg; and Italy is where the von Trapps actually landed. Says Maria von Trapp herself, "Didn't anyone bother to look at a map?"

That's funny: because *The Sound of Music* reads very strongly as an R & H show, not at all like the work of the men who contrived the text for the facetious *Call Me Madam* or the chaotic—in fact, the utterly meretricious—*Happy Hunting.* No, Hammerstein didn't rewrite L & C: he accepted their book as it was. Still, in every major respect *The Sound of Music* presents Hammerstein's view of human relations as a series of influential actions—sometimes calculated and sometimes unwitting—that change the course of people's lives. We have seen instances of this particularly in Hammerstein's shows with Rodgers; but *The Sound of Music* is crammed with it. Maria, of course, is the most influential of the characters: she brings a moribund widower out of his grief and thus "revives" his family. The von Trapps themselves similarly reclaim Maria, the introverted girl afraid of life who becomes an enthusiastic wife and mother. Even Max, the sybarite who would rather accommodate the Nazis than defy them, plays his part in the pageant of interlocked destinies by delaying the announcement of the winners of a song contest in order to enable the von Trapps to flee to Maria's former abbey. And Liesl, the oldest von Trapp daughter, has her "work" to do, in softening her Hitler Youth of a boyfriend, Rolf, so that, at the climactic moment, while the German soldiers search the abbey for the von Trapps, Rolf can, in one terrifying moment, abjure the monster he has been turned into and protect the von Trapps, allowing them to escape into Switzerland.

Another typical Hammersteinian "destiny maker" is the old sage character who explains the world to unknowing youth—Dr. Seldon in *Carousel,* the

A thorough artiste, Mary prepared for her role by visiting the real Maria von Trapp in Vermont (*below*), accompanied by director Vincent J. Donehue and, for some reason, Florence Henderson, who would later play the national tour. Note that everyone but Donehue is in official Trapp family garb. At left Mary romps on a Vermont hilltop with various von Trapp kids. In Tony Frissell's photograph they look like a tryout for the movie.

Above, the worldly element in the show is represented by Captain von Trapp (Theodore Bikel), his fiancée, the Baroness (Marion Marlowe), and his friend, the finagler (Kurt Kasznar). Below is the churchly side: the Mother Abbess (Patricia Neway) preaches "Climb Ev'ry Mountain." R & H shows have a highly developed sense of *community*.

mother and grandmother in *Allegro,* Fauna in *Pipe Dream,* and even Aunt Eller, in her crabby, makeshift way. In *The Sound of Music* this figure finds apotheosis in the Mother Abbess, operatic in sound (for enhanced authority), and first forcing Maria to confront her fears and later pointing the way out of Nazi Austria over the mountains: gradually instructing Maria in the uses of liberty.

The script doesn't secure all this quite as smoothly as Hammerstein would have done had he been able to write or at least collaborate on the book. A show with a Hammerstein text comprises a grid of action and feeling stated in the lines and developed, climaxed, by the songs. *The Sound of Music*'s lines are on the weak side, more a series of entrances and exits than an arch of scenes building upon each other. So the action and feeling must be stated almost entirely in the songs. This is why this show's score is exceptionally strong, and why the original idea—a Lindsay-and-Crouse play starring Mary Martin with von Trapp songs—would have been as forgotten today as the straight plays that Martin did.

In fact, *The Sound of Music* was the first R & H score since *The King and I* to become familiar not for a few numbers but as a whole. It is not an adventurous score. There are no musical scenes, no shocking outbursts along the lines of *Carousel*'s "The Highest Judge of All" or *Pipe Dream*'s "The Tide Pool," no character-opening soliloquies; and Rodgers' harmony is extremely basic, perhaps to taste of the folkish flavor of the songs that Maria would have known. But it is a highly melodious and heartfelt score, all the show's personality lodged, for once in R & H, not in the integration of text, songs, choreography, and design, but exclusively in…well, the sound of their music.

Therein lies a problem. For if *The Sound of Music* is for some an uncomfortably sweet show, it is most so in those songs—"Do-Re-Mi," the vapid catalogue of "My Favorite Things" ("bright copper kettles"?—Why would anyone even notice, much less relish, a kettle?), the children's a cappella reprise of "The Sound of Music," not to mention the "lark who is learning to pray," a truly terrifying concept. R & H do family shows, but they also killed off *Carousel*'s hero at a time when widowhood was a highly sensitive state and hammered at racism in *South Pacific.* "Raindrops on roses"? this is the team that wrote of hating "all the people your relatives hate"? The sheer wholesomeness of the piece seemed irrelevant in an era that witnessed the marvelously zany flippancy of *Once Upon a Mattress* (1959), or the savagely honest portrait of a devouring mother in *Gypsy* (1959), or the forthright sociopolitical scan of *Fiorello!* (1959), or the more contemporary sense of youth in *Bye Bye Birdie* (1960), or the bizarre primitivism of *Greenwillow* (1960), or the sexy vitality of *Tenderloin* (1960).

However, *The Sound of Music* is a somewhat autumnal show, withdrawn from the uproar of youth. Its principals share an unusually wide age span, from the adolescents through Rolf and Liesl on past the Captain and his friends to the nuns, of various years but in toto representing a venerable way of life. Of course, *Flower Drum Song* was also a show whose worldview is that of ancient sages, looking back, forgiving and omniscient. Consider what was to have been its key number, old Wang Chi-yang's "My Best Love (comes last)," dropped because Keye Luke's voice wasn't quite up to a long-lined ballad:

> How can a young man know where his heart will go?
> Only an old man knows what a man should know.
> All that was true for me shall be true for you.
> You are romantic—
> I was romantic, too.

But then *Flower Drum Song* was very clearly concerned with age and the war of "The Other Generation" (a song title, in fact) against the System. *The Sound of Music*'s kids aren't opposed to the System: their *father* is, at least when Nazis are running it. So *The Sound of Music* isn't about age, but it is nevertheless the product of age, the work of a man who is dying and a man who isn't certain what possibilities will be left him after his partner's death. I would call it a very youthful piece written by the elderly, because it is entirely about freedom, which youth always seeks and the aged feel the loss of. Maria fears freedom and hides in a convent, so the Mother Abbess forces her out not only to discover freedom but to redeem others' lives by that discovery. What else could a show that ends with a family fleeing the Nazis be about *but* freedom?

It is a wry show, too, R & H chuckling over a seventeen-year-old boy's advising a sixteen-year-old girl on the ways of the world, casting an ironic eye on the "every man for himself" school of ethics in "No Way to Stop It":

> So every star and every whirling planet,
> And every constellation in the sky
> Revolve around the center of the universe,
> A lovely thing called I!

and charting the relationship between passion and penury in "How Can Love Survive?," Max and the Baroness Elsa's duet on the lack of romance in a millionaire's way of life, Rodgers setting Hammerstein's nagging lyrics to a driving, anxious beat:

> How can I show what I feel for you?
> I cannot go out and steal for you,
> I cannot die like Camille for you—
> How can love survive?

### The Whole Show in Three Pictures

Maria enchants the kids (*right*) and revitalizes the moribund Captain, who gains not just a wife but a singing group (*below*), whereupon all flee to Switzerland (*bottom*).

Hammerstein isn't really talking money here: he's talking age. Von Trapp and the Baroness are too mature to get keen, too self-assured to *need*. Besides, the song is a plot clue: the woman whom the Captain will marry isn't well off, confident, or his social equal.

Did R & H never change style, never vary format? *What* format? What two shows could be less alike than *Oklahoma!* and *Carousel,* or than *Allegro* and *Me and Juliet*? One structural element did remain constant right through *The Sound of Music* — the long first act, stuffed with songs, followed by a much shorter second, getting by on a few new numbers plus reprises. *The Sound of Music* offers only three new numbers in Act Two. (*Flower Drum Song* offers only two.) But there is an R & H surprise at the first-act curtain. It occurs at the fundamental point of confrontation between a lead character and his or her destiny, which, in an R & H show, can happen literally anywhere. *Carousel* places it in the first dialogue scene, as Billy pulls Julie close for a kiss and their sorrowful future is determined. *Allegro* pushes it far to the end of the evening, in "Come Home," when Joe's dead mother appears to urge him to return to first principles, and *The King and I* similarly sites this moment far to the rear of the evening, when Anna "outfaces" the King from beating Tuptim.

In *The Sound of Music* this moment arrives when the Mother Abbess' message in "Climb Ev'ry Mountain" penetrates Maria's defenses and she realizes that she must abandon the religious life and own up to her feelings as a woman, for Captain von Trapp and his children. It takes the entire song to do it, but Maria at length capitulates, tearing the veil from her head. And suddenly — so suddenly that the Mother Abbess is still holding her last note — the curtain plummets. It's the most abrupt first-act curtain of its day... possibly excepting that of *Gypsy*, another show that plunges into its intermission as an older woman exhorts a younger one to go out and meet her fate.

It may be incomplete to discuss an R&H show that starred Mary Martin strictly in terms of composition, for by 1959 Martin was a phenomenally popular star of musicals, a figure whose very entrance upon a stage brought a host of associations along. Martin was Broadway's ageless gamine (to, basically, Ethel Merman's ageless "broad"), Annie Oakley merged with Peter Pan. This was especially true of Martin's Maria, ruthlessly charming with the kids and coy with the Captain, though deeply worried, inward, in her scenes with the Abbess. The performance was good enough to win Martin a Tony over Merman's Rose in *Gypsy,* a feat of *Guinness Book* proportions. Putting Nellie Forbush and Maria together, Martin becomes something like the essential R&H performer, not only because she was the only star to open two of their shows on Broadway but because after *South Pacific* she was constantly associated with them, hosting the 1954 General Foods R&H special, cutting an album with Rodgers of Rodgers songs, recording the *Cinderella* score, and recounting R&H anecdotes on television talk shows. Other performers can be identified with R&H—Julie Andrews, after all, created Cinderella and was seen by countless millions as Maria on film; and Gordon MacRae and Shirley Jones filmed the leads in both *Oklahoma!* and *Carousel,* pretty basic appearances. And others have made major history in R&H shows— Alfred Drake, John Raitt, Yana. But isn't it always Mary Martin who springs to mind when R&H are mentioned?

To a point, *The Sound of Music,* at first, was R&H & M, somewhat comparable to the star vehicle that the authors had written around Gertrude Lawrence—though this time the star part would always be Maria. Captain von Trapp is no King of Siam. The songs and Martin *were* the show, for *The Sound of Music* caps the break that R&H had made with the musical-comedy knowhow of the expert stagemaster who intuits the mode, the shape, the whole of the art—Julian Mitchell, John Murray Anderson, Hassard Short (to synopsize the rise of the musical's director from Victor Herbert to the very verge of R&H). When R&H began, they had Mamoulian and de Mille; indeed, they needed Mamoulian and de Mille. But by *South Pacific* the shows were basically staging themselves. Did *South Pacific* need Joshua Logan the way *West Side Story* needed Jerome Robbins? George Abbott couldn't help *Me and Juliet,* and the R&H directors who succeeded him—Clurman, Kelly, and Donehue—did not appreciably assist their productions. But then, the central performance in most musical comedies is that of the star, while the central performance in the musical play is that of the authors—and in this matter R&H were authors of musical plays. Ironically, their revolution paved the road for the concept musical, whose central performance is that of the authors in collaboration with the director and designer. We can envision different pro-

## Shocking But True

The photo at right of Rodgers and Hammerstein and Lindsay and Crouse flanking Mary Martin graced the souvenir book. So far so good. But each succeeding New York Maria was processed into the shot, her head grafted onto Mary's trunk. Opposite, here's Martha Wright, who took over in October of 1961—fourteen months after Hammerstein died!

ductions of *Gypsy,* as we can of *Oklahoma!* and *The King and I.* But when we reach *Fiddler on the Roof* and *Pacific Overtures,* don't we navigate inexorably around the original stagings, and don't revivals either replicate or imitate them? This is not to say that R & H emphasized content and that later shows emphasized style. It is that R & H so emphasized content that their heirs inherited a form absolutely secure in its purity of narration, and were thus able to move beyond the mechanics of telling the story into the wider world of analyzing the story *even as it is told.* In a word: *Company.*

How odd, then, to go back to *The Sound of Music*'s first night, November 16, 1959, at the Lunt-Fontanne Theatre,* and to consider what strange history this show was making even as critics—and Broadway in general—took it down as R & H on vacation. Too light. Too accommodating. Every so often someone goes "Heil Hitler!" and suddenly Mary Martin and these kids are walking into freedom. That's strange, suddenly neither light nor accommodating. Should this story even *be* a musical? A musical should be something on the order of, say, *The Music Man* (1958), last season's big hit, still playing at the Majestic Theatre—an R & H house, so to say. How do R & H stack up against the musical *today?* Against, for instance, *The Music Man,* so fleet and light and touching and all-American, an innocent piece that nevertheless boasts a con man hero, a look at small-town bigotry, and some deceptively ingenious numbers—"Rock Island," for instance, a dialogue of traveling salesmen in *Sprechstimme,* set to the rhythm of a moving train; or "Goodnight, My

*The Sound of Music* was the only R & H show not to open on "Hit Street": Forty-fourth between Seventh and Eighth Avenues.

Someone," a ballad sung to a child's piano exercises; or "My White Knight," an aria masquerading as a song? *The Music Man* seemed fresh next to *The Sound of Music*. But what would *The Music Man* have been like without R & H — if its model had been, oh, *Something for the Boys?* In some ways, the R & H era has been the story of how the musical educated itself. "You must find the life you were born to live," the Mother Abbess tells Maria. How? "Look for it." Examine, invent, alter.

That is exciting advice — but what was *The Sound of Music?* All those kids, those bright copper kettles! It was not all that well produced, but it was beautifully cast, with a very strongly sung Abbess from Patricia Neway. Listen to the album. Hers is a structural performance, one that understands that the entire show is about freedom, both the fear of it and the need for it. As von Trapp's friends, Kurt Kasznar was usefully Continental and Marion Marlowe another of those wonderful singers whom you ask about years later — what else did she do? (That is, besides officiating as one of television's first "crossover" sopranos, on *The Arthur Godfrey Show.)* Theodore Bikel may have been a bit wooden as an actor, but his Captain did bear a military air, and of course folksinger Bikel was a natural on the guitar. A very sound "Edelweiss."

Then Hammerstein died, and R & H were over. Rodgers was devastated, but so was the theatre in general. To my knowledge, none of the obituaries explained how systemic Hammerstein's revolution in musical-comedy narrative structure really was, how thoroughly he and his composer partners instated logic of action and sensitivity of character in what had been an art of anything goes. Hammerstein turned a vaudeville into stories with point. There were many influential composers and lyricists, but Hammerstein was

## Maria and the Kids From Egyptian Times to the Present

Below is the original cast: note the martinet Captain demonstrating the use of a whistle for summoning children. At bottom is Martha Wright (with her own body), who was Mary's replacement in *South Pacific* as well.

the only influential storyteller. And his revolution was more essential than that of the composers, because all the lovely and characterful music in the world can do nothing till it has something honest to work with. Hammerstein was, in fact, the single most influential figure in the American musical, more so even than its three outstanding musicians, Jerome Kern, Richard Rodgers, and Stephen Sondheim*—all of whom, as it happens, were Hammerstein associates.

Lights were dimmed in New York and Hollywood as obsequies for Hammerstein, and the world mourned a more or less beloved figure. Who wouldn't love the guy who wrote "When the Children Are Asleep" and "The Surrey with the Fringe on Top"—songs with lines that, in your childhood, stuck in your mind as concepts to be worked on, learning tools yet fun stuff that you would bellow from the back of the bus on a class trip? If you were the average American kid, the man had written the words to shows you put on in school, the few movie musicals you had seen and liked, the better of the songs you kept hearing that weren't rock. If you were slightly older, you had been raised during the R & H era, perhaps had been taken to some of the shows in New York or on tour. If you were much older, you could chart your show biz on Hammerstein, from *Rose-Marie* and *Show Boat* to *Oklahoma!* and *Carousel*. The man *was* an American art.

But what really put over Hammerstein, and Rodgers, as beloved Americans was the *Sound of Music* movie. Precise receipts are impossible to come by, and in Hollywood you divide everything you hear by nine. Still, Twentieth Century–Fox's 1965 film starring Julie Andrews, written by Ernest Lehman, and produced and directed by Robert Wise must stand, on a sheer head count of paid admissions, with *The Birth of a Nation* and *Gone with the Wind* as one of the most popular movies ever made. It came out at the height of the film musical's last great era, when lavish and even overproduced versions of stage shows—*Finian's Rainbow, Camelot, Hello, Dolly!, Funny Girl, Oliver!, Half a Sixpence*—tried to turn the special event into a staple. There were too many of them, and they cost so much that some of them barely turned a profit, or simply bombed.

Yet *The Sound of Music* turned out to be the ultimate movie musical, not only immensely profitable ($79 million in pre-inflation currency on an expense of $8.2 million) but omnipresent. Some spectactors didn't merely attend but absorbed it. One Myra Franklin of Wales holds the record for multiple viewings—as of 1988 she had seen the film 940 times—but countless others seem to have revisited *The Sound of Music* as if mesmerized.

*George Gershwin of course ranks with these three, but because much of his greatest work was done in opera and in the concert hall, he might well belong to a class all his own.

What is there to watch the twentieth time? Perhaps they study Julie Andrews' famous twirl in the opening sequence, just before she bursts into the title song, so they can duplicate it at home to the soundtrack recording, no doubt in a facsimile of Andrews' costume, a black number with a gray apron that appears to be organically attached. Perhaps they examine the Baird Marionettes in "The Lonely Goatherd" to see if they're biologically correct. Perhaps they memorize the lines—a man in Oregon sent Fox a copy of the script that he claimed to have set down from memory.

Has any other film inspired such devotion? An article in *The New York Times* stated that the theatre at which the film played Salt Lake City had clocked a total attendance of 509,516 by October 1966 (nineteen months after the film's original release). Yet according to the United States Census Salt Lake City had a population of 190,000. Apparently some people weren't going to the movies; they were going to *The Sound of Music*—especially in Moosehead, Minnesota, where, after forty-nine weeks of continuous road-show play in the town's only theatre, local college students threw up picket lines and demanded a change of bill.

A movie this prosperous gets Oscars. *The Sound of Music* copped ten nominations and won five, including Best Picture and Best Director. But is it a good movie? Is it good R & H? It isn't as authentic a filming as *Oklahoma!* or *The King and I,* with their preservations of de Mille and Robbins and their sharp casting. But neither is it a debauch like *Carousel.* Obviously, the addition of real mountains and Salzburg was useful, and surely the spirited and winning Julie Andrews gives this piece the very engaging center that the stage show had. Mary Martin was different—loving the audience in the fun parts and showing us a deep new Martin in the heavy parts...and too old for the role in the first place. But that's theatre.

Different rules apply in film, and Andrews observes the rules. She's sharp and eager and perfect. She does that twirl. The kids are acceptable and the Baird puppets, as always, wonderful. But why does Peggy Wood, forgotten but not gone, play the Mother Abbess? Wood had her heyday, justly deserved, as a Broadway and West End soprano, but this was a career that started in the chorus of *Naughty Marietta.* By the 1960s, at filming time, Wood's voice was shot, and she was so unattuned to dubbing technique that director Wise wreathed her in shadows during "Climb Ev'ry Mountain." Why didn't he have the Abbess take Maria to a café so she could sing the number behind a huge menu, perhaps a teeming pile of *Lebkuchen?* Why, while we're at it, didn't Wise hire the superb Patricia Neway from the original cast?

Top is Florence Henderson on the national tour. At Long Island's Westbury Music Fair in 1966 (*above*), Shirley Jones hands Stephen Elliot back his whistle.

Casting counts. As the public perceives it, what you write is no better than whom you hire to perform it. R & H may have gone astray here and there with a doughy Lun Tha or a questionable Fauna. But in general they were sharp at matching the available talent to the parts. Look, these men cast a perfect *Carousel* with nobodies; nowadays, no one can get up a *Carousel* using stars. Wise got up Christopher Plummer as Captain von Trapp: a fine actor who doesn't know what to do besides grimace or look as soigné as one can in those relentlessly green Austrian jackets which suggest that the wearer is about to break into a dance in which everyone slaps his shoes and yodels. *"The Sound of Mucus,"* Plummer called it; but he's one reason why. It's a depressing appearance.

As for textual variants, Ernest Lehman's script improves mildly on Lindsay and Crouse, and Rodgers wrote both words and music for two new songs, a new love duet called "Something Good," to replace the somewhat droning "An Ordinary Couple," and a character number for Maria, "I Have Confidence," a very Hammersteinian sort of soliloquy urged on by Rodgers in music that sounds like a charge up a hill:

> Somehow I will impress them.
> I will be firm but kind.
> And all those children—
> (Heaven bless them!)
> They will look up to me and mind me!

Unfortunately, the two cynical songs involving Max (Richard Haydn) and the Baroness (Eleanor Parker) were dropped. This did spare us seeing two other nonsingers hiding and turning away during their music in the Peggy Wood manner, but it has complicated the subsequent history of the stage show. With spectators so intimate with the movie, mustn't one include the movie's two added songs to avoid Audience Dejection—and doesn't the time factor then force one to omit some or all of the three songs dropped between stage and screen? A very successful London revival in 1981 starring Petula Clark did just that, as if attempting to stage the film rather than the show. Even the PR photographs were shot outdoors: movie stills.

It was almost shocking to reencounter the original text and score in the 1990 New York City Opera mounting, which James Hammerstein staged less as Maria's show than as *"The Von Trapp Story."* There were no movie songs, no Ernest Lehman cue-in lines. Hammerstein also dropped Rodgers' religious-prelude music and the opening abbey scene that culminates in the nuns' cries of "Maria! Where is Maria?," which, in 1959, led to the discovery of Mary Martin in a tree, to star-friendly applause. In 1990, the curtain rose on Debbie Boone in a tree, straight on, story beginning, no waste.*

### The Sound of Movie

Below, Julie leads the ascetic life, yet falls in love (with Christopher Plummer, *at bottom*).

---

*Hammerstein also reinstated the verse to "An Ordinary Couple," dropped somewhere between rehearsals and the premiere in 1959. Its inclusion enhances a number that even Mary Martin, Rodgers' biggest fan, thought a little dull.

Shocking, too, was the reminder that Liesl's boyfriend, Rolf, has not been so Nazified that he has lost his humanity. In the stage show, as I've said, he spots but protects the von Trapps during the Nazis' search of the abbey. In the Lehman version, however, he sounds the alarm before they can get away, which might be good naturalism but is not good R&H. It gives the film bite, yes—but immediately after this the nuns coyly confess to the Abbess that they have ripped the spark plugs out of the Nazis' cars, and this is the gooey side of *The Sound of Music*. "You must need the money," Burt Lancaster told Lehman in the Fox commissary. "Wasn't there perhaps one little von Trapp who didn't want to sing his head off?" Pauline Kael asked in *The New Yorker*, "or who screamed that he wouldn't act out little glockenspiel routines for Papa's party guests, or who got nervous and threw up if he had to get on a stage?"

They have a point. Any movie that wins the Best Film of the Year Award from both the National Catholic Office and the National Council of Churches must surely be a repressed and hypocritical piece of work. It's like being cited by Saddam Hussein for the Von Clausewitz Prize for Most Brilliant Military Tactics. This is not someone from whom anyone sensible or fair would want to win an award; it makes you wonder what your tactics are. The R&H shows are healing shows not because they are repressed or hypocritical but—on the contrary—because they are honest. They heal as most musicals don't because they test our assumptions as most musicals don't. They sing of a harmonious community only after challenging their folk, making them *strive* for community. What musical did, before R&H? As I said in regard to *Cinderella*, in R&H one doesn't deserve happiness: one works for it, and in ways the National Catholic Office wouldn't begin to understand.

Unfortunately, the sugary feeling of the *Sound of Music* movie has, through its popularity, extended to cover R&H as a whole. "We do family shows," remember? We do *Cinderella*, "You'll Never Walk Alone," beautiful mornin's, and raindrops on roses. The festering Jud Fry, the abused and abusing Billy Bigelow, *Allegro*'s casual leadership-class adultery, the volcanically sexual rapport between Anna and the King, and *Pipe Dream's* hookshop are forgotten. Even the Nazis aren't real by the time the "bright copper kettles" effect sets in. It's as if everything in the movie—and therefore everything in R&H—were one of my favorite things.

Listen. European art is honest: Italian art is about faith, English art is about class, and German art is about power. American art is dishonest—which explains why our major narrative invention is the musical, a fantasy form. R&H not only rationalized that fantasy but *realized* it, brought it close not to what life is like but what life is about. Like opera, the musical will

---

**Rodgers After Hammerstein**
Below are Richard Kiley, Diahann Carroll, and Mitchell Gregg in *No Strings*, a daring and undeservedly forgotten piece.

*As the title implies, the sound was all woods and brass, the blowing instruments. No strings.

always of necessity be a stylized form, but it has become realistic in its outlook. And the R & H era is when that happened.

This is one reason why Rodgers was so overcome when Hammerstein died. How do you replace the ultimate? Quirkily—but successfully—Rodgers wrote his next show with Rodgers: *No Strings* (1962), the music somewhat Rodgers-and-Hart in style but the lyrics couched in a strange voice entirely Rodgers' own. The show itself was something new, produced in a unique style as a free-flowing tour through the world of European fashion and money, with models setting the scene in turns and poses and the musicians, freed from their pit, wandering through the stage pictures to toot* as if at will. *No Strings* was a great show, and Rodgers could have gone on setting his own lyrics. But he found the composer-lyricist's life lonely and sought out partners, Hammerstein's heir Stephen Sondheim on *Do I Hear a Waltz?* (1965), Martin Charnin on *Two by Two* (1970) and *I Remember Mama* (1979), and Sheldon Harnick on *Rex* (1976). Do you ever start a new project fearful that the old magic will die on you, all of a sudden? Apparently Rodgers did, if only after those stupid reviews of *The King and I,* though he had been in effect a bottomless well of tunes for thirty years. He was in form for *No Strings* and at his best in *Do I Hear a Waltz?,* a box-office failure disdained by its creators but—take it from me—a wonderful show with a really lovely score.

*Two by Two,* however, was poor Rodgers and, uh, minor Charnin, and *Rex* and *I Remember Mama* found our man uninspired. They have their moments—*Rex* offers the last great Rodgers waltz in "No Song More Pleasing" and a flash of the old genius in "At the Field of Cloth of Gold," when the uneasy diplomacy of England and France is analyzed musically by clashing harmony, the English singing in F Major and the French in f minor, a hair-raising effect.

### Rodgers After Hammerstein, Continued

Another unusual show, *Do I Hear a Waltz?* (*below*), with Sergio Franchi and Elizabeth Allen, was underrated mainly because its gestation was notoriously unhappy—as we note at bottom, right, where Rodgers confers with collaborator Stephen Sondheim.

Life after partners as gifted as Hart and Hammerstein must be vexing enough, but this was life as the last giant: for all the other major musicians of Rodgers' generation — Kern, Porter, and Gershwin — were gone. (Irving Berlin was alive, but he had retired after *Mr. President* [1962] and was in any case not in these men's class as an artist.) Rodgers did keep in touch with the theatre — he especially admired *Fiddler on the Roof* — and, though ailing, he retained his sense of humor. At the badly staged 1975 Lincoln Center production of *A Doll's House* with Liv Ullmann, Dorothy Rodgers asked Dick when Ibsen died.

"Tonight," says Rodgers.

Tonight is R & H, this week and next year. Their works survive. Why? Great songs, unusual subjects, strong acting parts — that's part of it. The other part is that R & H believed what most of us want to believe, and present us with hard facts so we can yearn all the harder for a stimulating outcome. Hard facts have solutions — the dead Billy heartens his widow and daughter, Nellie conquers her racism out of compassion, the von Trapps escape. The solutions make R & H thrilling, but the hardness gives them grip. Strength. Greatness. Along with Florenz Ziegfeld, Eugene O'Neill, Katharine Cornell, Kaufman and Hart, *Our Town*, Tennessee Williams, Joseph Papp, Sondheim-Prince, and Charles Ludlam, R & H are unique and essential American theatre.

I've been saving a story for you. There's a production meeting on *The Sound of Music*, and Mary Martin's husband, Richard Halliday, a coproducer, announces that he has a tremendous idea for Martin's entrance scene. Yes, she'll appear in the tree, but she will *catch her bloomers on a branch as she climbs down*! What comedy! What Mary! Isn't it flawless and fabulous?

R & H tell Halliday that they don't think underpants humor has anything to do with the story or the character.

Thwarted and furious, Halliday stalks out, but turns at the door for his riposte.

"You know what's wrong with you guys?" he says. "All *you* care about is the *show*!"

*Two by Two* brought Rodgers back to the star vehicle. Below, librettist Peter Stone and Rodgers consider the poster, with star Danny Kaye's name as big as the title.

# Bibliography

There are a surprising number of books on R & H, separately and together, but they tend to a sameness, either because the authors interviewed the same subjects or because some of them have been composing over each others' shoulders. This book-to-book correspondence becomes risible when Rodgers' autobiography, *Musical Stages* (Random House, 1975), lifts almost verbatim a paragraph from David Ewen's Rodgers bio (Holt, 1957). Does Rodgers think Ewen knows more about Rodgers' life than Rodgers himself does?

It turns out that Stanley Green wrote *Musical Stages*, in conversation with Rodgers. Still, it's disconcerting. And, sad to say, Rodgers offers not much more insight than his biographers into how he and his partners wrote their shows, though every now and then a flash of something tells us how rich *Musical Stages* might have been if a more eliciting ghost than Green had been commissioned. Deems Taylor's *Some Enchanted Evenings* (Harper, 1953) came out so early that he covers only the first five shows; *Me and Juliet* checks in with a last-minute photograph, no more. Needless to say, Green's own *The Rodgers and Hammerstein Story* (John Day, 1963) has nothing to tell us beyond data. Green was probably the least boring and without question the most reliable of the first generation of musical-comedy historians who appeared in the wake of Cecil Smith's groundbreaking history, *Musical Comedy in America* (Theatre Arts, 1950). Some of Green's colleagues wrote with such little energy, such academic myopia, that one wondered if they had ever actually gone into a theatre and *seen* a musical. Even Green had this air of the impartial reporter. Come on, man, what do you *like*?

Books by younger writers are better, though less than ideal. Frederick Nolan's *The Sound of Their Music: The Story of Rodgers and Hammerstein* (Walker, 1978) is quixotic but comprehensive; and Nolan does sport an odd bit here and there that no other book has. (I have the list of *The King and I*'s investors on his authority; and I'd love to know where he got it.) On Hammerstein alone, Hugh Fordin's *Getting to Know Him* (Random House, 1977) is dependable, though Fordin hews to the famous parts of Hammerstein and ignores the mysteries—for instance, how he could have come up with flop after flop in that odd period between *Show Boat* and *Oklahoma!*. In the middle of that era he wrote *Three Sisters* with Jerome Kern for London. Now, the show did fail—but are we to assume that Kern and Hammerstein in their prime didn't create something marvelous, fail or no fail? My 78s of *Three Sisters* suggest something very unusual; but Fordin's report on the show is perfunctory, and the mystery stays mysterious.

I did not bother to include production data for the R & H shows, because all such information (along with critics' blurbs, awards listings, and so on) can be found in Stanley Green's compilation *The Rodgers and Hammerstein Fact Book* (Lynn Farnol, 1980), which details not only R & H shows but every show that either of the two worked on in his life. Strange to say, it's juicy; certainly I get more of a sense of what *Three Sisters* might have been like in these pages than I do in any other volume. "Do you have the *Fact Book*?" Dorothy Rodgers asked me, and for some reason the words sounded so strange that I didn't know what she meant—*The Peewee Reese Fact Book*? *The Schwanda the Bagpiper Fact Book*? But I quickly recovered myself, and we smoothed it out over a cordial.

We should consider as well books by the R & H associates—Josh Logan's (with dish about everybody but himself), George Abbott's (unbearably dull—this man directed *Wonderful Town*?), Mary Martin's (very personable), and several works by Agnes de Mille, who is an astonishingly fine writer. I should add to these Harold Messing's unpublished M.F.A. thesis on *Cinderella*, written upon quite privileged access to the original production from first to last.

What more? There are of course the published texts to nine of the eleven works (*State Fair* and *Cinderella* were never published, either in original or remake form), the piano-vocal scores, and recordings—especially the original cast readings, as R & H not only cast with insight but leaned toward singers who could act more than toward actors who could sing. May I suggest, to serious students, making a tour of some kind through some musical of the 1920s or 1930s, then through an R & H title, then through a modern show? One might try, along with scripts and scores, EMI's rather lifeless but beautifully sung back-to-the-original *Anything Goes* recording, then Victor's 1977 *King and I* revival (it has Brynner and an amazing amount of incidentals, virtually the entire score less "The Small House of Uncle Thomas," which can be heard on *Jerome Robbins' Broadway*), and at last That's Entertainment's *Pacific Overtures* (the English National Opera production, musically complete virtually to the note). And there you would have the history of the American musical: from fun to drama to opera. What? *City of Angels* isn't an opera? Sue me.

# Index

*Italic* page numbers refer to illustrations.

# Credits

## Photograph Credits

## Film Copyrights

## Song Credits

## Graphic Musical Notation Excerpts

# THE
# WHITE BARN INN
## COOKBOOK

FOUR SEASONS AT
THE CELEBRATED AMERICAN INN

Recipes by Jonathan Cartwright

Text by Susan Sully

Photographs by Philippe Schaff

RUNNING PRESS
PHILADELPHIA · LONDON

## ACKNOWLEDGMENTS

This book could not have been created without the enthusiasm, hard work, and generosity of many individuals and local Maine businesses. Much gratitude is owed to Dannah Fine Flowers in Kennebunkport for floral displays, Villeroy & Boch in Kittery for fine tableware, J. Jorgensen Antiques in Wells for fine antiques, Rocky Mountain Antique Quilts in York for quilts, and Victorian Affair in Kennebunkport for a peignoir—thank you for contributing to the exquisite settings for this book. Thanks to Snug Harbor Farm in Kennebunk and Patton's Berry Stand in Kennebunkport for seasonal color and produce, and to the Maritime Museum of Kennebunkport for the use of its dock. Thanks are also due to the Kennebunkport American Legion for presenting the Memorial Day parade, to the Franciscan Monastery for hosting the Christmas Carol program of the Christmas Prelude, and to the Kennebunk, Kennebunkport Chamber of Commerce for organizing the Christmas Prelude and the Blessing of the Fleet, events featured in the pages of this book that enrich the life of our community. Special thanks are offered to the staff of the Brick Store Museum in Kennebunk for sharing their treasure trove of historical information about the history of the region. And finally, deep gratitude is due to the staff of the White Barn Inn, as well as its sister properties Grissini, Stripers, Schooners, the Beach House, the Yachtsman Lodge and Marina, and the Breakwater Inn, for all the hard work and dedication to craft.

Library of Congress Control Number: 2002095690
ISBN 0-7624-1595-9

Cover and interior design by Frances J. Soo Ping Chow
Edited by Janet Bukovinsky Teacher
Typography: Bickham Script, ITC Berkeley,
   and Schneidlers Initials

This book may be ordered by mail from the publisher.
Please include $2.50 for postage and handling.
**But try your bookstore first!**

Running Press Book Publishers
125 South Twenty-second Street
Philadelphia, Pennsylvania 19103-4399

Visit us on the web!
www.runningpress.com

# TABLE OF CONTENTS

# Welcome to
# THE WHITE BARN INN

"This cozy little place is becoming very popular with its guests who enjoy home comforts, large cool rooms and an excellent table. [The proprietor] knows how to run a house of this kind to perfection." Although this description of the White Barn Inn was written in 1887, when Kennebunkport, Maine, was just gaining popularity as a fashionable seaside resort, it still perfectly expresses the appeal of this establishment that marries luxury with simplicity and tradition with contemporary flair. Established in 1887 as the Forest Hill House, the inn quickly attracted an upscale clientele that sought refuge from the summer heat and hectic lifestyle of nearby Boston and Portsmouth. Today the White Barn Inn, built during the heyday of America's resort movement, is one of only forty exclusive Relais & Château hotels in America. With a Relais Gourmand restaurant that is one of just three in New England to win the AAA Five Diamond award, the White Barn Inn is still recognized as the one of the region's finest lodgings and restaurants.

A nineteenth-century country house with an adjacent barn that gives the property its name, the inn combines rustic Maine ambience with European-style service and innovative New England cuisine. Fresh flowers add vibrant color in spring and summer. Fires burn in the living room hearths of the main house throughout fall and winter. Windows frame constantly changing views of each season's particular beauties, while the seasonal bounty is celebrated in gourmet presentations every night at the restaurant. With this book the staff of the White Barn Inn share the secrets of their special brand of hospitality with readers who wish to recall the delights of a holiday in Maine, re-create the pleasures they experienced at the White Barn Inn at home, or simply travel in their imaginations to one of the most sought-after resorts in America.

## A BRIEF HISTORY
## OF KENNEBUNKPORT AND THE
## WHITE BARN INN

Long before Europeans landed on the shores of Kennebunk Beach, Native Americans populated the region, hunting game on the Kennebunk Plains and harvesting the fruits of forest and sea. French and English explorers first visited the area's rocky shoreline and sandy beaches in the early 1600s, establishing fishing camps and trading posts by the 1620s. Early settlers began cutting local white pine and hardwoods, and by 1640 they established a shipbuilding and shipping trade that flourished for 250 years. Ships sailed from the mouth of the Kennebunk River to Boston, New York, and Philadelphia and across the seas to the West Indies,

Europe, and the Far East. More than 300 wooden sailing vessels were built in Kennebunk and Kennebunkport between 1854 and 1918, when the last of the great ships, a four-masted schooner called the Kennebunk, was launched into the sea.

Although the region's importance as a shipbuilding center had begun to dwindle by the end of the nineteenth century, a powerful new "industry" started to gain force by the mid-1800s: resort development. During the nineteenth century northeastern America became the home of thriving cities where industrialization changed the pace of life, ushering in a host of "modern" conveniences while creating a noisy, urban environment. Upper-middle-class city dwellers began to dream of escaping to the country or the shore, where they could reconnect with nature. The development of rail travel made it possible for them to travel with ease to formerly remote locations.

In 1872 a branch line of the Boston & Maine Railroad offered stops along a route from South Berwick to Portland, including a new station in Kennebunk. Suddenly, Bostonians discovered that they could reach the unspoiled beaches and charming old town of Kennebunk in a three-hour train ride. A group of Boston and Kennebunkport businessmen recognized the potential of this transportation development and quickly purchased several hundred acres of land along the coast that spread out on either side of the Kennebunk River. Doing business as the Boston and Kennebunkport Seashore Company, these developers built the grand Ocean Bluff Hotel on a hill (now the site of the Colony

Hotel) and offered for sale lots of lands subdivided for hotels and seasonal cottages.

Many more guesthouses and inns were established during the early decades of the resort movement, including the Forest Hill House, which would be renamed the White Barn Inn in the late twentieth century. Constructed in 1820 in a typical New England style, the building was purchased in the mid-1880s by the Boothby family, who transformed it into an inn, operating from spring through early fall, catering mainly to a Jewish clientele. The Boothbys divided the upper floors into large, well-appointed guestrooms and added a wraparound porch with Victorian details. On the ground floor they created spacious living and dining rooms cooled by summer breezes and warmed by wood-burning fires in autumn and spring. By 1887 the establishment was already celebrated through word of mouth and in the press as an extraordinary inn providing excellent accommodations and dining.

## Uncommon Charm

Today the common rooms of the White Barn Inn retain their old-fashioned appeal, with nineteenth-century-

been left unfinished, their timbers aged to a rich dark brown. Two walls have been replaced with picture windows that frame views of a walled garden and the surrounding landscape, which changes color and mood with each season. Starched white linen tablecloths, polished silver place settings, and glistening crystal stemware provide refined counterpoint to the interior. Above the tables former haylofts are filled with country antiques that glow beneath soft lights.

During the early years of the resort movement, the Seashore Company promoted the area including Kennebunk Beach, Kennebunkport, and Cape Arundel as an exclusive destination, inviting "none but the elite of cottagers to locate here." Their advertisements described the area as one "possessing natural scenery, such,

inspired upholstery and wallpapers, antique portraits, and oriental carpets laid across hardwood floors. The guestrooms combine traditional furnishings and decorations with such up-to-date luxuries as spa bathroom fixtures and gas-burning fires. An annex of spacious rooms and cottagelike suites, though constructed only recently, captures the same charm that characterizes the original inn and blends easily into the woods that surround the hilltop property. The inn's newest room, the Loft, nestles in the gables of the white barn that gives the property its name and features contemporary design and a large spa bathroom.

The main floor of the barn has been transformed into a dining room that marries rustic architecture with elegant accoutrements. Interior walls and trusses have

as perhaps, no other similar portion on the New England coast possesses." They extolled its "rugged beauty of scenery, delightful boating and bathing, abundant fishing, and convenient hotel accommodations. . . ." Within fifteen years a dozen large hotels were constructed in prime locations along the waterfront, and seasonal homes called "cottages"—a term that referred more to their fanciful architecture than to their scale—were built.

In addition to its natural charms, the area boasted Colonial- and Federal-style houses built by affluent chandlers and merchants of the eighteenth and early nineteenth centuries. By the late nineteenth century, Americans already disillusioned by the Industrial Age were intrigued by these antiquated buildings. Artists flocked to Kennebunkport to capture the charms of the old structures on canvas and paper, while architects, interior designers, and landscape designers of the Colonial Revival movement invoked the old-fashioned simplicity of these wooden houses in new cottages built for a wealthy clientele. By freely mixing elements inspired

by Colonial architecture with the emerging Queen Anne style, they created the rambling Shingle Style houses for which Maine's coastline is now famous.

## VARIOUS SOURCES OF AMUSEMENT

Just as Kennebunkport's architecture blended the old with the new, satisfying the desire for both nostalgia and fashion, so did its entertainments and pastimes. A typical advertisement from the Wentworth House hotel describes "[a] new 30-foot Yacht ready to take parties to sail or fish. Excellent facilities for Sailing, Bathing, Fishing and Driving, with Bowling Alleys and various sources of amusement. Horses and Carriages to let; also

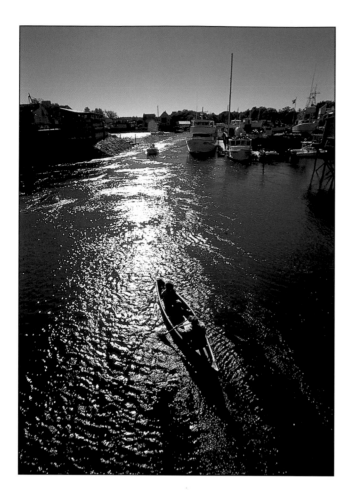

with recommendations for outings to consider. Suggestions might include sea-bound whale-watching excursions, hiking and biking tours, deep-sea fishing charters, or directions to local antiques stores and museums. The inn maintains a fleet of sturdy bicycles, and the staff is always prepared with maps and suggestions about touring routes that reveal the beauties of the area. The kitchen offers a picnic basket menu so guests can take a bit of the Inn's fine cuisine with them when they head out into the Maine waters or countryside.

## AN EXCELLENT TABLE

Kennebunkport's summer residents, who were called "rusticators" by the locals, sought not only healthy activities but also healthful foods that combined farm-fresh produce and local seafood and game with the sophistication of urban dining. A summer menu from one of the seaside hotels offers five courses, including such seasonal delights as "Broiled Salmon Steak [with] lemon butter," "Summer Squash," and "Blueberry Pie." "As there is a farm connected with the house," this hotel informed prospective clients, "we raise our own Vegetables, and take them as needed, fresh and of the best. Also, our Milk, Butter and Eggs are from the Farm."

Although nowadays produce grown directly on the property of the White Barn Inn is limited to fresh herbs, chef Jonathan Cartwright has sought out local foragers who bring freshly gathered mushrooms, fiddlehead ferns, and wild blueberries to the kitchen in season every day. Lobsters, diver-harvested sea scallops,

Coach and Buckboard to take large parties out on excursions." Facilities were developed for the newly popular sports of tennis and golf, including a score of tennis courts and three golf courses. Canoeing and sailing were common pursuits, along with sea bathing and fishing. Traditionalists enjoyed carriage outings that terminated in lavish picnics. By 1900, with the advent of an electric trolley, adventurous summer residents added "trolley tripping" to their amusements, bustling up and down the shore to attend a full schedule of dances and musical programs.

To keep today's guests amused, the manager of the White Barn Inn prepares a daily note that appears in each guest's room, including a weather forecast along and just-caught tuna, salmon, and striped sea bass are purchased directly from fishermen who daily ply the cold Maine waters. Local game, including guinea hens, turkey, and venison, garnished with wild mushrooms, New England cranberries, and preserved Maine blueberries, appear seasonally on the restaurant's ever-changing menu. A cheese board features artisanal selections from New England and European dairies.

While these ingredients reflect the changing seasons of Maine and surrounding New England, the sophisticated recipes at the White Barn Inn reveal the artistry of a European-trained chef who delights in combining classic preparations with contemporary creativity. A lobster spring roll featuring moist meat and julienned Asian vegetables bound in a golden fried wrapper is an ingenious hybrid of the traditional Maine lobster roll and a Thai spring roll. A grilled tournedo of local cod with spring pea purée, fried shrimp, and potato sticks combines local ingredients in a preparation that playfully recalls that English seaside favorite, fish and chips. A winter entrée of grilled venison

sauced with port and Madeira and served with a potato custard timbale incorporates traditional European and New England flavors in a stunning new way.

## DAYS OF GRACE AND LEISURE

The advent of the automobile significantly changed the way people summered in America. While the railroad was the traditional mode of travel, families were likely to relocate for weeks and months at a time at a single destination, living in seasonal cottages or taking rooms for long stays at large hotels. Once the automobile gained in popularity, summer vacationers were more mobile and less likely to stay for long in one holiday destination. As train travel dwindled and automobiles replaced both the newfangled trolley and the old-fashioned carriage, the pace of life sped up even more. Many of the large hotels lost much of their clientele and closed their doors.

Still, tourists, artists, and writers came to savor Kennebunkport's natural beauty and historic architecture. In 1927 a watercolor of a Federal-style doorway by Abbot Graves, an artist who frequented Kennebunkport, graced the cover of a summer issue of The Literary Digest. "It . . . might be anywhere in the old comfortable New England towns where Colonial architecture still abounds and is cared for," notes the magazine's editor. "It reminds us of the days of grace and leisure that have in recent years slipped away."

there are the stone-walled pastures that early summer powders cheerily with buttercups and daisies."

For those who belong to what one of the area's first developers described as "the most fastidious class of patronage"—travelers who seek unspoiled nature, a region filled with history and culture, luxurious accommodations, and gourmet cuisine—Kennebunkport remains an ideal destination. The White Barn Inn beautifully expresses the unique regional character of old Maine style, providing the perfect setting from which to explore the region in every season and to savor the best, freshest products from the surrounding land and sea.

## SEASONAL NEW ENGLAND CUISINE

The coast of Maine is a mercurial place, full of moods and marvelous surprises. Every few months the region reveals a different side of itself: the tender warmth and bounty of spring; the bright, exuberant days of summer; the mellow, mysterious shades of autumn; and the

Somehow, Kennebunkport and the surrounding coastal region possesses an uncanny ability to transcend time, retaining its rugged land and seascapes, protecting its elegant architecture, and still appealing to the world-weary visitor. This description of Kennebunkport from a 1930 novel by Booth Tarkington still perfectly describes the seaside town: "Away from the tumbled coast and the rocky woodland of pine and juniper, the village itself, like some outpost wandered into alien country, wears the very aspect of . . . old New England. There are little streets of clean white green-shuttered houses as old as the great wine-glass elms that dip shadows down upon the roofs; there are two white churches with columned porticoes and Christopher Wrenn steeples, and, for the landward borders,

alternately tempestuous and serenely silent winter. Each season has its own activities: long bicycle rides, beach picnics, hikes beneath the changing leaves, sleigh rides, and chestnut roasting parties. Each has its particular bounty from the waters, sky, and earth: lobsters, tuna, clams, and salmon; quail, pheasant, venison, and lamb; baby greens, mushrooms, berries, and apples. Each has its own comforts, whether bundling up by the fire, enjoying cool breezes on the beach, or swimming in the ocean or a woodland pool. And each has its own appetites: spring's taste for bright, green flavors; summer's desire for cooling soups and light, fresh dishes; autumn's pleasure in rich colors, textures, and tastes; and winter's hunger for savory stews and roasted game. At the White Barn Inn, every offering on the menu rep-

resents a perfect marriage of the freshest local ingredients with the spirit of the season.

The exquisite dishes created by the White Barn Inn's executive chef celebrate these seasonal elements in imaginative and deeply satisfying presentations. Seared scallops harvested by divers from Maine's icy waters and garnished with caviar, fresh asparagus, and a light foam of champagne sauce capture the colors, scents, and tastes of spring in Kennebunkport. A plate of strawberry shortcake, with towering layers of pale golden cake and juicy red strawberries and topped with a puffy cloud of cream, celebrates the uncomplicated pleasures of summer. A Thanksgiving dinner of roasted turkey garnished with cranberry-port compote recalls the autumnal largesse of Maine's forests, alive with wild game, colorful leaves, and berries. And a midwinter dinner of savory venison drizzled with Madeira sauce and studded with preserved blueberries provides the perfect antidote to the icy, white world that glistens beyond the inn's windows and doors.

The alchemist behind these vibrant pairings of seasonal ingredients is Jonathan Cartwright, an internationally trained chef who brings his love of European cuisine and passion for the offerings of New England's land and sea to his work. It is his goal to find the freshest local ingredients and to cook them in a style that blends a classic European approach with a contemporary attitude infused with imagination and the desire to delight and surprise even the most jaded palate. The result is a perfect balance of elegance and simplicity with just a hint of whimsy that enhances the essence of

cook can continue to enjoy the White Barn Inn experience at home by re-creating their favorite formal meals for friends or exploring the chef's suggestions for more relaxed offerings to be enjoyed in seasonal outdoor meals. Even though some of the special New England ingredients featured in these pages may be unavailable in certain parts of the country, the lessons shared here will inspire home chefs to begin experimenting more creatively with the local ingredients at hand. And many of the tips about cooking and entertaining that come from this Relais Gourmand kitchen can help any host transform a dinner party at home into an extraordinary, unforgettable meal. Share these menus with those you love and invite them to join in this celebration of sophisticated seasonal cuisine.

each season's offerings. While the chef creates intricate pairings of sauces and garnishes for the tables of the White Barn Inn, he never loses sight of the pure joy that can be found in preparing an easy, flavorful meal at home or for an informal outing. Cooking should not be too serious, he believes, because that takes all the fun out of it.

The menus and recipes that follow explore the full spectrum of the chef's genius and passion for seasonal cuisine. No true lover of food will want to miss the dramatic delights of dining at the White Barn Inn's restaurant, where attentive waiters deliver course after course with professional precision and, upon request, pair each perfectly with vintages chosen from an expertly selected, extensive wine cellar. But those who love to

# Spring at the
# WHITE BARN INN

Spring comes late to Maine, often not breaking free from winter's grip until the last few days of May. In Kennebunkport a gloriously patriotic Memorial Day parade heralds the official opening of the season. Although the parade route is short—just down the hill from the fire station on Temple Street, through Dock Square, over the bridge that spans the Kennebunk River, and back again—there is plenty of time for old-fashioned American flag waving, horn blowing, drum rolling, baton twirling, and speechifying— sometimes even featuring the heartfelt words of former President George H. Bush, a long-time summer resident of Kennebunkport. Children, teenage music makers, grown-up bagpipers, veterans, firefighters, and police officers all join the throng, honoring the heroes of bygone wars and basking in the long-awaited springtime warmth.

The earth finally thaws and brightly colored bulbs of crocus, narcissus, and daffodil work their way up to the sun. Cherry trees blossom with silent explosions of white, pale pink, and dark rose petals. Lilacs bristle with short-lived clusters in shades of lavender and deep violet. Lawns receive the first mowing of the year, filling the air with a vivid green perfume. Wild rose bushes that form a tangled hedge along the rocky coast bloom with citrus-scented flowers of pale pink and yellow. Seasonal residents and weekenders flock to Kennebunkport during the first weeks of spring, seeking the pleasures of fresh sea air, a colorful landscape, and a quaint New England village. The rooms of the White Barn Inn are booked well in advance, and the dining room tables are full.

Chef Jonathan Cartwright anticipates spring with pleasure, welcoming the arrival of fresh, local produce that transforms winter's menu into something altogether new. After months of preparing hearty ragouts and savory soups, he delights in concocting spring dishes packed with color and lighter, brighter tastes. Foragers arrive at the kitchen's back door bringing the first growth of fiddlehead ferns and forest mushrooms, and growers deliver tender chives, baby spinach, crisp watercress, and tart rhubarb, which they have coaxed into early harvest in local greenhouses. On the Kennebunkport docks, fishermen revel in the season's catch, especially delicately flavored salmon, buttery cod, and the last diver-harvested scallops. Lobsters are plentiful and spring lamb is right on time.

In keeping with the season, the White Barn Inn's appetizer menu features watercress soup garnished with

get outside and enjoy the spring air, so they offer a menu of picnic food that can be packed into hampers or backpacks and eaten outdoors. Offerings like cold grilled salmon, paired with an asparagus salad, provide light and flavorful refreshment for an alfresco lunch.

The following recipes provide a sampling of spring's culinary pleasures at the White Barn Inn. In the spirit of the season, you might want to invite friends over for a springtime feast and prepare one of the formal dinners featuring young lamb or a selection of seafood. By

*Offerings like cold grilled salmon, paired with an asparagus salad, offer light and flavorful refreshment for an alfresco lunch.*

a lobster tail, spring greens dressed with an aged balsamic vinaigrette, and a lobster spring roll, one of the chef's signature creations. Grilled guinea hen on creamed spinach with spring peas and a woodland mushroom sauce, an entrée, brings together the essences of spring's first earthy breath with tender green things. A rhubarb crêpe soufflé served with buttermilk ice cream marries the tart and sweet flavors of the season.

A formal, five-course meal is just one of the pleasures to be enjoyed during this season. The staff at the White Barn Inn understands that guests also want to

preparing a few ingredients in advance and buying time—serving a chilled soup, prepared hours earlier, between courses, for example—home cooks can host a memorable evening that captures the bounty of the table at the White Barn Inn while still enjoying their own party. A simpler picnic lunch menu offers great rewards of pure spring flavors and colors with limited effort. And although the breakfast of poached eggs on lobster hash requires cooks to make a batch of lobster bisque in advance, it is easily assembled and promises to delight.

# SPRING MENUS

## A Spring Celebration at the White Barn Inn

Carpaccio of Aged Tenderloin
with a Szechuan Pepper and Soy Vinaigrette on
a Salad of Beets and Daikon Radish

Hollandaise-Glazed Local Halibut on Spring Fiddleheads
and Forest Mushrooms

Iced Cantaloupe and Lychee Soup

Herb-Roasted Spring Lamb with Tomato Chardonnay Sauce on Ratatouille
and Pesto Potato Purée

*or*

Grilled Breast of Guinea Hen on Creamed Spinach
with Potatoes, Spring Peas, and a Woodland Mushroom Sauce

Lemon Balm Soufflé and Rosewater Ice Cream

## A Springtime Picnic

Rhubarb Smoothies

Grilled Salmon with Spring Fiddleheads, Asparagus, and Scallions

A Selection of Cheeses with Red Currant Chutney

•

## A Spring Cocktail

Stars and Stripes

•

## A Spring Seafood Menu

Diver-Harvested Scallops on Asparagus with Champagne Foam and Caviar

Lobster Spring Roll with Carrot, Daikon Radish, and Snow Peas
in a Thai-Inspired Spicy Sweet Sauce

Kalamansi Sour Lemon Sorbet

Grilled Tournedos of Local Cod Loin with Crispy Shrimp and
Calamari on a Spring Pea Purée with a Piquant Sauce

"Twice-Baked" Rhubarb Crêpe Soufflé with Buttermilk Ice Cream

•

## Breakfast by the Pool

Breakfast Fruit Bowl

Poached Eggs on Kennebunkport Lobster Hash

Freshly Baked Muffins

# A Spring Celebration at The White Barn Inn

Dinner at the White Barn Inn begins with an amuse bouche—a beautifully garnished, bite-size serving of something the chef dreamed up that day to "amuse the mouth" and tease the appetite. Try serving one of these diminutive dishes at a dinner party at home. It's a nice way to please your guests, while affording yourself an extra five minutes in the kitchen to finish assembling the appetizer course below.

## CARPACCIO OF AGED TENDERLOIN WITH A SZECHUAN PEPPER AND SOY VINAIGRETTE ON A SALAD OF BEETS AND DAIKON RADISH

*In the White Barn Inn's professionally equipped kitchen, the chef uses a slicing machine that makes it easy to carve paper-thin slices from the beef tenderloin. When preparing this at home, just use a very sharp knife and slice the beef, partially frozen for about one hour, as thinly as possible, at least ¼ inch thick. If desired, you can cover the slices with waxed paper and pound them more thinly using a meat mallet.*

*Serves 4*

1 teaspoon ground Szechuan red pepper

½ teaspoon cayenne pepper

1 pinch freshly ground white pepper

½ teaspoon paprika

1 pinch salt

10 ounces center cut beef tenderloin,
in one piece

1 tablespoon olive oil

Szechuan Pepper and Soy Vinaigrette (see page 24)

Salad of Beets and Daikon Radish (see page 25)

In a small bowl, combine the Szechuan, cayenne, and white peppers, paprika, and salt. Spread on a clean cutting board.

Roll the tenderloin in the spice mixture until evenly covered.

In a large skillet, heat the olive oil over high heat. When the oil is hot, add the beef and sear for a few seconds on each side, just long enough to brown the outside of the meat and seal the spice crust.

Place the seared beef on a large plate, cover with plastic wrap, and chill in the freezer for 1 hour.

Using a very sharp knife, slice the beef into paper-thin slices, cutting across the grain. Arrange the slices on four serving plates. Drizzle with the Szechuan Pepper and Soy Vinaigrette and surround with Salad of Beets and Daikon Radish.

---

## SZECHUAN PEPPER AND SOY VINAIGRETTE

*Makes about ½ cup*

2 tablespoons soy sauce

4 tablespoons blended oil (see Note)

1 teaspoon sherry vinegar

1 teaspoon ground Szechuan red pepper

Salt and freshly ground pepper

Combine the soy sauce, oil, vinegar, and Szechuan pepper in a small bowl. Blend thoroughly, using a hand-held blender or wire whisk. Season the dressing with salt and pepper to taste.

**Note**: Blended oil is a mixture of 90 percent vegetable oil and 10 percent olive oil.

SALAD OF BEETS AND DAIKON RADISH

*Serves 4*

½ pound red beets, peeled

½ pound daikon radish, peeled

1 tablespoon soy sauce

2 tablespoons blended oil (see Note)

1 teaspoon chopped fresh cilantro

Salt and freshly ground pepper

Using a mandoline or a Japanese vegetable slicer, cut the beets and the daikon radish into thin slices, then cut the slices into a fine julienne.

Using a whisk or a hand-held blender, whisk the soy sauce and the oil until the mixture is slightly thickened and forms an emulsion. Add the cilantro and mix well. Season to taste with salt and pepper.

Just before serving, combine the beet and the daikon radish in a large bowl and toss with the dressing.

**Note:** Blended oil is a mixture of 90 percent vegetable oil and 10 percent olive oil.

# Hollandaise-Glazed Local Halibut
## on Spring Fiddleheads and Forest Mushrooms

*North Atlantic halibut is a firm-textured fish with a mild flavor that perfectly comple-ments the fiddleheads and mushrooms. Glazing the hollandaise by running the just-sauced fish under a hot broiler gives this dish an appealing texture and appear-ance. It also prevents the sauce from dripping down the sides of the fish onto the vegetables that surround it. Fiddleheads and forest mushrooms have such nice flavor that they can stand on their own and don't need much sauce.*

*Serves 4*

### HOLLANDAISE

½ cup full-bodied white wine, such as chardonnay

½ cup champagne vinegar

1 teaspoon cracked black peppercorns

1 sprig fresh parsley

1 shallot, finely chopped

4 egg yolks

½ pound (2 sticks) unsalted butter, melted

1 teaspoon chopped fresh parsley


### HALIBUT AND VEGETABLES

1 cup fiddlehead ferns

1 tablespoon blended oil (see Note)

1½ pounds North Atlantic halibut filet, cut into four pieces

Salt and freshly ground white pepper

2 teaspoons unsalted butter

1 shallot, finely chopped

½ cup chanterelle or other wild mushrooms,
lightly rinsed, drained, and towel dried

¼ cup Parsley Oil (see page 29)

For the hollandaise: Combine the wine, vinegar, peppercorns, parsley, and shallots in a medium saucepan. Bring to a boil over high heat, then lower the heat and cook until the mixture is reduced by half, about 5 minutes. Strain through a fine sieve, discarding the shallots and peppercorns, and reserve the liquid reduction.

Place a heat-resistant mixing bowl over a pan of boiling water. Add the egg yolks and ⅜ cup of the hollandaise reduction and whisk until the mixture doubles in volume and turns pale yellow. At this stage, the whisk should leave a distinct trail when passed through the sauce. Remove the mixing bowl from the pan of water and gradually add the melted butter, whisking continuously. The finished hollandaise should have the consistency of ketchup. If it is too thick, add some of the reserved reduction to thin it. Season to taste with salt and pepper, and stir in the chopped parsley. Keep the hollandaise in a warm place (but do not set the pan on a stove burner) until ready to serve.

To prepare the vegetables: bring a medium saucepan filled with salted water to a boil. Rinse the fiddlehead ferns, add them to the pan, and blanch for 1 minute, or until tender but still bright green. Remove with a sieve or slotted spoon and refresh in a large bowl of ice water until cool, then drain.

Place the oil in a large skillet over high heat. Season the halibut filets with salt and freshly ground white pepper and place them in the hot oil, searing for 1 minute before reducing the heat to medium. Add 1 teaspoon of butter to the pan and continue cooking the filets for 3 to 4 minutes, or until golden brown on one side. Turn the filets and cook for 5 minutes longer, until cooked through. The thickness of the filets will determine the exact cooking time. The goal is to have a golden brown exterior with a moist center.

Melt the remaining teaspoon of butter in a large sauté pan over high heat. Add the chopped shallot and sauté until translucent but not browned. Add the mushrooms and cook over high heat for 3 minutes, tossing occasionally. Stir in the fiddlehead ferns and season to taste with salt and pepper.

To serve, preheat the broiler. If four shallow, heat-resistant serving bowls are available, divide the fiddlehead and mushroom mixture among them. Place a halibut filet on top of each serving and cover it with hollandaise. Run the bowls under a hot broiler for a few seconds, until the hollandaise turns golden brown. Alternatively, place the halibut filets on a baking sheet, cover each filet with hollandaise, and run the baking sheet under the broiler, just until the hollandaise turns golden brown. Arrange the glazed filets in four shallow bowls on top of the fiddlehead and mushroom mixture. Drizzle with Parsley Oil and serve.

**Note:** Blended oil is a mixture of 90 percent vegetable oil and 10 percent olive oil.

FIDDLEHEAD FERNS

IN SPRING THE FOREST FLOOR IS COVERED WITH BABY FERNS SHAPED
LIKE THE HEAD OF A FIDDLE. FIDDLEHEAD FERNS HAVE A UNIQUE FLAVOR THAT COMBINES
THE FRESH GREEN TASTE OF ASPARAGUS WITH THE RICHER NOTES OF ARTICHOKE.

PARSLEY OIL

*Makes 1 cup*

1 bunch fresh parsley

1 cup blended oil (see Note)

Fill a medium saucepan with water and bring it to a boil. Drop the parsley into the boiling water for a few seconds, then drain and refresh in a large bowl of ice water until cool.

Squeeze all excess liquid from the blanched parsley and place it in the jar of a blender with the oil. Blend the mixture on high for 30 seconds, until the parsley is pureed. Strain the oil through a fine sieve lined with cheesecloth. Store any remaining parsley oil in a covered container in the refrigerator.

**Note:** Blended oil is a mixture of 90 percent vegetable oil and 10 percent olive oil.

# ICED CANTALOUPE AND LYCHEE SOUP

*This chilled soup has such a delicious melony fragrance,*
*your guests will be tempted to take time out from eating simply to sit*
*and smell it. But encourage them to eat this soup*
*while it's still icy cold, as it provides a refreshing contrast*
*to the herbed lamb dish that follows. If you can't find fresh lychees,*
*frozen or canned lychees can be substituted.*

*Serves 4*

2 cups peeled, diced cantaloupe

1 cup peeled and pitted fresh lychees

1 cup white dessert wine, such as muscat

1 cup champagne, chilled

In the jar of a blender, combine the cantaloupe, lychees, and dessert wine. Purée, working in batches if necessary, until completely smooth.

Strain the puréed fruit mixture through a fine sieve into a stainless steel or glass pitcher and chill until ready to serve. Just before serving, gently stir the chilled champagne into the fruit mixture. Divide among four soup bowls and serve.

# HERB-ROASTED SPRING LAMB
## WITH TOMATO CHARDONNAY SAUCE
## ON RATATOUILLE AND PESTO POTATO PURÉE

*Because this dish has several components—the roasted lamb,
a sauce flavored with two different reduced meat stocks (or jus, as reduced stocks
are called in a French kitchen), and two vegetable accompaniments—it does require
advance planning. The stocks can be made days ahead of time and refrigerated
(or even weeks in advance and frozen) until you are ready to make the sauce.
The pesto will also keep for several days properly stored and refrigerated,
and the ratatouille actually tastes best if made a day before serving. Have your butcher
french the rack of lamb by scraping away any meat and fat from the upper portion
of the bones. The final presentation is so full of intense flavor and color that you
and your guests will find it well worth the advance effort.*

*Serves 4*

1 cup plain dried bread crumbs

2 tablespoons mixed dried herbs (rosemary, parsley,
chervil, and tarragon)

2 pounds lamb rump, trimmed of all fat

1½ pounds rack of lamb, frenched

Salt and freshly ground pepper

2 tablespoons unsalted butter

2 teaspoons Dijon mustard

2 cups Ratatouille (see page 34)

1½ cups Pesto Potato Purée (see page 35)

4 red baby bell peppers,
roasted, peeled, seeded, and halved

1 cup Tomato Chardonnay Sauce (see page 37)

4 Herb Chips, for garnish (see page 38)

Preheat the oven to 350°F.

Combine the bread crumbs and dried herbs in the bowl of a food processor and pulse until very finely chopped. Pass this mixture through a medium sieve set over a large bowl to remove any large pieces.

Season the lamb rump and rack of lamb with salt and pepper. Heat a large, heavy skillet over high heat and add 1 tablespoon butter. Working with one piece of lamb at a time, sear the meat in the hot pan, turning so that all sides are lightly browned. Spread the mustard on the back of the lamb rack and roll it in the herb-and-bread crumb mixture until evenly coated.

Place both pieces of lamb on a rack inside a baking pan and roast for about 10 minutes, or until a meat thermometer placed in the center of the lamb rack reads 110°F for medium rare or 140° for medium. Allow the lamb to rest in a warm place for 10 minutes before carving. Just before serving, cut the lamb rack into four equal portions and slice the rump into medallions.

To serve, place ½ cup of the Ratatouille in the center of each plate. Using two teaspoons, shape heaped spoonfuls of the hot Pesto Potato Purée into eight ovals, rounded on top and bottom, and place one inside each roasted red pepper half. Place two stuffed pepper halves on each plate. Arrange the individual portions of carved lamb on top of the Ratatouille. Whisk the remaining tablespoon of butter into the Tomato Chardonnay Sauce and drizzle 1 to 2 tablespoons over each serving of the lamb. Garnish each plate with an Herb Chip.

# Ratatouille

*This classic Provençal dish
of gently cooked vegetables improves in flavor
when made a day in advance.*

*Makes 4 cups*

1 medium eggplant, peeled

1 medium zucchini

1 medium yellow squash

1 red bell pepper

1 yellow bell pepper

1 yellow onion

1 clove garlic

$\frac{1}{4}$ cup olive oil

$\frac{1}{2}$ cup V-8 juice

Salt and freshly ground pepper

Cut the eggplant, zucchini, yellow squash, red pepper, and yellow pepper into $\frac{1}{4}$-inch dice, keeping each ingredient separate. Mince the onion and garlic.

Heat the olive oil in a large skillet over medium heat. Add the onion and garlic and cook for 3 minutes, until transparent but not brown.

Increase the heat to medium high and add the peppers, yellow squash, zucchini, and eggplant at 1-minute intervals, stirring continuously. Once all the ingredients have been added, cook the vegetable mixture 5 minutes longer.

Add the V-8 juice and cook over medium high heat for 5 minutes longer. Season to taste with salt and pepper.

PESTO POTATO PURÉE

*Makes about 2 cups*

½ pound Idaho potatoes, peeled and cut into rough dice

¼ cup olive oil

4 tablespoons (½ stick) unsalted butter

2 tablespoons Pesto (see page 36)

Fill a medium saucepan with salted water and bring to a boil. Add the potatoes and cook for 10 to 15 minutes, until easily pierced by a fork. Drain and place in a large bowl. Add the olive oil and butter, and mash just until the lumps disappear. Avoid overmashing the potatoes, which will release starches and make them gooey.

Cover the puréed potatoes and keep in a warm place while preparing the rest of the meal. Just before serving, add the Pesto and mix well.

A SENIOR MEMBER OF THE HOUSEKEEPING STAFF MAKES HER ROUNDS
TO KEEP PILLOWS PLUMPED, COVERS SMOOTHED, FLOWERS FRESH, AND EVERY DETAIL
CAREFULLY REVIEWED FOR THE COMFORT AND CONVENIENCE OF GUESTS.

## PESTO

*Properly stored, pesto will keep without changing color
for several days. Transfer the finished pesto to a nonreactive glass
or stainless steel container. Pour a thin layer of olive oil
over the pesto and cover the container with aluminum
foil to keep out light and air.*

*Makes about 1½ cups*

1 bunch fresh basil leaves

½ bunch fresh flat leaf parsley

1 clove garlic

¾ cup freshly grated
Parmesan cheese

1 cup olive oil

¼ cup shelled pistachios

¼ cup pine nuts

¼ cup shelled walnuts

Salt and freshly ground pepper

Combine the basil, parsley, garlic, cheese, and olive oil in the bowl of a food processor and pulse until finely chopped.

Add the nuts and chop for a few more seconds, being careful not to overprocess the mixture. The nuts should be chopped to a medium texture but not finely ground.

Season the pesto with salt and pepper to taste. Refrigerate until ready to use.

# Tomato Chardonnay Sauce

*Before mixed vegetable juices such as V-8 juice were commercially available,
cooks often used tomato purée to add flavor and texture to stocks and
sauces. Chef Cartwright likes to use mixed vegetable juice instead, because
it has a milder flavor than tomato purée. Another common addition
to the stockpot is mirepoix, a mixture of sautéed aromatic vegetables.
V-8 juice serves as a kind of instant mirepoix.*

*Makes about 1½ cups*

1 tablespoon unsalted butter

1 medium onion, diced

2 medium tomatoes, diced

6 sprigs fresh basil

6 sprigs fresh parsley

1 cup chardonnay
(or other full-bodied white wine)

1 cup V-8 juice

1 cup Veal Jus (see page 68)

1 cup Lamb Jus (see page 68)

Salt and freshly ground pepper

In a medium saucepan with a heavy bottom, melt the butter over medium high
heat. Add the onions, tomatoes, basil, and parsley and sauté for 3 to 4 minutes, until
the onions are transparent but not brown and the tomatoes begin to break down.

Add the chardonnay and cook over high heat until the mixture is reduced by
half. Add the V-8 juice, Veal Jus, and Lamb Jus, and continue cooking over high
heat until the mixture is slightly reduced, about 5 minutes.

Reduce the heat to medium low and simmer the sauce for 30 minutes. Strain
through a fine sieve and season with salt and pepper to taste.

HERB CHIPS

*If you don't have Silpat nonstick baking mats,*
*you can make these herb chips by placing the potato slices on a nonstick*
*baking sheet or a regular baking sheet coated with vegetable spray.*
*Then cover them during baking with a glass baking dish.*

*Makes 4*

1 large Idaho potato, peeled

4 sprigs fresh flat-leaf parsley or fresh chervil

Preheat the oven to 300° F.

Cut the potato into wafer-thin slices using a mandoline or a Japanese vegetable slicer. Reserve the eight largest slices and discard the rest.

Place a Silpat mat on a baking sheet. Place four potato slices on the mat. Lay a small herb sprig in the center of each potato slice. Top with another potato slice to form four "sandwiches," aligning the edges of the potato slices as closely as possible. Cover the potato slices with another Silpat mat.

Bake the chips for 5 to 10 minutes, until golden brown and crisp.

# GRILLED BREAST OF GUINEA HEN
## ON CREAMED SPINACH WITH POTATOES, SPRING PEAS,
## AND A WOODLAND MUSHROOM SAUCE

*This is a lovely spring-flavored game recipe that you can substitute
for the entrée in either of the formal menus in this section.
While many Americans don't like to eat heavier-tasting game birds,
they tend to love the light, savory meat of guinea hen, which tastes like
a very flavorful chicken. If you can't find guinea hens,
substitute free-range chicken.*

*Serves 4*

5 tablespoons unsalted butter

1 cup chanterelles or other wild mushrooms,
rinsed, drained, and towel dried

1 cup full-bodied white wine such as chardonnay

2 cups Guinea Hen Jus (see page 42)

1 tablespoon chopped shallots

1 pound fresh spinach, stemmed, washed, and drained

½ pound shelled English peas

½ pound shelled fava beans

12 new potatoes or small white potatoes, peeled

1 cup heavy cream

4 split guinea hen breasts, boned, with wing attached and skin on

Salt and freshly ground pepper

In a medium sauté pan, melt 1 tablespoon of butter over medium high heat. Add
the mushrooms and sauté for 2 minutes. Stir in the white wine. Remove the mushrooms with a slotted spoon and reserve. Increase the heat to high and boil until the
wine has almost completely evaporated. Add the Guinea Hen Jus and return to a
boil. Continue cooking over high heat until the sauce reduces and thickens enough
to coat the back of a spoon. Remove from the heat.

In a large sauté pan, melt 1 tablespoon of butter. Add the chopped shallots and sauté until soft and transparent. Add the spinach and cook for 1 minute, tossing until it is wilted and tender. Transfer the spinach to a sieve and press it to remove any excess liquid.

Bring 4 cups of water to a boil in a large saucepan. Add the peas and the fava beans and blanch for 2 minutes. Drain and rinse immediately with cold water. Remove the skins from the fava beans.

Preheat the oven to 400°F.

In a shallow ovenproof casserole large enough to hold the hen breasts and the potatoes, melt 2 tablespoons of butter over medium high heat. Add the peeled potatoes and turn to coat with butter. Place the casserole in the oven and bake for 15 minutes, or until the potatoes are easily pierced by a fork.

Pour the cream into a medium saucepan with a heavy bottom. Bring to a boil over medium high heat, then reduce the heat and simmer until the cream is reduced by half. Combine the reduced cream and the spinach in the bowl of a food processor and pulse several times to form a purée. Season to taste with salt and pepper.

Preheat a gas or charcoal grill. Grill the hen breasts for 3 minutes on each side, until lightly browned but not cooked through. Reduce the oven temperature to 350°F.

Transfer the guinea hen breasts to the center of the casserole with the potatoes. Surround with the potatoes. Place the casserole in the oven and bake for 8 minutes, until the juices run clear.

While the hen breasts are in the oven, warm the spinach purée in a medium saucepan with a heavy bottom. Melt the remaining tablespoon of butter in a large sauté pan over medium low heat and add the blanched English peas and fava beans, tossing just to warm through. Season to taste with salt and pepper. Return the mushrooms to the reduced sauce and warm over low heat.

To serve, spoon a portion of spinach purée in the center of each plate. Place a hen breast on top of the spinach. Divide the peas, fava beans, and potatoes into four portions, placing them around the edge of each plate. Spoon the mushroom sauce over the hen breasts and potatoes and serve.

GUINEA HEN JUS

*The exact proportions of vegetables and herbs are not what matters
in this stock recipe. Just use what you've got on hand
to create a well-balanced flavor.*

*Makes 3 cups*

4 pounds guinea hen bones or chicken bones

½ pound ( about 1 cup) diced mixed aromatic vegetables,
such as carrots, leeks, onions, and celery

1 clove garlic, crushed

12 sprigs fresh herbs, such as thyme, rosemary, and tarragon

1 cup dry, fruity white wine, such as sauvignon blanc

Preheat the oven to 450°F.

Place the bones in a large roasting pan and roast, turning occasionally, for 15 minutes, until golden brown. Add the vegetables to the pan and continue roasting for 5 minutes.

Transfer the bones and vegetables to a large stockpot and add the garlic, herbs, and white wine. Cover with water and bring to a boil over high heat, skimming off any scum that rises to the surface. Reduce the heat to medium and simmer the stock for 4 hours, until reduced by half.

Strain the stock through a fine sieve into a clean saucepan. Bring to a boil over medium high heat, then reduce the heat to medium and cook until reduced by half. The finished jus will have the consistency of a lightweight sauce.

Reserve 2 cups of jus for the Woodland Mushroom Sauce and freeze the remainder in ice cube trays. When frozen, transfer the cubes of stock to zipper-lock bags and store in the freezer for future use.

# LEMON BALM SOUFFLÉ AND
# ROSEWATER ICE CREAM

*There's a myth that soufflés are difficult to make. They're actually quite simple
as long as you follow the recipe carefully. Timing is important, too.
The uncooked soufflés can stand on the kitchen counter for up to 30 minutes before
you bake them. Just put them in the preheated oven 15 minutes before you
want to serve dessert, and they'll come out perfectly.*

*Serves 8*

## SOUFFLÉ BASE

2 cups milk

¾ cup sugar

8 to 10 sprigs fresh lemon balm

3 egg yolks

½ cup crème patissière powder
(or ¼ cup all-purpose flour sifted with ¼ cup cornstarch)

Combine the milk, half the sugar, and the lemon balm in a medium saucepan with
a heavy bottom. Bring to a boil over medium high heat, then transfer the mixture
to a nonreactive glass or stainless steel storage container and let cool to room temperature. Cover and refrigerate for 24 hours to allow the flavor to develop fully.

Strain the infused milk mixture through a sieve into a clean saucepan. Bring to
a boil over medium high heat, then immediately remove from the heat.

In a large bowl, beat the egg yolks until smooth. Beat in the remaining sugar and
the crème patissière powder (or flour-and-cornstarch mixture).

Add a few tablespoons of the hot milk mixture to the egg yolk mixture and beat
until combined. Beat in a few more tablespoons, and repeat this step once more to
bring the egg mixture gradually to the temperature of the hot milk mixture without
curdling the eggs.

Slowly add the warmed egg mixture to the hot milk, whisking constantly. Cook
over low heat, whisking constantly, until the mixture is thick enough to coat the
back of a spoon. Let cool to room temperature.

## SOUFFLÉ

2 tablespoons unsalted butter

3½ tablespoons sugar, plus additional for dusting

4 egg yolks

½ cup limoncello,
or other lemon-flavored liqueur

Soufflé Base (see page 43)

8 egg whites

Preheat the oven to 375°F. Butter eight ramekins (3½ inches in diameter, 1½ inches deep) and dust them with a small amount of sugar, shaking out any excess.

In a large bowl, combine the egg yolks and limoncello, and beat until the mixture is foamy and light in color. Add the Soufflé Base and stir vigorously.

In another large bowl, combine the egg whites with the sugar. Using an electric mixer, beat the mixture until it forms soft peaks. Carefully fold the beaten egg whites into the soufflé base mixture.

Fill the ramekins with the mixture and place them on a rack in the center of the oven. Bake for 15 minutes, or until golden and puffed.

Serve immediately. At the table, break a hole in the center of each soufflé and pour in a small amount of Lemon Sauce (see page 46).

LEMON SAUCE

*Makes 2 cups*

1 cup sugar

½ cup fresh lemon juice

5½ tablespoons limoncello or
other lemon-flavored liqueur

In a medium saucepan with a heavy bottom, combine the sugar and 1 cup of water. Bring to a boil over high heat, and continue to cook until the mixture caramelizes into a light golden brown syrup.

Remove from the heat and add the lemon juice. Return to medium heat, and whisk the syrup until the lemon juice is thoroughly incorporated.

Remove the syrup from the heat and whisk in the limoncello. Let cool to room temperature. The sauce will keep, covered and refrigerated, for two weeks.

ADVANCE PREPARATION IS THE KEY TO SUCCESS IN
A PROFESSIONAL KITCHEN WHERE AS MANY AS 15 COOKS WORK
TOGETHER THROUGHOUT THE DAY TO PREPARE DINNER.
MANY RECIPES IN THIS BOOK CAN BE PARTIALLY PREPARED HOURS,
AND IN SOME CASES, EVEN A DAY IN ADVANCE,
MAKING IT EASIER FOR HOME CHEFS TO ENJOY
THEIR OWN DINNER PARTIES.

# Rosewater Ice Cream

*The flavor of this ice cream is wonderfully subtle and
surprising. Paired with the lemon balm soufflé,
it is reminiscent of the citrusy smell of the wild rosebushes
that grow along the waterfront in Kennebunkport.*

*Makes 4 cups*

2 cups heavy cream

1½ cups half-and-half

¼ cup rosewater

1 cup sugar

1 dozen egg yolks

In a medium saucepan with a heavy bottom, combine the cream, half-and-half, rosewater, and sugar. Bring to a boil over medium high heat, stirring constantly to avoid scorching the mixture on the bottom of the pan.

In a large bowl, beat the egg yolks until foamy and light yellow in color. Add a few tablespoons of the hot cream mixture to the egg yolks and beat until combined. Beat in a few more tablespoons of the hot cream and repeat this step once more to bring the egg yolk mixture to the temperature of the hot cream mixture without curdling the yolks.

Slowly add the warmed egg yolk mixture to the hot cream mixture, whisking constantly. Cook over low heat, whisking constantly, until thick enough to coat the back of a spoon.

Strain the mixture through a sieve into a large bowl to remove any lumps and refrigerate until cool.

Freeze in an ice cream machine, following the manufacturer's instructions. Serve a small scoop of the ice cream on the dessert plate next to the Lemon Balm Soufflé.

## A Springtime Picnic

Grilled salmon is an elegant picnic dish that is also practical. If you are picnicking in a place with barbecue facilities, you can grill it on the spot (but be sure to keep the raw salmon on ice before you cook it). Otherwise, you can grill the salmon ahead of time and serve it cold over the vegetable salad.

# RHUBARB SMOOTHIES

*Smoothies transport easily in an insulated thermal container
and make a refreshing accompaniment to an outdoor meal.*

*Serves 4*

2 cups Rhubarb Purée

6 tablespoons plain yogurt

2 cups milk

4 scoops rhubarb or strawberry sorbet

Working in two batches, combine all the ingredients in the jar of a
blender. Blend just until smooth.

Serve at once in chilled glasses, or if transporting for a picnic,
pour into a chilled insulated thermal container.

---

# RHUBARB PURÉE

*Makes 2 cups*

3 cups diced rhubarb

6 tablespoons sugar

Combine the rhubarb, sugar, and 2 tablespoons of water in a medium saucepan. Bring the mixture to a boil over medium heat, stirring
occasionally. Reduce the heat to low and cover the pan. Cook over
low heat for 15 minutes, stirring occasionally.

Cool the mixture and purée it in a blender or food processor
until smooth. Strain the purée to remove any fibers and refrigerate
until ready to use.

# GRILLED SALMON WITH
## SPRING FIDDLEHEADS, ASPARAGUS,
## AND SCALLIONS

*The bright green flavors of fiddlehead ferns and asparagus dressed
in a very light vinaigrette really shine in this salad.
Slicing the asparagus tips in half reveals their delicate, leafy texture
and provides more surface for the dressing to cling to.*

*Serves 4*

1 cup fiddlehead ferns

1 bunch scallions

1 bunch medium asparagus,
woody ends trimmed

1 ripe tomato

1 teaspoon grainy mustard

¼ cup champagne vinegar

½ cup olive oil

Salt and freshly ground pepper

2 sprigs fresh chervil

1 pound center-cut salmon filet,
cut into four pieces

Preheat a gas or charcoal grill.

Rinse and drain the fiddlehead ferns. Slice the scallions on the diagonal into ¼-inch pieces. Cut the asparagus spears on the diagonal into ½-inch pieces. Seed the tomato and cut it into fine dice.

Bring a medium saucepan filled with salted water to a boil. Add the fiddlehead ferns and blanch for 1 minute, or until tender but still bright green. Remove them with a slotted spoon and refresh them in a large bowl of ice water until cool, then drain. Repeat this step with the scallions and then with the asparagus pieces.

Place the mustard in a medium, nonreactive glas or stainless steel bowl.

Whisk in the vinegar, then gradually whisk in the oil to form an emulsion. Season the dressing to taste with salt and pepper.

Drain the fiddleheads, scallions, and asparagus and combine them in a large salad bowl with 2 tablespoons of the diced tomato. Remove the leaves from the chervil sprigs and add them to the mixture. Add enough vinaigrette to dress the salad lightly and toss, seasoning to taste with salt and pepper. Divide the salad among four serving plates.

Season the salmon filets with salt and pepper to taste. Oil the grill grate and place the filets directly over the heat. Cook for 4 minutes on each side. Arrange the grilled filets on top of the salad and serve.

FRESH FISH IS FIRMLY FLESHED AND DELICATELY SCENTED OF THE SEA. EACH MORNING, THE CHEF OF THE WHITE BARN INN PERSONALLY SELECTS JUST-CAUGHT SEAFOOD FROM NEARBY DOCKS. HERE, HE FILETS WHOLE FISH TO SERVE FOR DINNER THAT EVENING.

# A Selection of Cheeses
# with Red Currant Chutney

For an interesting and flavorful selection of cheeses, combine hard and creamy-textured cheeses and choose those made from a variety of milks: cow, sheep, and goat. Blue cheese makes a nice tangy addition. We use Berkshire Blue, a creamy, aged Stilton-style cheese that's especially good in summer when the cows graze on rich green grass. We also serve Bonne Bouche, a smooth, ash-ripened goat cheese made in Vermont, as well as Vermont Shepherd, a beautiful, handmade sheep's milk cheese with a rich, dry flavor, and a blue Jersey cow's milk cheese from Massachusetts. American artisanal dairies are producing some delicious cheeses, so it's worth seeking out a high-grade domestic variety made on a nearby dairy farm. Domestic cheeses can often taste better than imported ones that may have been allowed to overripen. We serve our cheese course with homemade fruit chutneys that complement the flavors of the cheese as well as satisfy the desire for something sweet at the end of the meal.

# RED CURRANT CHUTNEY

*Makes about 1 cup*

½ cup sugar

¼ cup champagne vinegar

1 cup fresh red currants

Pinch ground ginger

Place the sugar in a medium sauté pan over medium heat and shake the pan, evenly distributing the sugar until it melts and turns into a golden brown syrup. Remove the pan from the heat and carefully add the vinegar. The mixture will bubble and "spit." When it settles, stir it gently. If some of the caramelized syrup has hardened, return the pan to the stove over medium heat and stir the mixture until the hardened bits dissolve.

Add the red currants and ginger. Cook the mixture over medium heat for 5 minutes, stirring occasionally, until some but not all of the currants break down. Remove from the heat and cool. The chutney will keep, covered and refrigerated, for up to ten days.

# A Spring Cocktail

## STARS AND STRIPES

*The inspiration for this cocktail comes from the red, white, and blue
striped bunting and flags hung around Kennebunkport in preparation for the Memorial
Day parade. The combination of orange-flavored vodka, tart Campari, and the sweet
citrus essence of Curaçao captures the tang of sea air on a breezy spring day.*

*Makes 1 large cocktail*

3½ ounces orange-flavored vodka

1 ounce Campari

½ ounce blue Curaçao

1 slice starfruit, for garnish

Mix the vodka and the Campari over ice in a shaker. Strain into a chilled martini glass.
Slowly pour the blue Curaçao into the center of the glass. It will form a blue layer float-
ing above the red layer in the bottom of the glass. Garnish with the slice of starfruit.

# A Spring Seafood Menu

When people visit Kennebunkport, they usually bring an appetite for fresh seafood. This menu reveals many different flavors of the sea, from sweet scallops and lobster meat to mild, buttery cod loin. Each recipe features sauces and garnishes that complement the taste and texture of the particular seafood, offering variety throughout the meal.

## DIVER-HARVESTED SCALLOPS ON ASPARAGUS WITH CHAMPAGNE FOAM AND CAVIAR

*This beautiful amuse bouche perfectly captures the salty-sweet essence of the Maine coast.
The champagne foam looks like the edge of a frothy wave. Diver-harvested scallops
are removed by hand from the ocean bed. This method results in large, well-shaped scallops
and, even more importantly, does not disturb the ocean floor.*

*Serves 4*

2 teaspoons unsalted butter

1 shallot, diced

1 cup champagne

1 cup heavy cream

Salt, freshly ground pepper, and cayenne

Fresh lemon juice

8 asparagus spears, woody ends trimmed

1 tablespoon blended oil (see Note)

4 diver harvested scallops

1 tablespoon osetra caviar

In a medium saucepan, melt 1 teaspoon of the butter. Add the shallots and sauté for 1 minute, or until translucent but not browned. Add ¾ cup champagne to the pan and reduce the mixture by half over medium high heat. Add the cream and reduce the heat to medium. Cook the sauce until it is thick enough to coat the back of a spoon. Season to taste with salt, pepper, cayenne, and a drop or two of lemon juice.

Bring a medium saucepan of salted water to a boil. Peel the asparagus stalks and cut into 1-inch pieces. Add to the boiling water and cook just until tender but still bright green, about 2 minutes. Refresh in a large bowl of ice water until cool, then drain.

Heat the oil in a small sauté pan. Season the scallops with salt and pepper and sear in the oil for 2 minutes on each side, or until golden brown and firm to the touch.

In a clean sauté pan, melt the remaining teaspoon of butter. Add the drained asparagus and toss gently to coat with the melted butter.

Divide the asparagus among four serving plates. Place one scallop on each plate, on top of the asparagus. Top each scallop with caviar.

Reheat the sauce and add the remaining champagne. Using a hand-held blender, beat the sauce to form a light foam. Spoon the sauce over each serving, using the foamiest part of the sauce to top the scallops and caviar.

**Note:** Blended oil is a mixture of 90 percent vegetable oil and 10 percent olive oil.

# Lobster Spring Roll
## with Carrot, Daikon Radish,
## and Snow Peas in a
## Thai-inspired Spicy Sweet Sauce

*This recipe takes its inspiration from the popular Thai spring roll.
The sweetness of the vegetables complements the taste of the lobster, and the spicy
sauce provides a little kick. Guests enjoy putting down their forks and knives
and eating this course with their fingers. Fry only as many rolls as you need for your
appetizer course. One roll per person is usually sufficient for a light appetizer.
You can refrigerate the remaining rolls on a plate, covered with a towel,
to cook the next day. Look for spring roll wrappers in the refrigerated section
of large supermarkets or Asian grocery stores.*

### Makes 8

1 teaspoon toasted sesame oil

2 large carrots, peeled and julienned

1 medium daikon radish, peeled and julienned

10 snow peas, julienned

1 (1-inch) piece of ginger, peeled and
finely chopped

1 teaspoon oyster sauce

1 tablespoon soy sauce

1 pound cooked lobster meat, chopped

8 spring roll wrappers

1 egg yolk, beaten

Vegetable oil, for frying

Cilantro Oil (see page 62)

Thai-Inspired Spicy Sweet Sauce (see page 62)

In a large sauté pan, heat the sesame oil over medium high heat. Add the carrots, daikon radish, and snow peas and stir-fry for 1 minute. Add the ginger, oyster sauce, and soy sauce and stir to combine. Remove the vegetables from the heat.

In a large bowl, combine half of the vegetable mixture with the lobster meat. Divide the mixture into eight equal portions, squeezing out any extra moisture.

On a dry work surface, lay out one spring roll wrapper. Using your hands, roll one of the portions of vegetable-and-lobster mixture into a cylinder and place in the center of the top edge of the wrapper.

Brush the egg yolk down the left and right edges of the wrapper and fold the edges over to cover the ends of the filling. Roll the filling down the length of the wrapper, tucking in the outside edges to make a tight roll. Seal the seam with more egg yolk. Repeat with the remaining wrappers and filling. The rolls can be fried immediately or kept covered with a towel in the refrigerator for up to 24 hours before frying.

Pour 2 inches of vegetable oil into a heavy skillet and heat over medium high heat until the oil reaches 350°F on a deep-fry thermometer. Carefully place the rolls in the hot oil and deep-fry for 5 minutes, or until golden brown on all sides.

Using tongs, remove the spring rolls from the oil and drain on paper towels. Slice them in half, cutting on the diagonal. Arrange the rolls on serving plates, surrounded with the remaining stir-fried vegetables. Drizzle Cilantro Oil and Thai-Inspired Spicy Sweet Sauce over the rolls.

## Cilantro Oil

*Makes 1 cup*

1 bunch fresh cilantro

1 cup vegetable oil

Fill a medium saucepan with water and bring it to a boil. Drop the cilantro into the boiling water for a few seconds, then drain and refresh in a large bowl of ice water until cool.

Squeeze all excess liquid from the blanched cilantro and place it in the jar of a blender with the oil. Blend on high for 30 seconds, until the cilantro is puréed. Strain the oil through a fine sieve lined with cheesecloth. Store any remaining cilantro oil in a covered container in the refrigerator.

---

## Thai-Inspired Spicy Sweet Sauce

*This recipe yields more sauce than you will need for
the Lobster Spring Roll. The remaining sauce will keep, covered, in the refrigerator
for up to two weeks. It makes a delicious stir-fry sauce for vegetables
or a flavorful dipping sauce for cooked shrimp, fried shrimp crackers, or crudités.*

*Makes 2 cups*

2 cups sugar

¼ cup soy sauce

¼ teaspoon hot pepper flakes (or half a dried hot pepper)

1 garlic clove, minced

In a large saucepan with a heavy bottom, combine 2 cups water with the sugar, soy sauce, hot pepper flakes, and garlic. Bring to a boil over high heat.

Reduce the heat to medium high and cook until the sauce is reduced slightly and coats the back of a spoon. Remove the dried hot pepper half, if used.

# KALAMANSI
# SOUR LEMON SORBET

*Now that many people have their own ice cream makers, home chefs
have discovered how easy it is to make fruit sorbets.
There's no reason to save sorbet for dessert. At the White Barn Inn,
we serve tart fruit sorbet as an intermezzo during a formal dinner. The flavor
clears the tastes of the previous course and lingers just a few minutes
on the tongue, priming the palate for the main course. This sorbet is made
from puréed kalamansi, a small, sour, limelike citrus common in the Philippines
that tastes like a cross between a lemon and a mandarin orange.
If you can't find kalamansi purée in a local gourmet store or catalog, then
substitute a mixture of pulpy lime and mandarin orange juice.*

*Makes 2 quarts*

2 cups sugar

4 cups kalamansi purée
(or 3 cups lime juice and 1 cup mandarin orange juice)

In a medium saucepan, combine the sugar with 3 cups of water and bring to a
boil over medium high heat. Place the kalamansi purée in a large, nonreactive
glass or stainless steel bowl and pour in the hot syrup, stirring to blend thoroughly. Alternatively, stir the lime and orange juices into the hot syrup, mixing
well. Refrigerate until cool.

Freeze in an ice cream machine, following the manufacturer's instructions.

# GRILLED TOURNEDOS OF LOCAL COD LOIN
## WITH CRISPY SHRIMP AND CALAMARI ON A SPRING PEA
## PURÉE WITH A PIQUANT SAUCE

*This recipe plays with the English idea of fish and chips in a very refined way.*
*The spring pea purée is reminiscent of the mushy peas commonly eaten*
*in England as an accompaniment to fried fish. The crispy shrimp and potatoes offer*
*that deep-fried crunch, and the piquant sauce adds a refreshing, spicy contrast.*
*To keep the potato sticks from falling apart when frying, it is important*
*to coat them thoroughly with the bread crumbs.*

*Serves 4*

¾ pound cod loin,
cut into four tournedos (1-inch-thick slices)

6 tablespoons olive oil,
plus extra for rubbing the tournedos

Salt, freshly ground black pepper,
and cayenne to taste

½ pound fresh spring peas (1 cup shelled peas)

¼ pound cleaned calamari,
cut into bite-size rings, with tentacles

1 teaspoon fresh lemon juice

1 large potato, peeled and diced

3 tablespoons unsalted butter

2 eggs

2 tablespoons flour

⅓ cup plain bread crumbs

¾ pound Maine shrimp or rock shrimp, peeled

Vegetable oil, for deep frying

Piquant Sauce (see page 67)

Preheat a gas or charcoal grill.

Using butcher's twine, tie each cod tournedo around the perimeter to keep its shape. Rub the tournedos with a little olive oil and season with salt and pepper. Grill for 1 or 2 minutes on each side. They will be partially cooked. Remove from the grill to a plate.

Fill a medium saucepan with water and bring to a boil. Drop the peas into the boiling water and cook until tender but still bright green, about 4 minutes. Drain and refresh in a large bowl of ice water until cool, then drain again. Purée the cooked peas in a food processor, then pass the mixture through a medium sieve to remove any lumps.

Heat the 6 tablespoons of olive oil in a medium skillet over high heat. Add the calamari pieces and sear for 3 minutes, tossing occasionally. Do not overcook. Remove from the heat immediately, sprinkle with the lemon juice, and season with salt and pepper.

Preheat the oven to 350°F.

Fill a medium saucepan with water and bring to a boil over high heat. Add the diced potatoes and boil until they are easily pierced by a fork. Drain the potatoes and dry them on a baking sheet in the hot oven for 3 to 4 minutes. In a large bowl, combine the potatoes with 2 tablespoons of the butter and mash until the lumps disappear. Season with salt and pepper.

Fill a pastry bag with the potato purée. Using a quarter-inch plain tip, pipe the purée onto a sheet of waxed paper into strips 2 inches long.

In a shallow bowl, beat the eggs. Fill another shallow bowl with the flour and a third with the bread crumbs.

Season the potato sticks and shrimp to taste with salt, pepper, and cayenne. Carefully dip the potato sticks in the flour, then the beaten eggs, then the bread crumbs. Take care that the potato sticks are completely coated in the bread crumbs.

Pour 2 inches of vegetable oil into a heavy pot and heat over medium high heat until the oil reaches 350°F on a deep-fry thermometer. Carefully place the potato sticks in the hot oil and deep-fry for 4 minutes, or until golden brown. Remove the cooked sticks from the oil with a skimmer or slotted spoon and drain on paper towels. Bread and fry the shrimp in the same manner.

Place the grilled cod tournedos in a nonreactive baking dish and bake for 5 minutes, or until cooked through. While the fish is baking, reheat the pea purée in a medium saucepan with the remaining tablespoon of butter. Season to taste with salt and pepper.

To serve, spoon the pea purée in a ring in the center of each plate. Place a cod tournedo in the center of each ring and arrange the potatoes, shrimp, and calamari in a pile on one side. Drizzle with Piquant Sauce.

## PIQUANT SAUCE

*Makes 1 cup*

4 tablespoons (½ stick) unsalted butter

¼ cup diced yellow onion

¼ cup dry, fruity white wine, such as sauvignon blanc

¼ cup champagne vinegar

8 crushed black peppercorns

2 cups Veal Jus (see page 68)

1 tablespoon Dijon mustard

Salt and freshly ground pepper

In a medium saucepan with a heavy bottom, melt the butter over medium heat. Add the onion and sauté for about 5 minutes, until translucent but not browned. Stir in the wine, vinegar, and crushed peppercorns. Cook over medium heat for 5 minutes, or until reduced by half.

Add the Veal Jus, increase the heat to medium high, and bring the mixture to a boil. Reduce over high heat until the sauce becomes thick enough to coat the back of a spoon.

Remove the pan from the heat, whisk in the mustard until it is completely incorporated, and season to taste with salt and pepper. Strain through a fine sieve.

# VEAL OR LAMB JUS

*In French kitchens, reduced meat stock, called jus, forms the base for many sauces.
Use this formula to prepare lamb jus for the recipe on page 37 by substituting lamb bones
for the veal bones. If you are serious about cooking, it's a good idea to keep
a supply of different meat stocks and jus on hand. Whenever you are at the butcher shop,
buy extra bones and roast them. Then simmer them on the stove with
aromatic vegetables and herbs. When the stock has cooked for several hours,
cool it to room temperature, then freeze it.*

*Makes 6 cups.*

10 pounds veal or lamb bones

½ pound (about 1 cup) diced mixed aromatic vegetables,
such as carrot, leek, onion, and celery

1 cup dry red wine

4 medium tomatoes, diced

1 garlic clove, crushed

2 dozen fresh herb stems, such as thyme, rosemary, and tarragon

Preheat the oven to 450°F.

Place the bones in one or more large roasting pans and roast for about 30 minutes, turning occasionally, until golden brown. Add the diced vegetables and continue to roast for 5 minutes more.

Transfer the roasted bones and vegetables to a large stockpot. Add the wine and enough water to cover the bones. Bring to a boil over high heat. Skim off and discard any scum that rises to the surface.

Add the tomatoes, garlic, and herb stems to the stock. Reduce the heat to low and simmer for 4 to 6 hours, until the stock becomes dark and rich. Strain the stock through a colander, discarding the solids, and pour it into a clean saucepan. Cook over medium heat for about 40 minutes, until reduced by half.

Fill the kitchen sink half-full with ice and cold water. Cool the jus by placing the saucepan in the ice bath until cooled to room temperature. The jus will keep in the refrigerator for a couple of days, or in an airtight container in the freezer for up to two months.

# "TWICE-BAKED" RHUBARB CRÊPE SOUFFLÉ
# WITH BUTTERMILK ICE CREAM

*Although it sounds complicated, most of this dish can be prepared three hours
ahead of time. It combines the texture of a crêpe with the fluffiness of
a soufflé and tempers the tartness of rhubarb with sugar and apple liqueur.*

*Serves 4*

## CRÊPES

2 eggs

3 tablespoons sugar

½ cup half and half cream

2 tablespoons toasted almond flour or finely ground
toasted almonds

2 tablespoons flour

2 tablespoons unsalted butter, melted

In a large bowl, beat the eggs until foamy. Add the sugar and beat until combined. Add the cream, almond flour, flour, and melted butter, beating continuously to form a smooth batter.

Heat a 6-inch nonstick skillet over medium heat. Ladle about 3 tablespoons of the crêpe mixture into the skillet and swirl to cover the bottom of the pan. Cook over medium heat until the edges begin to turn light brown. Carefully flip the crêpe and continue cooking for 30 seconds. Transfer the crêpe to a plate and repeat until all the batter has been used.

## SOUFFLÉ

1 cup milk

3 tablespoons unsalted butter

3 tablespoons flour

¾ ounce Calvados

3 tablespoons granulated sugar, plus additional, for dusting

½ cup Rhubarb Purée (see page 49)

4 eggs, separated

Confectioners' sugar

Buttermilk Ice Cream (see page 72)

In a small saucepan with a heavy bottom, bring the milk to a boil. Remove from the heat and keep warm.

In a medium saucepan, melt the butter over medium low heat and whisk in the flour. Gradually pour in the hot milk to form a smooth sauce, whisking constantly to remove any lumps.

Remove from the heat and stir in the Calvados, sugar, and Rhubarb Purée. Beat the egg yolks and whisk them into the mixture, continuing to whisk until the soufflé base returns to room temperature.

Preheat the oven to 350°F.

In a large bowl, whisk the egg whites until they form stiff peaks. Carefully fold the beaten egg whites into the soufflé base.

Butter four ramekins (3½ inches in diameter, 1½ inches deep) and coat them with granulated sugar, shaking out any excess. Line each ramekin with one crêpe, tucking it carefully into the sides and bottom. Pour the soufflé mixture into the prepared ramekins. Place the ramekins in a baking pan and pour boiling water into the pan to reach almost halfway up the sides of the ramekins. Carefully place the pan in the oven and bake for 30 minutes, until the soufflés are golden on top and puffed.

Remove the pan from the oven. Remove the soufflés from the water bath and allow them to cool. They can be prepared 3 hours ahead of time up to this point.

Before serving, preheat the oven to 425°F.

Place the soufflés on a baking dish and bake for 5 minutes. The soufflés will collapse. Remove the soufflés from the oven and turn them out, crêpe side up, onto dessert plates. Sprinkle with confectioners' sugar and serve hot, with Buttermilk Ice Cream.

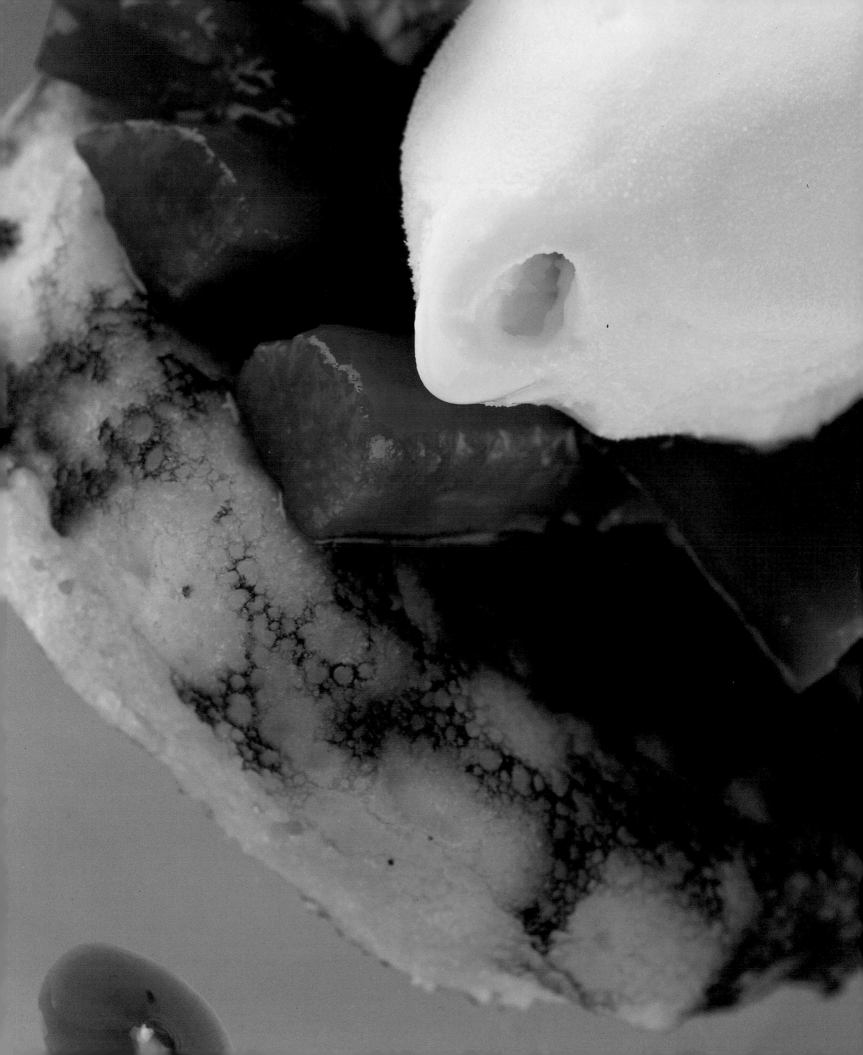

## BUTTERMILK ICE CREAM

*Buttermilk has such a rich, tangy flavor.*
*When made into ice cream,*
*it tastes a little like Devonshire clotted cream.*

*Makes about 1½ quarts*

2 cups heavy cream

2 cups buttermilk

1 vanilla bean

1 cup sugar

12 egg yolks

In a large saucepan with a heavy bottom, combine the heavy cream and buttermilk. Split the vanilla bean and scrape the seeds into the pan, then add the bean. Add ½ cup of the sugar and bring to a boil over medium high heat, stirring regularly to make sure that the mixture does not scorch on the bottom of the pan. Remove from the heat and let cool for a few minutes.

In a large bowl, beat the egg yolks. Add the remaining sugar and stir just to combine. Pour a small amount of the warm cream mixture into the egg yolks, stirring to temper and warm the egg yolks slightly. Then gradually pour the egg mixture into the saucepan with the cream mixture, stirring until thoroughly blended. Cook over medium heat, stirring constantly, until thick enough to coat the back of a wooden spoon.

Strain the custard through a fine sieve and allow it to cool completely. Freeze in an ice cream machine, following the manufacturer's instructions.

# *Breakfast by the Pool*

## BREAKFAST FRUIT BOWL

*By cutting several different kinds of fruit into half-inch dice and
tossing them together, you can create a confetti-like salad that accentuates
the fresh colors and textures of seasonal produce.*

*Serves 8*

1 cup sugar

1 cinnamon stick

1 vanilla bean

1 cantaloupe

1 honeydew melon

1 pineapple

4 oranges

2 kiwis

1 cup raspberries

In a medium saucepan, combine the sugar and cinnamon stick with 2 cups of water. Split the vanilla bean, scraping the seeds into the pan, and add the bean. Bring to a boil over medium high heat, stirring to dissolve the sugar. Remove the syrup from the heat. When it is cool, strain and discard the vanilla bean and cinnamon stick.

Remove the rind and seeds from the melons and cut into $\frac{1}{2}$-inch dice. Remove the skin and core from the pineapple and cut the fruit into $\frac{1}{2}$-inch dice. Peel the oranges, divide the fruit into sections, and cut each section in half. Peel and slice the kiwis. Rinse and drain the raspberries.

In a large bowl, gently combine the fruits with the syrup. The fruit salad will keep in the refrigerator, covered, for 2 hours before serving.

# POACHED EGGS ON
# KENNEBUNKPORT LOBSTER HASH

*This dish is inspired by the quintessential New England dish, hash.
Lobster is considered the queen of seafood, so it may seem a bit decadent to make
hash out of it—but a bit of decadence is what guests have come
to expect from the White Barn Inn. This version combines bits of lobster
with potato, bound with a sauce made from lobster bisque. If you prepare the
lobster bisque a day ahead of time, this recipe makes a quickly assembled brunch
dish sure to surprise and impress your guests. The eggs can be poached
2 to 3 hours ahead of time and kept in chilled water, to be reheated just before
serving. Any remaining lobster bisque can be enjoyed later for dinner.*

*Serves 4*

1 teaspoon white vinegar

Salt and freshly ground pepper

4 eggs

1 tablespoon olive oil

2 cups peeled and diced potato

2 tablespoons unsalted butter

1 cup diced, cooked lobster meat

4 cooked lobster claws, shelled, with meat in one piece

1 cup Lobster Bisque (see page 77)

1 tablespoon chopped mixed fresh herbs,
such as chives, tarragon, and parsley

4 long fresh chives, for garnish

Fill a shallow pan with water and add the white vinegar and a pinch of salt. Bring to a simmer over medium heat. Gently break the eggs into the simmering water. Cook over medium heat for 3 to 4 minutes, until soft-poached. Using a slotted spoon, remove the eggs to a pan filled with ice water and reserve until ready to reheat just before serving. Reserve the poaching liquid.

Heat the olive oil in a large sauté pan over medium high heat. Add the potatoes and cook, turning frequently, for about 8 minutes, until golden brown.

Add the butter to the pan and reduce the heat to medium. Gently stir in the lobster meat, lobster claws, and Lobster Bisque, and cook for 3 to 4 minutes. Add the fresh herbs and season to taste with salt and pepper.

Reheat the eggs in the poaching liquid for 2 to 3 minutes. While the eggs are reheating, remove the claws from the pan and divide the hash among four serving plates. Top each serving with a poached egg and garnish with a lobster claw and a chive.

THICK TOWELS, NUBBY LOOFAHS,
AND AN ARRAY OF LIGHTLY SCENTED BODY PRODUCTS
ENHANCE THE PLEASURE OF BATHING AT
THE WHITE BARN INN, WHERE ALL SUITES INCLUDE
SPACIOUS BATHROOMS WITH DEEP
WHIRLPOOL TUBS.

## Lobster Bisque

*Makes 2 quarts*

4 tablespoons (½ stick) unsalted butter

1 medium onion, diced

1 garlic clove

6 medium tomatoes, diced

1 sprig fresh thyme

1 sprig fresh parsley

1 sprig fresh tarragon

½ cup white dessert wine, such as muscat

1 cup brandy

4 cups heavy cream

4 cups Lobster Stock (see page 78)

1 teaspoon lobster roe, if available

Salt, freshly ground pepper, and cayenne

Juice of ½ lemon

In a large saucepan with a heavy bottom, melt the butter over medium heat. Add the onion, garlic, tomatoes, and herbs and sauté for about 5 minutes, until the onions are translucent but not browned.

Add the wine and brandy and increase the heat to medium high, cooking the mixture until it is reduced by half. Add the cream and lobster stock and bring to a boil. Reduce the heat to medium and cook for about 15 minutes, whisking occasionally, until thick enough to coat the back of a spoon.

Whisk in the lobster roe, if available, and bring the soup back to a boil. Strain the soup through a fine sieve into a clean saucepan and season to taste with salt, pepper, cayenne, and lemon juice before serving.

## LOBSTER STOCK

*You will need 6½ pounds of lobster to yield 5 pounds of lobster shells.*
*The Lobster Hash recipe calls for just 1 cup of lobster meat, so if*
*you make this stock a day in advance, you can enjoy a dinner of boiled lobster*
*as a dividend. In a restaurant kitchen, nothing is wasted—hence the addition*
*of fresh herb stems to this flavorful stock.*

*Makes 1 quart*

5 pounds lobster shells, head cavity cleaned

1 pound (about 1 cup) diced mixed aromatic vegetables,
such as carrot, leek, onion, and celery

10 medium ripe tomatoes, chopped

2 cups dry white wine, such as chardonnay

1 cup V-8 juice

1 dozen mixed fresh herb stems,
such as thyme, parsley, tarragon, and dill

1 garlic clove

Preheat the oven to 450°F.

In a roasting pan, combine the lobster shells, vegetables, and tomatoes and roast for 15 minutes, stirring occasionally, until the shells have a dry, cooked appearance and the vegetables are lightly browned.

Transfer the roasted shells and vegetables to a large stockpot. Add the wine, V-8 juice, and enough water to cover all the ingredients. Bring the stock to a boil over high heat, skimming off any scum that rises to the surface.

Reduce the heat to a simmer and add the herbs and garlic. Simmer the stock for at least 3 hours, until it turns a deep reddish-brown and has a rich flavor and aroma.

Strain the stock into a clean pot and cook over high heat until reduced by half. The stock will keep in the refrigerator for a few days, or up to two months in an air-tight container in the freezer.

# PoppySeed Muffins

*In this recipe, the pastry flour is sifted twice*
*to ensure a light, moist muffin.*

*Makes 16 small or 8 regular muffins*

2 cups pastry flour, sifted twice

1/4 teaspoon salt

1/2 cup sugar

1 teaspoon baking powder

4 tablespoons poppyseeds

3 1/2 tablespoons unsalted butter, melted

1/2 cup sour cream

2 eggs

1 drop maple extract

Preheat the oven to 400°F. Butter a muffin tin. In a large bowl, sift together the flour, salt, sugar, baking powder, and poppyseeds.

In a medium bowl, combine the melted butter, sour cream, and eggs and beat for 7 minutes. Add the egg mixture to the dry ingredients and beat with an electric mixer on low speed until thoroughly combined. Add the maple extract and beat until combined. Spoon the batter into the buttered muffin cups, filling them to the top. Bake for about 10 minutes, until the muffins have risen and are light gold on top.

# CHOCOLATE CHIP
# MUFFINS

*Makes 16 small or 8 regular muffins*

10 tablespoons (1¼ sticks) unsalted butter,
at room temperature

2 cups sugar

½ cup milk, at room temperature

2¼ cups all-purpose flour

¼ cup unsweetened cocoa powder

¼ teaspoon salt

1 tablespoon baking powder

4 large eggs

1 cup chocolate chips

Preheat the oven to 400°F. Butter a muffin tin. In a large bowl, cream the butter with the sugar. Gradually add the milk and mix until thoroughly combined.

In a large bowl, sift together the flour, cocoa powder, salt, and baking powder.

Using an electric mixer on low speed, gradually add half the beaten eggs to the butter mixture. Add half of the dry ingredients and mix until thoroughly incorporated. Repeat with the remaining beaten eggs and dry ingredients. Add the chocolate chips and mix on medium speed for 7 minutes to aerate the muffins.

Spoon the batter into the buttered muffin cups, filling them to the top. Bake for about 10 minutes, until the muffins have risen and are light gold on top.

# Spring Ingredients

### FOREST MUSHROOMS

These little mushrooms grow on the forest floor in the spring and early summer. They have a wonderful, woodsy taste—slightly nutty, with a peppery finish. Serve them very lightly sautéed to capture their delicate flavor. Chanterelles, or yellow-foot mushrooms, known as girolles in France, are raised domestically year-round on the East Coast.

### FIDDLEHEAD FERNS

In spring the forest floor is covered with baby ferns shaped like the head of a fiddle. Fiddlehead ferns have a unique flavor that combines the fresh green taste of asparagus with the richer notes of artichoke. Unless you are an experienced forager, it's best to buy packaged fiddlehead ferns in spring rather than forage for them, as not all forest ferns are edible.

### ASPARAGUS

The first asparagus of spring are delicate and delicious. The tender tops, lightly steamed, are a wonderful addition to a cold salad of cooked vegetables. They also make a beautiful bed of color beneath grilled fish.

### WATERCRESS

Watercress has a robust, peppery flavor with a touch of bitterness. Served raw and dressed with a champagne vinaigrette, it makes a delicious salad with steamed beets. When cooked, watercress assumes a soft, velvety texture and makes a wonderful base for a cream soup.

### SPINACH

Spinach is a very versatile ingredient—fresh-tasting, like watercress, but milder in flavor. Baby spinach leaves form the basis for a great spring salad. Creamed spinach is a delightful spring comfort food that celebrates the bright color and tender texture of this leafy green.

### RHUBARB

Rhubarb is considered by many to be a rather plain vegetable, but it has a beautiful color and versatile flavor that adds tartness to both sweet and savory recipes.

### CHIVES

Chives are one of the first herbs to grow in spring. Their mild, oniony flavor and fresh green color provide great accents in soups, salads, and sauces. Their long, slender shape makes chives an ideal garnish.

# Summer at the
# WHITE BARN INN

Summer is short in Maine—which is all the more reason to surrender completely to its pleasures. One of the best places to surrender is on a boat, skimming along the water with a light wind cooling your skin. From the vantage point of the sea, the Maine shore reveals its varied nature, with rocky promontories where waves toss veils of foam into the sky, protected coves where surf laps against sandy beaches, and bright green lawns that spill down to the sea from rambling Shingle Style cottages.

Hot summer days call for light lunches that can be easily prepared and eaten on the go. Maine's famous lobster roll—tender morsels of lobster meat tossed with a lemony mayonnaise and spooned into a roll—is a perfect expression of summer's simpler fare. When guests require a picnic lunch, White Barn Inn chef Jonathan Cartwright transforms this ubiquitous sandwich into something special by serving it on a roll with a sturdy texture that stands up better to the moist filling than the commercial rolls typically used.

Deep-sea fishermen look forward to the summer months with eager anticipation, dreaming of pulling in one of the giant bluefin tuna that ply the waters, or landing a striped bass, a magnificent fighting fish that leaps through the surf. Scallops, mussels, and clams are easily gathered, and lobsters fill the lobstermen's traps. A formal dinner at the White Barn Inn offers an opportunity to taste the bounty of summer's sea without having to go to the trouble of catching it. On summer menus the chef pairs each fish with sauces ranging from the delicate to the spicy, as well as such locally grown produce as heirloom tomatoes, bright red peppers, and tender peas.

Next to boats, porches offer summer's best perches. Nearly all the houses along Maine's coast boast porches where grills stand in as outdoor stoves, picnic tables serve as second dining rooms, and comfortable wicker rocking chairs invite long spells of sitting, reading, or chatting with friends. On the Fourth of July, year-round and seasonal residents gather on porches and lawns for elaborate picnics made easy by the sharing of cooking and cleaning tasks. Thanks to its hard shell and firm flesh, lobster stands up well to the grill. While planning crops of tomatoes, squash, beans, and corn. Fruit farmers open their fields to amateur pickers, who delight in gathering their own strawberries and eating them straight from the plant. Cold fruit soups—served year-round at the White Barn Inn as intermezzos between heavier courses—take on a special appeal in summer when so much sun-sweetened fruit is available. A chilled soup of strawberries puréed with mandarin orange juice and champagne or watermelon blended with the juice of Bing cherries perfectly captures the

*Fruit farmers open their fields to amateur pickers, who delight in gathering their own strawberries and eating them straight from the plant.*

a menu for a Fourth of July cookout, chef Cartwright created a mayonnaise infused with smoked tomato to complement the flavor of grilled lobster. Served with a trio of salads featuring baby lettuces, sweet corn, and wild rice, and followed with strawberry shortcake, this entrée celebrates the robust colors, textures, and flavors of the season.

Each summer, stands spring up along the country roads where local farmers sell a selection of freshly harvested produce that changes weekly as their fields yield

essence of summer. For hot summer afternoons, the chef also recommends iced fruit teas flavored with peaches, raspberries, or whatever fruit is at hand.

The following menus and recipes suggest just a few ways of celebrating New England's summer harvest. Mix and match them to create meals that involve as much or little effort as you want to expend. No matter where you live, summer always delivers plentiful, colorful, flavorful produce that is a pleasure to cook and to eat. Enjoy it while it lasts.

# SUMMER MENUS

## Fourth of July Party

Edible Martinis

Iced Watermelon and Bing Cherry Soup

Grilled Maine Lobster with Barbecue Mayonnaise,
Wild Rice Salad, and Grilled Corn Salad

Local Summer Greens with
Carrot Vinaigrette

Strawberry Shortcake

·

## A Simple Boating Lunch

Maine Lobster Roll

Carrot Hummus Roll-ups

Peach Iced Tea

Miniature Berry Muffins

## A Summer Tea Party

Raspberry Iced Tea

Homemade Lemonade

Tomato and Cheddar Sandwiches

Cold-Smoked Salmon Sandwiches

Egg Salad Sandwiches

Scones with Strawberry Jam

Warm Blueberry Petit Fours

•

## A Summer Seafood Dinner

Tandoori-Crusted Soft-Shell Crab with Avocado and Lime Salsa

Grilled Yellowfin Tuna Loin on Summer Corn and Shellfish Hash
with Smoked Tomato Coulis

Strawberry, Mandarin Orange, and Champagne Soup

Pan-Roasted Striped Bass and Lobster Ravioli with
Summer Zucchini Ribbons and Saffron Foam

A Selection of Summer Sorbets

•

## A Summer Cocktail

Watermelon Cosmopolitan

# Fourth of July Party

This menu offers a wonderful way to celebrate Independence Day, or any summer day when you feel like lighting the grill and inviting friends over for a special meal. If you prepare the Cold-Smoked Salmon and Barbecue Mayonnaise in advance, you can finish cooking this meal in an hour or two. Or divide the recipes among your friends and host a casual summer potluck party.

## EDIBLE MARTINIS

*This dish is part cocktail, part canapé. Eat the salmon first,*
*then drink the dill-infused vodka while it's still icy cold. Save the remaining*
*smoked salmon to make tea sandwiches (see pages 116–117) or serve it*
*with poached eggs for a special breakfast.*

*Serves 4*

½ cup Dill-Infused Vodka (see page 92)

8 slices Cold-Smoked Salmon (see page 91)

4 lemon twists

8 Sicilian jumbo green olives

Chilled cooked crab claws, for garnish (optional)

Ice four large martini glasses. In a cocktail shaker, combine the Dill-Infused Vodka with ice and shake to chill.

Curl two slices of salmon in the bottom of each martini glass. Spear two olives and a lemon twist on each of four cocktail picks and place one in each glass with the salmon.

Pour 1 ounce (⅛ cup) iced vodka into each glass over the salmon. Garnish with a chilled, cooked crab claw.

## COLD-SMOKED SALMON

*This simple, flavorful salmon can be stored in an airtight container
in the refrigerator for up to ten days after it's been smoked.*

*Makes 2 pounds*

1½ cups kosher salt

2 cups sugar

2 pounds salmon filet, in one piece

2 pounds wood chips, for smoking (hickory, maple, or apple)

In a large bowl, combine the salt and sugar. Press the salmon filet into the mixture, coating it evenly. Place the seasoned salmon on a large plate or in a nonreactive glass or stainless steel baking dish and cover it with plastic wrap. Place the salmon in the refrigerator to cure for 24 hours.

Rinse the salt and sugar off the salmon under cold water. To cold-smoke the salmon using an outdoor charcoal grill, place half the wood chips in the bottom of the grill and light them. Place the salmon skin-side down on the grill grate and cover the grill, leaving a small gap or adjusting the chimney to a slightly open position. Check from time to time to make sure that the chips are smoking and that the salmon is not getting so hot that it is cooking. (If this happens, the flesh will start to turn a lighter shade.) If the salmon is cooking, place a metal tray filled with ice between the salmon and the wood chips and continue smoking. Add more chips and relight as necessary to smoke the salmon for a total of 2½ hours.

Let the smoked salmon cool, then cover with plastic wrap. Refrigerate for at least 12 hours. To serve, remove the rib and pin bones with your fingers or tweezers. Slice the salmon thinly using a very sharp knife.

## DILL-INFUSED VODKA

*Any remaining flavored vodka will keep in the refrigerator
for several weeks and makes a wonderful addition to Bloody Marys.*

*Makes 32 ounces*

1 bunch fresh dill

10 wide strips lemon zest

1 (32-ounce) bottle lemon-flavored vodka

Wash the dill and combine with the lemon zest in a large jar or pitcher. Add the vodka. Cover and leave to infuse in the refrigerator for 24 hours. Strain the vodka, discarding the dill and lemon zest, and store in the freezer or refrigerator for up to two months.

---

## ICED WATERMELON AND BING CHERRY SOUP

*The trick to making chilled fruit soups is to keep them light and well balanced in flavor. A soup that's too sweet will overwhelm the palate. The addition of champagne adds an effervescent note. Be sure to serve this as soon as you stir in the chilled champagne.*

*Serves 4*

2 pounds watermelon, peeled, seeded, and cut into chunks

1 pound Bing cherries, pitted

1 cup white dessert wine, such as muscat

1 cup chilled champagne

In a food processor, purée the watermelon, cherries, and white wine until smooth. Strain through a fine sieve into a serving bowl or pitcher, cover, and refrigerate. Just before serving, stir in the chilled champagne.

# GRILLED MAINE LOBSTER WITH
# BARBECUE MAYONNAISE, WILD RICE SALAD,
# AND GRILLED CORN SALAD

*It's important to relax and socialize with your guests when hosting a barbecue.
Because the lobsters are steamed before being grilled, you can prepare them
partially in advance. The grilling takes only 10 minutes,
which permits the hosts plenty of time to relax.*

*Serves 4*

2 (1½ pound) Maine lobsters

1 cup Barbecue Mayonnaise (see page 96)

Local Summer Greens with Carrot Vinaigrette (see page 97)

Grilled Corn Salad (see page 100)

Wild Rice Salad (see page 101)

Bring a large stockpot filled with water to a boil and plunge the live lobsters head-first into the pot, cooking them for 5 minutes in the rapidly boiling water. Remove from the water and drain.

Using a large, heavy chef's knife, split the cooked lobsters in half lengthwise. Clean out the head cavities, discarding the contents. With the knife, make long slits in the shells of the claws and knuckles (but do not remove the shells.) The cooled, steamed lobsters can be kept covered with plastic wrap in the refrigerator for up 24 hours before grilling.

Preheat a charcoal grill to high. Place the partially steamed lobsters flesh-side down on the oiled grate of the grill and cook directly over the coals for 5 minutes.

Turn the lobsters, placing them shell side down on the grill grate. Brush the exposed lobster meat liberally with Barbecue Mayonnaise and cook directly over the coals for 5 minutes.

To serve, place the grilled lobster halves on a bed of Local Summer Greens with Carrot Vinaigrette. Fill the head cavity with Grilled Corn Salad and place a mound of Wild Rice Salad next to the lobster.

# BARBECUE MAYONNAISE

*Any remaining Barbecue Mayonnaise can be kept in the refrigerator for a week and makes a wonderful substitute for regular mayonnaise in lobster rolls or other sandwiches.*

*Makes 2 cups*

Wood chips, for smoking (hickory, maple, or apple)

6 ripe tomatoes

1 cup plus 1 tablespoon olive oil

1 garlic clove, minced

¼ cup chopped shallots

1 teaspoon prepared horseradish

2 egg yolks

1 teaspoon Dijon mustard

¼ cup red wine vinegar

2 drops Tabasco sauce

2 drops Worcestershire sauce

1 teaspoon fresh lemon juice, or to taste

Salt and freshly ground pepper

Light two handfuls of wood chips in the bottom of a charcoal grill. Cut the tomatoes in half and place them skin-side down on the grill grate over the wood chips. Cover the grill, leaving a small gap or adjusting the chimney to a slightly open position, and smoke the tomatoes for 20 minutes.

In a medium sauté pan, heat 1 tablespoon of olive oil over medium heat. Add the garlic and shallots and cook until transparent but not brown.

In the jar of a blender or food processor, combine the cooled, smoked tomatoes, the cooked garlic and shallots, and the horseradish and purée until smooth. With the motor running, add the egg yolks, mustard, vinegar, and Tabasco.

With the motor still running, gradually add the remaining olive oil, Worcestershire sauce, and lemon juice.

Season to taste with salt, pepper, and lemon juice. This mayonnaise can be stored in an airtight container in the refrigerator for one week.

# LOCAL SUMMER GREENS
# WITH CARROT VINAIGRETTE

*When serving tender baby lettuce, it is important*
*not to overdress the salad. Use just a bit of dressing, toss, and taste.*
*If all the greens are lightly coated with dressing, then serve*
*the salad at once. If the greens seem dry, add a little more dressing and*
*toss lightly. Make sure that the pansies and nasturtiums*
*are free of any garden pesticides or sprays.*

*Serves 4*

3 heads baby Lola Rossa lettuce

3 heads baby red Bibb lettuce

3 heads baby green Bibb lettuce

1 small bunch arugula

2 small heads curly endive

3 pansies

20 baby asparagus

1 golden beet

1 cup Carrot Vinaigrette (see page 98)

4 nasturtium flowers

20 cherry tomatoes

Small bunch chives, finely chopped

1 small carrot, grated

Wash and dry all the greens. Remove the petals from the pansies and reserve.

Bring a medium skillet of water to a boil over medium high heat and add the asparagus. Blanch until tender, 2 to 3 minutes. Refresh in cold water and drain well.

Preheat the oven to 400°F.

Wrap the beet in aluminum foil and place it in a roasting pan in the center of the oven. Roast for about 30 minutes, or until tender. Allow it to cool, then peel and slice thinly.

In a large salad bowl, toss the greens with the Carrot Vinaigrette.

To serve, divide the dressed greens among four serving plates. Surround with the asparagus, beet slices, and tomatoes, drizzling with additional dressing. Garnish the salad with pansy petals, whole nasturtiums, chives, and grated carrot.

---

## CARROT VINAIGRETTE

*Fresh juice infuses this light vinaigrette with the sweet taste of spring's first carrots. If you don't have an appliance to make your own carrot juice, buy freshly made carrot juice. Don't use prebottled juice, as it will not have the sweet, fresh flavor required for this vinaigrette.*

*Makes about 2 cups*

3 medium carrots, juiced (½ cup
fresh carrot juice)

½ teaspoon Dijon mustard

1 cup extra-virgin olive oil

½ cup white wine vinegar

Salt and freshly ground pepper

Pour the carrot juice into a medium bowl and whisk in the mustard. Gradually add the olive oil, continuing to whisk until the mixture is emulsified.

Whisk in the vinegar and add salt and pepper to taste. This dressing will keep in the refrigerator, tightly covered, for three days.

## GRILLED CORN SALAD

*This salad is a perfect way to showcase
the sweet flavor of summer corn.*

*Serves 4*

4 ears fresh corn, husks on

1 red onion, diced

2 ripe medium tomatoes, diced

1 teaspoon chopped fresh parsley

1 tablespoon rice wine vinegar

¼ cup olive oil

Salt and freshly ground pepper

Preheat a charcoal grill.

Without removing the husks, place the ears of corn on the grate of the hot grill and cook for 10 minutes, turning occasionally. The husks will turn black. Remove the corn from the grill and allow to cool. Remove the husks and silks and cut the kernels off the cob into a large bowl.

Add the diced red onion and tomatoes to the corn. Then add the parsley, vinegar, olive oil, salt, and pepper and toss well to combine. The salad can be prepared up to one day in advance. Cover and refrigerate until ready to serve.

# WILD RICE SALAD

*Although this recipe calls for carrots, other summer vegetables*
*such as peppers, zucchini, tomatoes, and celery can be added. Just use*
*your imagination and the freshest farm produce available.*

*Serves 4*

1½ cups raw wild rice (early harvest, if available)

1 large carrot, diced

½ medium yellow onion, diced

3 tablespoons Homemade Mayonnaise (see page 108),
or a good-quality commercial brand

1 teaspoon chopped mixed fresh herbs, such as chives, tarragon, and chervil

Salt and freshly ground pepper

In a large saucepan, bring 6 cups of salted water to a boil. Add the rice, reduce the heat to low, and cover. Cook for 15 minutes, or until the grains are just beginning to split open and you see the white inside. Drain the rice and let cool.

In a large bowl, combine the cooled rice with the carrot, onion, mayonnaise, and herbs and toss thoroughly. Season to taste with salt and pepper. Cover and refrigerate until ready to serve.

### CHIVES

THE WHITE BARN INN KITCHEN STAFF MAINTAINS
AN HERB GARDEN, SO THAT SEASONAL FLAVORINGS CAN
BE USED WITHIN HOURS OF BEING HARVESTED.
CHIVES THRIVE IN THE GARDEN AND MAKE A FLAVORFUL,
ATTRACTIVE GARNISH FOR SPRING
AND SUMMER DISHES.

# STRAWBERRY SHORTCAKE

*This classic dessert is one of the best ways to enjoy
perfectly ripe summer strawberries.
The crumbly shortcake biscuits absorb some of the
marinated strawberries' juices, and the vanilla-flavored
whipped cream provides a mellow contrast
to the berries' tangy flavor.*

*Serves 6*

6 Shortcake Biscuits (see page 104)

2 cups Marinated Strawberries (see page 105)

Vanilla-Flavored Whipped Cream (see page 105)

Place one biscuit, split in half, on each of six serving plates. Spoon equal amounts of Marinated Strawberries over each biscuit. Drizzle any remaining juice over each serving. Top with a heaping spoonful of Vanilla-Flavored Whipped Cream. Serve immediately.

# SHORTCAKE BISCUITS

*In the White Barn Inn kitchen, we have a variety of flours
on hand. Some flours are made from hard wheat, which has a higher gluten
(or starch) content, and others from soft wheat. This recipe calls for
a mixture of bread and pastry flour. Four cups of all-purpose flour can be
substituted for the combination of these two flours.*

*Makes 10*

1½ cups bread flour

2½ cups pastry flour

½ teaspoon salt

4 tablespoons baking powder

¾ cup sugar

12 tablespoons (1½ sticks) cold
unsalted butter

3 eggs

1 teaspoon poppy seeds (optional)

1 egg yolk, beaten

2 tablespoons milk

In a large bowl, sift together the flours, salt, baking powder, and sugar. Cut in the butter and mix until crumbs begin to form.

In a small bowl, beat the eggs. Combine the eggs gradually with the flour mixture to form a dough. Cover and allow to rest in a cool place for 10 minutes.

Preheat the oven to 350°F.

Lightly flour a dry surface and a rolling pin. Roll the dough out to a thickness of ½ inch. Using a 3-inch cookie cutter, cut the dough into ten round biscuits. In a small bowl, mix the egg yolk with the milk. Brush the top of each biscuit with the egg yolk mixture. Bake for 8 minutes, until golden brown.

## MARINATED STRAWBERRIES

*The sugar draws the juices out of the strawberries.*
*If you marinate the strawberries for less than six hours, the juices*
*will not be completely released. Do not marinate the strawberries*
*for much longer, however, as the fruit will turn mushy.*

*Makes 2 cups*

2 cups strawberries, hulled

½ cup sugar

Cut any large strawberries in half and leave the smaller ones whole. In a large bowl, sprinkle the sugar over the strawberries and toss to combine. Cover and refrigerate for 6 hours, stirring occasionally.

---

## VANILLA-FLAVORED WHIPPED CREAM

*You can prepare the whipped cream up to 3 hours ahead of serving time and keep it*
*in the refrigerator, covered in plastic wrap, until you are ready to serve dessert.*

*Makes about 3 cups*

2 cups heavy cream

¼ vanilla bean, halved lengthwise

3 tablespoons confectioners' sugar

Pour the cream into a large bowl. Scrape the seeds from the vanilla bean into the cream, reserving the bean for another use.

Add the sugar and, using an electric mixer, whip until the cream forms soft peaks. Serve immediately or cover and refrigerate until ready to use.

# A Simple Boating Lunch

When planning a picnic to eat on the water, it's nice to avoid packing cutlery. This simple, delectable lunch features finger food that is easy to transport and to eat.

## MAINE LOBSTER ROLL

*Because the filling in this salad is moist,*
*wait until you're ready to eat to spoon it into the rolls.*
*A firm-textured roll stands up best to this filling, so it's best*
*to buy freshly baked rolls from a local bakery*
*for these sandwiches. Be sure to keep the mayonnaise-based*
*filling chilled until serving time.*

*Makes 4*

1 pound (2 cups) freshly cooked lobster meat,
roughly chopped

3 tablespoons Homemade Mayonnaise (see page 108),
or a good-quality commercial brand

4 tablespoons peeled, diced cucumber

Salt and freshly ground pepper

4 firm, 6-inch-long rolls

In a large bowl, combine the lobster, mayonnaise, and cucumber. Season with salt and pepper. Cover and refrigerate for up to 4 hours, until ready to serve. Just before serving, cut the rolls lengthwise and fill with lobster salad.

# HOMEMADE MAYONNAISE

*This is absolutely delicious, and so easy to make by hand.
As with all emulsion sauces, however, there are a few potential pitfalls
to watch out for. If the mayonnaise seems to become
too thick while you're adding the olive oil, just whisk in an extra
tablespoon of vinegar before adding the remaining oil.
Then add only one tablespoon of vinegar, instead of two, at the end
of the recipe. If the oil looks like it is separating from the other
ingredients, whisk in the tablespoon of hot water
during that stage instead of at the end of the preparation.
These tips should help ensure that your homemade mayonnaise
is a success. Homemade mayonnaise will keep 4 to 5 days
refrigerated in an airtight container.*

*Makes 1½ cups*

2 egg yolks

1 tablespoon Dijon mustard

4 tablespoons champagne vinegar

1 cup extra-virgin olive oil

Salt and freshly ground pepper

In a large mixing bowl, whisk together the egg yolks, mustard, and 2 tablespoons of the vinegar. Whisking vigorously, gradually add the oil, pouring it into the bowl in a thin stream. When all the oil is incorporated, whisk in the remaining vinegar and 1 tablespoon of hot water. Season to taste with salt and pepper. Cover and refrigerate until ready to use.

## CARROT HUMMUS ROLL-UPS

*A vegetable roll-up is very satisfying—and a great way to make sure*
*you eat your vegetables. The addition of carrots to the hummus*
*gives this sandwich a vibrant color, and the grilled vegetables*
*stand out brightly and beautifully, too.*

*Makes 4 roll-ups*

1 cup peeled, sliced carrots

1 tablespoon tahini

1 garlic clove

1 zucchini, sliced ⅛ inch thick

1 eggplant, sliced ⅛ inch thick

1 yellow squash, sliced ⅛ inch thick

1 bunch asparagus, woody ends trimmed

1 red bell pepper, cored, seeded,
and cut into 2-inch squares

1 cup extra-virgin olive oil

Salt and freshly ground pepper

4 pieces lavash flatbread, each about 10 x 12 inches

2 tomatoes, sliced

2 cups mixed lettuce leaves

Bring a medium saucepan of salted water to boil. Add the sliced carrots and cook just until tender, 10 to 15 minutes. Drain and cool.

In the bowl of a food processor, combine the cooked carrots, tahini, and garlic, and purée to form a smooth spread.

Preheat a gas or charcoal grill. Toss the zucchini, eggplant, squash, asparagus, and pepper with olive oil, salt, and red pepper. Arrange them on the grill grate directly over the heat and cook until tender but not burned. Each vegetable may require a different cooking time, so watch carefully and remove as soon as it is grilled to tenderness. Remove the blackened pepper skins, if you like.

Lay the flatbread on a work surface. Spread each piece with carrot hummus. Arrange some of the grilled vegetables on top of the hummus. Top the vegetables with tomato slices and lettuce leaves and season with salt and pepper to taste. Roll each sandwich up into a tight cylinder, securing with toothpicks, if necessary.

# PEACH ICED TEA

*If you're taking this tea on a picnic, pour the peach and tea infusion
into a pitcher and chill it before transferring it to an insulated thermal container.
Rub some extra lemon juice on the peach wedges to keep them from discoloring,
and store them in a separate container.*

*Makes about 3 quarts*

1 cup sugar

Juice of ½ lemon

4 firm, ripe peaches

4 tablespoons Darjeeling tea leaves

In a medium saucepan, combine the sugar with 1 cup of water and bring to a boil over high heat. Continue to cook over medium heat, stirring to dissolve the sugar. When the sugar is dissolved, add the lemon juice and remove from the heat.

Meanwhile, remove the pits from two peaches and roughly dice the flesh, leaving the peaches unpeeled.

In the jar of a blender, combine the sugar syrup and diced peaches and purée until smooth. Strain through a sieve and reserve in a small pitcher.

In a kettle, bring 4 cups of water to a boil. While the water is boiling, remove the pit from one peach and roughly dice the flesh. Place the tea leaves and diced peach in a heat-resistant pitcher. Add the boiling water and infuse for 3 minutes.

Add 4 cups of cold water to the pitcher and stir vigorously with a wooden spoon, smashing the peach pieces to a pulp.

Remove the pit from the remaining peach and cut it into six wedges, leaving the peach unpeeled. Combine the wedges in a serving pitcher with 4 cups of ice. Put another 4 cups of ice in a large sieve and place it over the serving pitcher. Strain the peach and tea infusion through the ice-filled sieve into the pitcher. Add peach syrup to taste and stir to mix. Serve immediately. The remaining syrup can be served with the iced tea for those who prefer their tea sweeter.

# MINIATURE BERRY MUFFINS

*Adding a cupful of chopped blueberries, cranberries, raspberries,
or strawberries to this versatile sweet muffin recipe is an easy way to create a batch
of freshly baked seasonal treats—perfect for breakfast or afternoon tea.*

*Makes 16 small or 8 regular muffins*

2¼ cups pastry flour, sifted

¾ tablespoon baking powder

¾ cup sugar

¼ tablespoon salt

2 eggs

¾ cup milk

½ cup vegetable oil

1 cup chopped seasonal berries

Preheat the oven to 375°F. Butter a muffin tin.

In a large bowl, sift together the flour, baking powder, sugar, and salt.

In a medium bowl, combine the eggs, milk, and oil, and whisk to combine. Add the egg mixture to the dry ingredients and using an electric mixer, beat on low speed until thoroughly combined. Gently fold in the chopped berries.

Spoon the batter into the buttered muffin cups, filling them to the top. Bake for about 10 minutes, until the muffins have risen and are light gold on top.

# A Summer Tea Party

Overnight guests often arrive at the White Barn Inn in the early afternoon, after several hours of traveling. An afternoon tea service featuring hot beverages, freshly baked scones, and sandwiches provides a revitalizing snack. Although the British drink hot tea even in summer, Americans usually prefer iced tea when it's hot outside. This menu offers several suggestions for chilled drinks spiked with fresh fruit.

## RASPBERRY ICED TEA

*Chefs are trained to do everything they can to add flavor to each recipe.*
*Here, in addition to dropping fresh berries into the tea, the chef extracts their essence*
*by simmering them in a sugar syrup before passing it through a sieve.*
*The syrup sweetens the tea and infuses it with the pure flavor of raspberries.*
*Try making this recipe with strawberries, too.*

*Makes 2½ quarts*

1 cup sugar

Juice of ½ lemon

1 cup fresh raspberries, gently rinsed and drained

4 tablespoons English Breakfast tea leaves

In a medium saucepan, combine the sugar with 1 cup of water and bring to a boil over high heat. Continue to cook over medium heat, stirring to dissolve the sugar. When the sugar is dissolved, add the lemon juice and remove from heat.

In the jar of a blender, combine the sugar syrup and ½ cup of raspberries and purée until smooth. Strain through a sieve and reserve in a small pitcher.

In a kettle, bring 4 cups of water to a boil. Place the tea leaves and half of the remaining raspberries in a heat-resistant pitcher. Add the boiling water and infuse for 3 minutes.

Add 4 cups of cold water to the raspberry tea and stir vigorously with a wooden spoon, smashing the raspberries to a pulp.

Combine the remaining raspberries in a serving pitcher with 4 cups of ice. Put another 4 cups of ice in a large sieve and place it over the serving pitcher. Strain the raspberry and tea infusion through the ice-filled sieve into the pitcher. Add raspberry syrup to taste and stir to mix. Serve immediately. The remaining syrup can be served with the iced tea for those who prefer their tea sweeter.

## HOMEMADE LEMONADE

*Not everyone wants to drink something caffeinated.*
*Lemonade is a refreshing and delicious alternative to iced tea.*
*For extra flavor, garnish this beverage with fresh mint.*

*Makes 4 cups*

½ cup fresh lemon juice

½ cup sugar (or to taste)

1 cup ice

In a medium pitcher, combine the lemon juice and sugar with 2½ cups of cold water and stir until the sugar dissolves. This mixture can be made a day ahead and refrigerated.

When ready to serve, add the ice to the pitcher of lemonade, stir, and serve immediately.

# TOMATO AND CHEDDAR SANDWICHES

*Heirloom tomatoes grown on farms in Maine have beautiful color
and a firm texture. One delicious way to eat tomatoes is simply to slice them,
sprinkle them with salt and pepper, and sandwich them between thin slices
of freshly baked bread with a slice of cheddar cheese.*

*Makes 6 finger sandwiches*

4 slices white bread

4 slices cheddar cheese

2 ripe tomatoes, thinly sliced

Salt and freshly ground pepper

Place two slices of bread on a work surface. Layer two slices of cheddar cheese and several tomato slices on each piece of bread. Season with salt and pepper. Top with the remaining bread. Using a serrated knife, remove the crusts and slice each sandwiche into three "fingers." Serve immediately.

---

# COLD-SMOKED SALMON SANDWICHES

*Makes 6 finger sandwiches*

4 slices brown bread

1 tablespoon butter, softened

4 slices Cold-Smoked Salmon (see page 91)

Freshly ground pepper

Butter all four slices of bread on one side. Place two slices, buttered-side up, on a work surface. Cover each piece of bread with two salmon slices. Season with freshly ground pepper, if desired. Top with the remaining slices of bread, buttered-side down. Using a serrated knife, remove the crusts and slice each sandwich into three "fingers." Serve immediately.

## EGG SALAD SANDWICHES

*The addition of freshly cut chives or watercress brightens up the color
and adds another dimension of flavor to these satisfying little sandwiches.*

*Makes 6 finger sandwiches*

2 hard-cooked eggs, peeled

2 tablespoons Homemade Mayonnaise (see page 108),
or a good-quality commercial brand

Salt and freshly ground pepper

1 tablespoon chopped fresh chives or watercress (optional)

4 slices multigrain bread

In a medium bowl, mash the eggs with a fork. Add the mayonnaise. Continue mashing until the mixture forms a roughly textured paste. Season with salt and pepper. Add the chopped watercress or chives, if using.

Place two slices of bread on a work surface. Spread with the egg salad. Cover with the remaining slices of bread. Using a serrated knife, remove the crusts and slice each sandwich into three "fingers." Serve immediately.

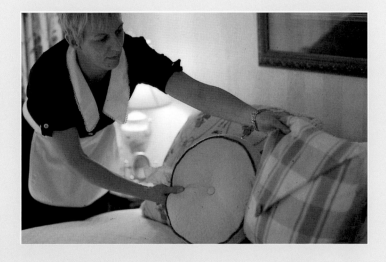

DOWN FEATHERBEDS AND COMFORTERS
AND A CHOICE OF PILLOWS TRANSFORM THE WHITE BARN
INN'S BEDS INTO IRRESISTIBLE NESTS. DRESSED
WITH COVERLETS AND THROWS IN DESIGNER FABRICS,
THEY ARE AS BEAUTIFUL TO BEHOLD AS THEY ARE
COMFORTABLE TO CURL UP IN.

# SCONES WITH STRAWBERRY JAM

*Scones are among the easiest baked goods to make,*
*and berry preserves are simple to prepare, as well. Homemade preserves melt*
*right into the rich, fluffy heart of these fresh-from-the-oven scones.*

*Makes 12 scones*

3¼ cups all-purpose flour

½ cup sugar

1 teaspoon baking powder

¼ teaspoon baking soda

2¼ sticks cold unsalted butter

¾ cup buttermilk

½ cup dried currants

Strawberry Jam (see page 120)

Preheat the oven to 350°F. Butter a baking sheet.

In a large bowl, sift together the flour, sugar, baking powder, and baking soda. Cut in the butter to form coarse crumbs.

Add the buttermilk and currants and stir to combine. Cover with a damp cloth and allow the dough to rest in a cool place for 15 minutes.

Lightly flour a dry surface and rolling pin. Roll the dough out to a thickness of ½ inch. Using a 2-inch round cookie cutter, cut the dough into scones.

Place the scones on the buttered baking sheet. Bake for 15 minutes, until slightly risen and golden. Serve with Strawberry Jam.

# STRAWBERRY JAM

*Nothing will make afternoon tea guests feel more special than a bowl
filled with just-made jam. This strawberry preserve is easy to make and can be
eaten as soon as it cools. Any remaining jam may be canned in glass jars,
following proper canning procedures, and stored for up to 6 months.*

*Makes 1 quart*

4 cups ripe strawberries, rinsed, cored, and quartered

3 cups sugar

Juice of 1 lemon

In a large saucepan with a heavy bottom, combine the strawberries, sugar,
and lemon juice. Bring to a boil over medium high heat. Reduce the heat to
medium low and simmer, uncovered, for 30 minutes, stirring occasionally,
until the mixture is reduced by half. Cool and serve, or can in glass jars
according to proper canning techniques.

DURING THE LATE SPRING, SUMMER,
AND FALL MONTHS, GUESTS MAY ENJOY REFRESHMENTS
OR LUNCHEON BY THE NEGATIVE-EDGE POOL
THAT BRIMS WITH WATER LIKE A FOREST POND. MASSAGES
AND OTHER SPA TREATMENTS ARE ALSO AVAILABLE
IN POOLSIDE CABANAS.

# WARM BLUEBERRY
## PETITS FOURS

*These little blueberry muffins are one of the best ways*
*to enjoy Maine's small, flavorful wild blueberries. They are best served warm,*
*when the blueberries are meltingly tender. Flexible muffin tins are best*
*for this recipe, which produces a soft-textured muffin.*

*Makes 24 miniature muffins*

7 eggs

2½ cups sugar

3 cups flour

4½ teaspoons baking powder

1 cup heavy cream

12 tablespoons (1½ sticks) unsalted
butter, melted

½ cup blueberries

Preheat the oven to 350°F. Butter two miniature muffin tins.

In a large bowl, beat the eggs with the sugar, using an electric mixer on high, for 6 minutes, until the mixture doubles in volume and the beater leaves a distinct trail when lifted from the batter.

In another large bowl, sift together the flour and baking powder. In a large measuring cup, combine the cream and the melted butter. Alternately fold the dry ingredients and the cream mixture into the beaten eggs, mixing only until all the ingredients are completely incorporated. Gently stir in the blueberries.

Spoon the batter into miniature muffin cups, filling them to the top. Bake for 10 minutes, until golden brown.

# A Summer Seafood Dinner

Many diners at the White Barn Inn request the chef's recommendation for an all-seafood dinner featuring the best seasonal fish from Maine waters. This menu includes two fish that swim off the coast of Maine each summer—tuna and striped bass—as well as soft-shell crab, a specialty from Maryland's Chesapeake Bay.

## TANDOORI-CRUSTED SOFT SHELL CRAB WITH AVOCADO AND LIME SALSA

*This dish celebrates contrasting textures and flavors. The smooth coolness of the avocado-lime salsa sets off the crunch and spice of the soft shell crab. Tandoori powder, traditionally used on foods cooked in a tandoori oven, is an Indian spice mixture including dried and ground coriander, fenugreek, cumin, cayenne, nutmeg, and paprika or some other spice that produces a red color. It is available from Indian and international grocers, or by mail order from gourmet spice merchants.*

*Serves 4*

1 cup milk

Salt, freshly ground pepper, and cayenne

4 jumbo soft-shell crabs, cleaned

2 ripe avocados

2 limes

1 cup plain yogurt

1 teaspoon crushed garlic

½ small cucumber, peeled, seeded, and diced

½ cup cornmeal

1 tablespoon tandoori powder

½ cup blended oil (see Note)

In a large bowl, combine the milk with a pinch of salt and pinch of cayenne. Place the crabs in the milk and refrigerate while preparing the rest of the ingredients.

Peel the avocados and cut the flesh into quarter-inch dice. Place the diced avocado in a medium bowl. Cut off the skin of the lime and dice the flesh. Add the diced lime and any juice to the avocado. Season to taste with salt, pepper, and cayenne.

In a medium bowl, combine the yogurt and crushed garlic. Stir in the cucumber and season with salt, pepper, and cayenne.

In a shallow bowl, combine the cornmeal and tandoori powder. In a large sauté pan, heat the oil over high heat. Remove the crabs from the milk and dredge them in the seasoned cornmeal. Place the crabs in the pan and sauté for about 3 minutes on each side, until golden brown.

To serve, place some avocado and lime salsa in the center of each of four plates. Drizzle the yogurt mixture around the outside of each plate. Place the crabs on top of the salsa.

**Note:** Blended oil is a mixture of 90 percent vegetable oil and 10 percent olive oil.

# GRILLED YELLOWFIN TUNA LOIN
## ON SUMMER CORN AND SHELLFISH HASH WITH
## SMOKED TOMATO COULIS

*Both bluefin and yellowfin tuna are caught in Maine waters.*
*Chef Cartwright prefers yellowfin tuna for this dish because its firm flesh*
*holds up well on the grill. Start by smoking the tomatoes for the coulis.*
*While the tomatoes are smoking, make the shellfish hash. You can reheat*
*the hash and the coulis while grilling the tuna.*

*Serves 4*

1½ pounds yellowfin tuna loin, cut into 4 steaks

1 tablespoon extra-virgin olive oil

Salt and freshly ground pepper

Summer Corn and Shellfish Hash (see page 126)

Smoked Tomato Coulis (see page 128)

Preheat a charcoal grill to high.

Coat the tuna steaks with olive oil and season with salt and pepper. Place the tuna on the grate of the grill directly over the heat and cook for 2 to 3 minutes on each side for medium rare.

To serve, spoon some Summer Corn and Shellfish Hash in the center of each of four plates. Using a sharp knife, cut each tuna steak in half and arrange the two halves on each plate on top of the hash. Drizzle the Smoked Tomato Coulis over the tuna and the hash.

## SUMMER CORN AND SHELLFISH HASH

*Serves 4*

3 tablespoons blended oil (see Note)

½ medium onion, diced

1 sprig fresh thyme

1 cup dry, fruity white wine, such as sauvignon blanc

16 littleneck clams, scrubbed under cool running water

16 Maine mussels, scrubbed under cool running water

2 small potatoes, peeled and cut into quarter-inch dice

1 teaspoon butter

Kernels from 2 ears young white corn

4 large sea scallops, cut into quarters

In a sauté pan large enough to hold the clams, heat 1 tablespoon of oil over high heat. Add a third of the diced onion, half the thyme sprig, $\frac{1}{2}$ cup of white wine, and the clams. Cover and cook for 4 to 5 minutes over high heat, until the clams open. Remove the pan from the heat and allow to cool.

In a sauté pan large enough to hold the mussels, heat 1 tablespoon of oil over high heat. Add a third of the diced onion, the remaining thyme sprig, the remaining white wine, and the mussels. Cover and cook for 4 to 5 minutes over high heat, until the mussels open. Remove the pan from the heat and allow to cool.

Remove the clams and mussels from the pan juices, remove the meat, and discard the shells. Combine the pan juices and strain through a fine sieve lined with cheesecloth into a bowl.

In a large sauté pan, heat the remaining oil over high heat. Add the remaining diced onion and the diced potatoes. Cook over high heat for 2 to 3 minutes, until the potatoes are lightly browned. Reduce the heat to medium and add the butter and corn kernels. Cook, stirring, for 2 minutes. Add the strained shellfish pan juices and cook over medium heat for 8 to 10 minutes, until the potatoes and corn are tender and the liquid has reduced to a thick sauce that clings to the vegetables. Add the scallops, clams, and mussels and cook over medium heat for 1 minute. Season with salt and pepper and remove from the heat.

**Note:** Blended oil is a mixture of 90 percent vegetable oil and 10 percent olive oil.

# SMOKED TOMATO COULIS

*Makes about 1½ cups*

Wood chips for smoking,
such as hickory, maple, or apple

8 ripe tomatoes

1 sprig fresh basil

1 tablespoon blended oil (see Note)

½ medium onion, diced

1 cup V-8 juice

Salt and freshly ground pepper

Light two handfuls of wood chips in the bottom of a charcoal grill. Cut the tomatoes in half and place them skin-side down on the grill grate over the wood chips. Cover the grill, leaving a small gap or adjusting the chimney in a slightly open position, and smoke the tomatoes for 20 minutes.

Remove the leaves from the sprig of basil. Reserve four leaves, cutting them into fine julienne, to garnish the finished dish.

In a medium saucepan, combine the blended oil, stem and remaining leaves of basil, and diced onion. Cook for 5 minutes, until the onion is translucent but not brown. Add the smoked tomatoes and V-8 juice and bring to a boil over medium high heat. Reduce the heat to medium low and simmer for 10 minutes, until the tomatoes break down and the sauce thickens.

Purée the sauce in a food processor. Strain through a fine sieve into a bowl, discarding the seeds and skins, and season the coulis with salt and pepper.

**Note:** Blended oil is a mixture of 90 percent vegetable oil and 10 percent olive oil.

# Strawberry, Mandarin Orange, and Champagne Soup

*This soup can be prepared earlier in the day and finished with the addition
of the chilled champagne at the last minute. If you can't find mandarin orange purée
at a gourmet store or through a catalog, you can substitute 2 cups of
pulpy orange juice, preferably from mandarin oranges*

*Makes 5 cups*

2 cups mandarin orange purée

1 cup cored and chopped strawberries

1 cup white dessert wine, such as muscat

4 sprigs fresh mint

1 cup champagne, chilled

In a blender combine the mandarin orange purée, strawberries, white wine, and
mint. Purée until smooth. Strain through a fine sieve into a bowl or pitcher, cover,
and refrigerate. Just before serving, stir in the chilled champagne.

To create presentations that celebrate each season,
fine products are flown in from
around the country to complement locally
grown fruit and vegetables. Plump mandarin oranges
give sparkle to summer's cold soups,
sorbets, and beverages.

# Pan-Roasted Striped Bass and
## Lobster Ravioli with Summer Zucchini Ribbons and Saffron Foam

*Striped bass is a robust game fish with a beautiful skin
that turns crisp when pan-roasted, adding extra taste and texture
to this dish. With thinly sliced ribbons of squash, lightly sautéed
baby spinach, and a saffron-colored sauce, this fish entrée is full of
fresh summer flavors and colors. For additional appeal,
we garnish this dish with lobster oil and fried shallots
at the White Barn Inn.*

*Serves 4*

2 medium zucchini

2 medium yellow squash

3 tablespoons plus 2 teaspoons unsalted butter

1 shallot, diced

1 cup champagne

Pinch of saffron (about 20 threads)

1 cup heavy cream

Salt, freshly ground pepper, and cayenne

2 drops fresh lemon juice

1 pound striped wild bass, cut into 4 filets

4 cups baby spinach, stemmed and rinsed

2 tablespoons olive oil

4 Lobster Ravioli (see page 133), cooked

Cut the zucchini and yellow squash in half lengthwise. Using a mandoline or Asian vegetable slicer, cut both vegetables into thin, long, ribbonlike slices about ½ inch wide.

In a medium sauté pan, heat 2 tablespoons of the butter over medium heat. Add the diced shallot and sauté for 1 minute, until translucent.

Stir in the saffron and ¾ cup champagne and cook over medium high heat until reduced by half. Reduce the heat to medium and add the cream. Cook for 5 minutes, until the sauce coats the back of a spoon. Strain through a fine sieve, season to taste with salt, pepper, cayenne, and lemon juice, and set aside

Heat a large sauté pan over medium high heat. Place the bass, skin-side down, in the dry, hot pan and sear for 3 to 4 minutes, until the skin becomes crisp. Reduce the heat to medium and add 1 teaspoon of butter to the pan. When the butter turns a rich brown, turn the filets and reduce the heat to low. Cook for 5 minutes.

In a large sauté pan over medium high heat, melt 1 teaspoon of butter. Add the spinach and cook, tossing gently, for 2 minutes or until wilted. Set aside in a warm place.

In a clean sauté pan over medium heat, melt the remaining tablespoon of butter. Add the squash ribbons and cook for 2 minutes, stirring gently, until tender. Set aside in a warm place.

Reheat the sauce over high heat. Add the remaining champagne and bring to a boil.

To serve, place the squash ribbons on one side of each of four dinner plates (oval plates are best, if available). Place the spinach on the other side of the plate. Top the squash with the bass filet. Top the spinach with the ravioli. Using a hand-held blender, beat the sauce until it foams. Spoon the foam and sauce on top of the fish and ravioli, and serve at once.

# LOBSTER RAVIOLI

*Ravioli can be made up to six weeks ahead of time and frozen.*
*Since the Pan-Roasted Striped Bass recipe calls for only four ravioli, the remaining*
*ravioli can be enjoyed in a separate meal. One of my favorite light dinners*
*is a bowl of lobster bisque garnished with a raviolo, as a single ravioli is called.*

*Makes 8 to 10 3-inch ravioli*

## FILLING

¼ pound salmon filet

1 tablespoon salt

¼ cup heavy cream

2 tablespoons diced cooked lobster meat

1 tablespoon lobster roe

1 teaspoon chopped fresh parsley

Freshly ground pepper and cayenne

In the bowl of a food processor, combine the salmon and salt and pulse to combine. With the motor running, slowly add the cream. Stop processing when the cream is incorporated into the salmon. Add the lobster, lobster roe, and parsley and season with pepper and cayenne. Pulse a few times until the lobster is incorporated and the mixture has a rough, pastelike consistency.

## RAVIOLI

1¾ cups bread flour or
all-purpose flour

6 egg yolks

2 tablespoons olive oil

1 pinch salt

1 tablespoon milk

In the bowl of a food processor, combine the flour, 5 egg yolks, olive oil, and salt. Pulse for 30 seconds, or until the mixture has the texture of wet sand. Turn the mixture out onto a work surface and knead it with the palms of your hands to form a dough. Continue kneading the dough until it is smooth and pliable. Gather it up loosely into a ball, cover with plastic wrap, and let it rest for 30 minutes in the refrigerator.

Make an egg wash by beating together the remaining egg yolk and the milk in a small bowl.

Lightly flour a work surface and rolling pin (or put the dough in a pasta machine on the #1 setting). If rolling by hand, roll the dough as thinly as possible into a rectangular sheet roughly 12 by 14 inches.

Brush the entire sheet of pasta with the egg wash. Cut the sheet in half lengthwise, leaving both pieces on the work surface. Working down the edge of one sheet, place one tablespoon of the lobster filling 2 inches in from the side and top. Place another tablespoon of filling 4 inches below this. Repeat this step until you reach the bottom of the sheet. Make another vertical row of filling 4 inches from the first row. Repeat until you have used all the lobster filling to create evenly spaced portions on the sheet of pasta.

Fold the second sheet of pasta over the sheet with the filling. Press down to seal the pasta around the filling.

Using a 3-inch fluted cutter, cut round ravioli, making sure the edges are fully sealed.

The ravioli can be placed on a baking sheet and frozen. Store the frozen ravioli in an airtight container or zipper-lock bag for up to six weeks.

To cook the ravioli, bring a large pot of salted water to a boil. Drop the ravioli in the boiling water. As soon as the water returns to a boil, reduce the heat to medium. Fresh ravioli will cook in 2 minutes; frozen ravioli will take 5 to 6 minutes. The ravioli is done when the pasta and filling are tender. Remove the cooked ravioli with a slotted spoon.

# A Selection of Summer Sorbets

Sorbets keep nicely in the freezer for several days. You can make this selection of fruit sorbets earlier in the week and delight your guests with a multicolored dessert. Or just serve a single sorbet garnished with a mint sprig or edible flower for an equally delightful finish to the meal. These recipes call for fruit purée, which is available from specialty stores. If you can't find fruit purée, you can make it by stewing a mixture of fruit and sugar over low heat until the fruit breaks down. Purée the fruit in a food processor and pass it through a sieve to remove any seeds or fibers. To calculate the correct ratio of fruit and sugar, you'll need a kitchen scale to weigh the fruit. Then add enough sugar to equal one-tenth the weight of the fruit.

## GRIOTTE SORBET

*A griotte is a dark, sour cherry, similar to the cherries*
*used to make the famous Black Forest cake of Germany.*
*Bing cherries may be substituted, but they may be*
*too sweet. A better choice is Early Richmond*
*or Montmorency cherries.*

### Makes 2½ quarts

1½ cups sugar

5 cups griotte purée

In a large saucepan, combine the sugar with 2¾ cups water and bring to a boil, stirring until the sugar is dissolved.

Place the purée in a large bowl. Pour the hot sugar syrup over the purée and stir well to blend. Let cool to room temperature. Freeze in an ice cream machine, following the manufacturer's instructions.

## APRICOT SORBET

*Makes about 2 quarts*

1¾ cups sugar

4 cups apricot purée

In a large saucepan, combine the sugar with 2 cups of water and bring to a boil, stirring until the sugar is dissolved.

Place the purée in a large bowl. Pour the hot sugar syrup over the purée and stir well to blend. Let cool to room temperature. Freeze in an ice cream machine, following the manufacturer's instructions.

---

## BLUEBERRY SORBET

*Makes about 2 quarts*

1¾ cups sugar

3¼ cups blueberry purée

In a large saucepan, combine the sugar with 1¾ cups water and bring to a boil, stirring until the sugar is dissolved.

Place the purée in a large bowl. Pour the hot sugar syrup over the purée and stir well to blend. Let cool to room temperature. Freeze in an ice cream machine, following the manufacturer's instructions.

# STRAWBERRY CHAMPAGNE SORBET

*Makes 2½ quarts*

3 cups sugar

2 cups champagne

2 cups strawberry purée

In a large saucepan, combine the sugar with 1 cup of champagne and 2 cups of water. Bring to a boil, stirring until the sugar is dissolved.

Place the purée in a large bowl. Pour the hot sugar syrup over the purée and stir well to blend. Stir in the remaining cup of champagne. Let cool to room temperature.

Freeze in an ice cream machine, following the manufacturer's instructions. Because this sorbet includes alcohol, which slows the freezing process, it will be necessary to run the ice cream machine a few minutes longer than with the other sorbets.

# A Summer Cocktail

## WATERMELON COSMOPOLITAN

*This beverage translates watermelon's irresistible flavor
and color into a refreshing cocktail.*

*Makes 2 cocktails*

4 ounces vodka

⅓ cup crushed, seeded watermelon

¾ ounce watermelon schnapps

¾ ounce freshly squeezed lime juice

1 ounce triple sec

2 small wedges watermelon, for garnish

Chill two large martini glasses. In a cocktail shaker, combine all of the
ingredients and add crushed ice. Shake, then strain into chilled martini
glasses. Garnish with a small wedge of watermelon.

# Summer Ingredients

### CORN

Corn changes color and flavor throughout the growing season. The first summer corn is light in color, sweet, and succulent. Grilled on the cob then cut into kernels, it makes a delicious cold salad.

### BLUEBERRIES

If you ask anyone from Maine, they will tell you that Maine wild blueberries are the best in the world. Sweet and juicy, they grow only during a five-week season from mid-July to late August.

### STRAWBERRIES

Strawberries are harvested throughout the summer months in Maine. Full of flavor and firmly textured, they are delicious served in uncomplicated fruit salads and also form the basis for intense purées that can flavor sorbets, iced teas, and soups.

### RED PEPPERS

Ranging in flavor from sweet to spicy, these versatile vegetables add colorful highlights to cooked and raw preparations. They also hold up well on the grill. Cooked and puréed, they make a brightly colored coulis to serve with fish and meat dishes.

### TOMATOES

Brightly colored and filled with flavorful juice, the tomato is the ultimate summer vegetable. Harvested from July until the first frost, locally grown varieties include a number of heirloom tomatoes that vary widely in color, flavor, and shape.

### SQUASH

Mild-tasting, firm-textured, and varied in color and shape, squash is the perfect foil for light summer sauces and an ideal garnish for grilled meats and fish. Varieties including zucchini, yellow squash, and pattypan are plentiful throughout the summer.

### CHERRIES

After Maine's cherry trees bloom in spring, they prepare for a brief summertime harvest that is welcomed with a burst of pie-making and canning.

# Autumn at the
# WHITE BARN INN

Autumn arrives quietly in Maine before gathering force to explode in a colorful crescendo by mid-October. In the last days of August or early September, the sky begins to burn a brighter, deeper blue. The sun sets with a redder glow and darkness descends a little earlier each day, with a chill that calls for sweaters and wood-burning fires. One morning waves gently lick the sand at Gooch's Beach into a silver sheen. The next day dawns with the sound of heavy surf pounding the shore, shooting geysers of foam high into the air. Shreds of red seaweed scuttle like bits of torn lace along the breezy beach, and the wind teases leaves from trees that have begun to trade their summer green for fiery autumn hues.

Masses of seaweed and moss that hug the rocks along Ocean Avenue turn gold overnight, glowing with a burnished light against the brown-black stone. Wildflowers and grasses along country roads fade and go to seed, creating a tapestry of deeply varied brown interwoven with spiked pods and silky puffs adorned with tiny seeds. The trees succumb to autumn's pull, their tips turning red, maroon, and gold, then blush slowly downward until they stand like towering candles in full flame. At its peak autumn ignites the forests and fields into a pulse-quickening conflagration that burns through the countryside, leaving behind the rustling of dead leaves and the sharp scent of autumn bonfires.

With its clear light and warm afternoons, autumn is the perfect season for the year's final boat outings. The view of the bright tree-lined shore from across the waves is one of Maine's finest prospects, and the cool fall waters produce a plentiful harvest. Mussels, oysters, clams, and lobsters grow firm and sweet in the cold autumn waters. The woods and skies offer up a harvest feast, with turkey, duck, and venison satisfying the season's hunger for flavorful game. Within the woods knowledgeable foragers scan the forest floor, searching for cèpes, hen-of-the-woods, and oyster mushrooms that thrive in fall's cooler, moister climate. Along the roadsides farm stands contribute to the harvest mood with their bright displays of pumpkins, butternut and acorn squash, baskets of crisp apples and pears, and jugs of just-pressed cider.

In the kitchen of the White Barn Inn, Chef Cartwright plans menus that celebrate autumn's rich colors and mellow flavors. For a vegetarian offering, he creates a puff pastry bursting with tangy goat cheese and forest mushrooms. Served on a bed of tender greens and herbs, this hearty appetizer is followed by an entrée of ravioli filled with purees of butternut squash, roasted beets, and pesto-flavored potatoes that echo the colors of the autumn landscape. Whole steamed lobster, shelled and

ish their celebration with pumpkin pie, the chef opens his menu with pumpkin, featured in a delicately flavored, velvety soup. It is followed by a salad dressed with pumpkinseed oil and spiked with Roquefort and spice-dusted pecans. Such classics as cornbread stuffing and tart cranberry relish promise to satisfy the traditionalist, while Black Cherry and Kirsch Baked Alaska brings the meal to a stylishly retro close.

On the day after Thanksgiving, the chef transforms the excess from this feast into a delicious picnic menu to take along on a driving, walking, or cycling expedition.

*On the day after Thanksgiving, the chef transforms the excess from this feast into a delicious picnic menu to take along on a driving, walking, or cycling expedition.*

arranged atop a bed of fettuccine coated with cognac coral butter sauce is a signature dish served year-round at the White Barn Inn. It is especially delicious in fall when Maine lobsters are their sweetest and most succulent.

With a New England turkey dinner served throughout the afternoon and into the evening, Thanksgiving is the busiest day of the year at the White Barn Inn. The chef enjoys combining the traditional ingredients of the Thanksgiving feast with innovative preparations to surprise and delight his guests. While many Americans fin-

But for those whose idea of autumn pleasures is a cozy afternoon or evening spent inside by the fire, another menu celebrates the season's bounty with mushroom salad and a simple yet sophisticated shellfish ragout that can be enjoyed fireside. On a nostalgic note, the meal ends with s'mores—that addictive campfire favorite combining graham crackers (homemade this time), marshmallows (also homemade), and rich, dark chocolate. Accompanied by Irish coffee and hot mulled cider, this dessert promises to take the chill off even the coolest autumn evening.

# AUTUMN MENUS

## Thanksgiving Day Dinner

Pumpkin Soup with Seared Diver Scallops and Five-Spice Cream

An Autumn Assortment of Lettuces
in a Pumpkin Seed Vinaigrette with Roquefort Cheese
and Spiced Pecans

Roasted Maine Turkey with Sage and Onion Stuffing
and Gravy, Sweet Potato Hash, Cranberry Relish,
Brussels Sprouts with Sautéed Shallots, and Whipped Potatoes

Black Cherry and Kirsch Baked Alaska

•

## Day after Thanksgiving
## Driving Tour Picnic

Spiced Pumpkin Soup

Turkey Sandwich with Stuffing and Cranberry Relish

Belgium Endive and Frisée Salad with Maine Goat Cheese
and Grainy Mustard Vinaigrette

Butternut Squash Cookies

## Fall Vegetarian Dinner

Local Forest Mushroom and New England Goat Cheese Pithiviers with
Arugula and Herb Salad with Chanterelle Vinaigrette

Roasted Red Pepper Sorbet

Ravioli of Butternut Squash, Roasted Beet,
and Pesto Potato on Spinach with Truffle Sauce

or

Steamed Maine Lobster Nestled on a Bed of Homemade Fettucine with
Carrot, Ginger, Snow Peas, and a Cognac Coral Butter Sauce

Poire William Crème Brûlée on a Sablé Biscuit and Pear Sorbet
with Spiced Port Wine Sauce

•

## Romantic Fireside Dinner

Warm Fall Mushroom Salad with Sherry Vinaigrette

Ragout of Maine Salmon with Local Shellfish Medley
and Saffron Champagne Sauce

S'mores

Mulled Apple Cider

Irish Coffee

# Thanksgiving Day Dinner

The tradition of the Thanksgiving Day feast began in New England, so it is an especially meaningful time in Maine for celebrating not only the history of the region, but also its natural bounty: pumpkins, potatoes, cranberries, and turkey. The colors of the meal are beautiful, and the flavors range from sweet to savory, with tart and spicy notes. Several of the dishes served for Thanksgiving at the White Barn Inn are American classics, including sage and cornbread stuffing, creamy whipped potatoes, and butter-basted turkey. But the pumpkin soup, garnished with a local scallop and a dollop of Asian-spiced whipped cream, is an unexpected way of integrating that most autumnal of squashes into the meal. A green salad tossed with pumpkinseed oil vinaigrette is garnished with crumbled Roquefort and spiced pecans. And baked Alaska, with its barely warmed meringue exterior and chilly center infused with cherries, kirsch, and chocolate, offers a beautiful surprise for dessert.

## PUMPKIN SOUP WITH SEARED DIVER SCALLOPS AND FIVE-SPICE CREAM

*Simmered with cream and chicken broth (or vegetable stock, for an equally savory vegetarian version), pumpkin makes an elegant soup with a smooth texture and rich golden color. Maine shellfish is at its best when the waters are cold, so diver-harvested scallops make an especially delicious addition. Five-spice powder in the whipped cream introduces warm Asian flavors, and the fried ginger garnish adds another dimension of taste and texture to the bowl of steaming soup.*

*Serves 8*

2 tablespoons unsalted butter

4 heaping cups peeled, diced raw pumpkin

1 small onion, diced (about ¼ cup)

1 carrot, peeled and diced (about ¼ cup)

1 McIntosh apple, peeled and diced
(about 1 cup)

1 clove garlic

1 sprig fresh thyme

½ cup white wine

4 cups chicken stock

1 cup heavy cream

¼ teaspoon ground nutmeg

⅛ teaspoon ground cinnamon

Salt and freshly ground pepper, to taste

2 teaspoons olive oil

8 diver-harvested scallops

Five-Spice Cream (see page 150)

Crispy Fried Ginger strips (see page 150)

In a stockpot with a heavy bottom, melt the butter over medium heat. Add the pumpkin, onion, carrot, apple, garlic, and thyme and reduce the head to low. Sauté for about 10 minutes, stirring occasionally. Increase the heat to medium and add the white wine. Cook until the wine nearly evaporates. Add the chicken stock and cook the soup at a low simmer, stirring occasionally, for 30 minutes, until all the vegetables are soft. Using a food processor or a hand-held blender, purée the soup and strain it through a fine sieve. Stir in the cream and season with the nutmeg, cinnamon, salt, and pepper.

Heat the olive oil in a medium nonstick skillet over high heat. Season the scallops with salt and pepper, and place in the hot oil. Sear until golden, turning once, about 2 minutes per side. The scallops will continue to cook in the hot soup. Remove the scallops from the pan and drain on paper towels to remove excess oil.

To serve, place a seared scallop in the center of each of eight shallow soup bowls and cover with the soup. Garnish with a dollop of Five-Spice Cream and a few Crispy Fried Ginger strips.

## Five-Spice Cream

*Makes 2 cups*

1 cup heavy cream

1 teaspoon five-spice powder

Pinch salt

In a medium mixing bowl, combine the cream and five-spice powder and whip until the mixture forms stiff peaks. Season to taste with salt.

---

## Crispy Fried Ginger

*Makes about 2 tablespoons*

1 (2-inch) piece ginger root, peeled

3 cups blended oil or canola oil (see Note)

Pinch salt

Using a mandoline or an Asian vegetable slicer, slice down the length of the ginger root to make several very fine slices. With a sharp chef's knife, cut the slices lengthwise into very thin julienne strips the size of a quartered wooden matchstick.

In a deep medium skillet, heat the oil to 350°F on a deep-fry thermometer. Carefully drop the ginger strips into the oil and fry for 3 to 4 minutes, until golden-brown. Using a slotted spoon, remove the ginger from the oil, shaking off any excess, and drain on paper towels. Sprinkle lightly with salt while hot.

**Note:** Blended oil is a mixture of 90 percent vegetable oil and 10 percent olive oil.

# An Autumn Assortment of Lettuces in a Pumpkin Seed Vinaigrette with Roquefort Cheese and Spiced Pecans

*Many of our local farmers are growing lettuces in greenhouses,
so we can still get fresh greens in the fall. Autumn greens are a little heartier
than summer ones. I like to serve endive in the fall, along with radicchio and arugula,
all of which add a sharp, slightly bitter flavor to salads. I combine these
with soft leaves of Boston or Bibb lettuce to balance the texture and flavor. I love the
taste of roasted pumpkin seeds in the fall. Pumpkinseed oil lends that same toasted,
nutty flavor to the vinaigrette. The best pumpkinseed oil comes from Austria
and is available in some gourmet stores. If you can't find it, substitute ¼ cup
extra-virgin olive oil and toss 2 tablespoons of toasted pumpkin seeds into the salad
with the dressing. Roquefort adds nice, creamy depth with a sharpness that stands
up well to the lettuces, while spiced pecans contribute fire and crunch.*

*Serves 8*

1 head radicchio

2 heads Belgian endive

1 small head curly endive

1 small bunch arugula

1 head Boston or Bibb lettuce

1 teaspoon Dijon mustard

¼ cup sherry vinegar

¼ cup extra-virgin olive oil

¼ cup pumpkinseed oil

Salt and freshly ground pepper, to taste

½ cup crumbled Roquefort cheese

1 cup Spiced Pecans (see page 152)

Wash and dry all the greens. Tear into bite-sized pieces and toss to combine. Wrap and refrigerate until ready to serve.

In a small mixing bowl, combine the mustard and vinegar. Gradually add the olive oil and the pumpkinseed oil, whisking until the mixture is emulsified. Season to taste with salt and pepper.

Place the greens in a large bowl and toss with the vinaigrette, using only enough dressing to coat the leaves lightly. Season with additional salt and pepper, if desired. Divide the salad among eight plates, sprinkle evenly with crumbled Roquefort, and top with Spiced Pecans. Any remaining dressing will keep tightly covered in the refrigerator for up to a month.

## SPICED PECANS

*If you like fiery flavors, increase the quantities of the spices called for in this recipe. It will make more nuts than you need to garnish the salad, but the remaining nuts make a wonderful appetizer to serve with drinks before dinner.*

### Makes 3 cups

2 tablespoons unsalted butter, melted

¾ pound whole shelled pecans (about 3 cups)

⅛ teaspoon cayenne pepper, or more to taste

⅛ teaspoon chili powder, or more to taste

⅛ teaspoon curry powder, or more to taste

⅛ teaspoon salt, or more to taste

⅛ teaspoon freshly ground black pepper,
or more to taste

Preheat the oven to 400°F.

Melt the butter in a large skillet over medium heat. Add the pecans, cayenne, chili powder, curry powder, salt, and pepper and toss to coat the nuts evenly with the butter and the spices.

Transfer the nuts to a baking sheet and toast for 1 to 2 minutes, until lightly browned and sizzling. Serve warm.

## ROASTED MAINE TURKEY WITH
## SAGE AND ONION STUFFING AND GRAVY

*Near the White Barn Inn, several local farms breed flavorful turkeys
for Thanksgiving. If you can't find a local turkey producer, purchase a fresh turkey
from your supermarket or butcher. The flavor and texture will be far superior
to that of a frozen turkey. Stuffing a quartered apple in the neck cavity provides added
moisture and subtle flavor from within during roasting, and basting the turkey with
plenty of butter helps ensure that the breast remains moist and tender.*

*Serves 8, with plenty of leftovers*

1 (15-pound) fresh turkey, dressed

1 McIntosh apple

Sage and Onion Stuffing (see page 155)

8 tablespoons (1 stick) unsalted butter, at room temperature

2 tablespoons all-purpose flour

2 cups strong Turkey Stock (see page 160)

Salt and freshly ground pepper

Preheat the oven to 400°F.

Season the turkey inside and out with salt and pepper and place on a rack in a deep roasting pan. Cut the apple into quarters and place in the neck cavity. Loosely pack the main cavity with Sage and Onion Stuffing. Place the remaining stuffing in a buttered baking dish and cover with aluminum foil.

Rub the turkey breast with the butter. Pour 1 cup of water into the bottom of the roasting pan and place the pan in the preheated oven. Bake for 20 minutes, baste the turkey with the pan juices, and return it to the oven. Bake for another 10 minutes, checking to make sure that the breast is not getting too dark. Baste with pan juices and return to the oven, reducing the heat to 325°F. Cook for a total of 3 hours, or until the turkey reaches an internal temperature of 160°F on a meat thermometer. Continue basting with pan juices every 20 minutes, checking periodically to make sure the breast is not getting too browned. If the breast and legs start to turn dark brown, cover them with a loose tent of aluminum foil, and continue baking and basting.

About 1 hour before the turkey is fully cooked, place the baking dish of stuffing in the oven. Fifteen minutes before removing the turkey from the oven, remove the aluminum foil (if used) from the breast and legs and the pan of stuffing, and allow both to brown lightly.

Remove the turkey from the oven. Lift it from the pan and transfer it to a large serving platter or a carving board with a channel to collect any juices.

To make the gravy, sprinkle the flour over the pan juices, scraping up any browned bits from the bottom of the pan, and whisk to dissolve any lumps. Place the pan in a hot oven and roast for 5 minutes. Remove from the oven and place on the stovetop over medium heat. Slowly whisk in the Turkey Stock. Transfer the gravy to a saucepan and cook over low heat for 15 minutes. Skim off any fat that rises to the surface and season with salt and pepper to taste. Strain through a fine sieve into a gravy boat and serve hot.

# SAGE AND ONION STUFFING

*This stuffing is made with homemade cornbread.*
*The recipe that follows makes a dry cornbread that is not*
*suitable for eating by itself but is perfect for absorbing*
*all the butter and turkey stock that flavors it so richly.*
*Sage adds a subtle herbal note.*

*Serves 8, with leftovers*

1 cup (2 sticks) unsalted butter

1 cup diced onion

1/4 cup chopped fresh sage

1 cup milk

1 cup Turkey Stock (see page 160,
or use a good-quality canned chicken stock)

3 heaping cups crumbled, dried Cornbread for Stuffing
(see page 156)

2 large eggs, beaten

Salt and freshly ground pepper

Preheat the oven to 350°F.

In a skillet with a heavy bottom, melt the butter over medium heat. Add the onion and sauté until soft and translucent but not browned. Add the sage and remove from the heat.

Combine the milk and stock in a saucepan and bring to a boil over medium heat. Remove from the heat as soon as it boils.

Place the crumbled Cornbread for Stuffing in a large bowl. Add the sautéed onion, beaten eggs, and the hot stock mixture. Stir to combine all the ingredients thoroughly. Season to taste with the salt and pepper.

Butter an 8-inch baking dish and fill with the stuffing. Cover with aluminum foil and bake for 45 minutes. Remove the foil to let the stuffing brown, and bake for 15 minutes longer.

1½ cups yellow cornmeal

1 cup all-purpose flour

1 tablespoon baking powder

1 teaspoon salt

1 cup milk

1 large egg, beaten

3 tablespoons unsalted butter, melted

Preheat the oven to 425°F.

Butter an 8-inch baking pan. In a large bowl, whisk together the cornmeal, flour, baking powder, and salt. In another bowl, whisk together the milk, egg, and butter. Add the wet ingredients to the dry ingredients, stirring just until combined.

Pour the batter into the prepared pan and bake on the center rack of the oven for 20 to 25 minutes, or until the top turns pale gold and a tester comes out clean. Cool the cornbread in the pan on a rack for 5 minutes. Remove from the pan and continue cooling on the rack until it reaches room temperature.

Coarsely crumble the cornbread into a large baking pan. Let it stand at room temperature, uncovered, for at least three hours or overnight, until it becomes slightly stale and hardened.

Preheat the oven to 300°F.

Place the pan of crumbled cornbread on the center rack of the oven and bake, stirring occasionally, until the crumbs are dried and golden, about 30 minutes.

# SWEET POTATO HASH

*Every year I experiment with recipes that use leftover turkey in creative ways.*
*This one was so delicious that I decided to make it part of my Thanksgiving Day menu.*
*Since the recipe calls for just 2 cups of dark meat (a little less than one leg*
*of a 15-pound turkey), you can easily cut off the meat required for this side dish*
*while carving the turkey. The moist hash makes a perfect accompaniment to a slice*
*of white meat. If you prefer, however, you can make it the day after Thanksgiving*
*and serve it with stuffing and cranberry relish. However you serve it,*
*it's a wonderful way to enjoy the rich and flavorful leg meat.*

*Serves 8*

2 tablespoons blended oil (see Note)

2 tablespoons diced onion

1 clove garlic

1 tablespoon unsalted butter

2 cups diced, peeled sweet potatoes (about 2 medium potatoes)

2 cups diced cooked turkey leg meat

1 cup turkey gravy

½ cup Turkey Stock (see page 160)

In a medium saucepan heat the blended oil over medium heat. Add the onion and garlic and sauté until translucent but not browned. Add the butter and the diced sweet potatoes and continue cooking over medium low heat for 5 minutes, or until the potatoes begin to darken and soften on the outside (they will still be hard inside).

Add the turkey, gravy, and Turkey Stock and cook over low heat for about 20 minutes, or until the sweet potatoes are cooked through.

**Note:** Blended oil is a mixture of 90 percent vegetable oil and 10 percent olive oil.

# CRANBERRY RELISH

*Onion, port, and champagne vinegar add savory notes to this sweet-and-tart relish,*
*which is equally delicious served warm with hot turkey or other game,*
*or right from the refrigerator on day-after-Thanksgiving turkey sandwiches.*

*Makes 4 cups*

1 pound fresh New England cranberries

2 teaspoons diced onion

1 cup sugar

½ cup port wine

¼ cup champagne vinegar

In the top of a large double boiler over medium heat, combine the cranberries, onion, sugar, port, and vinegar. Stir to combine and cover. Cook over simmering water for 45 minutes, stirring occasionally, until some of the cranberries pop, creating a thick, saucelike consistency. The relish will thicken as it cools. It may be stored in an airtight container in the refrigerator for one week.

AT THE WHITE BARN INN'S BAR, MURALS OF FARMYARD
ANIMALS RECALL THE STRUCTURE'S FORMER LIFE
AS A RUSTIC BARN, WHILE SHELVES OF THE FINEST SPIRITS
OFFER JUST ABOUT ANY REFRESHMENT
A GUEST MIGHT REQUEST.

# TURKEY STOCK

*Makes 3 cups*

4 pounds roasted turkey bones

½ pound mixed aromatic vegetables,
such as carrots, leeks, onions, and celery, diced

1 clove garlic, crushed

12 sprigs fresh herbs, such as thyme, rosemary, and tarragon

1 cup dry white wine, such as Sauvignon Blanc

Preheat the oven to 450°F.

Place the bones in a large roasting pan and roast, turning occasionally, for 15 minutes, until golden brown. Add the vegetables to the pan and continue roasting for 5 minutes.

Transfer the bones and vegetables to a large stockpot and add the garlic, herbs, and white wine. Cover with water and bring to a boil over high heat, skimming off any impurities that rise to the surface. Reduce the heat to medium and simmer the stock for four hours, until reduced by half.

Strain the mixture through a fine sieve. For a further reduced stock suitable for sauces, simmer the strained stock over medium heat until it is reduced by half. Store in an airtight container in the refrigerator for up to three days or freeze in ice cube trays, transferring the cubes of frozen stock to zipper-lock bags for up to a month.

# Brussels Sprouts
## with Sautéed Shallots

*I love every vegetable in the cabbage family,*
*including brussels sprouts, which make me think of*
*little whole cabbages. They are best cooked*
*until tender but not mushy, and tossed with plenty*
*of butter, salt, and pepper. Butter balances*
*the sharp flavor of sprouts and in this recipe,*
*sautéed shallots add a savory note.*

*Serves 8*

1 pound brussels sprouts

Salt and freshly ground white pepper

2 tablespoons unsalted butter

2 large shallots, diced (about 3 tablespoons)

Bring a large pot of water to a boil and salt it generously. Add the sprouts and cook just until soft, but not mushy. Depending upon the age and size of the sprouts, this will take from 7 to 10 minutes. Drain the sprouts and cut them in half.

In a skillet with a heavy bottom, melt the butter over medium low heat. Add the shallots and cook for about 5 minutes, until softened but not browned.

Toss the sprouts with the shallots and the butter. Season to taste with salt and freshly ground white pepper.

## WHIPPED POTATOES

*Many Americans are hesitant to use large quantities of butter, but it adds great flavor and texture to whipped potatoes. In fact, the more buttery and creamy whipped potatoes are, the better they taste. Thanksgiving only comes once a year, so why not take advantage of the occasion to enjoy a generous amount of butter?*

*Serves 8*

4 Yukon gold potatoes, peeled and diced (about 4 heaping cups)

¾ cup (1½ sticks) unsalted butter

½ cup heavy cream

Salt and freshly ground pepper

Pinch freshly grated nutmeg (optional)

Preheat the oven to 300°F.

Bring a large pot of water to a boil and salt it generously. Add the potatoes and return to a boil. Reduce the heat to medium and simmer for 10 to 12 minutes, or until the potatoes are easily pierced by a fork. Drain the potatoes and place them on a baking sheet in the oven to dry for 5 minutes. Transfer the hot potatoes to a large bowl and mash until most of the lumps are removed.

In a medium saucepan with a heavy-bottom, combine the butter and cream over medium heat and warm until the butter is completely melted. Gradually add the cream mixture to the mashed potatoes and whisk until smooth. Season to taste with salt, pepper, and nutmeg, if desired. Serve immediately, or keep covered in a warm place until ready to serve.

# BLACK CHERRY AND
# KIRSCH BAKED ALASKA

*Baked Alaska is a visually stunning dessert that makes a fitting end
to a festive meal. The cool texture of the iced cream center hidden beneath a layer
of just-warmed meringue is a delightful surprise. Although this impressive dessert
does require several steps, it is surprisingly easy to reproduce at home.
If you prefer, substitute fresh berries for the black cherries.*

*Serves 8*

12 egg yolks

2¼ cups sugar

2 cups heavy cream

1 cup diced Chocolate Sponge (see page 165)

3 tablespoons kirsch

1 cup black sweet cherries (fresh, thawed if frozen, or canned)

1 cup egg whites (from about 6 large eggs)

In a medium heat-resistant bowl, combine the egg yolks and ½ cup of the sugar. Beat with an electric mixer on high speed until smooth and light yellow. Place the bowl over a pan of boiling water and cook, continuing to mix at high speed or by hand, for 4 to 5 minutes. The egg yolks will turn pale yellow and glossy. When the mixture forms a ribbon when dropped from the whisk (or when it reaches a temperature of 120°F on a candy thermometer), remove from the heat. Continue beating the mixture until it reaches room temperature.

In a medium bowl, whip the cream to form soft peaks. Fold the whipped cream into the cooled egg yolk mixture.

Cut the Chocolate Sponge into 1½-inch squares and drizzle the kirsch over them. Once the chopped cake has absorbed the kirsch, fold it into the whipped cream and egg mixture along with the black cherries. The cake will break up into the mixture. If you are using frozen or canned cherries, drain them before adding them to the mixture.

Butter a 20 x 3 x 2-inch log mold (also called a büche de Noël mold), then line it with plastic wrap, making sure that the lining is smooth and that no air bubbles are trapped between the plastic wrap and the mold. Pour the mixture into the mold, cover with plastic wrap, and freeze for at least 12 hours and up to 2 weeks.

After 12 hours, remove the frozen log from the mold, place on a heat-resistant serving platter, cover with plastic wrap, and return to the freezer.

Place the egg whites in a clean bowl with high sides. Using an electric mixer, whip the egg whites on medium speed until they start to foam. Add the remaining ¾ cup sugar. When the sugar is incorporated, whip the egg whites on high speed until they form stiff peaks.

Gently spoon the egg white mixture into a pastry bag fitted with a medium star tip. Remove the log from the freezer and pipe the mixture to cover it completely. Cover with plastic wrap and return the log to the freezer until ready to serve. It can be frozen at this point for up to 1 week.

To serve, preheat the broiler. Place the frozen, meringue-covered log on a baking sheet at least 6 inches below the heat source for just a few seconds, until the meringue is glazed and lightly browned. Watch carefully to avoid burning the meringue. Bring the whole Baked Alaska to the table and slice into individual servings.

## CHOCOLATE SPONGE

*Once it has cooled completely,*
*this airy cake can be wrapped tightly in plastic wrap*
*and stored in the refrigerator for 2 to 3 days or*
*in the freezer for up to a month.*

*Makes 1 (12 x 16-inch) cake*

2 eggs

½ cup sugar

⅓ cup flour

2 tablespoons cornstarch

4 tablespoons dark cocoa powder

1 teaspoon baking powder

Preheat the oven to 375°F. Butter a 12 x 16-inch baking pan.

In a large bowl, combine the eggs with 2 tablespoons of cold water and beat with an electric mixer on high speed until foamy. Gradually add the sugar while continuing to mix.

Sift together the flour, cornstarch, cocoa, and baking powder. Carefully fold the dry ingredients into the egg yolk mixture until well combined.

Pour the batter into the prepared baking pan and bake for 15 minutes, or until a tester comes out clean. Turn the cake out onto a rack to cool.

# Day after Thanksgiving
# Driving Tour Picnic

The Friday after Thanksgiving can be a perfect time to work off some of the extra calories from the previous day's feast with an outdoor expedition. Fortunately, Thanksgiving dinner usually yields a plentiful array of excess from which to create delicious lunches and casual suppers. This simple picnic lunch, which features several dishes from the Thanksgiving Day menu, can be easily prepared and taken on a driving, biking, or walking tour.

## SPICED PUMPKIN SOUP

*Simply reheat yesterday's soup, or, for a spicier, richer first course,*
*stir in any remaining Five-Spice Cream before packing this*
*in a thermal container and heading for the outdoors.*

*Serves 4*

4 cups Pumpkin Soup (see page 147)

¼ to ½ cup Five-Spice Cream (see page 150)

Salt and pepper

In a medium saucepan over medium low heat, reheat the soup. Stir in the leftover Five-Spice Cream, if using. Season to taste with salt and pepper. Transfer to a thermal container until ready to serve.

# TURKEY SANDWICH WITH STUFFING
## AND CRANBERRY RELISH

*One of the best ways to enjoy the remains of Thanksgiving dinner*
*is in a satisfying sandwich stacked high with sliced turkey,*
*a layer of cold stuffing, and a bright red garnish of cranberry relish.*
*The relish, savory with onion and vinegar, makes a deliciously*
*sweet-and-sour addition to a hearty fall sandwich.*
*If you are packing these sandwiches for a picnic, keep them cold*
*in a portable cooler, and add the cranberry relish just before*
*you are ready to eat them.*

*Serves 4*

8 slices firm-textured, seeded rye bread

2 tablespoons unsalted butter at room temperature (optional)

8 slices turkey, dark and white meat

Salt and freshly ground pepper

1 cup Sage and Onion Stuffing (see page 155)

1 cup Cranberry Relish (see page 159)

Spread four slices of bread lightly with butter, if using. Place two slices of turkey on each slice of buttered bread and season to taste with salt and pepper. Top with ¼ cup of stuffing and ¼ cup of cranberry relish. Cover the sandwiches with the remaining bread slices, cut in half on the diagonal, and serve.

# Belgium Endive and Frisée Salad with Maine Goat Cheese and Grainy Mustard Vinaigrette

*When shopping for the ingredients for this salad,
look for an aged goat cheese with a dry texture that will
crumble nicely. Good New England goat cheeses
to use include an aged* crottin *from Vermont or
a Blue Bonnet from Massachusetts.*

*Serves 4*

2 heads frisée, dark outer leaves removed

1 head Belgian endive

1 bunch chives

1 teaspoon grainy Dijon mustard

¼ cup champagne vinegar

½ cup extra-virgin olive oil

4 tablespoons crumbled aged goat cheese

Salt and freshly ground pepper

Wash and dry the greens, tearing the pale, tender inner leaves of the frisée and cutting the endive leaves into bite-size pieces. Cover and refrigerate until ready to serve. Finely chop the lower portion of the chives, reserving the top 2½ inches of each chive for garnish.

Place the mustard in a small mixing bowl and whisk in the vinegar. Gradually add the oil, whisking to emulsify the dressing. Season to taste with salt and pepper.

Just before serving, place the greens in a large bowl. Add the crumbled goat cheese and chopped chives to the chilled greens. Dress lightly with vinaigrette, reserving any unused dressing in a covered container in the refrigerator for future use. Season the salad with salt and pepper, if necessary.

Divide the salad among four plates and garnish with the reserved chives.

# BUTTERNUT SQUASH COOKIES

*These cookies have a soft texture somewhere between that of a muffin and a cookie.
Butternut squash and pumpkin purée create a beautiful fall color and a surprising, mildly
sweet flavor. They are best when baked an hour or two before serving,
but the prepared dough can be shaped into a roll, wrapped tightly, and frozen for up
to two weeks. That way, you can cut cookies from the roll and bake as needed.*

*Makes 2 dozen*

1 cup peeled, finely diced butternut squash

1¼ cups packed brown sugar

½ cup (1 stick) unsalted butter

2 eggs, beaten

½ teaspoon vanilla extract

1½ cups canned pumpkin purée

2½ cups all-purpose flour

4 teaspoons baking powder

½ teaspoon salt

½ teaspoon ground cinnamon

½ teaspoon ground nutmeg

½ cup chopped pecans (optional)

Preheat the oven to 350°F. Butter a baking sheet.

Bring a medium saucepan of salted water to a boil and add the squash. Cook for 5 minutes, or until fork-tender. Drain and reserve.

In a large bowl, cream the butter with the sugar until smooth. Add the eggs and beat thoroughly. Mix in the vanilla extract and pumpkin purée.

In another large bowl, whisk together the flour, baking powder, salt, cinnamon, and nutmeg. Combine the dry ingredients with the pumpkin mixture and stir just to combine. Stir in the diced squash and pecans, if using.

Drop well-rounded tablespoons of dough 2 inches apart on the buttered baking sheet.

Flatten each cookie slightly with the bottom of a glass that has been dipped in sugar.

Bake the cookies in the middle of the oven until lightly browned.

# Fall Vegetarian Dinner

Many guests of the White Barn Inn stay for several days during peak leaf season to watch autumn unfold while sampling the offerings of the inn's kitchen. Often they will choose the vegetarian menu for dinner one night. This menu provides an excellent opportunity to celebrate the variety of seasonal vegetables. It features several dishes which can—and should—be made in advance, since it would be challenging for one person to prepare all the courses of this meal in a single day and still sit down to enjoy them with guests that night. If you prefer not to serve an entirely vegetarian menu, then substitute the lobster recipe on page 183 for the ravioli.

## LOCAL FOREST MUSHROOM AND NEW ENGLAND GOAT CHEESE PITHIVIERS WITH ARUGULA AND HERB SALAD WITH CHANTERELLE VINAIGRETTE

*For an appetizer full of variety in texture, color, and taste,
these buttery pithiviers—puff pastry pillows stuffed with tangy goat cheese
and sautéed mushrooms—are served warm with a salad of spicy arugula,
sweet Thai basil, and fresh parsley. If wild mushrooms are unavailable, substitute
a combination of cremini, white button, portobello, or oyster mushrooms. This recipe
can be easily made using the packaged frozen puff pastry sold in grocery stores.
The unbaked pithiviers can be assembled in advance and kept in an airtight
storage container in the freezer for up to 1 month.*

*Serves 4*

1 tablespoon olive oil

1 tablespoon finely diced shallots

1 cup roughly chopped mixed wild mushrooms, such as chanterelle, chicken- and hen-of-the-woods, porcini, matsutake, or lobster mushrooms

1 pound frozen puff pastry, thawed

½ cup soft goat cheese, at room temperature

1 tablespoon chopped fresh herbs, such as chervil, chives, and parsley

1 egg, beaten

Preheat the oven to 350°F.

Heat the olive oil in a medium sauté pan over medium heat. Add the shallots and sauté for 1 to 2 minutes, until translucent but not browned. Add the mushrooms and sauté for 5 minutes, until tender. Season with salt and pepper and allow to cool.

On a clean, dry work surface, roll out a single ¼-inch layer of puff pastry. Using a 3-inch round cookie cutter, cut out eight pastry rounds.

In a medium bowl, combine the cooled mushrooms with the goat cheese and herbs, seasoning to taste with salt and pepper. Place a heaping tablespoon of the mushroom mixture in the center of four of the pastry rounds.

Lightly brush the outsides of the cheese-topped rounds with the beaten egg. Top with the remaining four rounds of puff pastry, pressing the edges to seal in the mixture. Brush the top of each pithivier with beaten egg. Using a sharp knife, lightly score the top of each pastry in a pinwheel pattern (the lines should be approximately ¼ inch apart on the outer edges of the circle).

Place on a buttered baking sheet and bake in the preheated oven for 10 to 12 minutes, until the pastry has risen and turned golden-brown. Serve at once with Arugula and Herb Salad with Chanterelle Vinaigrette (recipe follows).

The pithiviers can also be frozen on a baking sheet and stored in an airtight container in the freezer for up to a month before baking. If freezing, do not brush the pithiviers with egg wash. Defrost for ½ hour before baking, brush with egg wash, and bake for about 15 minutes, until puffed and golden brown.

# Arugula and Herb Salad
## with Chanterelle Vinaigrette

*If you can't find Thai basil or chervil,*
*substitute cilantro for an equally refreshing mix of greens.*
*Oyster mushrooms, portobello, or even*
*white button mushrooms may be substituted*
*for the fresh chanterelles.*

*Serves 4*

1 cup arugula

1 bunch fresh Thai basil

1 bunch flat-leaf parsley

1 bunch fresh chervil

2 ripe tomatoes

10 tablespoons olive oil

1 tablespoon diced shallots

½ cup sliced chanterelle mushrooms

4 tablespoons champagne vinegar

Salt and freshly ground pepper, to taste

Rinse and dry the arugula and fresh herbs, removing any yellowed leaves. Cover and refrigerate until ready to serve.

Bring a small saucepan of water to a boil and add the whole tomatoes. Blanch for 30 seconds to 1 minute, just until the skins start to split. Transfer to a bowl of cold water. When cool, remove the skins, seed the tomatoes (discarding the seeds and juice, or reserving to add to stocks, if desired), and cut the flesh into ⅛-inch dice.

In a medium skillet, heat 1 tablespoon of the olive oil over medium heat. Add the shallots and cook for 1 minute, until translucent but not browned. Add the chanterelles and cook for 5 minutes, until tender. Stir in the vinegar and season to taste with salt and pepper.

Pour the mushroom mixture into a fine sieve, reserving the pan juices in a small bowl. Gradually whisk the remaining olive oil into the juices to create an emulsion.

Combine the cooked mushrooms and the diced tomatoes, seasoning to taste with salt and pepper.

Gently toss the arugula and fresh herbs with a small amount of the dressing and a few spoonfuls of the mushroom-and-tomato mixture. Divide the salad among four plates. Arrange the remaining mushroom-and-tomato mixture around the outer edge of each plate. Place one hot pithivier next to the salad greens, and drizzle a small amount of the vinaigrette over the plate. Serve at once.

### CHANTERELLE MUSHROOMS

THE FRESHEST SEASONAL INGREDIENTS, PAINSTAKINGLY PREPARED,
FORM THE BASIS FOR EACH DISH AT THE WHITE BARN INN. FOREST MUSHROOMS,
JUST HARVESTED THAT MORNING, ARE CAREFULLY SCRAPED TO REMOVE
THE STEMS' OUTSIDE COATING BEFORE BEING COOKED WHOLE.

# ROASTED RED PEPPER
## SORBET

*This sorbet has an amazing vermilion color and
an equally surprising taste that combines the sweet, tangy,
and slightly spicy flavors of roasted red peppers.
Serve it to your guests in chilled bowls while you slip back
into the kitchen to finish preparing the ravioli (or lobster) entrée.
You will be sure to hear exclamations of delight
when you return to the table.*

*Makes 2 cups*

½ cup sugar

1 cup Roasted Red Pepper Purée (see page 177)

Pinch salt

Pinch freshly ground pepper

In a medium saucepan, combine 1 cup of water and the sugar and cook over high heat, stirring occasionally, until the sugar dissolves. Place the Red Pepper Purée in a large bowl and stir in the hot syrup until combined. Season with a pinch of salt and pepper and let cool.

Freeze the mixture in an ice cream machine, following the manufacturer's instructions. Serve at once, or store in a covered container in the freezer for up to one day in advance.

*This purée can be prepared up to four days
in advance and refrigerated.*

*Makes 1 cup*

6 red bell peppers, halved and seeded

1 tablespoon sunflower oil

¼ cup water

Preheat the oven to 350°F.

Place the peppers in a glass baking dish large enough to hold them in a single layer. Pour the oil over the peppers and toss to coat well. Cover the baking dish with aluminum foil and roast for 30 minutes, until the peppers are soft but have not yet begun to brown.

Transfer the peppers to the bowl of a food processor, adding ¼ cup water. Purée until smooth. Pass the purée through a fine sieve to remove any pieces of skin.

# Ravioli of Butternut Squash, Roasted Beet, and Pesto Potato on Spinach with Truffle Sauce

*The firm, supple sheets of pasta used to make ravioli may
be rolled out by hand or in a pasta machine.
For best results, use blended flour, a mixture of equal parts
bread flour, made from hard, glutinous wheat, and cake or pastry flour,
made from soft wheat. Sift the flour before measuring to ensure
the proper ratio of ingredients. Since egg yolks vary widely
in size, be sure to measure the yolks in a
measuring cup before adding them to the flour.*

*Serves 4*

### RAVIOLI FILLINGS

½ pound Yukon Gold potatoes
(about 2 small potatoes),
peeled and diced

4 tablespoons (½ stick) unsalted butter

5 tablespoons olive oil

Salt and freshly ground pepper

2 tablespoons Pesto (see page 36)

½ pound butternut squash
(about ½ medium squash),
peeled and diced

Pinch freshly ground nutmeg

½ pound beets (about 2 medium beets),
washed, left whole with skin on

1 tablespoon olive oil

## RAVIOLI

1¾ cups blended flour, sifted

½ cup lightly beaten egg yolks
(5 to 7 yolks from large eggs)

2 tablespoons olive oil

1 pinch fine salt

Truffle Cream Sauce (see page 181)

**To make the fillings:** Preheat the oven to 300°F.

Place the diced potatoes in a medium saucepan, cover with water, and bring to a boil over high heat. Reduce the heat to medium and cook until the potatoes can be easily pierced with a fork, 12 to 15 minutes. Drain the potatoes and place them on an ungreased baking sheet in the oven to dry for 5 minutes. Transfer the potatoes to a mixing bowl and mash until smooth, adding the butter and 4 tablespoons of olive oil. Season to taste with salt and freshly ground pepper. Set aside until ready to fill the ravioli. Just before filling them, add 2 tablespoons of Pesto to the potatoes and mix well.

Place the squash in a medium saucepan, cover with water, and bring to a boil over high heat. Reduce the heat to medium and cook until the squash is easily pierced with a fork, 7 to 9 minutes. Drain the squash cubes and place them on an ungreased baking sheet in the oven to dry for 5 minutes. Transfer to the bowl of a food processor and purée until smooth. Season to taste with salt, pepper, and a small pinch of nutmeg.

Increase the oven heat to 350°F. Rub the beets with the tablespoon of olive oil, season with salt and pepper, and wrap tightly in aluminum foil. Place in a baking dish and roast for 30 minutes, or until very tender when gently squeezed.

Remove the beets from the foil, cool, and peel. Dice the beets coarsely and place them in the bowl of a food processor. Purée until smooth, seasoning to taste with salt and pepper.

**To make the ravioli:** In the bowl of a food processor, combine the flour, 5 egg yolks, olive oil, and salt. Pulse for 30 seconds, or until the mixture has the texture of wet sand. Turn the mixture out onto a work surface and knead it with the palms of your hands to form a dough. Continue kneading for 2 to 3 minutes, until it is smooth and pliable. If you plan to roll out the dough by hand, rather than in a pasta machine, knead for several minutes longer. If the mixture is too dry to gather up into a ball after a minute or two of kneading, mix in an additional egg yolk. Gather the dough loosely into a ball, cover with plastic wrap, and let rest in the refrigerator for about 30 minutes.

If rolling by hand, use a wooden rolling pin on a clean, dry work surface. Roll out the dough as thinly as possible, forming a rectangular sheet roughly 12 x 14 inches. If using a pasta machine, roll the dough to the thinnest setting recommended by the manufacturer for making ravioli.

Cut the sheet in half, leaving both pieces on the work surface. Working down the edge of one sheet, place 1 tablespoon of the filling 1½ inches in from the side and top. Place another tablespoon of filling 3 inches below it. Repeat this step until you reach the bottom of the sheet. Make another vertical row of filling 3 inches from the first row. (If you are using pasta sheets rolled in a pasta machine, you may only be able to fit one row of ravioli on each sheet.) Repeat this step until you have used all the fillings to create eight evenly spaced portions of each filling, covering half of the total pasta sheets.

Lightly brush water around the mounds of filling. Gently lift the remaining pasta by loosely folding it, and unfold it over the sheet with the mounds of filling. Press down to seal the layers of pasta around the filling.

Using a 3-inch fluted cutter, cut round ravioli, making sure the edges are fully sealed. The ravioli can be made a day in advance kept, tightly covered with plastic wrap, in the refrigerator. They may also be frozen on a baking sheet, transferred to an airtight container or zipper-lock bag, and frozen for up to six weeks. Just before serving, bring a large pot of salted water to a boil. Gently slide the ravioli into the water and reduce the heat to medium, keeping the water at a very low boil for 3 minutes. If using frozen ravioli, do not thaw them before cooking, but add an extra minute to the cooking time. Gently remove the ravioli from the hot water and serve immediately with the Truffle Cream Sauce.

## TRUFFLE CREAM SAUCE

*Truffle oil infuses this champagne cream sauce with a rich, full, irresistible flavor. The sauce is also delicious served with fettuccine or penne. We usually make our own truffle oil by steeping the peelings of white or black truffles in olive oil. When buying truffle oil at a gourmet store, look for a good-quality white truffle oil with no artificial flavoring. Some of the best truffle oils come from Italy.*

*Makes 1½ cups*

1 tablespoon unsalted butter

1 shallot, finely chopped (about 1½ tablespoons)

1 clove garlic, finely chopped

1 cup Vegetable Stock (see recipe on page 223)

1 cup heavy cream

1 cup champagne

Salt and freshly ground pepper, to taste

1 pound fresh baby spinach, picked over and washed

1 teaspoon truffle oil

¼ ounce fresh black truffle, very thinly sliced (optional)

Melt the butter in a medium sauté pan over low heat. Add the shallot and garlic and sauté for 3 minutes, until transparent but not browned. Add the Vegetable Stock, increase the heat to high, and cook until the liquid is reduced by half. Add the cream and ½ cup of champagne. Reduce over medium heat until the sauce has thickened enough to coat the back of a spoon. Season to taste with salt and pepper and strain through a fine sieve.

Bring two large pots of salted water to a boil. Add the spinach to one pot and cook for 2 minutes, until bright green and tender. Drain well. Add the ravioli to the other pot and cook as directed above for 3 minutes. Drain well.

While the spinach and ravioli are cooking, reheat the sauce, add the remaining ½ cup of champagne and the truffle oil, and stir to combine.

To serve, divide the spinach among four plates, placing it in the center of each plate. Gently slide the cooked ravioli into the sauce, then divide the ravioli among the plates. Drizzle the remaining sauce over the ravioli and spinach and serve immediately, topping with the truffle slices, if using.

EVERY NIGHT BEFORE DINNER,
THE SERVICE STAFF GATHERS FOR A PRE-MEAL
MEETING TO DISCUSS THE SPECIAL
NEEDS OF ANY GUESTS AND TO PLAN AHEAD
FOR THE SEAMLESS PRESENTATION
OF A COMPLEX MEAL.

## STEAMED MAINE LOBSTER NESTLED ON A BED OF HOMEMADE FETTUCCINE WITH CARROT, GINGER, SNOW PEAS, AND A COGNAC CORAL BUTTER SAUCE

*This beautifully composed dish is one of the chef's signature presentations and a year-round favorite at the White Barn Inn. The steamed lobster is carefully shelled to keep the claw and tail meat intact. These are rearranged in the shape of a lobster atop a bed of lightly sauced fettucine, giving diners the pleasure of eating an entire lobster without the work of shelling it themselves.*

*Serves 4*

4 (1½ pound) lobsters

½ cup heavy cream

1 cup Lobster Stock (see recipe on page 78)

½ cup cognac

2 sticks (½ pound) plus 2 tablespoons
unsalted butter, chilled

Salt and freshly ground pepper, to taste

1 (1-inch) piece ginger root, peeled

2 medium carrots, peeled

1 cup snow peas

1 pound fresh fettuccine

1 tablespoon extra-virgin olive oil

Bring a large stockpot filled with water to a boil. Plunge the lobsters headfirst into the water, submerging them completely, and boil for 9 minutes. Remove the lobsters from the boiling water and refresh in a bath of salted ice water. Break off the head cavity of each lobster, removing and reserving any coral or roe. Clean out the head, discarding the contents. Using kitchen shears, remove the lower part of the head shell, reserving the top of the shell with the antennae intact for garnish. Remove the tail and shell the claws, keeping the flesh whole, if possible. Using kitchen shears, cut off the bottom part of the tail shells and reserve for garnish.

In a large, heavy skillet, combine the cream, Lobster Stock, and cognac. Cook at a low boil over medium heat until reduced by half. Dice two sticks (½ pound) of the chilled butter and whisk into the sauce, along with the reserved lobster coral. Strain the sauce through a fine sieve into a medium saucepan, season to taste with salt and pepper, and keep warm over very low heat.

Cut the ginger, carrots, and snow peas into fine julienne, keeping each vegetable separate.

Place the ginger in a small saucepan of cold water and bring to a boil. Drain and repeat this process two more times, using fresh, cold water.

Fill a large stockpot and a large saucepan with salted water and bring to a boil. Add the fettuccine to the stockpot and cook for 5 minutes, or until tender but still firm. Drain and toss with the olive oil. Add the carrots to the saucepan of boiling water and cook for 2 minutes. Add the snow peas and continue cooking for 1 minute more. Drain and toss the vegetables with the remaining 2 tablespoons of butter, seasoning to taste with salt and pepper. Combine the fettuccine and vegetables in a large bowl and toss very gently to mix. Arrange in nests on the center of four dinner plates.

Gently reheat the lobster meat in the lobster coral sauce. Arrange the tail and claw meat in the shape of a whole lobster on top of each pasta nest, using the head and tail shells for garnish. Spoon the remaining sauce over the plates and serve immediately.

# POIRE WILLIAM CRÈME BRÛLÉE ON A SABLÉ BISCUIT AND PEAR SORBET WITH SPICED PORT WINE SAUCE

*This elegant, layered dessert combines the warm, creamy texture*
*of crème brûlée with the cool, ever-so-slightly granular consistency of pear sorbet.*
*A crisp, sweet biscuit separates the two layers and adds yet another dimension of flavor and*
*texture. Each element of the dessert—the Poire William-infused crème brûlée*
*the pear sorbet, and the poached pears—brings out a subtly different aspect*
*of the fruit's flavor. Because the crème brûlée must be refrigerated overnight and the sorbet*
*needs to freeze for at least four hours before serving, this recipe is best started the day*
*before you plan to serve it. For a simpler dessert, prepare just the crème brûlée*
*or the sorbet, and serve with a garnish of poached pears.*

## POIRE WILLIAM CRÈME BRÛLÉE

*Serves 8*

4 cups (1 quart) heavy cream

1½ cups milk

3 tablespoons Poire William, or other clear pear brandy

1½ cups egg yolks (15 to 18 yolks from large eggs)

1⅓ cups sugar, plus extra for the brûlée topping

2 eggs

8 Sablé Biscuits (see page 187)

Pear Sorbet (see page 188)

Poached Pears (see page 256)

Spiced Port Wine Sauce (see page 189)

Preheat the oven to 300°F.

In a medium saucepan with a heavy bottom, combine the cream, milk, and Poire William. Bring to a boil over medium heat.

In a large bowl, combine the egg yolks, whole eggs, and sugar. Using an electric mixer or whisking by hand, beat at medium speed for 5 minutes, until the mixture turns pale yellow.

Whisking constantly, add a quarter of the hot cream mixture to the egg mixture. When fully combined, gradually add the remaining cream mixture to the egg mixture, whisking continuously. Strain through a sieve to remove any lumps.

Pour the mixture into a 12 x 6-inch glass baking dish. Cover with aluminum foil. Place this dish inside a larger, deeper baking dish and add water to come halfway up the outside of the glass baking dish. Place in the center of the oven and bake for 1 hour to 1 hour and 15 minutes, until the custard becomes firm at the edges but still trembles slightly in the center. Remove from the oven, let cool to room temperature, and place in the refrigerator until it is fully chilled. Cover with plastic wrap and refrigerate overnight.

Just before serving, prepare a kitchen torch or preheat the oven to broil.

Arrange the Sablé Biscuits on an ungreased baking sheet. Using a 3-inch round cutter, cut disks of the chilled custard and place one on top of each biscuit. Sprinkle a light, even coating of sugar on top of each custard. Caramelize the sugar with a kitchen torch or place the baking sheet under a broiler, 3 to 5 inches below the heat source, until the sugar browns. Watch carefully to avoid burning. Arrange each serving of biscuit and crème brûlée on top of a disk of Pear Sorbet. Place in the center of a dessert plate, surround with the slices of Poached Pear, and drizzle with Spiced Port Wine Sauce.

## SABLÉ BISCUITS

*Sablé is a French culinary term for sweet dough.
In this recipe, it yields a sweet, crisp biscuit that provides
the perfect layer between the cold sorbet and the just-browned
Crème Brûlée. This recipe is made with plenty of butter and
a light flour suitable for pastries or cakes.*

*Makes 12 biscuits*

1¾ sticks unsalted butter

¾ cup confectioners' sugar

2 egg yolks

1⅔ cups pastry or cake flour, sifted

Preheat oven to 350°F. Butter a baking sheet.

Place the butter and sugar in the bowl of a standing mixer. On medium speed, cream the mixture for about 5 minutes, until white and fluffy. Add the egg yolks and mix thoroughly. Add the sifted flour and mix by hand, stopping as soon as it is fully incorporated; take care not to overmix. Wrap the dough in plastic wrap and place in the refrigerator for 15 minutes.

Using a floured rolling pin, roll out the dough ¼ inch thick on a lightly floured cool surface, such as marble. Using a 3-inch cookie cutter, cut the dough into rounds, and arrange them 1 inch apart on a greased baking sheet. Bake for 8 to 10 minutes, until the cookies turn golden brown around the edges. Cool on a wire rack. These cookies are best served the day they are made, but they can be stored in an airtight container for one to two days, if necessary.

## Pear Sorbet

*At the White Barn Inn, we make this sorbet with pear purée
purchased from a gourmet purveyor. To make your own purée, peel and core
three pears. Quarter the pears and place in a glass baking dish.
Cover with foil and bake in a 350°F oven for 20 minutes, until tender
but not browned. Purée until smooth in a food processor.*

*Serves 8*

2 cups pear purée

¾ cup sugar

Place the pear purée in a large, heatproof bowl. Combine the sugar with ½ cup of water in a medium saucepan and bring to a boil over medium high heat, stirring until the sugar is completely dissolved. Remove from heat and pour over the purée. If you are using homemade pear purée, allow the syrup to cool before adding to the purée. Let the mixture cool to room temperature, then cover and refrigerate.

Freeze the mixture in an ice cream machine, following the manufacturer's directions. Transfer the sorbet to a 12 x 6-inch glass dish, spreading it evenly, and place in the freezer for at least 4 hours, until firm. To serve with the Crème Brûlée above, cut the sorbet into 3-inch disks using a cookie cutter. Otherwise, serve small scoops of the sorbet as an intermediate course or a dessert. It keeps for up to two weeks in a covered container in the freezer.

## Spiced Port Wine Sauce

*Makes 1 cup*

1 cup port

1 cup sugar

1 (6-inch) stick cinnamon

1 piece star anise

Pinch freshly ground white pepper

Pinch ground allspice

In a medium saucepan, combine 1 cup of water with the port, sugar, cinnamon, star anise, white pepper, and allspice. Bring to a boil over high heat. Reduce the heat to medium low and simmer for 15 to 20 minutes, until the sauce is reduced by half and has thickened enough to coat the back of a spoon. Remove from the heat and let cool. The sauce will thicken further upon cooling. The sauce can be kept in the refrigerator in an airtight container for three to four days.

OFFERING 8,000 BOTTLES FROM EVERY MAJOR WINE PRODUCING REGION IN THE WORLD, THE WINE CELLAR AT THE WHITE BARN INN INCLUDES THE PERFECT VINTAGE TO COMPLEMENT EVERY DISH. WITH A TUSCAN VINEYARD MURAL BY WELL-KNOWN LOCAL ARTIST JUDITH HARDENBROOK, THE WINE CELLAR SEATS UP TO 15 FOR PRIVATE PARTIES.

# Romantic Fireside Dinner

The salad and entrée for this meal are relatively simple to prepare—perfect for a relaxed dinner with friends or a romantic evening at home. While the s 'mores will require advance planning if you make the graham crackers and marshmallows from scratch, they are sure to delight everyone.

## WARM FALL MUSHROOM SALAD WITH SHERRY VINAIGRETTE

*Lightly sautéed and dressed with a slightly sweet sherry vinaigrette,*
*fall mushrooms lend a deliciously earthy flavor to this salad. At the White Barn Inn,*
*an expert forager provides us with an ever-changing supply of seasonal mushrooms.*
*Fall offerings include hen-of-the-woods, matsutake, black chanterelles, and*
*cèpes. If you don't have access to wild mushrooms, a mixture of cultivated mushrooms*
*such as porcini, cremini, oyster, or portobello makes a good substitute.*

*Serves 4*

4 cups mesclun mix or
other mixed greens

1 cup mixed wild mushrooms,
lightly washed, drained, and towel dried

¼ cup sherry vinegar

½ cup extra-virgin olive oil

1 tablespoon blended oil (see Note)

Salt and freshly ground pepper

1 tablespoon diced shallot

2 tablespoons chopped chives

Wash and dry the mesclun and refrigerate until ready to serve. Trim the stems from the mushrooms and cut the mushrooms into bite-size pieces.

Measure the sherry vinegar into a small bowl and gradually whisk in the olive oil. Season to taste with salt and pepper.

In a medium skillet, warm the blended oil over medium heat. Add the shallots and sauté for a few seconds. Add the mushrooms and sauté, turning gently, for 2 to 3 minutes, until the mushrooms are soft. Add 2 tablespoons of the sherry dressing, season to taste with salt and pepper, and remove from the heat. Allow the mushrooms to cool for 3 to 5 minutes.

In a large bowl, combine the mesclun, mushrooms, and chopped chives. Add just enough dressing to coat the salad lightly, toss gently, and taste for seasoning. Divide the salad among four plates and serve immediately.

**Note:** Blended oil is a mixture of 90 percent vegetable oil and 10 percent olive oil.

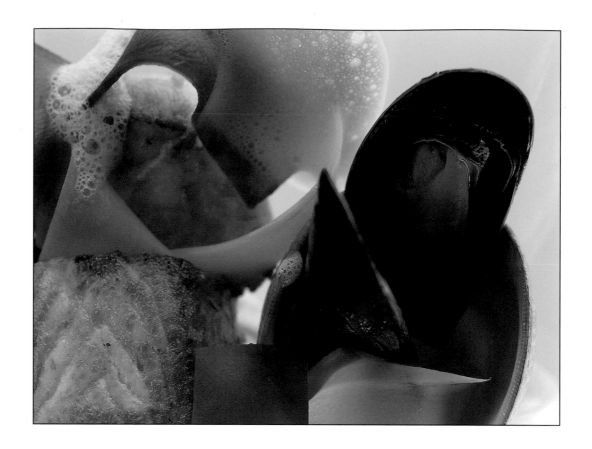

# Ragout of Maine Salmon with Local Shellfish Medley and Saffron Champagne Sauce

*This elegant seafood mélange delights the eyes and the tongue.*
*Served in the shell, the clams and mussels have great visual appeal. Saffron lends*
*a golden tone to the sauce, and the colorful ribbons of lightly sautéed vegetables*
*are evocative of seaweed. If desired, accompany this dish with rice pilaf or boiled*
*potatoes tossed with plenty of butter and chopped dill or parsley.*

*Serves 4*

1 cup fruity white wine, such as Riesling

16 mahogany clams or other medium clams in the shell, scrubbed

16 mussels in the shell, scrubbed and debearded if necessary

2 tablespoons unsalted butter

1 shallot, diced

1 clove garlic, minced

Pinch saffron (about 20 threads)

1 cup heavy cream

1 cup champagne

Salt and freshly ground pepper

1 large celery root, peeled

1 large carrot, peeled

1 large Yukon Gold potato, peeled

1 large beet, peeled

1 pound skinless salmon filet, cut into 1-inch cubes

8 diver-harvested scallops

In a large skillet with a heavy bottom, bring the wine to a boil over medium high heat. Add the clams and mussels and cover. Cook, shaking the pan occasionally, until the shells open. Discard any clams or mussels with unopened shells. Strain the pan juices through a fine sieve lined with cheesecloth to remove any sand, and reserve.

Heat 1 tablespoon butter in a medium skillet over low heat and add the shallots, garlic, and saffron. Sauté for 3 minutes, until the shallots are translucent but not browned. Add 1 cup of the reserved pan juices, increase the heat to high, and boil, uncovered, until the mixture is reduced by half. Add the cream and $\frac{1}{2}$ cup of champagne. Reduce the heat to medium and simmer until the sauce thickens enough to coat the back of a spoon. Add salt and pepper to taste and strain through a fine sieve.

Using a mandoline or an Asian vegetable slicer, cut the celery root, carrot, potato, and beet into ribbons 1 inch wide. Heat the remaining butter in a medium sauté pan over medium heat. Add the celery root, carrot, and potato, and cook, turning gently, for 1 or 2 minutes, just until tender. Add the beet ribbons and cook turning gently, for 1 to 2 minutes, just until tender. Remove from the heat.

Season the salmon and scallops with salt and pepper. In a deep skillet or casserole set over medium heat, combine the salmon and scallops with the remaining $\frac{1}{2}$ cup of champagne. Bring to a boil, then reduce the heat to medium and cook for 2 to 3 minutes, just until the salmon and scallops are tender, with rare centers.

Add the cooked mussels and clams, reserved sauce, and vegetable ribbons to the skillet, stirring gently to combine without breaking up the salmon. Serve immediately in large, warmed soup bowls.

# S'MORES

*Growing up in England, I had never encountered s'mores until I came
to America. Toasting these sweet little sandwiches by the fire is the perfect way
to take the nip out of a cold day. If you make the graham crackers and
marshmallows from scratch, you can transform this simple campfire recipe
into a gourmet treat to enjoy on a romantic fireside evening.*

*Makes 12*

24 Cinnamon Graham Crackers (see page 195)

12 good-quality milk chocolate bars (1 ounce each)

12 Marshmallows (see page 196)

Arrange the Cinnamon Graham Crackers on a large platter. Place one chocolate bar on twelve of the graham crackers.

Using a long-handled barbecue fork, toast each marshmallow over an open fire until golden brown. Immediately place a toasted marshmallow on a chocolate-topped graham cracker. Cover with another cracker and press gently to make a sandwich.

Let stand for 1 minute to soften the chocolate, then eat while warm. Repeat with the remaining ingredients.

WHILE THE KITCHEN STAFF PREPARES THE ELEMENTS
OF EACH EVENING'S DINNER, THE SERVICE STAFF ATTENDS TO
ALL THE DETAILS OF AN ELEGANT TABLE INCLUDING
CRISPLY PRESSED LINENS AND WELL-POLISHED TABLEWARE.

*Makes 24 crackers*

2 cups whole wheat flour

1 cup all-purpose flour

1 teaspoon baking powder

½ teaspoon baking soda

Pinch salt

¾ cup brown sugar, packed

½ cup vegetable shortening

⅓ cup honey

1 teaspoon vanilla extract

½ cup milk

3 tablespoons sugar

1 teaspoon ground cinnamon

In a large bowl, whisk together the flours, baking powder, baking soda, and salt. In another large bowl, combine the brown sugar with the shortening, and cream until smooth. Using an electric mixer or a wooden spoon, beat in the honey and vanilla until light and fluffy.

Add the dry ingredients to the shortening mixture, alternating with the milk mixture. Beat well after each addition until the ingredients are fully incorporated.

Wrap the dough in plastic wrap and refrigerate for several hours or overnight.

Preheat the oven to 350°F.

Divide the chilled dough into quarters. On a well-floured surface, roll each quarter into a 15 x 5-inch rectangle. Cut each rectangle into six small rectangles measuring 5 x 2½ inches each. Place the rectangles on an ungreased baking sheet. Make a line across the center of each rectangle with the tines of fork and score a regular pattern of holes on each cracker. You can also score initials or decorative patterns.

In a small bowl, combine the sugar and cinnamon. Sprinkle the mixture evenly over the crackers. Bake the crackers for 13 to 15 minutes, until golden-brown at the edges and firm to the touch. Remove from the baking sheet at once and cool on a wire rack.

# MARSHMALLOWS

*These homemade marshmallows can be prepared a week in advance
and stored in an airtight container in the refrigerator.*

*Makes 12 marshmallows*

2 cups sugar

2 tablespoons powdered gelatin
soaked in ½ cup cold water

1 teaspoon vanilla extract

¼ teaspoon salt

2 tablespoons confectioners' sugar,
plus additional for dusting

2 tablespoons cornstarch

In a medium saucepan with a heavy bottom, combine the granulated sugar
and ¾ cup water. Bring to a boil and cook to the soft-ball stage (238°F on a
candy thermometer). Soft-ball stage is achieved when a small amount of
syrup dropped into a cup of cold water forms a soft ball that flattens out but
does not fall apart when picked up with a spoon. Remove from the heat and
stir in the dissolved gelatin.

Transfer the mixture to a glass bowl and let cool to room temperature.
Using an electric mixer, whip the mixture until thick and white. Stir in the
vanilla extract, salt, confectioners' sugar, and cornstarch.

Spread the mixture evenly into a 9-inch square pan. Cool, uncovered, in
the refrigerator until firm. Using a wet knife to prevent sticking, cut into
twelve squares. Dust lightly with confectioners' sugar and enjoy.

# MULLED APPLE CIDER

*There's nothing like a hot mug of mulled cider or Irish coffee
to warm up a cold evening. This recipe, infused with spices and orange peel,
is delicious with or without the addition of rum.*

*Serves 2*

2 cups fresh apple cider

1 (6-inch) cinnamon stick

$\frac{1}{8}$ teaspoon ground nutmeg

Peel of 1 medium orange

2 ounces dark rum or spiced rum (optional)

In a medium saucepan, combine the cider, cinnamon, nutmeg, and orange peel and bring to a boil over medium heat. Remove the pan from the heat and allow the mixture to infuse for 20 minutes. Strain through a medium sieve into a clean saucepan. Heat over medium heat until hot. Add the rum, if using, and divide between two glass mugs.

CONSTANT COMMUNICATION
BETWEEN THE KITCHEN STAFF AND THE SERVICE STAFF
ENSURES THAT EVERY DETAIL IS ADDRESSED, AND
THAT EACH COURSE IS PRESENTED WITH PRECISE ATTENTION
TO TIMING, TEMPERATURE, AND APPEARANCE.

# IRISH COFFEE

*At the White Barn Inn, we serve our Irish coffee with*
*a generous amount of whiskey. If you prefer a less alcoholic drink,*
*try adding just one ounce of whiskey instead of two.*

*Serves 2*

4 ounces Jameson Irish whiskey

2 cups hot, freshly brewed coffee

6 teaspoons whipped cream (lightly sweetened, if desired)

Cocoa powder

Warm two heat-resistant glass cups with hot water. Pour out the hot water and divide the whiskey between the cups. Fill with hot coffee and top with whipped cream. Sprinkle with cocoa powder and serve immediately.

# Autumn Ingredients

### WILD MUSHROOMS

Hen-of-the-woods, also called maitake, are large, ridged mushrooms that grow beneath maples and oaks and flourish in the cool fall weather. The even larger cauliflower mushrooms (mature ones can measure 6 to 8 inches in width) spring up beneath trees that are dropping their leaves. Colorful cèpes with tall caps nestle among the roots of blue spruce trees, and the white matsutake grow only on sleep slopes under hemlock trees.

### CRANBERRIES

These bright berries are synonymous with autumn in New England. One of the few fruits native to North America (along with blueberries and Concord grapes), they thrive in low temperatures and can be harvested from cranberry bogs as late as November. Their tart taste, balanced with a judicious amount of sugar, creates a delicious accompaniment to the season's earthy, savory flavors.

### PEARS

Pears are an abundant early autumn fruit that make wonderful additions to seasonal tossed green salads. They come in many sizes, shapes, and textures, from tiny, firm Seckel pears to the larger, softer-fleshed Comice pears. Roasted pears make flavorful garnishes for meat entrees, and pear purée forms the basis for a delicious fall sorbet.

### APPLES

Many varieties of apples are harvested in Maine's orchards from late August through October, including McIntosh, Cortland, Macoun, and Northern Spy. Apples add sweetness and fall flavor, whether sliced raw into salads, simmered in a ragout of root vegetables, or sautéed with sugar for dessert.

### LOBSTER

Lobsters grow by molting their shells, shedding every year up to the age of seven. They grow their new shells during the warmer summer months. By the time the ocean cools down in the fall, lobsters have formed new shells and their flesh becomes firm and particularly succulent. The chef at The White Barn Inn considers autumn the best time for eating the crustaceans, whether steaming them and enjoying them straight out of the shell with lemon butter or pairing the sweet meat with delicately flavored cream sauces.

### PUMPKIN

The bright flesh of pumpkins is remarkably versatile. It may be blended with cream to make a mild-flavored soup with an extraordinary pale orange color, or with spices and eggs to form a zesty pie filling. The seeds of the pumpkin add a deliciously nutty flavor to salads, whether roasted and scattered on top as a garnish or infused into a richly flavored dressing made with pumpkinseed oil.

# Winter at the
# WHITE BARN INN

In Maine, winter is called the Silent Season, perhaps because so many of the state's seasonal residents, both avian and human, flock to warmer climates, leaving behind an eerily serene landscape. In early December Canadian geese soar in wavering formations across the sky, their haunting cries piercing the thin, cold air. Great nor'easters sweep in, bringing powerful winds that buffet the sea and shore, and clouds of snow that swirl in white-on-white frenzy. Days of exquisite calm often follow, when a crescent moon hangs like a sliver of ice in the afternoon sky and a faint pink glow along the western horizon presages early sunset.

Kennebunkport's year-round residents and a devoted population of off-season visitors cherish winter's particular pleasures. Wrapped in sweaters and hats, they take dogs for long romps on Mother's Beach, where the surf freezes along the water's edge and frozen sea foam skitters across the sand. Or they strike out for exhilarating walks along Ocean Avenue, savoring the crystalline light that accentuates the colors and textures of the ever-changing seascape. At Spouting Rock, deep blue and luminous green waves explode with arcs of spray against snow-limned ledges of black and purple stone. Along the marshes lining the Kennebunk River, snow clings to the windblown plants, its pale dust contrasting against golden blades of marsh grass, the soft brown rods of cattails, and clusters of crimson berries.

Although most of the pleasure craft are stowed for the season, lobster boats still ply the icy waters, their brightly painted hulls and droning motors venturing out at dawn while most sleepers still snuggle deeply into down-lined beds. Other fishermen gather succulent fruits of the winter sea, including Maine oysters, mussels, and North Atlantic shrimp caught several hundred miles offshore. Deep in the woods, hunters claim deer and pheasant that will be savored at the Christmas table alongside the season's hearty vegetables: sweet potatoes, celery root, turnips, and cabbage, both red and green.

These ingredients shine in sophisticated presentations at the White Barn Inn during Christmas Prelude, a weeklong celebration in early December when the entire town of Kennebunkport heralds the beginning of

Inn to celebrate Christmas, ring in the New Year, or indulge in a Valentine's Day escape-for-two.

Throughout the holiday season, chef Jonathan Cartwright revels in the delights of the winter table, ranging from the decadent excess of Christmas and New Year's Eve feasts replete with oysters, foie gras, and wine-rich sauces to the simple pleasure of a bowl of hearty soup. Since winter is a time when family and

*. . . the White Barn Inn during Christmas Prelude, a weeklong celebration in early December when the entire town of Kennebunkport heralds the beginning of the holidays. Miles of evergreen garland decorate sidewalks and doorways, and at night, glittering strands of light illumine the homes and shops.*

the holidays. Miles of evergreen garland decorate sidewalks and doorways, and at night, glittering strands of light illumine the homes and shops. On the first Friday of the Prelude, guests gather at the Inn for a festive cocktail party, where champagne flows and caviar-topped canapés of oysters and salmon tartare are nibbled from silver spoons. The following evening they join the townspeople for roasted chestnuts and Christmas carols on the grounds of the local Franciscan monastery. Many guests return year after year to the

friends enjoy meeting over food and drinks, the chef also suggests two party menus, for a holiday cocktail gathering and a New Year's Day brunch, that promise to dazzle guests. Together, these recipes and entertaining ideas reveal the full spectrum of winter's joys, from the sociable feast to the quietly romantic stroll in the snow. The chef recommends a bracing walk by the sea as the perfect antidote to holiday feasting, with a pocketful of warm, freshly roasted chestnuts and a thermal flask of spiced wine or rum-spiked tea.

# WINTER MENUS

### Winter by the Sea

Spiced Nuts

Grissini Breadsticks

Roasted Chestnuts

Christmas Present Hunters' Tea

Glühwein

Velvety Pheasant and Chestnut Soup

•

### Christmas Prelude Dinner at
### the White Barn Inn

Kennebunkport Lobster on Mango Salsa
with Golden Osetra Caviar and Lobster Mayonnaise

Truffled Celeriac Soup

Pan Seared New England Venison Cutlet
with a Caramelized Sweet Potato Timbale, Red Cabbage,
and Elderberry Sauce

or

Tenderloin of Beef Glazed in a Foie Gras Crust
on a Potato Rösti with Madeira Sauce

Warm Chocolate Cake with Warm Chocolate Sauce
and Vanilla Bean Ice Cream

## A Holiday Cocktail Party

Northern Lights Cocktail

Maine Oyster Canapés

Pan-seared North Atlantic Shrimp
and Quail Egg Canapés

Duck Confit and Apple Pasties

Feta Cheese and Spinach Rolls

Maine Peekie Toe Crab Cakes

Marinated Salmon Tartar with Golden Osetra Caviar

•

## A New Year's Day Brunch

Cold-Smoked Maine Salmon with
Creamy Scrambled Eggs

Apple French Toast

Pineapple Coconut Granola

Ham and Mozzarella Quiche

Poached Pears

Prunes Poached with Cinnamon and Port

# Winter by the Sea

It's tempting to stay indoors when the weather turns cold, but a walk along the water's edge at sunset can be the perfect antidote to winter's ennui or holiday overindulgence. By planning ahead and filling your pockets with a bag of roasted nuts and a thermal flask with a hot drink, you can transform a chilly walk into a delightful outing. When you return, there is no better way to reward a well-honed appetite than with a hot bowl of soup and just-baked breadsticks.

## SPICED NUTS

*This delicious snack combines the textures
of pecans, cashews, almonds, and pumpkin seeds with a
spice mix of dried red chiles, black pepper, and
yellow curry powder. Diners at the White Barn Inn enjoy
these nuts served warm at the bar with cocktails.
They can be prepared in minutes and make a healthy snack
to munch on a wintertime walk, as well as
a perfect cocktail nibble for dinner
parties at home.*

*Makes 1¾ cups*

½ cup shelled pecans

½ cup unsalted cashews

½ cup unsalted almonds

4 tablespoons pumpkin seeds

1 tablespoon olive oil

⅛ teaspoon cayenne pepper

$^1/_8$ teaspoon chili powder

$^1/_4$ teaspoon curry powder

$^1/_4$ teaspoon salt

$^1/_4$ teaspoon freshly ground black pepper

Preheat the oven to 450°F.

In a large bowl, combine all of the ingredients. Toss until the nuts and seeds are completely coated with the spice mixture. Taste for seasoning and add more cayenne, chili, and curry powder if you prefer a spicier taste. Transfer the nuts to a baking sheet and bake for 1 to 2 minutes, just until the nuts begin to sizzle and the seeds begin to pop. Watch carefully to avoid burning the nuts. Serve warm, or cool on the baking sheet and transfer to an airtight container. Nuts will keep at room temperature in a sealed container for two weeks.

# Grissini Breadsticks

*These crisp, thin breadsticks make a delicious accompaniment to salads and soups or a great cocktail snack that won't spoil guests' appetites. They are a favorite at Grissini, the White Barn Inn's sister restaurant in nearby Kennebunk, which takes its name from the Italian word for breadsticks. There, they are baked in a wood-fired oven alongside pizza, grilled steak, seafood, and fowl. But they may be prepared just as effectively in a conventional oven at home and are a simple bread to master.*

*Makes 30 12-inch breadsticks*

2½ cups sifted bread flour

1 cup semolina flour

2 teaspoons (½ ounce) dry yeast

2 teaspoons salt

1½ tablespoons olive oil

Dried Italian herb mixture,
poppy or sesame seeds, or sea salt (optional)

In an electric mixer fitted with a dough hook, combine the flours, yeast, and salt. Mixing at low speed, gradually add the oil and 1¼ cups water until the wet and dry ingredients are fully combined and form a soft dough. Knead for a few minutes, until smooth and pliable. Cover the dough with a dry towel and let it rest at room temperature for 20 minutes.

Preheat the oven to 375°F.

Divide the dough into ten evenly sized balls. On a floured work surface, roll each dough ball into a cylinder 36 inches in length. Cut each into three 12-inch sticks. Arrange 1 inch apart on an ungreased baking sheet. If desired, sprinkle lightly with dried Italian herb mixture, poppy or sesame seeds, or sea salt. Bake for 40 minutes, until golden brown and crisp. Cool slightly on the baking sheet and serve warm. Breadsticks are best eaten the day they are made but can be stored in an airtight container for 3 days.

## ROASTED CHESTNUTS

*In England and New England, chestnuts roasting by an open fire
have been a quintessential part of Christmas for centuries. At the White Barn Inn,
where 200 pounds of chestnuts are roasted and served to carolers during
the Christmas Prelude each year, they are true harbingers of the holiday season.
Throughout most of the country, raw chestnuts are available in the produce
section of quality grocery stores. They are simple to prepare, and you will find
the sweetly nutty aroma they exude during roasting irresistible.*

*Makes 2 pounds*

2 pounds fresh chestnuts

Preheat a charcoal grill. Using the tip of a sharp knife, pierce a cross on the pointed
tip of each chestnut, opposite the dark flat circle on the nut's base. Once all the
flames have subsided, arrange the chestnuts in a single layer on the grill over the
glowing coals. If the bars of the grill are spaced too widely, use a grilling basket to
keep the nuts from falling into the fire. Alternately, chestnuts can be roasted in a
metal basket or on a grate placed near the embers of an open fireplace. Cook the
chestnuts for 10 to 12 minutes, turning frequently, until the cut edges of the shell
curl slightly and the chestnut meat is tender but still moist.

# CHRISTMAS PRESENT HUNTERS' TEA

*European hunters have long enjoyed hot tea fortified with alcohol
during or after a day spent stalking game in cold fields and forests. This version of
hunters' tea, spiked with mint-flavored schnapps and rum, is guaranteed
to soothe the winter shivers, whether brought on by a day of hunting or an afternoon
of holiday shopping. When serving this tea to guests, the ceremony of igniting
the rum-soaked sugar cubes adds a festive and memorable touch to the presentation.*

*Serves 4*

4 slices lemon

8 sugar cubes

4 cups freshly brewed black tea, such as Darjeeling

2 teaspoons peppermint schnapps

4 teaspoons white rum

Place one slice of lemon and one sugar cube in each of four heat-resistant glass cups.
Divide the hot tea evenly among the cups. Add ½ teaspoon of peppermint schnapps
to each cup. Place the remaining sugar cubes on four teaspoons arranged on a heatproof plate. Pour 1 teaspoon of rum over each sugar cube. Set the sugar cubes on
fire and add the burning cubes to the tea.

# GLÜHWEIN

*Glühwein (glue-vine), a citrus-and-spice-mulled red wine, is a*
*traditional German winter beverage. It is best prepared with Cabernet Sauvignon*
*or Merlot, but even an inexpensive table wine makes a tasty cup of glühwein.*
*Some people prefer it mulled with orange peel and juice instead of*
*lemon, and others add more alcohol, such as spiced rum or flavored schnapps.*
*Experiment with this throughout the winter months to create*
*your own favorite version.*

*Serves 4*

4 cups full-bodied red wine,
such as Merlot or Cabernet Sauvignon

1 cup sugar

1 (3-inch) stick cinnamon

2 whole cloves

½ lemon, peeled and juiced

In a large saucepan over medium high heat, combine all of the ingredients and bring
to a boil. Remove from the heat and serve immediately in heat-resistant glass cups,
or store in a thermal container until ready to drink.

GLEAMING DECANTERS OF BRANDY
AND A FULL AFTERNOON TEA SERVICE COMPLETE WITH
FINGER SANDWICHES AND SCONES GREET GUESTS
EACH AFTERNOON. THESE REFRESHMENTS CAN BE ENJOYED
IN THE BREAKFAST ROOM OR SAVORED BESIDE
A FIRE IN THE COOLER MONTHS.

# VELVETY PHEASANT AND CHESTNUT SOUP

*Chestnuts make an exceptionally rich soup when puréed with flavorful stock
and cream. This recipe combines savory, slow-cooked stock made from
roasted pheasant with the sweet nuttiness of chestnuts. While the chopped pheasant
breast makes a lovely addition to the soup, it is optional, which makes this soup
a wonderful way to use the remains of a pheasant enjoyed for dinner the night
before (or even frozen from a previous meal). If you don't want to go
to the trouble of roasting and peeling chestnuts, you can use packaged,
precooked chestnuts, available in gourmet stores.*

*Serves 4*

1 Roast Pheasant, about 3 pounds before cooking (see page 214)

4 tablespoons (½ stick) unsalted butter

1 medium carrot, peeled and diced

1 medium onion, diced

2 celery stalks, diced

3 sprigs fresh rosemary

3 sprigs fresh thyme

2 cloves garlic

1 cup fruity white wine, such as Riesling

¾ pound (about 2½ cups) shelled, roasted chestnuts (see page 210)

1 cup heavy cream

Salt and freshly ground black pepper

Preheat the oven to 450°F.

Remove the breasts from the roasted pheasant and reserve. Place the pheasant
carcass with legs attached in a large roasting pan. Roast, turning occasionally, for 15
minutes, until golden brown.

Melt the butter in a large stockpot over medium heat. Add the carrot, onion, celery, rosemary, thyme, and garlic and sauté until the vegetables are soft but not
browned. Remove the pheasant from the oven and add it to the stockpot. Add the
wine, plus enough water to cover the bones. Simmer over medium low heat for 6

hours, until the stock is dark golden brown and richly flavored. Strain through a fine sieve. You should have about 4 cups of stock.

In a blender or food processor, combine the stock with all but ½ cup of the shelled chestnuts. Purée the mixture for a few minutes until it is smooth.

Pour the soup into a clean saucepan and bring to a simmer over medium heat. Add the cream and season to taste with salt and pepper.

Cut the reserved pheasant breasts and reserved chestnuts into ½ inch dice. Serve the soup hot, garnished with diced pheasant breast and chestnuts.

## ROAST PHEASANT

*Serves 2 to 4*

1 pheasant (about 3 pounds)

Salt and freshly ground pepper

1 clove garlic

1 small sprig fresh rosemary

1 small spring fresh thyme

2 tablespoons blended oil (see Note)

Preheat the oven to 350°F.

Season the pheasant inside and out with salt and pepper. Place the garlic, rosemary, and thyme in the cavity of the pheasant and rub the outside with the oil. Place on one side in a roasting pan and roast for five minutes. Turn the pheasant over and roast for five minutes more. Turn breast-side up and continue roasting for 45 minutes, until the pheasant is golden brown and the juices run clear when the breast is pierced with a fork. Allow to rest for ten minutes, then carve as desired.

**Note:** Blended oil is a mixture of 90 percent vegetable oil and 10 percent olive oil.

# Christmas Prelude Dinner at the White Barn Inn

Guests at the White Barn Inn begin their holiday feasting early with the Christmas Prelude dinner, a five-course meal that combines many of the traditional delights of the winter table: sweet morsels of lobster, creamy soup, lean and flavorful game paired with robust vegetables, and a warm chocolate dessert. Gourmet touches such as a drizzle of truffle oil and the transformation of the lowly sweet potato into a custardy timbale add festive elegance to this menu.

## KENNEBUNKPORT LOBSTER ON MANGO SALSA WITH GOLDEN OSETRA CAVIAR AND LOBSTER MAYONNAISE

*This colorful dish can be served in bite-size portions that tease the tongue,*
*or in a larger serving that can replace the Truffled Celeriac Soup as a first course.*
*In addition to pleasing the eye with its beautiful shades of red and orange,*
*this dish explodes with a combination of sweet, tart, and salty flavors,*
*plus contrasting crisp and creamy textures.*

*Serves 4 as a first course or*
*8 as an amuse-bouche*

2 (1¼-pound) lobsters

¼ cup Lobster Oil (see page 219)

1 ripe mango, peeled, seeded, and cut into ⅛-inch dice

1 red bell pepper, seeded and cut into ⅛-inch dice

1 shallot, finely diced

1 tablespoon chopped chives

1 tablespoon champagne vinegar

2 tablespoons blended oil (see Note)

Pinch cayenne pepper

1 lime

2 tablespoons sherry vinegar

1 large egg yolk

1 teaspoon Dijon mustard

Salt and freshly ground black pepper

¼ ounce golden osetra caviar

Bring 2 large pots of salted water to a boil over high heat. Add one lobster, head first, to each pot. Cook at a boil for 8 minutes. Remove the pots from the heat and let the lobsters cool to room temperature in the cooking liquid. Drain and shell the lobsters, reserving the shell and any coral for the Lobster Oil. (Lobster coral, or roe, is the cluster of eggs found at the top of the tail of the female lobster. Uncooked coral is dark blue; once steamed, it takes on a reddish hue.) Although lobster tastes best on the day it is cooked, the shelled meat will keep tightly wrapped in plastic in the refrigerator for up to three days. For best flavor, bring it to room temperature before serving.

Prepare the Lobster Oil (see page 219).

In a medium nonreactive glass or stainless steel bowl, combine the mango, red bell pepper, shallot, and chives. Add the champagne vinegar and blended oil and season to taste with a pinch of cayenne pepper and the juice of ½ lime.

In a medium nonreactive bowl, whisk together the sherry vinegar, egg yolk, and Dijon mustard. Gradually add the Lobster Oil, whisking continuously to form an emulsion.

Season the mayonnaise to taste with salt and pepper and, if desired, a pinch of cayenne pepper and a few drops of lime juice.

Divide the mango salsa evenly among the plates. Divide the lobster into equal portions consisting of tail, claw, and knuckle meat and arrange on top of the salsa. Garnish the lobster with caviar and drizzle the mayonnaise around the outside of the plate.

**Note:** Blended oil is a mixture of 90 percent vegetable oil and 10 percent olive oil.

## LOBSTER OIL

*This infused oil contributes the essence of lobster*
*to sauces and salad dressings. For more intense flavor,*
*try adding it to the mayonnaise used for Lobster Rolls (see page 106).*
*The lobster shells create a reddish-gold tint, making the oil*
*a colorful element in such recipes as the Lobster Spring Roll on page 59.*
*Lobster oil can be stored in an airtight container*
*in the refrigerator for 2 weeks.*

1 pound lobster shells

1 teaspoon lobster coral (if available)

½ cup blended oil (see Note)

Preheat the oven to 300°F.

Clean out the head cavities of the shells, discarding the contents. Cut the shells into 1-inch pieces and place them on a baking sheet. Bake for 10 minutes to dry.

Reduce the oven temperature to 160°F. Transfer the dried shells to a wide, shallow, ovenproof pan. Add the coral and blended oil and toss to coat the shells with oil. Gently heat on the stove top over low heat until the oil is warm but not sizzling, then transfer the pan to the oven. Cook for at least 2 hours and no longer than 3 hours, stirring occasionally, to infuse the oil with the flavor of the lobster shells. When the oil has turned a rich golden red, strain it through a fine sieve, pressing on the shells to extract all the oil. Discard the solids, let the oil cool to room temperature, and refrigerate until ready to use.

**Note:** Blended oil is a mixture of 90 percent vegetable oil and 10 percent olive oil.

## TRUFFLED CELERIAC SOUP

*While sharing the mild flavor of the familiar celery stalk,*
*the root known as celeriac has the added benefit of a smooth, starchy texture*
*that can be transformed into delicious purées and creamy soups.*
*A touch of truffle oil enriches the flavor, adding an intense note that is at once*
*earthy and ethereal. The optional shavings of fresh truffle provide another*
*degree of elegance for this sensational winter soup.*

*Serves 8*

2 tablespoons unsalted butter

1 tablespoon olive oil

½ medium onion, diced

2 pounds celery root (celeriac),
peeled and cut into 1-inch dice (2 large roots)

1 sprig fresh thyme

1 sprig fresh rosemary

1 cup dry white wine, such as chardonnay

1 cup Chicken Stock or Vegetable Stock (see page 222 or 223)

4 cups heavy cream

Salt and freshly ground black pepper

Truffle oil, to taste

1 black truffle, thinly sliced (optional)

In a large pot, melt the butter with the olive oil over medium heat. Add the onion and celery root and sauté for 3 minutes, until the onion begins to soften. Add the thyme and rosemary and sauté for 3 minutes. Cover, reduce the heat to low, and cook for 5 minutes, stirring occasionally. Add the wine and stock and bring the soup to a boil over medium heat. Add the cream and continue to boil for 2 minutes. Reduce the heat to low, cover, and simmer for 15 minutes, until the celery root is tender.

Working in batches, purée the soup in a blender or food processor until smooth. Strain it through a fine sieve into a clean pan. Season to taste with salt and pepper. Just before serving, return the soup to a boil to reheat it. Whisk in 1 tablespoon of truffle oil by hand or with a handheld blender. Taste the soup; if you prefer a stronger truffle flavor, add a little more truffle oil. Serve in individual soup bowls, garnished with slices of black truffle if desired.

CHAIRS CLAD IN GLOVE-SOFT ESPRESSO-COLORED ITALIAN LEATHER AWAIT DINNER GUESTS AT THE WHITE BARN INN. PEWTER CHARGERS AND FANCIFUL SCULPTURES MADE FROM SILVER CUTLERY BY FRENCH ARTIST GIRARD BOUVIER PROVIDE GLEAMING HIGHLIGHTS WITHIN THE RUSTIC SETTING OF THE CONVERTED COUNTRY BARN.

## Chicken Stock

*Makes 3 cups*

4 pounds chicken bones

½ pound mixed aromatic vegetables,
such as carrots, leeks, onions, and celery, diced

1 clove garlic, crushed

12 sprigs fresh herbs,
such as thyme, rosemary, and tarragon

1 cup dry white wine, such as chardonnay

Preheat the oven to 450°F.

Place the bones in a large roasting pan and roast, turning occasionally, for 15 minutes, until golden brown. Add the vegetables to the pan and continue roasting for 5 minutes.

Transfer the bones and vegetables to a large stockpot and add the garlic, herbs, and white wine. Cover with water and bring to a boil over high heat, skimming off any scum that rises to the surface. Reduce the heat to medium and simmer for four hours, until reduced by half.

Strain the stock through a fine sieve. To use for sauces, simmer the strained stock over medium heat until it is reduced by half. Store in an airtight container in the refrigerator for up to three days or freeze in ice cube trays, then transfer the stock cubes to zipper-lock bags and freeze for up to 1 month.

# Vegetable Stock

*This versatile stock can be used as the base for many soups.*
*Feel free to vary the ingredients to reflect what is available in your*
*vegetable bin. Also, you may want to add more of the vegetable*
*that will be the primary flavor of the finished soup.*

¼ cup vegetable oil

1 medium butternut squash, peeled,
seeded, and chopped

2 celery stalks, chopped

1 leek, chopped

1 medium onion, peeled and chopped

1 medium carrot, peeled and chopped

4 medium tomatoes, chopped

1 sprig fresh thyme

1 sprig fresh parsley

1 clove garlic, chopped

1 cup dry white wine, such as chardonnay

5 whole peppercorns

Salt and freshly ground pepper

In a large stockpot, warm the oil over medium heat. Add the vegetables, herbs, and garlic and stir to coat with the oil. Cover and cook, stirring occasionally, for 5 minutes. Add the wine and 3 quarts of water and bring to a boil. Reduce the heat to medium low, add the peppercorns, and simmer for 2 hours. Strain through a fine sieve and season to taste with salt and pepper. Store in an airtight container in the refrigerator for up to three days or freeze in ice cube trays, transferring the cubes of stock to zipper-lock bags, and freeze for up to 1 month.

# Pan Seared New England Venison Cutlet
## with a Caramelized Sweet Potato Timbale,
## Red Cabbage, and Elderberry Sauce

*Thanks to the increased availability of farm-raised venison, this lean and flavorful meat is now available year-round. But the traditional season for hunting—and eating—game is winter. Relatively simple to prepare (especially if you already have Veal Jus on hand or make one by diluting a high-quality commercially prepared meat glaze), this beautiful main course is highly rewarding. For the sauce, I like to use preserved elderberries, which are available at gourmet shops, but preserved blueberries are equally delicious, and the sauce also tastes great without any berries at all.*

*Serves 4*

2 tablespoons red wine vinegar

2 tablespoons plus ¼ cup full-bodied red wine,
such as Merlot or Cabernet Sauvignon

1 tablespoon honey

Salt and freshly ground black pepper

½ head red cabbage, outer leaves and core discarded, thinly sliced

3 tablespoons unsalted butter

¼ cup diced onion

2 ounces (about ⅓ cup) lean trimmings from
beef, venison, or other red meat

1 sprig fresh thyme

1 teaspoon cracked black peppercorns

2 tablespoons port

2 cups Veal Jus (see page 68)

¼ cup preserved elderberries

1 cup brussels sprouts, outer leaves discarded, halved

4 venison rack chops or tenderloin filets (about 5 ounces each)

1 tablespoon blended oil (see Note)

4 Caramelized Sweet Potato Timbales (see page 227)

In a large nonreactive glass or stainless steel bowl, whisk together the vinegar, 2 tablespoons wine, and honey with salt and pepper to taste. Add the sliced cabbage and toss to combine. Cover with plastic wrap and marinate at room temperature for 12 hours.

Heat 1 tablespoon of butter in a medium saucepan over low heat. Add the diced onion and sauté for 3 to 4 minutes, until translucent but not browned. Add the venison trimmings and cook for 1 minute on high heat, until the trimmings are seared. Add the remaining ¼ cup wine, thyme, and cracked peppercorns. Bring to a boil, then reduce the heat to medium and simmer for 2 to 3 minutes. Add the port and the Veal Jus and return the sauce to a boil over high heat. Reduce the heat to medium and simmer for 5 to 8 minutes, until the sauce is glossy and has thickened enough to coat the back of a spoon. Strain the sauce through a fine sieve and season to taste with salt and pepper. Stir in the elderberries.

Bring a medium saucepan of salted water to a boil. Add the brussels sprouts and boil for 6 to 8 minutes, just until tender. Drain.

Season the venison with salt and pepper. Heat the blended oil in a large skillet over high heat. Add the venison and sear for 5 to 10 seconds. Add ½ tablespoon of butter to the pan and continue to cook over high heat for 3 to 5 minutes on each side for medium-rare venison. For medium venison, cook for 7 minutes on each side.

While the venison is cooking, melt 1 tablespoon of butter in a saucepan over medium heat. Add the brussels sprouts and reheat gently, tossing to coat them with the butter, and season to taste with salt and pepper.

Melt the remaining ½ tablespoon of butter in a large skillet over medium heat. Add the red cabbage and any marinating liquid and sauté for 2 to 3 minutes, until tender but still slightly crisp. Season to taste with salt and pepper.

To serve, place one Caramelized Sweet Potato Timbale and a mound of red cabbage on each plate. If using chops, make a cut in each chop from the bottom up to the bone. Open the meat up, seasoning the cut surface with salt and pepper, and place it on top of the cabbage. If using tenderloin, serve filets whole. Spoon the elderberry sauce over and around the venison. Arrange a spoonful of brussels sprouts on one side of the plate.

**Note:** Blended oil is a mixture of 90 percent vegetable oil and 10 percent olive oil.

CARAMELIZED SWEET POTATO TIMBALE

*The sweet potato is a colorful, tasty root vegetable that is often overlooked. It gives these timbales a beautiful pale-orange color. Their well-rounded, gently sweet flavor is heightened by the layer of caramelized sugar that makes them taste like slightly savory portions of crème caramel. To prepare in advance, store the caramelized timbales and sweet potato custard mixture separately in the refrigerator for up to three days. Bring to room temperature and bake as instructed below.*

*Makes 8 timbales*

1½ pounds sweet potatoes
(about 1 large or 2 small potatoes), peeled

¾ cup sugar

5 eggs

2 cups heavy cream

¼ teaspoon salt

Freshly ground black pepper

Nutmeg

Preheat the oven to 300°F.

Slice the sweet potatoes ½ inch thick. Place in a steamer rack set over a saucepan of rapidly simmering water, cover, and steam for 10 minutes, or until tender. Transfer to a medium bowl and mash until smooth, then set aside.

In a small saucepan over medium high heat, combine the sugar with 1 cup of water and bring to a boil. Continue to boil for 10 minutes, or until the mixture forms a golden brown syrup. Immediately remove the caramelized sugar from the heat and divide it among six timbale molds or ramekins (see Note). Swirl the ramekins to distribute the caramelized sugar evenly around the bottoms and lower sides. Allow to cool.

In a large bowl, combine the eggs, cream, salt, a pinch of pepper, and a pinch of nutmeg. Add the mashed sweet potatoes and mix thoroughly.

Butter the sides of the ramekins and fill them with the sweet potato custard mixture. Place the ramekins in a baking dish and add enough hot water to reach halfway up the sides of the ramekins. Cover the baking dish with aluminum foil and bake the timbales for 30 minutes, or until the custard is firmly set.

To serve, invert each timbale onto a plate.

**Note:** Timbale molds are slightly taller and narrower than standard ramekins.

THE SPACIOUS WHIRLPOOL BATHS
IN THE WHITE BARN INN'S SUITES PROVIDE
THE PERFECT PLACE TO SOAK AWAY
THE STRESS OF EVERYDAY LIFE AND ENJOY AN
AFTERNOON OF PAMPERING.

# TENDERLOIN OF BEEF GLAZED IN A FOIE GRAS CRUST ON A POTATO RÖSTI WITH MADEIRA SAUCE

*This wonderfully wintery beef entrée is a perfect alternative
to the venison recipe. The golden foie gras crust adds another level of richness
and flavor to an already superb cut of beef. Crisp potato rösti, a lovely contrast
in texture, provide a perfect foil for the Madeira sauce. Hearty vegetables
such as cauliflower or carrots tossed in oil and roasted until tender in a 400°F oven
make a nice accompaniment to this dish. Foie gras crust can be stored up
to 5 days in the refrigerator and makes a superb topping for mashed potatoes. If you
prefer, substitute the Pepper Crust on page 240 for the foie gras crust.*

*Serves 4*

4 ounces diced fresh foie gras or foie gras terrine (about ½ cup)

10½ tablespoons unsalted butter, at room temperature

⅔ cup grated Vermont cheddar cheese

3 tablespoons grated Parmesan cheese

½ cup fresh bread crumbs

Salt and freshly ground black pepper to taste

¼ cup diced mixed aromatic vegetables
(onion, carrot, and leek)

⅛ cup Madeira

¼ cup port

2 crushed black peppercorns

2 cups Veal Jus (see page 68)

4 beef tenderloin filets (7 ounces each)

1 tablespoon olive oil

4 Potato Rösti (see page 231)

In a large bowl, combine the foie gras, 6 tablespoons of butter, the grated cheeses, and bread crumbs and mix until thoroughly combined. Season to taste with salt and pepper. Form the mixture into a ball and place it on a sheet of waxed paper. Roll the ball into a 3-inch cylinder and wrap it tightly in the waxed paper. Reserve in the refrigerator for up to 5 days, until ready to slice and use.

In a medium saucepan, melt 4 tablespoons of the remaining butter over medium heat. Add the mixed vegetables and sauté for 5 minutes, until the onion is translucent but not browned. Add the Madeira, port, and crushed peppercorns and cook at a low simmer over medium heat for 5 minutes, or until reduced by half. Add the Veal Jus and continue to cook at a low boil for 5 minutes, or until the sauce is reduced by half and coats the back of a spoon. Strain through a fine sieve and season to taste with salt and pepper.

Preheat the broiler. Season the beef filets with salt and pepper and roll them in the olive oil. Heat a large skillet over high heat. Add the beef and sear for 5 minutes on each side. Add the remaining $\frac{1}{2}$ tablespoon of butter to the pan and continue to cook over high heat for 3 to 5 minutes on each side for medium-rare beef. For medium beef, cook for 7 to 8 minutes on each side.

Divide the foie gras crust into four slices, place a slice on top of each filet, and place under the broiler for 1 to 2 minutes, just until the crust turns golden brown and begins to bubble.

To serve, place a Potato Rösti in the center of each plate. Top with a beef filet and spoon the sauce over the beef and potatoes.

## POTATO RÖSTI

*These golden, butter-crisped potato pancakes*
*are easy to make and hard to resist.*
*If you are serving hearty eaters, you might double*
*this recipe and give each diner two rösti.*

*Makes 4*

2 medium Yukon Gold potatoes, peeled and grated

Salt and freshly ground black pepper

1 tablespoon blended oil (see Note)

2 tablespoons unsalted butter

Squeeze any moisture out of the grated potatoes and season with salt and pepper. Using a 3-inch circular mold, form four $\frac{1}{2}$-inch-thick potato cakes, pressing to firm the cakes. Heat the oil in a large, nonstick sauté pan over medium high heat. When the oil reaches the smoking point, slide the potato cakes into the pan. Reduce the heat to medium and add the butter. Cook the rösti for 3 to 4 minutes on each side, until golden brown. Remove from the pan and drain on paper towels before serving.

**Note:** Blended oil is a mixture of 90 percent vegetable oil and 10 percent olive oil.

# WARM CHOCOLATE CAKE WITH WARM CHOCOLATE SAUCE AND VANILLA BEAN ICE CREAM

*Who can resist a warm chocolate cake with a molten center—especially*
*when paired with homemade Vanilla Bean Ice Cream? Since all the components*
*of this dessert can be made several days in advance, it's a perfect way*
*to end a festive winter meal. Just put the cakes into the oven when you serve the*
*main course, and they will be ready to devour when it's time for dessert.*

*Serves 8*

Warm Chocolate Sauce (see page 234)

Butter and sugar for preparing the ramekins

10 ounces semisweet chocolate

$^5/_8$ pounds (2$^1/_2$ sticks) unsalted butter

5 large eggs

5 egg yolks

$^1/_3$ cup sugar

$^3/_4$ cup sifted all-purpose flour

Vanilla Bean Ice Cream (see page 235)

Prepare the Warm Chocolate Sauce and set aside.

Butter eight shallow 4-ounce ramekins, sprinkle with sugar, and set aside.

Combine the chocolate and butter in the top of a double boiler over low heat or in a microwave at half power until the chocolate melts. Allow to cool slightly.

In a large bowl, combine the eggs, egg yolks, and sugar. Using an electric mixer, beat for about 5 minutes, until the mixture is very pale yellow in color and falls in flat ribbons when the beaters are lifted. Fold in the chocolate mixture, then fold in the flour.

Divide the batter evenly among the eight molds and reserve until ready to bake. Unbaked cakes will keep at room temperature for up to 1 hour and in the refrigerator for up to 5 hours.

Thirty minutes before serving, preheat the oven to 375°F.

Bake the cakes for 10 minutes if at room temperature (20 minutes if they have been refrigerated). Allow the cakes to rest for about 5 minutes after removing from the oven, then invert them onto warmed dessert plates. Serve with Warm Chocolate Sauce and Vanilla Bean Ice Cream.

## WARM CHOCOLATE SAUCE

*Drizzling this rich, dark sauce over
chocolate cake is gilding the lily, but that is what
holiday dinner parties are all about.
You can also serve this with ice cream alone or over
Poached Pears (see page 256) and ice cream.*

*Makes 2 cups*

1 cup milk

1 cup sugar

1⅓ cups Dutch cocoa

4 ounces good-quality semisweet chocolate

In a large, heavy-bottomed saucepan, combine the milk, sugar, cocoa, and chocolate with 1 cup of water over medium low heat, whisking frequently. When the chocolate melts and the mixture comes to a boil, remove it from the heat. Serve warm or reserve and reheat gently before serving. The sauce will keep for 1 hour at room temperature or for 2 to 3 days, covered and refrigerated.

## Vanilla Bean Ice Cream

*It's hard to beat the flavor of a homemade ice cream*
*prepared with heavy cream and plenty of fresh vanilla bean—*
*especially when paired with Warm Chocolate Sauce.*

*Makes 1½ quarts*

2 cups milk

2 cups heavy cream

1 cup sugar

1 vanilla bean, split lengthwise

8 egg yolks

In a large saucepan with a heavy bottom, combine the milk, cream, ½ cup of sugar, and the vanilla bean, scraping out the seeds with a teaspoon and adding them as well as the bean halves to the pan. Bring to a simmer over medium heat.

In a large heat-resistant bowl, combine the remaining ½ cup of sugar with the egg yolks and stir to combine.

Pour ½ cup of the hot milk and cream into the sugar-and-egg-yolk mixture and stir to mix. Whisking constantly, slowly add the remainder of the hot milk and cream (including the vanilla bean) to the bowl.

Return the mixture to the pan and cook over medium heat, stirring constantly, until the mixture thickens enough to coat the back of a wooden spoon. If you can run your finger down the back of the spoon and leave a trail, the custard is done. Do not allow the mixture to boil.

Strain the custard through a fine sieve into a clean bowl and refrigerate until chilled. Freeze in an ice cream machine, following the manufacturer's instructions.

# A Holiday Cocktail Party

The White Barn Inn hosts a cocktail party for its Christmas Prelude guests, many of whom come year after year to launch their holiday season with a festive weekend in Kennebunkport. Champagne corks pop and silver trays full of canapés are passed while old friends and new gather to celebrate. This menu brings together several favorite recipes that highlight the winter flavors of Maine's shellfish and game.

## NORTHERN LIGHTS COCKTAIL

*Linda Allen, bartender at the White Barn Inn, created
this champagne cocktail after witnessing the glow of northern lights
during a nighttime stroll on Gooch's Beach. A variation
on a kir royale, this mixture of pear purée, crème de cassis,
and champagne fills the champagne flute
with rosy translucence.*

### Makes 1 cocktail

1 ounce pear nectar

1 teaspoon crème de cassis

½ cup chilled champagne

Combine the ingredients in a cocktail shaker filled with ice. Stir until the shaker begins to turn frosty on the outside. Strain the mixture into a cocktail glass and serve immediately.

# MAINE OYSTER CANAPÉS

*Though labor intensive, oysters are well worth
the trouble of cleaning and shucking. To serve this dish at a cocktail party,
open the oysters just before guests arrive and keep them chilled on trays of ice;
garnishing takes only a few minutes. The Pepper Crust used as a topping
can be made several days in advance, so the baked oysters can also be prepared and
glazed in a matter of minutes. If you prefer to keep things simpler,
just prepare one or two variations. For this recipe I use local Glidden Point oysters,
which are cultivated above the ocean bed, so they are not gritty at all.
However, any good-quality medium to large oyster
with plump, flavorful flesh will work well.*

### Makes 20 canapés

½ cup crème fraîche or sour cream

1 tablespoon prepared horseradish

Salt and freshly ground pepper

1 teaspoon wasabi powder

20 medium or large oysters, cleaned and shucked,
with bottom shells reserved

4 small sprigs fresh dill

4 small sprigs fresh chervil

8 slices Pepper Crust (see page 240)

1 tablespoon golden osetra
or regular osetra caviar (see Note)

Coarse kosher salt (optional)

In a small bowl, combine ¼ cup of crème fraîche with the horseradish and season
to taste with salt and pepper.

In another small bowl, mix the wasabi powder with a few drops of water to form
a smooth paste. Combine with the remaining 4 tablespoons of crème fraîche.

Preheat the oven to 450°F.

Remove four oysters from their bottom shells and place a tablespoon of the wasabi-crème fraîche mixture into the shell. Replace the oysters on top and garnish with dill sprigs.

Remove four more oysters from their bottom shells and place a tablespoon of the horseradish-crème fraîche mixture into the shell. Replace the oysters on top and garnish with chervil sprigs.

Top four more oysters with $\frac{1}{2}$ teaspoon of crème fraîche and $\frac{1}{4}$ tablespoon of the caviar.

Place the remaining eight oysters in a shallow baking dish. Cut eight $\frac{1}{4}$-inch slices of Pepper Crust and arrange on top of the oysters. Bake these oysters for 3 minutes, until the crust turns golden brown and starts to bubble.

While baking the oysters, divide the raw oysters among serving plates or arrange them on a large serving platter. A bed of lightly moistened course kosher salt can be used to keep the oysters level. Add the baked oysters to the serving plates or platter and serve at once.

**Note:** Golden osetra caviar is better in quality and lighter in color than regular osetra caviar; you can substitute any type of good-quality caviar.

## PEPPER CRUST

*This crust, made with Parmesan and butter and seasoned
with mild-flavored green and pink peppercorns, is rich and subtly piquant.
In addition to making a wonderful topping for baked oysters,
it also forms a delicious glaze for salmon and beef filets. Just cover a cooked filet
with a slice or two of the crust and run under a preheated broiler for one
to two minutes, until the crust is hot and bubbling.*

*Makes about 30 slices*

¼ pound grated Parmesan cheese (about ¾ cup)

½ pound (2 sticks) unsalted butter, at room temperature

2 tablespoons green peppercorns, drained

4 tablespoons pink peppercorns

½ pound fresh bread crumbs (about 4 cups)

Salt and freshly ground black pepper

In a large bowl, combine all of the ingredients and mix until thoroughly blended. Season to taste with salt and pepper. Form the mixture into a ball and place it on a sheet of waxed paper. Roll the ball into a cylinder 2 inches in diameter and wrap it tightly in the waxed paper. Reserve in the refrigerator for up to 2 weeks.

# Pan-seared North Atlantic Shrimp and Quail Egg Canapés

*North Atlantic deep sea shrimp caught off the Massachusetts coast are crisp and sweet. If you can't find them, just use the freshest shrimp available. At the White Barn Inn's holiday party, we pass these on silver spoons. Garnished with a tiny quarter of hard-cooked quail egg, they make a perfect bite-size canapé. If you can't find quail eggs, a hard-cooked hen's egg, finely diced, may be substituted.*

*Make 8 canapés*

2 quail eggs

1 tablespoon ketchup

1 teaspoon grated horseradish

Salt and freshly ground black pepper

1 teaspoon butter

8 small shrimp, peeled and deveined

8 small sprigs fresh dill

Bring a small saucepan of water to a boil over high heat. Add the quail eggs, reduce the heat to medium, and simmer for $2\frac{1}{2}$ minutes. Cool to room temperature, peel, and cut into quarters with a sharp knife.

In a small bowl, combine the ketchup and horseradish and season to taste with salt and pepper.

Melt the butter in a small skillet over medium high heat. Add the shrimp and sear for 1 to 2 minutes, until firm and pink.

Divide the horseradish sauce among eight dessert spoons. Place a seared shrimp on each spoon. Top with the quartered quail eggs and garnish with dill sprigs.

# DUCK CONFIT AND APPLE PASTIES

*In England, hot pastry pockets stuffed with savory meat fillings
called* pasties *are a winter favorite. These little pasties encase tender bits
of duck confit sweetened with diced apples. They can be prepared
up to a month in advance and frozen, making them a perfect holiday food
to keep on hand for small cocktail gatherings or big parties.*

*Makes 8 pasties*

1 tablespoon unsalted butter

1 McIntosh apple, peeled, cored, and diced

2 legs duck confit (see page 243),
about 8 ounces on the bone, skinned, boned, and diced

1 tablespoon apple cider

1 pound frozen puff pastry, thawed

1 egg, beaten

Preheat the oven to 350°F.

In a medium skillet, melt the butter over medium heat. Add the diced apple and sauté for 2 to 3 minutes, until the apple begins to soften. Add the duck confit and the apple cider and sauté for 2 minutes, until the apple is completely tender but still holds its shape. Remove from the heat and cool to room temperature.

On a cool, floured surface, roll out the puff pastry ⅛ inch thick. Using a 1½-inch fluted cutter, cut sixteen rounds of pastry. Place 1 teaspoon of the duck-and-apple mixture on eight of the rounds. Using a pastry brush, brush the beaten egg on the pastry around the filling. Top with the remaining eight rounds of pastry and press the outer edges together to form a firmly sealed packet. Refrigerate for up to three days before baking.

Place the pasties on a buttered baking sheet and bake for 10 to 12 minutes, or until puffed and golden brown. Serve hot.

Unbaked pasties may be frozen on a baking sheet and then stored in an airtight container in the freezer. Defrost for 30 minutes and bake for 13 to 16 minutes, until puffed and golden brown.

# DUCK CONFIT

*Duck confit is available in some gourmet stores and through mail order, but it is also fairly easy to make and is a great way to use leftover legs when preparing a recipe that calls only for the duck breast. To render the duck fat called for in this recipe, trim the fatty parts of the duck and bring to a low boil, along with ½ cup of water, in a saucepan over a medium heat for about 20 minutes. Let cool slightly, strain, and refrigerate. Leftover duck fat will keep, tightly covered, in the refrigerator for two weeks and makes an excellent medium for searing poultry, as it has a very high smoke point. It is also useful as a protective layer for homemade pâtés and meat terrines.*

*Makes 2 legs*

2 duck legs

½ cup kosher salt

1 sprig fresh thyme

2 black peppercorns

1 clove garlic

½ cup duck fat or olive oil

In a small nonreactive glass or stainless steel bowl, combine the legs with the salt, thyme, peppercorns, and garlic, rubbing the salt to coat the legs evenly. Cover and refrigerate for 24 hours.

After 24 hours, rinse the salt thoroughly off the legs, reserving the thyme, peppercorns, and garlic.

Preheat the oven to 250°F.

Place the legs, thyme, peppercorns, and garlic in a small casserole and cover with duck fat or olive oil or a mixture of both. Bring to a boil over medium high heat.

Remove the casserole from the heat, cover loosely with waxed paper or a lid, and bake for about 2 hours. To test for doneness, slide a roasting fork into the meat. If the meat drops easily off the fork, it is done.

If cooked in duck fat, the duck legs can be covered with the fat and packed in an airtight container for up to 2 weeks in the refrigerator; if cooked in olive oil, they will keep for up to 1 week. The legs can also be drained, boned, and frozen in an airtight container, reserving the duck fat for another use.

# FETA CHEESE
# AND SPINACH ROLLS

*These bite-size canapés are a cross between
Greek spanakopita and Asian eggrolls. They can be prepared
up to three days in advance and kept, uncooked,
in an airtight container in the refrigerator, or frozen uncooked
for up to a month. Just bring them to room temperature
before frying as instructed below.*

*Makes 12 canapés*

1 teaspoon unsalted butter

½ red bell pepper, cored, seeded,
and finely diced

1 cup baby spinach leaves, washed

2 tablespoons feta cheese, crumbled

Salt and freshly ground black pepper

Pinch freshly grated nutmeg

3 (4 x 4-inch) spring roll wrappers

1 egg, beaten

2 cups canola oil

In a skillet, melt the butter over medium heat. Add the diced pepper and cook for 2 to 3 minutes, until it begins to soften. Increase the heat to high and add the spinach, cooking for another minute, stirring occasionally, until the spinach wilts. Cool to room temperature and squeeze out any excess moisture.

Transfer the mixture to a medium mixing bowl. Add the feta cheese, and season to taste with salt, pepper, and nutmeg, being careful not to oversalt, since the feta cheese has a high salt content.

Quarter the spring roll wrappers, making two perpendicular cuts. Lay the quarters on a clean work surface. Place a teaspoon of the feta mixture inside one corner of each wrapper quarter. Brush the opposite corner with the beaten egg. Fold the sides of the wrapper in to cover the filling and roll tightly, making sure the top is well sealed with the beaten egg.

Heat the oil to 350°F over medium high heat in a deep frying pan or an electric deep-fryer. Fry the rolls at 350°F for 3 minutes or until golden brown. Drain on paper towels and serve warm. If you prefer baking to frying, you can brush the rolls with oil and bake in a 350°F oven for 6 to 8 minutes, until golden brown and warmed through.

GRACIOUS DINNERS AT THE WHITE BARN INN OFTEN BEGIN WITH
SAVORY LITTLE BITE-SIZED CANAPES TO WHET THE APPETITE AND ACCOMPANY A COCKTAIL,
INCLUDING CRISP FETA CHEESE AND SPINACH ROLLS, A CROSS BETWEEN
GREEK SPANAKOPITA AND ASIAN EGG ROLLS.

# MAINE PEEKIE TOE CRAB CAKES

*Peekie toe crab is another name for the sand crabs that are plentiful along Maine's beaches.
These plump-clawed crabs yield tender, sweet flesh that is perfectly suited for crab cakes.
You will have a hard time making enough of these moist morsels to go around.*

*Makes 4 main-course servings or 16 canapés*

8 ounces Maine peekie toe crabmeat or other white crabmeat

1 small shallot, diced

1 tablespoon fresh homemade mayonnaise (see page 108),
or a good-quality commercial brand

1 tablespoon chopped chives

1 large egg yolk

1 cup fine white bread crumbs

1 dash Tabasco sauce

Salt and freshly ground pepper

2 tablespoons flour

1 large egg

2 tablespoons blended oil (see Note)

In a medium mixing bowl, combine the crab, shallot, mayonnaise, chives, and egg yolk. Add 2 tablespoons of the bread crumbs and mix well. Add the Tabasco and season with salt and pepper. Shape the mixture into eight or sixteen crab cakes, depending upon whether you will be serving them as a main course or canapé.

Place the flour in a shallow bowl and season to taste with salt and pepper. Beat the egg in a separate shallow bowl. Place the remaining bread crumbs in a third shallow bowl. Dip each cake carefully in the seasoned flour, then the beaten egg, and finally in the bread crumbs, making sure it is completely coated in bread crumbs and retains its shape.

In a medium skillet heat the oil until it shimmers. Add the crab cakes, working in two batches, and fry until golden brown, 3 to 4 minutes on each side. Drain on paper towels and serve warm.

**Note:** Blended oil is a mixture of 90 percent vegetable oil and 10 percent olive oil.

# MARINATED SALMON TARTARE WITH GOLDEN OSETRA CAVIAR

*Made with salt- and citrus-cured salmon, this delicious tartare*
*retains the deep orange color and moist meatiness of just-caught salmon.*
*By forming the chopped salmon into oval-shaped individual portions,*
*and presenting them on spoons, you can keep the focus on the*
*tartare's intense flavor and succulent texture instead of serving it*
*on the more traditional toast or cracker.*

*Makes 8 canapés*

¼ pound Citrus-Cured Salmon ( see page 248)

1 teaspoon chopped fresh dill

1 teaspoon sour cream

1 teaspoon golden osetra caviar

Finely dice the cured salmon; you should have about ¾ cup. In a medium bowl, combine it with the dill. Divide the mixture into eight even portions. Using two teaspoons, shape each portion into a rounded oval. Place each oval on a clean teaspoon. Garnish with sour cream and caviar and serve.

# CITRUS-CURED SALMON

*Cured with a mixture of salt, citrus peel and juices, gin, and juniper berry, this salmon has a bright, refreshing flavor. It is also a lot easier to make than cold-smoked salmon, which requires steady vigilance over the smoker. In addition to chopping it finely for tartare, you can also cut this salmon into thin slices and form the slices into rosettes for serving. It will keep tightly covered in the refrigerator for up to one week.*

*Makes 2 pounds*

2 pounds Maine salmon filet, bones removed, with skin on

1 tablespoon olive oil

4 tablespoons sea salt

4 tablespoons sugar

½ teaspoon coarsely crushed black peppercorns

2 juniper berries

2 oranges

2 lemons

1 ounce gin

Chopped fresh dill (optional)

Place the salmon skin-side down in a shallow, nonreactive glass or stainless steel dish large enough to hold the filet flat. Rub the filet with the olive oil.

In a medium bowl, combine the salt, sugar, pepper, and juniper berries. Cover the salmon filet with this mixture, heaping more curing mixture on the thicker parts of the filet.

Peel the oranges and lemons, cutting the peel into slices about ½ inch wide and 1½ to 2 inches long. Cover the salmon with the peels.

Juice one orange and both lemons into a medium bowl. Stir in the gin and pour over the salmon. Cover the dish tightly with plastic wrap and refrigerate for 18 hours.

After 18 hours, rinse the salmon quickly under cold water to remove the peel and salt mixture. Pat dry with paper towels. If serving whole, slice thinly on the diagonal, arrange slices in an overlapping pattern on a serving platter, and garnish with chopped fresh dill.

# A New Year's Day Brunch

New Year's Day tends to dwell in the shadow of New Year's Eve, yet it is a wonderful time to gather with family and friends. Many of the recipes for this colorful, flavorful brunch may be prepared days in advance, and several dishes can be served either warm or at room temperature, making them ideal for a buffet. While the scrambled eggs and French toast should be eaten hot, they can be prepared at the last minute and put on the table just before guests are summoned to fill their plates.

## COLD-SMOKED MAINE SALMON WITH CREAMY SCRAMBLED EGGS

*Well-scrambled eggs with a touch of cream and butter are always delicious.
Paired with thinly sliced smoked salmon, this simple dish
becomes both elegant and irresistible. Try to use free-range eggs when
making this dish, as the flavor is superior.*

*Serves 6*

12 large free-range eggs

½ cup heavy cream

1 tablespoon unsalted butter

Salt and freshly ground pepper

1 pound Cold-Smoked Salmon, thinly sliced,
at room temperature (see page 91)

In a large mixing bowl, combine the eggs and cream and whisk until thoroughly combined and frothy.

In a large nonstick pan, melt the butter over medium heat. Add the egg-and-cream mixture and stir with a wooden spoon. Season with salt and pepper. Continue gently stirring the eggs for 4 to 6 minutes, or just until they form soft curds.

To serve, arrange the salmon and eggs attractively on a warmed serving platter or divide among six individual plates.

## APPLE FRENCH TOAST

*This French toast has a surprise inside: a pocket full of warm diced apple*
*sautéed with apple brandy. For best results, buy an unsliced loaf*
*of firm-textured white bread from an artisanal bakery. This recipe makes enough*
*to serve six people as part of a larger brunch menu. If you are serving this alone,*
*make enough for two slices per person.*

*Makes 6 pieces*

6 (1-inch) slices firm white bread

3½ tablespoons unsalted butter

1 ½ cups peeled, cored and diced Granny Smith apples
(about 2 apples)

⅓ cup plus 1 ½ tablespoons sugar

3 tablespoons Calvados brandy

$\frac{1}{3}$ cup pure maple syrup

$\frac{3}{4}$ teaspoon ground cinnamon

6 eggs

$\frac{3}{4}$ cup heavy cream

Using a sharp knife, make a pocket in each slice of bread by cutting from the bottom of each piece to about 2 inches from the top.

In a sauté pan melt $1\frac{1}{2}$ tablespoons of the butter over medium heat. Add the apples and $1\frac{1}{2}$ tablespoons of sugar and sauté for 2 to 3 minutes, until the apples begin to soften. Add $1\frac{1}{2}$ tablespoons of the Calvados, $1\frac{1}{2}$ tablespoons of the maple syrup, and the cinnamon, and sauté 2 to 3 minutes longer, until the apple is completely tender but still holds its shape.

Divide the apple mixture into two equal parts, reserving half for the sauce and using the remaining half to fill the bread slices. Loosely pack the apple mixture into each bread pocket, pressing the edges of the bread together to seal.

In a medium mixing bowl, whisk together the eggs, cream, and remaining $\frac{1}{3}$ cup of sugar.

Melt the remaining 2 tablespoons of butter in a large skillet over medium heat. Gently dip the bread slices in the batter and slide them into the skillet. Sauté, turning once, until golden brown, 3 to 5 minutes per side.

In a small saucepan, combine the reserved apple compote with the remaining Calvados and maple syrup and bring to a boil over medium heat. Remove from the heat. To serve, slice the pieces of French toast diagonally and arrange on a serving platter. Drizzle with sauce and serve additional sauce on the side.

# PINEAPPLE COCONUT GRANOLA

*Granola is full of satisfying flavors and textures.*
*Served with fresh fruit, or poached fruits like those included in this menu,*
*it is a healthful addition to a brunch buffet. Don't be surprised*
*if your guests ask for this recipe.*

*Serves 10*

4 cups unsweetened bran flakes

2 cups rolled oats

2 cups sliced unsalted almonds

1½ cups sweetened coconut

1 cup well-drained crushed pineapple

½ cup honey

Preheat the oven to 200°F.

In a very large bowl, combine all the ingredients and mix well with a wooden spoon until thoroughly combined. Transfer the mixture to two baking sheets and bake for 20 minutes.

After 20 minutes, stir the granola and open the oven door by about 6 inches to allow steam to escape and the granola to dry. Continue baking with the door ajar for 1 hour more, stirring every 20 minutes to ensure even baking. The granola is done when it is no longer damp but slightly chewy.

Remove the granola from the oven and cool on the baking sheets. It will continue to dry as it cools. Transfer to an airtight container, where it can be stored at room temperature for up to 10 days.

## HAM AND
## MOZZARELLA QUICHE

*Quiche is a great make-ahead dish that also works well on a buffet table,
as the flavor and texture hold up even at room temperature.
Feel free to add lightly cooked, well drained vegetables, such as spinach,
asparagus, onions, or mushrooms to this recipe. You can bake the crust up to
two days in advance and keep it covered in the refrigerator. The filling
is easily assembled while the oven preheats. While quiche tastes best hot out
of the oven, it can also be baked ahead and frozen. Bring it to
room temperature, then reheat it, loosely covered, in a microwave
oven for 90 seconds, or until heated through.*

*Makes 1 (12-inch) quiche*

2½ cups all-purpose flour

½ teaspoon salt

⅜ pound (1½ sticks) unsalted butter,
chilled and cut into pieces

10 eggs

4¼ cups heavy cream

2½ cups shredded mozzarella cheese

1½ cups diced ham

Salt and freshly ground pepper

In a large mixing bowl, combine the flour and salt. Using a pastry blender or two knives, cut the butter into the dry ingredients to form a fine cornmeal consistency. Gradually add ½ cup of cold water, mixing until a stiff dough forms. Let the dough rest in the refrigerator for 30 minutes.

Preheat the oven to 350°F.

Roll out the dough ¼ inch thick. Lifting it carefully, transfer to a 12-inch quiche pan with a removable bottom. Let the crust overlap the edges of the pan to prevent it from shrinking during baking. Bake for 30 minutes, using aluminum pie weights or dried beans to prevent the crust from rising and forming bubbles. The crust is done when the bottom is golden brown.

In a large bowl, beat the eggs until the yolks and whites are well combined. Add the cream and mix well. Season with salt and pepper. Evenly sprinkle the cheese and ham across the bottom of the baked crust. Pour the egg-and-cream mixture over the filling. Bake for 1 hour and 15 minutes, or until the filling is firmly set.

**Note:** If your quiche pan is smaller or shallower than 2 inches, reduce the amount of filling accordingly.

# POACHED PEARS

*Pears are often poached in red wine. Here, a crisply fruity Sauvignon Blanc
accentuates the fruit's delicate flavor and allows the pears to retain
their creamy color. These make a lovely brunch dish, whether as a first course alongside hot or cold cereal, or as a dessert, served with Vanilla Bean Ice Cream and
drizzled with Warm Chocolate Sauce (see pages 235 and 234).*

*Makes 6 cups*

1 cup fruity white wine, such as Sauvignon Blanc

½ cup sugar

1 lemon, sliced and seeded

5 Bartlett pears

In a large saucepan, combine the wine, sugar, and lemon slices with 2 cups of water.
Peel, core, and quarter the pears, placing the pieces immediately into the saucepan
to prevent them from turning brown. Bring to a boil over high heat. Once the liquid comes to a boil, remove the pan from the heat and allow it to cool. Chill until
ready to serve. The pears can be made in advance and stored in a covered nonreactive glass or stainless container for up to three days.

AT THE RESTAURANT BAR, RUSTIC WOODEN BEAMS
ORIGINAL TO THE BARN CONTRAST WITH
SOFTLY GLEAMING METAL VENEER CREATED BY A
LOCAL METALSMITH, WHO WAS INSPIRED BY THE SLEEK
ELEGANCE OF ART MODERNE DESIGN.

## PRUNES POACHED
## WITH CINNAMON AND PORT

*Dried plums, better known as prunes, are an overlooked fruit.
Poached in a mixture of red wine, port, and cinnamon, the prunes become plump,
moist, and delicious. Guests who might have passed up a serving of plain dried
or stewed prunes will come back for seconds of these. For an elegant dessert, top these
with Vanilla Bean Ice Cream (see page 235) and serve with a glass of cognac.*

*Makes 3 cups*

1 pound pitted prunes (about 2½ cups)

1 cup red wine

½ cup port

1 (3-inch) stick cinnamon

1 orange, sliced and seeded

Combine all of the ingredients in a large saucepan and bring to a boil over
high heat. Remove the pan from the heat and allow the contents to cool.
Chill until ready to serve. The prunes may be refrigerated in a covered nonreactive glass or stainless steel container for up to three days.

# Winter Ingredients

### CABBAGE

Cabbage is a hearty vegetable that continues to thrive in cold weather; it even grows beneath a layer of winter's snow. Thinly sliced and lightly sautéed, it adds crunch and color to many dishes. The German tradition of marinating cabbage in wine lends even more flavor to this satisfying winter ingredient.

### CELERIAC

Celeriac, also known as celery root, combines the delicate taste of celery stalks with the earthy flavor and texture of a root vegetable. Simmered or steamed until tender, it can be whipped into purées or incorporated into velvety-textured cream-based soups.

### CHESTNUTS

Chestnut trees were plentiful in Maine before the onslaught of a blight that decimated the trees in the early twentieth century. Fortunately, some trees continue to grow in Maine, dropping nuts encased in a spiny outer shell in late autumn. The meat of the chestnut is moist and rich in flavor, delicious hot off the fire or puréed for a side dish or a full-bodied soup.

### OYSTERS

Maine's cold waters harbor some of the most delicious oysters in the country, ranging in size from compact to plump, and in flavor from sweet to salty. Edible year-round, they have the best taste and texture in winter. Whether served raw, lightly poached, or baked in the shell, oysters are always a festive addition to the table.

### POTATOES

Maine is home to more than 500 potato farms, many of which are located in northernmost Aroostook County. Maine farmers raise a wide variety of potatoes, including common russets, popular Yukon Golds, Russian banana fingerlings, and exotic blue varieties. Steamed, boiled, baked, fried, or sautéed, they never fail to satisfy winter cravings for hearty food.

### SWEET POTATOES

These beautifully colored tubers are popular in cold and warm climates alike. Whether further sweetened with maple syrup or brown sugar, or served in savory presentations with herbs and a touch of garlic, sweet potatoes make a colorful and flavorful addition to winter meals.

### VENISON

Thanks to the increasing availability of farm-raised venison, this lean and full-flavored meat can now be purchased fresh year-round. The perfect complement to winter's mellow root vegetables, venison is a cold-weather favorite on the menu of the White Barn Inn.

# Source Guide

*More and more supermarkets are carrying exotic produce, fresh shellfish, and other foods
called for in some of the recipes in this book. Here are a few sources for mail-order and online shopping.*

## QZINA

83 Meyer Street

Hackensack, NJ 07601

Phone: 201–996–1939

www.Qzina.com

This online gourmet market favored by professional chefs carries crème pâtissière powder, griottes in syrup, kalamansi purée, fine chocolate, and many other products.

## STONEWALL KITCHEN

Stonewall Lane

York, Maine 03909

Phone: 207–351–2713

www.stonewallkitchen.com

This specialty foods company makes jams, jellies, and marmalades, including Maine wild blueberry jam.

## D'ARTAGNAN

280 Wilson Avenue

Newark, NJ 07105

Phone: 800–327–8246

www.dartagnan.com

Venison rib racks and tenderloins, whole guinea hens, guinea hen breasts, pheasant, foie gras, and other game meats and specialty foods, including truffle oil, truffles, forest mushrooms, and prepared chestnuts, are available from this top-quality purveyor, a favorite with restaurant chefs around the world.

## EARTHY DELIGHTS

1161 East Clark Road, Suite 260

DeWitt, Michigan 48820 USA

Phone: 800–367–4709

www.earthy.com

Caviar and foie gras, Austrian pumpkin seed oil, truffles, fresh wild mushrooms, and artisanal goat cheeses are among the products available from this specialty foods company.

## SPARROW ENTERPRISES

Phone: 800–783–4116

www.chocolatebysparrow.com

This gourmet chocolate company offers online access to the finest quality chocolate and fruit purées.

## HARBOR FISH MARKET, INC.

9 Custom House Wharf

Portland, Maine 04101

Phone: 800–370–1790

Within Maine: 207–775–0251

www.cascobaybiz.com/harborfishmarket

This retail and online mail-order source offers the highest-quality native diver-harvested scallops, live lobsters, oysters, mussels, clams, farm-raised and wild salmon, and other seafood products (note: some items are only available in season).

## THE LOBSTER COMPANY

1272 Portland Road, Route 1

Arundel, ME 04046

Phone: 207–985–3456

This seafood store offers fine Maine seafood, including live lobster, diver-harvested scallops, oysters, mussels, clams, and fish. Shipping not available.

## SIMPLY SEAFOOD SUPERSTORE

1111 NW 45th St. Suite B

Seattle, WA 98107

877–706–4022

This Seattle-based company offers a retail location and an internet catalog for mail-ordering George's Bank giant sea scallops, Maine lobster, Pacific oysters, Pacific salmon, and other fresh seafood products.

## THE GREAT CHEESES OF NEW ENGLAND

www.newenglandcheese.com

This web site, sponsored by The Great Cheeses of New England, New England Dairy Promotion Board, includes comprehensive information about New England cheese and cheese makers, including extensive details about how to purchase cheese online and in retail stores across the country.

## WILLIAMS-SONOMA

Phone: 877–812–6235

www.williams-sonoma.com

With retail stores in major cities around the country and an online catalog with mail order service, this company offers ready access to cookware, bakeware (including timbale molds and ramekins), gourmet oils and vinegars, meat glazes, and more.

## PREVIN INC.

2044 Rittenhouse Square

Philadelphia, PA 19103

Phone: 215–985–1996

www.previninc.com

Upon request, this company, specializing in supplying fine restaurants with kitchen and baking equipment, will ship individual items by mail, including bûche de noël molds, large quiche pans, timbale molds, and ramekins.